Out of the Underground:

Homosexuals, the Radical Press and the Rise and Fall of the Gay Liberation Front.

ST SUKIE DE LA CROIX

Rattling Good Yarns Press

33490 Date Palm Drive #3065

Cathedral City CA 92235

USA

ISBN: 978-0-578-44238-9

For Simon Thorn, a fellow traveler

CONTENTS

ACKNOWLEDGMENTS

This book would never have been written if it hadn't been for the diligent staff at the Harold Washington Library in Chicago. On many cold wintry days I trudged through the snow and parked myself at a microfilm reader on the third floor. There I sat for hours, days, and weeks-on-end, sipping from my smuggled-in cup of hot chocolate and dipping into a bag of Bavarian crèmes from Dunkin Donuts. I never got caught once.

I would also like to thank the staff at the Library of Health Sciences, Cook County Law Library, Chicago History Museum, University of Chicago Library and Archives, Northwestern University Archives, University of Illinois at Chicago Library, Loyola University–Chicago Library, Sulzer Regional Library, Roosevelt University Library, and Gerber/Hart Library.

And finally, thanks to Ian Henzel, my husband, and to friends who helped me through this long process. Rick R. Reed, Gregg Shapiro, Owen Keehnan, Corey Black, John "Smokey" Condon, and all the hippies and yippies I've known growing up.

PREFACE

The June 28, 1969 Stonewall Riots came at the end of a turbulent decade when, for better or worse, the world turned itself upside down. The 1960s saw the Cuban Missile Crisis, the Bay of Pigs; the Prague Spring; the birth of the Cultural Revolution in China; in May 1968, students and labor unions attempted to overthrow the government in France; the Berlin Wall was built; in Greece a group of colonels established a military dictatorship; in the Middle East the Six-Day War between Israel and several Arab States; and in Africa, Communist-led nationalist armies in Angola and Mozambique rebelled against Portuguese colonialists.

Then there was the Vietnam War.

And the assassinations: Civil rights NAACP worker Medgar Evers shot by Ku Klux Klansman Byron De La Beckwith on June 12, 1963; John F. Kennedy, President of the United States, shot by Lee Harvey Oswald on November 22, 1963; human rights activist Malcolm X shot by Nation of Islam members Talmadge Hayer, Norman 3X Butler and Thomas 15X Johnson on February 21, 1965; Martin Luther King Jr. shot by James Earl Ray on April 4, 1968; and US Sen. Robert F. Kennedy shot by Jordanian citizen Sirhan Bishara Sirhan on June 5, 1968, to protest the senator's support for Israel.

If they had lived, these New Left heroes may have triumphed, or they may have "sold out," become "tools of the fascist pig establishment." It's tempting to guess their views on homosexuality, but the truth is nobody knows if these men would have supported the Gay Liberation Front (GLF). Instead the frozen images of Medgar Evers, John F. Kennedy, Malcolm X, Martin Luther King Jr., and Robert F. Kennedy, hang on the walls of the 1960s Cultural-Icon Art Gallery like Andy Warhol prints.

One iconic image of the 1960s that left pinholes in the walls of student dorms, hippie crash pads, and free-love communes, was *Guerrillero Heroica,*

Alberto Korda's photograph of Marxist revolutionary Ernesto "Che" Guevara, who also fell victim to the assassin's bullet. Korda's image of the handsome guerilla leader with shoulder-length hair, a black beret, eyes filled with pain and stoicism, prompted some gay men to seek refuge in the arms of the New Left. Some GLF members joined the Venceremos Brigade, traveled to Cuba, and labored in the sugarcane fields in solidarity with the workers.

For some gay men, Guevara was as much an icon and role model as Bette Davis and Joan Crawford was for others. It's no coincidence that one of the earliest post-Stonewall gay rights groups in Britain was named CHE (Campaign for Homosexual Equality). In the British underground newspaper *Ink*, a feminized version of Korda's photograph appears on the cover, under the headline "Gay!" Guevara is depicted wearing heavy blue eye shadow and red lipstick, with a GLF fist-in-the-air button pinned to his beret. However, given Guevara's political views, he likely harbored a negative opinion of homosexuals. One of his inspirations, Friedrich Engels, co-author with Karl Marx of *Das Kommunistische Manifest,* wrote that homosexuality was "morally deteriorated," "abominable," "loathsome," and "degrading."

Out of the Underground: Homosexuals, the Radical Press and the Rise and Fall of the Gay Liberation Front explores homosexuality in the underground press between 1966, thru the emergence of GLF, to its dying gasps around the time of the second Gay Pride Parade in 1971. It covers GLF in several cities, including Milwaukee, Atlanta, Austin, Detroit, San Jose, as well as gay metropolises like New York, San Francisco, Los Angeles, and Chicago. The book begins with a chapter on the early radical press and Adolf Brand, the German anarchist who published *Der Eigene*–possibly the first homosexual magazine in the world.

Prior to a regular and reliable gay press, the only positive images of homosexuals appeared in the underground rags. Most young gay men, threatened with the draft, couldn't relate to the stuffy newsletters of Mattachine-era groups, or the Society for Individual Rights, as they were "old aunties," or "establishment" gays. Young lesbians too, while acknowledging the achievements of their elders, were drawn to the direct action of the Radical Lesbians and Women's Liberation Front, rather than the gab and java get-togethers of the Daughters of Bilitis (DOB). Those young radicals were more likely to read the *Great Speckled Bird*, the *Ann Arbor Argus,* the *San Francisco Oracle*, the feminist *It Ain't Me Babe*, and the anarchic *Berkeley Tribe*, than the *Ladder*, the DOB newsletter.

Out of the Underground looks at the relationship between GLF and the New Left, Yippies, Black Panthers, and Women's Liberation Front. As with my previous book, *Chicago Whispers: A History of LGBT Chicago Before Stonewall,* I stay close to my sources. For me, history comes alive when its plots and intrigues unfold in the writings of the time, authored by the people living it. I like to hear their voices, sometimes angry, frustrated, naive, joyful, petulant, hopeful, playful, and hysterical. It's true that the writing skills of the "reporters" in the underground press varied from excellent to barely literate, but their articles were always full of love and passion.

The underground press covered gay news, publicized gay events, gave free range to LGBT writers, and offered a readership numbering hundreds of thousands. These papers reported stories that would have been lost to history: the homosexual film festival in Los Angeles in 1968, a radical group threatening to bomb underground papers that didn't cover gay news, gay radicals smashing up a straight bar in Washington DC, a female impersonator writing for an Atlanta underground paper in 1968, and gay couples holding hands in Philadelphia, a few days after the Stonewall Riots.

Out of the Underground is also about the culture, music, politics, and art, that radicalized young LGBT's and brought them out of the underground and into the light. Clearly, not all LGBTs were left-wing revolutionaries. Some were conservative and others worked within established gay groups. The majority were married to members of the opposite sex and deeply closeted.

This book isn't about them.

OUT OF THE UNDERGROUND

INTRODUCTION

A PORTRAIT OF THE AUTHOR AS AN ANGRY YOUNG MAN

September 16, 1951

I was born at St. Martin's Hospital in Bath, Great Britain, a city built by the Romans circa AD 60 after the invasion by Emperor Julius Caesar, a man known as "every woman's husband and every man's wife." I'm the only child of poor working class parents, life-long Labour Party supporters. My father's diatribes against the monarchy, the Tories, the powers-that-be, matched the fire and spittle of Leon Trotsky. Although, the erudite Bolshevik leader benefited from a boarding school education paid for by his well-to-do Jewish parents, whereas my father installed sewage pipes as a plumber's apprentice at age fourteen. My father's verbal assaults on the "ruling class" were sprinkled with colorful Anglo-Saxon words like "fuck," and "shit." All his visceral opinions were growled in a thick West Country accent as impenetrable as the US Bullion Depository in Fort Knox, KY. In truth, nobody outside a ten-mile radius of Bath understood what my father was saying.

So my childhood was infused with raw foul-mouthed Socialism. Gifted with girly-boy ways, I embraced the radical politics of the 1960s, grew my hair long, wore unisex clothes, and cast my sexuality to the wind. The first woman I fell in lust with was a bikini-clad Brigitte Bardot. The first man, Che Guevara. The first book I read twice was Jack Kerouac's *On the Road*. And the first 45 rpm disc I wore out was the Rolling Stones' *Play With Fire*. I grew up watching the Cuban Missile Crisis and the US Civil Rights Movement on a black and white "lobotomy box," in the corner of a tiny sitting room, as reported by BBC newscasters. My impression of America came from *I Love Lucy* and *The Lone Ranger*, slapstick laughs of the wacky redhead, and a sturdy masculine code of ethics and honor … *Ke-mo sah-bee*. This fantasy world stood in stark contrast to the grim reality of the Vietnam War and "coloreds" brutally beaten and hosed with water cannons. Images that haunt me still, after all these years.

And homosexuality? Even as a child I was aware of the word "homosexual," though I didn't know what it was, or understand the central role it would play in my life. I vaguely remember Sen. Joseph McCarthy's attempt to rid the US of communists and homosexuals. I thought they were the same thing. Why wouldn't I? I lived through the intrigue of the Cambridge Five, a ring of college educated spies, recruited at university in the 1930s, who sold British secrets to the Russians; Kim Philby, Donald Maclean, Guy Burgess, Anthony Blunt, the fifth man was never caught. Of the four known spies, three were homosexuals. In 1962 another homosexual spy story broke. While serving at the British embassy in Moscow, John Vassall was lured into a gay orgy, a honey-trap organized by the KGB, where he was photographed *in flagrante delicto* with swarthy Russians. He was blackmailed until his arrest in 1962.

In 1960, when Peter Finch played the doomed Irish playwright in the film *The Trials of Oscar Wilde*, Britain was confronted with an embarrassing episode in its history. The image of a fragile artist trampled on for minor indiscretions by jack-booted government philistines, resurfaced with the Rolling Stones.

In 1967, after the notorious bust at the Redlands estate, and the subsequent court case, the Stones recorded *We Love You* to thank their fans for supporting them through the trials. In the accompanying video, Keith Richards plays the judge, condemning Mick Jagger, as Oscar Wilde, to jail. Marianne Faithful plays the part of Lord Alfred Douglas, Wilde's love interest. *You will never win "we," Your uniforms don't fit "we"* sing the defiant rebels. The previous year the band wore old-lady drag in a promotional film for the single, *Have You Seen Your Mother, Baby, Standing in the Shadows?* Clearly the 1960s were looking to be a radical departure from the 1950s. Bobby sox and poodle skirts were out. Cross-dressing and psychedelic drugs were in.

I woolgathered my early teens in the sterile classrooms of an all-boys secondary-modern school, where mutual masturbation and oral sex were *de rigueur*. At age sixteen I left school, took the less-traveled path, began reading the underground press, and sang my own rendition of *You will never win "we." Your uniforms don't fit "we."*

Like most cities in the world, Bath had its bohemian neighborhood. New York had Greenwich Village with its beatniks, folk singers, and drunken Irish poets tumbling off barstools. In San Francisco's Haight

Ashbury, hippies "turned on, tuned in and dropped out." Atlanta had Piedmont Park and battles with the "pigs." Chicago's Old Town was under constant surveillance from the Red Squad. In London, squats of White Panthers lived in Notting Hill Gate. And in Bath, there was Walcot Street and its tribe of yips and hips.

The counter-cultural life in Bath thrived along a short strip bookended by two public houses, the Bell and the Hat and Feather, and was fueled by the Natural Theater Company, Bath Arts Workshop, and *Spark* newspaper, where my juvenile scribbling began. There were several stores in my hometown where I could buy British papers like *International Times*, *OZ*, *Black Dwarf*, and US publications like *Rolling Stone*, and the *Berkeley Barb*. Other papers from the US appeared from goodness-knows-where and were passed around like sacred texts. I saw copies of Chicago's *Seed*, the *Ann Arbor Argus*, even the *Black Panther* surfaced in my social circle. Through this radical print medium my view of the world took shape. There I read about homosexuals being a part of the revolution, about Stonewall and the Gay Liberation Front.

On Saturday June 28, 1969, on the day of the Stonewall Riots in New York, I was at Bath Blues Festival tripping on acid and enjoying Fleetwood Mac, John Mayall, Ten Years After, Led Zeppelin, the Nice, Chicken Shack, Taste, Savoy Brown Blues Band, Roy Harper and others. I would never have known about the riots if it hadn't been for the underground press.

In the August 1, 1969 issue of the London-based *International Times*, I read an anonymously penned "Letter From America." After reading some gossip about Ed Sanders and the Fugs recording a Country & Western album, and the Mothers of Invention performing a ballet at the Fillmore East, I read:

"The 'Stonewall' gay bar & gentlemen's club was busted two nights running. On the third night Allen Ginsberg and I went to investigate on behalf of the international underground press (and also because we were passing the door). Inside is like a scene from 'The Fabulous Wedding of Miss Destiny' if you remember your John Retchy [sic]: a gaggle of giggling fairies clustered around the juke-box, some very exotic gay dancing going down, all very quiet considering the night before the police arrested 28 people and beat some of them up badly. They smashed the place to pieces, wrecking a juke-box and amplification equipment so badly that half the club is now boarded off till repairs can be made. Allen shouted a few things about 'Fairy Power' and 'Gay Power Erects Its Head.' Outside a cop responded to Allen's greeting by saying 'Peace.' A few prowl cars kept Sheridan Square empty of its usual male population."

Another man who read about Stonewall in *International Times* was an American named Jeremy, who interpreted the riots as "politics as usual." In

February 1970 he wrote in Milwaukee's *Kaleidoscope*:

"I was in London this past summer when the news of the gay riots at the Stonewall first broke. Paging thru a copy of *International Times*, I noticed a brief paragraph describing police raids on the Stonewall, one of New York's best known gay bars: cops busting up the bar; kids getting beaten and arrested. 'The usual stuff,' I remarked to my lover. 'It's election time in New York, and [Mayor John] Lindsay's gotta prove to the voters that he's tough as [Mario] Proccacino and [John] Marchi by sending his goons out to bust up the gay bars.' Nothing too unusual, these election year busts. Chicago, Denver, Minneapolis. It happens everywhere. Just one of the occupational hazards of being homosexual–something like the crabs, I guess. Inevitable."

In August 1969 Jeremy returned to Milwaukee:

"I settled down to a summerful of *Kaleidoscope, Rolling Stone,* and *Village Voice* back issues. The July 3 issue of the *Village Voice* provided my first belated introduction to the concept of Gay Power. The *Voice* articles–two of them on the front page–recounted the stories of the police raids on the Stonewall that I had read previously about in London. But what a difference! Not just cops busting heads and arresting blushing queens, but defiant gay kids standing their ground and fighting back. Defending their territory with cans and bottles. Teen queens leading chants in the streets: 'GAY GAY POWER TO THE PEOPLE!' Ginsberg yelling 'Defend the Fairies!' Cops, scared shitless and calling for reinforcements to protect them from the angry crowd. All in all, quite a change from the days of the surprise bust and trying to sneak out the back door of the bar to get away."

Jeremy, on the subject of Gay Power:

"We know that there's a world revolution on–a movement against oppression and for freedom, dignity, and equality of all human beings. We believe in the eventual victory of that revolution and want to be part of it. We can dig it when Che says that a revolutionary must be motivated by love, and we refuse to accept the limits that your puritan sexuality places on our love. We will no longer accept the guilt, fear, pity, and self-hatred that you have told us to feel. We won't be 'queer' for you anymore."

I was there at the birth of *International Times* in 1966 and saw its first tentative steps. I lived through the petulant, "We want the world and we want it now" teen years and the fist-in-the-air revolutionary young adult phase. I mourned the paper's untimely death in 1974, squashed by the fat ass of the British establishment. The paper has been revived over the years, and may or may not be currently in print. In the first issue I was introduced to the gay art scene in New York:

"Andy Warhol's Exploding Plastic Inevitables are back at the Velvet Underground with Super-girl Nico and The Man With the Snake. Speaking of Andy, when he did his famous series of hand-coloured illustrated books–'The Jump Book,' 'The Gold Book,' 'The Feet Book,' etc.–in order to save money on the hand-painted illustrations, he would have a very big IN party for his twelve most with-it friends and seat them around a table with little paper cups of paint, each numbered to correspond with pictures in the books in front of them, and he would proceed to have his friends–who might range from some diamond braceleted socialite to Cecil Beaton–fill in the illustrations–each book sold for 35 dollars."

International Times is where I educated myself on American politics: an interview with black comedian and civil rights worker Dick Gregory, eight hundred students arrested on the Berkeley campus of the University of California, the trial of Black Panther Huey Newton, and police brutality at the Democratic National Convention in Chicago in the summer of 1968. The articles were in a street language I understood e.g. under the headline, "Presidents and Pigs," David Mairowitz wrote of the Chicago police riot: "Outside in the streets, blood was creating a reality to counter the fantasy world inside. Newsmen and photographers were beaten senseless and that is a lesson I'm delighted to see them learning after all these years of sucking off the cops."

The acceptance of homosexuality in *International Times* may be partially due to one of the paper's founders, American Jack Moore, being gay. However, it was "homosexuality" that got the paper into trouble with the law. In August 1967, a letter from a Miss Fiske, a student at the University of Sussex, read: "I consider that the *International Times* is an enticement to sexual perversions and drug-taking." The paper didn't argue with the accusations–drug-use was encouraged, and "sexual perversion" made an appearance in the classified ads: "Gay muscle-boy movies in standard 8 mm. Rugged ... Riotous ... Uninhibited youths at play plus the greatest in European girlie movies ... and lots more ... send S.A.E. to Tony Campino, 50 Lordship Park, London N. 16."

Two issues after Miss Fiske's letter, the cover of *International Times* depicted a duo of full-frontal male nudes with the headline "Consenting Adults–The IT Boys."

Before the first issue of *Gay News* in June 1972, the only positive news about homosexuality in Britain was found in the pages of *International Times,* or *OZ,* the psychedelic hippie magazine. The August/September 1969 *OZ* was the "Homosexual 'Suck for Peace' Issue," guest-edited by homosexuals. On the cover it quotes, "Yet each man kills the thing he loves" from Oscar Wilde's *The Ballad of Reading Gaol* under a photograph of a naked, one black, one white, male couple embracing. Inside are extracts from *The Homosexual Handbook* by Angelo d'Arcangelo, and the "Suck for

Peace" article is about American "hustlers," accompanied by a photograph of two men standing side-by-side at a public urinal. *OZ* escaped the obscenity laws for its gay coverage, but ended up in court for their "Schoolkidz OZ" issue, guest-edited by school kids.

However, it was *International Times* that was taken to court for its homosexual content. By September 1968 *International Times* was selling 40,000 copies a week, and included a gay classified ads section under "MALES" Ads like: "LEATHER boy, 22, wants way out rocker friends with bikes." And: "BROADMINDED, quiet, intelligent youth (21) wants boyfriend under 23 for friendship."

On April 28, 1969 the offices of *International Times* at 27 Endell Street, London WC2, were raided and all materials pertaining to the "MALES" ads was confiscated, including sealed letters and replies to box numbers. In a front-page editorial in May, *International Times* predicted other underground publications would soon be raided, like *OZ, Black Dwarf,* and *Gandalf's Garden.* Their conclusion read: "If you want revolution—sexual freedom, freedom of thought, freedom to discover who you really are—in short if you want a new world and won't settle for less, then these journals are your only overt communication media. One suggestion: start more of them."

In 1969 homosexuality in England was legal between two consenting adults in private, but enticing others into "sexual perversion" with classified ads was not. In truth, the raid had nothing to do with homosexuals, but was an attempt to stifle the underground press. Homosexuality wasn't the issue, challenging the status quo was. Anarchist graffiti in my hometown read: "Where there is real communication, there is no State." Communicating ideas, exploring different ways of thinking, adopting unorthodox spirituality and alternative lifestyles, made the British establishment uneasy. Underground newspaper headlines like, "We are the people our parents warned us against" didn't allay their concerns. Soon after the raid on *International Times,* the police busted *Black Dwarf* and *Black Dimensions,* after they criticized police mistreatment of "colored people" in Notting Hill Gate.

The cover of the December 5, 1969 *International Times* read:

"It is with heavy hearts that we have to report that as a result of the police raid on the offices of *IT* last April, two conspiracy charges have been brought against Knuller (Publishing, Printing & Promotions) Ltd. and three directors, Dave Hall, Graham Keen, and Peter Stansill.

"Both charges relate to ads which appeared in the "males" column in issues 51-56.

"The first charge alleges that they conspired with persons inserting ads and with other persons to induce readers to resort to the said advertisements for the purpose of homosexual practices and thereby to debauch and corrupt public morals, contrary to Common Law.

"The second charge alleges that they conspired to outrage public decency by inserting advertisements in the said issues containing lewd, disgusting, and offensive matter contrary to Common Law. The preliminary hearing will be on January 16th at Wells Street Magistrates Court after which we can expect the case to proceed to the Old Bailey."

In January 1970, at Wells Street Magistrates Court, Hall, Keen, and Stansill were charged with corrupting morals. Fifteen men who inserted or replied to gay ads in *International Times* were offered immunity from prosecution in return for giving evidence. These men were anonymously named Mr. A, B, C, etc. The issue was the wording of the advertisements. The trial was not without comedic moments. One witness was asked the meaning of the term "well hung." He replied that it meant he had no "hang-ups." And in another exchange:

Witness B: "I am a clerk. I know the publication *IT* and have bought a copy from public bookshops in Manchester. I put in an advertisement. I am a homosexual."

Prosecuting Counsel Peter Spencer: "I am going to ask you to look at your advertisement. What did you mean by passive gay?"

B: "I meant non-aggressive in the homosexual act. I didn't mean anything else than gentle and passive. The passive partner plays, in the homosexual relationship, what might be called the feminine role in the relationship."

Spencer: "It goes on 'needs randy butch guy 21/26.'"

B: "Randy=sexually potent. Butch=homosexual, aggressive. Guy=slang term for a man; Age Group 21/26."

Spencer: "It goes on 'for friendship/sex.'"

B: "That means just what it says. I prefer the sort of person who would prefer to wear jeans and studded jackets. I understand this to indicate the type of person previously indicated in the advertisement. I filled out the form from a previous issue to place the advertisement. I paid about 15/- by cheque for it. I received no acknowledgement from the paper. The next I heard was when I got the replies. About two weeks later I got the letters. I bought a copy of *IT*. They arrived by post, addressed to me in an envelope. They were sealed and did not appear to have been tampered with or previously opened. They were from men. They were within the age group mentioned. One in his 50's. I destroyed the replies because they were lewd and disgusting and of no interest to me."

Leon Brittan, barrister for *International Times*, argued the ads would not corrupt the average reader because they were phrased in a coded language and understood only by a practicing homosexual. On November 10, 1970 *International Times* was found guilty and Knuller (Publishing, Printing & Promotions) Ltd. fined £1500 and ordered to pay £500 costs. Directors Dave Hall, Graham Keen, and Peter Stansill, each received an eighteen month jail sentence suspended for two years, and were ordered to pay £200 each toward the costs. The publicity from the court case affected advertising revenue, and the paper never regained its former strength. *International Times* struggled on until mid-1974 when it ceased publication.

1

HOMOSEXUALITY IN THE EARLY RADICAL PRESS

A recurring theme in the long battle for gay rights has been its association with Marxism, anarchism, and other movements on the Left. Not surprising when you consider that after the signing of the Declaration of Independence on July 4, 1776, it soon became clear that the phrase, "We hold these truths to be self-evident, that all men are created equal, that they are endowed by their Creator with certain unalienable Rights, that among these are Life, Liberty and the pursuit of Happiness" did not include African-Americans, women, Native Americans, homosexuals, and other disenfranchised groups. Out of these disgruntled masses grew a dissident press.

"One cannot tell by looking whether a person is queer. Before queers can build a community, fight for civil rights, or even form friendships or more intimate relationships, they have to find each other. Before they can find each other, they have to find themselves in a culture that tells them in myriad ways to hide."–Bob Ostertag in *People's Movements, People's Press: The Journalism of Social Justice Movements.*

The underground press of the 1960s and 1970s appeared to be groundbreaking at the time, but that assortment of rags was just another chapter in a long history of radical publications dating back to America's first newspaper. On September 25, 1690, Benjamin Harris' *Publick Occurrences, Both Foreign and Domestick* was published, but Boston officials deemed it too critical, and it went down after only one issue. The press had to be sanctioned, licensed, and controlled by the authorities. In that respect, nothing changed between 1690 and 1960. In his book, *The Paper Revolutionaries: The Rise and Fall of the Underground Press,* Laurence Leamer wrote: "Thirty years later [after *Publick Occurences*] Benjamin Franklin's brother James found himself thrown into prison for satirizing the local government in his *New England Courant.* During the Revolutionary War there was a 'fugitive press' and before the Civil War an 'abolitionist press' suffered severe harassment."

In Chicago, a century before the psychedelic *Seed,* the leftist *Second City,* and the radical *Kaleidoscope,* an anarchist paper called the *Alarm* sold 15,000 copies a week. The *Alarm,* first published October 4, 1884, was edited by Albert Parsons, who believed man's laws were in violation of nature's laws, therefore should be abolished. Two years later Parsons was arrested in connection with the "Haymarket Riot."

In Haymarket Square, on May 4, 1886, a rally in support of striking workers turned violent when a bomb was thrown into the police ranks. The explosion, subsequent panic, and gunfire, resulted in the deaths of seven police officers. Dozens of protestors were injured. Eight anarchists were arrested, six were sentenced to death, one died in prison, and one received a jail sentence of fifteen years, even though none of these men threw the bomb. Gov. Richard J. Oglesby commuted the death sentences for Samuel Fielden, Oscar Neebe, and Michael Schwab, to life in prison. On June 26, 1893, the three men were pardoned by John Peter Altgeld, the new governor. Of the remaining five, Louis Lingg committed suicide in prison, while Albert Parsons, August Spies, Adolph Fischer and George Engel were executed. Of the four who hung, three worked for left-wing newspapers: Parsons edited *Alarm,* August Spies edited the German-language *Arbeiter-Zeitung,* and Adolph Fischer was a typesetter for the same paper. Of the three pardoned, Michael Schwab was the assistant editor of *Arbeiter-Zeitung* and Oscar Neebe, the office manager. In total, of the eight anarchists arrested, five worked for radical papers.

Sexual variance was rarely written about in American anarchist periodicals in the late 19th and early 20th centuries, though it was understood and accepted by sex radicals like John William Lloyd, Emma Goldman, and others. (See *Free Comrades: Anarchism and Homosexuality in the United States, 1895-1917* by Terence Kissick). However, articles on the subject appeared regularly in the European radical press. Emil Szittya, the Hungarian anarchist, bohemian, writer, reporter, and Dadaist, wrote for several magazines, including the French modernist *Les Hommes Nouveaux* and the German anarchist *Horizont-füzet.* In his 1923 book, *Das Kuriositäten-Kabinett,* Szittya made reference to homosexual radicals: "Very many anarchists have this tendency. Thus I found in Paris a Hungarian anarchist, Alexander

Sommi, who founded a homosexual anarchist group on the basis of this idea." Also, German sexologist and homosexual rights campaigner, Magnus Hirschfeld, noted in his book *Die Homosexualität des Mannes und des Weibes*: "In the ranks of a relatively small party, the anarchist, it seemed to me as if proportionately more homosexuals and effeminates are found than in others."

Adolf Brand, a German anarchist, published *Der Eigene*, thought to be the first homosexual magazine in the world. The periodical ran from 1896 to 1932, when it was eventually shut down by Adolf Hitler and the Nazis. Not only was *Der Eigene* homosexually-oriented, but a number of the contributors were Jewish, like sexologist Benedict Friedlaender, anarchist poet and playwright Erich Mühsam, philosopher Theodor Lessing, and writers Kurt Hiller and Klaus Mann whose mother was Jewish. His bisexual father, Thomas Mann, author of the gay novel *Death in Venice*, was Lutheran, and also a contributor to *Der Eigene*. Other contributors were the painter Fidus (real name Hugo Reinhold Karl Johann Höppener) who died in 1948, but whose work was rediscovered in the 1960s and influenced the psychedelic posters of rock concerts. Other artists included Wilhelm von Gloeden, known for his photographs of nude Sicilian boys, and homosexual artist and bodybuilder, Sascha Schneider, whose 1894 drawing "The Anarchist" depicts a naked muscular male figure throwing a bomb.

Another homosexual radical was the Prussian born Johannes Holzmann, who wrote under the name Senna Hoy. He edited the journal *Der Kampf: Zeitschrift für gesunden Menschenverstand* that included many of his own articles on homosexuality. In 1995 an article appeared in the *Journal of Homosexuality* called "Anarchism and Homosexuality in Wilhelmine Germany: Senna Hoy, Erich Mühsam, John Henry Mackay," by Walter Fähnders. In it, the author quotes from a Holzmann article called "Die Homosexualität als Kulturbewegung," where he argued that "no one has the right to intrude in the private matters of another, to meddle in another's personal views and orientations, and that ultimately it is no one's business what two freely consenting adults do in their homes."

There were also female revolutionaries, like lesbian feminist, poet, and writer, Lucía Sánchez-Saornil, founder of the Spain's Mujeres Libres, an organization of anarchist women working for women's liberation and social revolution. Even earlier than 1919, she wrote articles on homosexuality for publications like *Los Quijotes, Tableros, Plural, Manantial* and *La Gaceta Literaria*. Because of the controversial subject matter she was forced to write under a man's name. Sánchez-Saornil was a friend of Emma Goldman, the American anarchist who spoke in defense of homosexuality and the plight of working-class women. In 1896 Goldman published an article called "Anarchy and the Sex Question" in Chicago's *Alarm*. It began:

"The workingman, whose strength and muscles are so admired by the pale, puny off-springs of the rich, yet whose labour barely brings him enough to keep the wolf of starvation from the door, marries only to have a wife and house-keeper, who must slave from morning till night, who must make every effort to keep down expenses. Her nerves are so tired by the continual effort to make the pitiful wages of her husband support both of them that she grows irritable and no longer is successful in concealing her want of affection for her lord and master, who, alas! soon comes to the conclusion that his hopes and plans have gone astray, and so practically begins to think that marriage is a failure."

Another anarchist newspaper in Chicago was *Lucifer the Light-Bearer*, edited by Moses Harman, a tireless campaigner for free love and women's rights. The Free Love movement was anti-marriage and believed the laws of the State and antiquated morals of the Church should be kept out of sexual matters, notably age of consent, birth control, homosexuality, abortion, and prostitution. *Lucifer the Light-Bearer* was first published in Valley Falls, KS, in 1883, but moved to Chicago in 1896. In 1885, *One Thousand and One Nights (The Arabian Nights)*, a collection of stories translated from Arabic by British writer Sir Richard Francis Burton, and also a version by British poet John Payne, was banned in the United States, because of its explicit sex and homosexual stories, like *The Tale of the Youth and his Tutor* and *The Tale of Abu Nuwas and the Three Youths*. In March 1885, in *Lucifer the Light-Bearer* "W" wrote:

"Anthony Comstock [US Postal Inspector and politician], agent of the Vice Society, a moral smelling club composed partly of hypocrites and partly of ignoramuses, has recently pounced upon an unexpurgated edition of the *Arabian Nights*, and bullied the New York agent, Mr. Worthington, into promising not to sell any more copies of it."

In her book *The Gender-Feminist Attack on Women*, author Wendy McElroy writes that on February 23, 1887, the editor and staff of *Lucifer* were arrested for obscenity. The charges were in connection with three published letters to the editor. The letter from W.G. Markland caused the most trouble, quoting from a letter he received:

"Today's mail brought me a letter from a dear lady friend, from which I quote and query: About a year ago F _____ gave birth to a babe, and was severely torn by the use of instruments in incompetent hands ... last night, her husband came down, forced himself into her bed and the stitches were torn from her healing flesh, leaving her in a worse condition than ever. I don't know what to do."

Markland goes on to pose questions:

"Can there be legal rape? Did this man rape his wife? Would it have been rape had he not been married to her? Does the law protect the person of woman in marriage? Does it protect her person out of marriage? ... If a man stabs his wife to death with a knife, does not the law hold him for murder? If he murders her with his penis, what does the law do? ... Can a Czar have more absolute power over a subject than a man has over the genitals of his wife? ... Has freedom gender? ... "

Moses Harman was sentenced to five years in jail for publishing the letter, but only served eight months on a technicality. In 1895 he was sentenced again to one year in jail, after which he moved *Lucifer* to Chicago. In the *Chicago Tribune* on February 27, 1906 a headline read, "Penitentiary for an editor": "Moses Harman, 500 Fulton street, editor of *Lucifer, the Light Bearer*, who was convicted several months ago and sentenced to the penitentiary for sending objectionable literature through the mails, will be taken to the penitentiary at Joliet over the Alton road at 10 o'clock this morning."

Harman was seventy-five years old at the time, yet he survived the one-year sentence of hard labor, breaking rocks for eight hours a day, sometimes in the harsh Illinois winter. Free again he relocated to Los Angeles and renamed *Lucifer the Light-Bearer* as the *American Journal of Eugenics*. Harman died January 30, 1910. His obituary in the *Chicago Tribune* read: "Harman's beliefs and teachings which led him to conflict with the views of the postal authorities had for their ideal the rearing of better children. He believed a woman was her own mistress."

In the 19th century Johannes Holzmann saying "it is no one's business what two freely consenting adults do in their homes" and W.G. Markland asking if a woman can be raped by her husband, are the same issues raised by the Gay Liberation and Women's Liberation Fronts in the late 20th century. In the 1960s the concerns and issues of homosexuals, women, and African-Americans were only aired on the pages of the radical and underground press. It was life-changing for homosexuals, as the few gay publications that existed in the 1960s were staid and had a limited readership.

In late 19th, early 20th Century, America, information about the "crime against nature" only surfaced in medical journals, in essays that sounded like anthropological studies of a sub-human species. At that time, the mainstream press ignored homosexuality, and the law reviled it. In *Honselman vs. People*, an 1897 Chicago sodomy case, Justice James Cartwright described homosexuality as "the abominable crime not fit to be named by Christians."

However, one defense of homosexuality was published in the *Little Review*, a Chicago literary journal, edited by lesbian anarchist Margaret Anderson. On February 4, 1915, Edith Mary Oldham Lees Ellis, the lesbian wife of British sexologist Havelock Ellis, visited Chicago to give a lecture at Orchestra Hall. Her talk comprised two papers, "Masculinism and Feminism," written by her husband, and her self-penned "Sexuality and Eugenics." Anderson was not impressed by Ellis' lecture and wrote an editorial in the March 1915 *Little Review* entitled "Mrs. Ellis' Failure." "There was one great fault to be found with Mrs. Ellis' lecture: it was not illuminating," charged Anderson. In her opinion Ellis had not come through with her promise to tell the truth about sex. Ellis had said: "I have read all my husband's manuscripts before they were published and I know he has never told anything but the truth about sex ... I shall tell the truth as I know it, if I am sent to jail or put out of Chicago for it."

Margaret Anderson adopted "isms." Futurism, Bergsonism, the New Paganism, Imagism, Dadaism, and Surrealism all found a home in the *Little Review*. The journal was primarily a magazine of art, poetry and literature, but also embraced feminism and anarchism. Emma Goldman wrote articles for the paper, and many writers were first published in its pages, including Ernest Hemingway. In 1917 the *Little Review* moved to New York's Greenwich Village where it serialized James Joyce's *Ulysses* from 1918 to 1921, for which the editor was taken to court for obscenity. Not everyone was as brave, or perhaps foolhardy, as Margaret Anderson, to openly defend homosexuality in print. Others veiled their support in the guise of articles advocating "free-love."

Another radical Greenwich Village magazine was *Masses*, started in 1911 by Piet Vlag, a Dutchman. The *Masses* soon fell apart and was adopted by a group of Village bohemians, with Max Eastman as editor. Eastman was a socialist and free-love advocate, who believed the upcoming revolution should be both cultural and political. The magazine included fiction, poetry, and art by leading radicals, some of them advocates of free-love, like Chicago's *Friday Night Review* editor Floyd Dell, reporter John Reed, and bisexual Mabel Dodge Luhan, who wrote about her "women friends" in her 1933 autobiography, *Intimate Memories*. Cigar-smoking lesbian poet Amy Lowell also contributed to the magazine. In 1916 *Masses* was banned from sale on New York newsstands due to its pacifist stand against America's pending involvement in the war in Europe. In 1917 it was barred from the mails. In the end, *Masses* was charged with violating the Espionage Act (Pub. L. 65-24, 40 Stat. 217, enacted June 15, 1917) for publishing "treasonable material" in the 1917 August issue. Max Eastman, Floyd Dell, John Reed, Josephine Bell, H.J. Glintenkamp, Art Young, and Merrill Rogers were all charged with seeking to "unlawfully and willfully ... obstruct the recruiting and enlistment of the United States' military." Fifty years later the same charges were leveled at the underground press for urging readers to burn their Vietnam War draft cards. Eastman and his "band of traitors" faced $10,000 fines and twenty years in jail, but escaped prosecution with a hung jury. One rebellious juror was a socialist.

Masses ceased publication soon afterwards. The *Liberator* and *New Masses* followed, but they were serious socialist papers. After the Bolsheviks toppled the Russian Tsarist autocracy in 1917, American socialists adopted a hardline Marxist approach, discarding the freethinking, free love advocates, bohemians, poets and artists. It would be decades before Greenwich Village saw another radical paper that embraced the arts. Not the *Village Voice* but the *East Village Other*.

On October 26, 1955 the first issue of *Village Voice* hit the newsstands, launched by Ed Fancher, Dan Wolf, British journalist John Wilcock, and Norman Mailer. Though not politically radical, its place in gay history is secured by its coverage of the Stonewall Riots, though prior to that, homosexuality was not mentioned. In a 1967 article about the Underground Press Syndicate (UPS), *Provo*, a Los Angeles bi-weekly underground paper, criticized the *Village Voice*:

> "As underground papers wax successful the devil tempts them to fall into settled arrangements, to grow complacent and to join the Establishment. The *Village Voice* was founded during the days of the 'Beat Generation.' Now it is too good for UPS and supports Mayor Lindsay, Bobby Kennedy and Captain Fink of the New York Police Department."

The real successor to *Masses* was the *East Village Other*, co-founded in October 1965 by Walter Bowart, Ishmael Reed, Allen Katzman, Dan Rattiner, Sherry Needham and the *Village Voice*'s John Wilcock, who later co-founded *Interview* magazine with Andy Warhol. The *East Village Other* was a countercultural psychedelic paper with local, national, and international news, rock music, dope, Dada cut-up artwork and bizarre headlines. The *East Village Other* also included comic strips of explicit sex, including anal bestiality, and storylines about "offing the pigs." In the *New York Times* obituary for the *East Village Other*'s first publisher, Walter Bowart, the author remembers the *East Village Other* was once described by a New York newspaper as, "So countercultural that it made the *Village Voice* look like a church circular."

Unlike the pre-Stonewall *Village Voice*, the *East Village Other* embraced homosexuals as an integral part of the political and spiritual counterculture movement. As early as 1968, the paper published gay classified ads for everything from Male Nude movies to lesbian consciousness-raising groups.

2

SEXUAL FREEDOM

Wisconsin Sen. Joseph McCarthy's 1950s witch-hunt of communists and homosexuals infiltrating American life was prophetic as a decade later a generation of college-educated gay men and women adopted socialism as the cause du jour. From the tightly bound chrysalis of the 1950s a butterfly emerged: the New Left. With it came a tidal wave of radical publications against the Vietnam War, that advocated free love, experimenting with drugs, and adopted the slogan: "The most revolutionary thing you can do is change your mind." With this new openness, magazines like *Time* and *Life* cast a jaundiced eye over the twilight world of homosexuals with salacious exposés. This coincided with the emergence of the Sexual Freedom League and a discourse on sexuality in the underground press.

"Sexual intercourse began in 1963 ... between the end of the Chatterley ban and the Beatles' first LP."–British author Philip Larkin in his poem *Annus Mirabilis*.

World War II had a dramatic effect on the lives of young Americans: men were drafted into a virtually all-male environment to fight in foreign wars, while many women wore the overalls of Rosie the Riveter, working long hours in the munitions factories. Men found friendship, a camaraderie, affection, and brotherhood. Women formed sisterly bonds while packing bullets into boxes on the production line. Far from the scrutiny of family, neighbors, and church ministers, it's not surprising that latent homosexual desires surfaced. The war shifted sexuality on its axis and muddied the tranquil waters of "traditional marriage." At the end of the war, after VE and VJ Days, African-Americans were expected to return to the back of the bus, women to the role of homemakers, homosexuals back into the closet, leaving the country to be run by white heterosexual males, as it had been since the Founding Fathers.

In the 1950s Wisconsin Sen. Joseph McCarthy embarked on a witch-hunt to purge government of communists and homosexuals. The result of that persecution of Reds and Pinks was the emergence of the revolutionary New Left and Gay Liberation Front of the 1960s. In 1965, Jack Weinberg, a leader in the Free Speech Movement at the University of California, Berkeley, told the *San Francisco Chronicle*: "We have a saying in the movement that we don't trust anybody over 30." In the 1960s a new term was coined: "The Generation Gap." Older Americans clung to traditional gender roles, where John Wayne kills a bad guy, smiles, and blows smoke from the barrel of his gun. While women wear aprons and bake cookies in the cookie-cutter studio-set world of *The Donna Reed Show*. The ideal woman was Barbie, launched in 1959. White Barbie, that is, "Black Barbie" didn't arrive until 1980. In 1967, Frank Zappa sang *Plastic People*, his take on Barbie women: *A fine little girl/She waits for me/She's as plastic/As she can be/She paints her face/With plastic goo/And wrecks her hair/With some shampoo*. At the end of the song, Zappa sings: *Go home/and check yourself/you think we're singing 'bout someone else?*

In 1948 Dr. Alfred Charles Kinsey's *Sexual Behavior in the Human Male* exposed high rates of masturbation, adultery, and pre-marital sex among the 18,000 men interviewed. Kinsey also noted thirty-seven percent of men had engaged in at least one homosexual act since puberty, that four percent were homosexual throughout their whole lives, and ten percent had been exclusively homosexual for the last three years. In the 1950s the American male had dueling identities: Traditional Family Values Man v. *Rebel Without a Cause*. The latter snapped their fingers to the free-form be-bop jazz of Charlie "Bird" Parker's *Bird Gets the Worm*. Marlon Brando and James Dean presented on-screen images of tortured souls, and were lauded by Benzedrine soaked Beat Poets. Kenneth Anger produced homoerotic films like *Fireworks*, Allen Ginsberg's *Howl* was published in 1956, William Burroughs' *Naked Lunch* in 1959. The social movement of free-love was alive and well and living in Greenwich Village with Jackson Pollock, Mark Rothko, Willem de Kooning, Jack Kerouac, Lawrence Ferlinghetti et al. The generation gap grew wider still after the rebels without a cause found a cause: the Vietnam War.

In the summer of 1958 the first issue of New York's monthly *Realist* appeared with a front-page headline, "An Angry Young Magazine," and an editorial boasting that the paper would be "devoted to the reporting and analysis of timely and significant conflicts that are ignored or treated superficially by the general press." The founder, publisher, and editor, Paul Krassner, later joined Ken Kesey's Merry Pranksters, and co-founded the Yippies. In his autobiography, *Confessions of a Raving Unconfined Nut*, one story goes that when *People* magazine named Krassner "the father of the underground press," he demanded a paternity test. The *Realist* was a mix of politics, cartoons, articles, and satire. In *Playboy*, Jacob Brackman described the *Realist* as the "*Village Voice* with its fly open." Krassner's most notorious satire, "Parts That Were Left Out of the Kennedy Book," appeared in the May 1967 issue, titled after the censorship of William Manchester's book, *The Death of a President*. The end of the satire has Jackie Kennedy talking about LBJ:

> "That man was crouching over the corpse, no longer chuckling but breathing hard and moving his body rhythmically. At first I thought he must be performing some mysterious symbolic rite he'd learned from Mexicans or Indians as a boy. And then I realized–there is only one way to say this–he was literally fucking my husband in the throat. In the bullet wound in the front of his throat. He reached a climax and dismounted. The next thing I remember, he was being sworn in as the new President."

On July 16, 1962 WBAI radio broadcast an interview with six homosexuals about their lives, careers, police problems, and promiscuity. Over August, September, and October, the *Realist* published the entire transcript of the program as "Live and Let Live: Parts One, Two and Three." Here are some of the highlights:

> Question: "Well, do you think that your choice of a homosexual role is partially attributable to your revulsion against normal domesticity? ... Well, I'm not saying normal–let's say bourgeois domesticity."

> Answer: "This I find very untrue. I think it is the nature of all human beings to be bisexual, and that this perverted nature results in strict homosexuals and strict heterosexuals, both of whom have puritanical attitudes toward the other. In fact, you can find homosexuals any day who will say to heterosexuals, 'Oh, you made it with a girl! Oh, how terrible! This is awful!' And the same thing: I'll speak to a heterosexual friend and he'll say, 'How terrible! How can two boys have sex together! This is awful! This is perversion!' This is puritanism. And both sides–both heterosexuals and homosexuals are guilty of it, which I find quite revolting to me. I think people should be free. Personally, I find that I have more homosexual relationships, and it's because of the freedom–call it promiscuity if you will; I call it freedom. I think that there is more freedom, more honesty between people in a homosexual relationship, because the social rules have built up within a framework which is not widespread and therefore including people who are

completely frigid and anti-sex–but I find an equal amount of satisfaction with a girl who is equally free. And since ... there are very few girls who are sexually free ... this doesn't happen as often, for obvious reasons."

Question: "I want to talk about harassment, which I think is practiced."

Answer: "Yeah, but let's talk about anarchy so we can settle this. The heterosexual sees homosexuality as anarchy, but they really see it as a competing system, and this is not true. It's not trying to compete. We're not trying to overthrow heterosexual society."

Another guest answers: "As a group, homosexuals are not of any particular political mind. This I have found out much to my horror, but they are not. I feel they all should be–every blooming homosexual in the world should be anti-state, anti-establishment, anti-government, because every government–with the exception of Napoleon's of course–has put down homosexuals. If I may say one thing about the government attitude here towards the equation of homosexuality and Communism, the Communist Party–which of course is a radical group, and I belong to other radical groups, although the Communist Party, in my opinion, is counter revolutionary–the Communist Party is probably the most puritanical group in the United States of America. It's more puritanical than the Women's Temperance Union. They're impossible. ... They're like a bunch of early Salem, Massachusetts puritans. ... Then basically, inherent in our democracy is a tolerance towards minorities. ... Well, let's just say a tolerance towards homosexuality is just a democratic idea."

Question: "I'd like to ask one final question ... if you could address the corporate straight world ... what would you say to them regarding the homosexual? What attitude would you like them to adopt toward homosexual society?"

Answer: "Well, I'd sum it up in a phrase. I'd say, just: "Live and let live.""

The veneer of secrecy covering the twilight world of the homosexual was scratched again by *Life* magazine on June 26, 1964 with Paul Welch's expose, "Homosexuality in America." It begins:

"These brawny young men in their leather caps, shirts, jackets and pants are practicing homosexuals, men who turn to other men for affection and sexual satisfaction. They are part of what they call the 'gay world,' which is actually a sad and often sordid world. ... Homosexuality shears across the spectrum of American life–the professions, the arts, business and labor. It always has. But today, especially in big cities, homosexuals are discarding their furtive ways and openly admitting, even flaunting, their deviation. Homosexuals have their own drinking places, their special assignation streets, even their own organizations. And for every obvious homosexual, there are probably nine nearly impossible to detect. This social disorder, which society tries to suppress, has forced itself into the public eye because it does present a problem–and parents especially are concerned. The myth and misconception with which homosexuality has so long been clothed must be cleared away, not to condone it but to cope with it."

Subheadings in the piece include: "A secret world grows open and bolder. Society is forced to look at it and try to understand it," "The 'Gay' World Takes to the City Streets," "Rejected by the 'Straight' World, Homosexuals Build a Society of Their Own," "In a Constant Conflict with the Law, the Homosexual Faces Arrest, Disgrace," and "A Legal-Religious Debate Grows Over Personal Immorality." Welch's expose ends with an article by Ernest Havemann, titled "Scientists search for the answers to a touchy and puzzling question: Why?"

Throughout the 1950s and 1960s gay rights groups like One Inc., Mattachine Society, and Daughters of Bilitis, tried to educate the public about homosexual concerns. However, within the cloistered walls of academia, university students were sheltered from homosexual life in the outside world. Too young to frequent gay bars and socializing mostly within their own peer group, students were more likely to learn about homosexuality from the Free Universities that emerged after the Free Speech Movement at the University of California, Berkeley. One of the most successful was Midpeninsula Free University (MFU) in Palo Alto, CA, where, for a $10 membership fee, between 150 and 300 courses were offered to everyone. One early speaker at MFU was Paul Goodman, the bisexual novelist, playwright, poet, and anarchist intellectual. Goodman's essay, "Memoirs of an Ancient Activist," was published in New York's *Win* in November 1969. (A revised version entitled "The Politics of Being Queer" appears in *Crazy Hope and Finite Experience: Final Essays of Paul Goodman*, edited by Taylor Stoehr). It begins with the line: "In essential ways, my homosexual needs have made me a nigger."

In June 1968, in the *Midpeninsula Observer*, Vic Lovell writes, "Free U course asks 'all sexual questions.'" Lovell and Robb Crist are offering a course in "Sexual Morality Now." The course description reads:

"Among the young these days many traditional questions regarding 'sexual morality' are no longer relevant. Few, for example, would find much worth discussing the question of whether unmarried people should make love or whether teenage girls should be provided with birth control pills if they want them. That was yesterday's revolution.

"Though liberals may deny it, radicals know that the domino theory is true, in sex as in politics. The new climate of permissiveness creates as many problems as it solves. For example, should (or can) you love more than one person at the same time, and if you do, can possessiveness and jealousy be eliminated by sleeping with both at the same time, (i.e. in the same bed and at the same time)? The demand for exclusivity in sexual relationships creates many problems, but is inclusivity a feasible alternative?

"We will try to consider all sexual questions, no matter how freaky or outlandish they may be, including the value of orgies, group marriage, bisexuality, homosexuality, and the future of conventional marriage and family structures. Everybody's doing something about it, but nobody's talking. If you feel the need for gentle but candid verbal communication, come join us."

One organization that students read about in college papers and the underground press was the Sexual Freedom League (SFL). Founded in New York City in 1963 by Jefferson Poland (later J. "Fuck" Poland) and Dr. Leo Koch, SFL was a nudist and orgy group that campaigned for sex education and repeal of laws against censorship, abortion, and sodomy. Koch, a professor of biology, was fired from his job for advocating pre-marital sex, and Poland was described by *Time* magazine in 1966 as "a restless student who says he is studying to be 'either a lawyer or an agitator.'" Koch's troubles began in April 1960 when University of Illinois President David D. Henry and the board of trustees fired him from his job after his letter advocating pre-marital sex was published in the *Daily Illini*, the student newspaper. In the letter he wrote: "With modern contraceptives and medical advice readily available at the nearest drugstore, or at least a family physician, there is no valid reason why sexual intercourse should not be condoned among those sufficiently mature to engage in it without social consequences and without violating their own codes of morality or ethics."

Frank Hughes in the *Chicago Tribune* wrote that Koch "went on a literary sex binge in the columns of a student newspaper." A meeting of the university board of trustees, nine men and one woman, found Koch's letter "odious, detrimental to the university, a flouting of Illinois law, and grounds for dismissal." Koch's defense was that there needed to be a public discussion about sex. As a result of his firing, thousands of students protested and police were summoned to remove them from the administrative building. In July 1960, 229 faculty and staff members wrote a letter of protest to Henry and the trustees, saying they did the school a "disservice" firing Koch and were setting "a precedent that infringes on free enquiry, teaching and discussion." Three years later, on April 26, 1963, the American Association of University Professors voted to censure Henry and the University of Illinois board of trustees for firing Koch.

Jefferson Poland moved to San Francisco and founded an SFL chapter at the University of California, Berkeley. In the *Berkeley Barb* in February 1966, Poland asked why human sexuality was taboo at the University:

"Cal teaches Marxism ... which is evidently less frightening to the Regents. The psychology department offers instruction on a wide variety of human activities–

perception, motivation, adjustment, group processes, language, cognition, childhood, adolescence, behavior disorders–but doesn't consider the psychology of sex sufficiently important to be the subject of a course. ... At LA's Free University of California, Lawrence Lipton lectures on 'The New Morality and the Sexual Revolution.'"

Lipton was a journalist, writer, beat poet, and father of James Lipton, host of the TV series *Inside the Actor's Studio*. In the 1920s Lipton was a figure in the Chicago Renaissance, friends with writers Edgar Lee Masters, Sherwood Anderson, Harriet Monroe, Ben Hecht, and Carl Sandburg who congregated in Towertown, Chicago's gay neighborhood. Lipton also wrote for underground papers like the *Los Angeles Free Press*, and was the author of *Holy Barbarians*, a 1959 book about the Beat poets. The cover of the first edition reads: "At last the complete story of the 'Beat'–that hip, cool, frantic generation of new Bohemians who are turning the American scale of values inside out." In the book, a Beat named Chris Nelson, talks about Allen Ginsberg's friend, Carl Solomon, and the fluid sexuality of the bohemians in Greenwich Village:

"Their homosexuality, I don't know, I feel it's weird, sort of–what I mean, it isn't real, really. I've seen these guys from the sticks make it in New York who don't know how to be homosexuals and they learn from other fags how to be homosexuals. These guys are like this intellectual type homosexual. They are well read and they know all the things that the famous homosexuals have written in literature. But these same guys, they still make it with chicks."

In Lipton's 1965 book *The Erotic Revolution*, he wrote:

"Repeal all the laws regulating pre-marital sex; Make legal marriage optional; Repeal all laws making homosexuality illegal; Repeal all the so-called 'unnatural laws' regarding the sexual act; Make contraceptives legal everywhere and free to low income groups; Make all abortions legal and free to those unable to pay."

Jefferson Poland's article in the *Berkeley Barb* opened a discourse on the letters pages, on subjects like "what is, and what isn't 'sick sex,'" and "pansensualism," topics that were never mentioned in the mainstream press. The *Berkeley Barb* was a weekly newspaper edited by Max Scherr, first published in August 1965. In his book, *The Paper Revolutionaries*, Laurence Leamer described Scherr as "a middle-aged radical with a full, silver-flecked beard, and a quaint, almost rigid sense of individuality." The *Berkeley Barb* was one of the most influential underground papers, covering anti-war protests, radical politics, and civil rights issues. It also embraced nudity in its graphics, and carried sex ads for X-rated films, porno bookstores, and masseurs, both gay and straight.

In April 1965, the *Los Angeles Free Press* published "Sexual Liberty Movement to Follow Civil Rights," an article about psychologist Dr. Albert Ellis visiting the Los Angeles chapter of the Institute for Rational Living. In his lecture, Ellis repeatedly called for women's rights and sexual liberty groups to form using the template of the racial freedom groups. He said:

"Most people live lives today that do not tap one-tenth of their psychological and sexual capacities for life enjoyment and fulfillment on earth, yet we are reaching for the moon. ... The widespread erroneous beliefs in women's inferiority and the evil wrong of our sex drives except in marriage and for procreation–these false concepts would be a good place to begin along with civil rights."

After years of derision in the mainstream press, where homosexuality was judged criminal or a medical anomaly, negative attitudes toward sexual variance were now being openly challenged in the underground press. In October 1965 One Inc. placed an ad in the *Los Angeles Free Press* that read:

"For a completely new and up to date look at our hypocritical and prejudicial opinions concerning sex, we invite you to read the most serious and provocative book on the subject to appear since Freud and Kinsey.

"To order your copy of IN DEFENSE OF HOMOSEXUALITY (Julian Press), send $6.25 (includes 4% tax) to ONE Bookservice, 3473 1/2 Cahuenga Bld., Hollywood, California. List of other books on homosexuality on request."

In December 1965, the *Los Angeles Free Press* published the "ACLU Policy Statement About Sexual Behavior," adopted by the Board of Directors of the American Civil Liberties Union of Southern California, written by writer, historian, and sexologist, Vern Bullough, at the time Chairman of the ACLU's Committee on Sex and Civil Liberties. It begins:

"The ACLU of Southern California believes that the right to privacy in sexual relations is a basic constitutional right. In respect to private conduct by adults, each individual has the right to decide what kind of sexual practices he or she will or will not engage in, what techniques will be used, and whether or not a contraceptive should be used. Public regulation of sexual conduct should be concerned only with preventing rape and assault and the protection of minors."

The Statement goes on to say:

"We do recognize, however, that the most controversial aspect of the policy relates to homosexuality. We therefore feel justified in making certain observations about homosexual conduct. It should be made clear from the first that at present it is not a crime to be a homosexual, but it is a crime to perform a homosexual act. Some states provide separate definitions of and penalty for particular homosexual offenses; others set forth a vaguely phrased, catch-all offensive such as unnatural crimes, the infamous crime against nature, any unnatural copulation, the abominable and detestable crime against nature with mankind or beast, any unnatural and lascivious act."

The Statement notes that police, pressured into curbing homosexual practices, have "fallen back on an amalgam of unsavory vice squad techniques or of 'looking the other way.'" It goes on to say that in large cities, police patrol homosexual meeting places and make arrests. "Often the police become agent provocateurs because it is argued that only by such techniques can the existing law be enforced. ... Plainclothesmen are stationed in bars as decoys and when men are arrested, the bars are charged with 'disorderly conduct.'"

It wasn't until the end of 1967 that the ACLU officially called for an end to laws prohibiting homosexuality. The Los Angeles paper *Open City* reported on a statement issued by the ACLU Board of Directors acknowledging the widespread harassment of homosexuals:

"The right of privacy should extend to all private sexual conduct and should not be a matter for invoking penal statutes. ... The existence of such laws, moreover, stimulates governmental harassment of persons who engage in non-typical sexual behavior, even though no criminal charge is placed against them. Police, license officials and other government administrative personnel continually subject homosexuals to a variety of pressures in bars, parks, night clubs and other places where they assemble solely on the grounds that homosexuals congregate there and without any evidence of a crime being committed."

The mainstream media's take on the Sexual Freedom League can be found in a March 11, 1966 prurient article in *Time* magazine:

"As they do at countless collegiate parties everywhere, the couples wriggled to the watusi and gyrated to the jerk, while recorded drums and saxophones resounded in the dimly lit apartment of a University of California student in Berkeley. Unlike parties most anywhere, however, the boys and girls were naked. ... The promoters of nude parties contend that their motivation is intellectual and philosophical, not merely sensual. Nonstudent Richard Thorne, 29, a Negro, who heads an off campus East Bay Sexual Freedom League, argues that 'man will only become free when he can overcome his own guilt and when society stops trying to manage his sex life for him.' His idea of freedom is parties in which individuals can engage in any sexual act 'that doesn't impose on the desire of other people.'"

Time goes on to suggest the trend is spreading with student committees promoting sexual freedom at Stanford, the University of Texas and UCLA:

> "In Austin, the Texas Student League for Responsible Sexual Freedom has 18 members so far, led by Senior Tom Maddux. He contends that limiting birth control pills to married women is 'ridiculous,' society's attitude toward homosexuality is 'hypocritical,' and laws against sodomy should be 'stricken or radically changed.'"

Maddux's views on sex proved too controversial for the University of Texas. In August, Austin's *Rag* reported the Texas Student League for Responsible Sexual Freedom "is dead." Gary Chason, co-chairman of the League, wrote that university approval of the group was withdrawn after the *Time* article. The Texas Civil Liberties Union took up the case, but closed it after Thomas Maddux, the scheduled plaintiff, abruptly withdrew. His withdrawal came after a series of "coincidences." Maddux, who was due to become a teaching assistant in the Spanish Department, was inexplicably denied the post. Another "coincidence" occurred when the Admissions office failed to notify Maddux's draft board that he was attending school, leaving him eligible for military service. Also, State Senator Grady Hazlewood described League members as a "bunch of queer-minded social misfits," and threatened, as a member of the Senate Appropriations Committee, to cut University allocations unless the group was denied the Administration's approval. Another "coincidence" was when League faculty sponsors, Dr. Irwin Spear of the Botany Department and Dr. Robert Montgomery of the English Department, pulled their support for the League, after parents started a campaign to get them fired. However, from this suppression, emerged the Texas Students for Free Speech, a group that protested in open defiance of the Administration, carrying signs "End Censorship" and "Bring the Constitution to the Campus."

On April 2, 1966 the East Bay Sexual Freedom League held a nude beach party at San Gregorio Beach State Park, attended by sixty-five people and sanctioned by the police. However, that honeymoon didn't last as police raided a private SFL party a month later, claiming someone reported them for serving alcohol to minors. They weren't. The group placed this ad in the *Berkeley Barb* to clarify rules of entry: "East Bay Sexual Freedom League now invites all persons to join if they believe in individual freedom of choice in sexual matters, and are at least 18: male, female, heterosexual, homosexual, couples, or singles."

In May 1966, Jefferson Poland wrote a letter to the *Berkeley Barb*, slamming beatniks for holding traditional sexual values, one man and one woman at a time. "Changing restrictive laws can be only a part of the sexual freedom movement. It is also necessary to free bohemia from monogamy, possessiveness, jealousy, and sexual 'faithfulness.'" The orgies and nude beach parties continued for the next eighteen months. In the late-fall of 1967, an article in *Modern Utopian,* a Berkeley-based magazine, edited and published by Richard Fairfield, claimed the Sexual Freedom League was expanding, along the West Coast and throughout the nation. There were now SFL chapters in Chicago, San Diego, San Francisco, New York, and soon, Los Angeles. *Modern Utopian* reported that Virginia Miller, SFL President, had written about homosexuality in their newsletter: "If the men want to bring their boy-friends to our parties, or if the women want to bring their girl-friends, they should feel free to do so. Don't let up-tight members discourage you."

As gay men and lesbians emerged from the closet and formed their own social and sexual groups, the less of a role they played in the Sexual Freedom League. Even bisexuals were leaving. In a December 1967 *Berkeley Barb,* a graduate psychology student named Leo Laurence, opined: "'Bisexuality is a natural aspect of the normally developed man or woman. … Yet it isn't openly accepted at the SFL parties."

In July 1968, *Open City* described Tony Palmer, director of the San Francisco branch of the Sexual Freedom League, as "a slightly overweight satyr of 39 whose younger wife has plump calves, dark and sadistic eyes and a proclivity for watching her husband fuck other broads while primly disdaining such activities for herself." Palmer told the paper there were two active SFL groups on the West Coast: the San Francisco League with 400 members and Los Angeles, which has 175. He explained the demographics: "We're mostly heterosexual. There are some bi-sexuals in the group. And they consider the heterosexuals hung up, inhibited. But I guess this is just what you'd call a sexual norm … and most of us are normal."

In January 1969 a headline in the *Berkeley Barb* read: "Bi-Sexual Bi-Circle Dissolves." "Bisexuals in the Sexual Freedom League have dissolved their 'bi-circle,' which held mixed gay/straight parties. The circle leader, a male transvestite named Sally, says interest had declined, especially among females." While West Coast gays, lesbians, and bisexuals were off "doing their own thing," the Sexual Freedom League was actively recruiting gays in other cities. In an August 1968 article in Milwaukee's *Kaleidoscope*, SFL President Jay Richards said the Milwaukee chapter had twenty-five members. He told the paper the group "has many goals. … To put out some literature, work on abortion reforms and end discrimination for homosexuals." By October 1971 there were SFL chapters in seven cities. In the *Daily Planet*, out of Coconut Grove, FL, Allen Levi wrote that Mark Stires, local SFL coordinator, said the aim of the organization is "to change the puritan oriented sex laws which remain on the books. [The SFL] goal is a free society where each person can express his or her sexual desires freely and without legal harassment." Some of the activities planned by SFL Miami included "encounter groups to help one understand one's sexual hang-ups and how to overcome them." They included sexual sensitivity and growth classes, and "a weekend retreat from artificiality" was being planned at the Indies Inn and Yacht Club at Duck Key, halfway between Miami and Key West, for August 27-29. "Encounter groups, dining, dances (one a ladies choice), drinks, swimming and, of course, sex are on the agenda. ... All are welcome, regardless of sexual persuasion, hetero, gay, unisexual or transsexual."

3

NUDITY

The ancient Greeks and Romans were first to celebrate the male physique as an art form, stretching man's physical and mental abilities to the limit, in the areas of sport, philosophy, and the arts. In those ancient cultures, male homosexuality was a noble love. However, after the two pagan societies fell, and Christianity took hold, the male nude in art vanished beneath a censorious cloak. It was revived during the Renaissance, when the Roman Catholic Church commissioned works like Michelangelo's marble statue, "Pieta," Christ draped across his mother's lap, and the muscular full-frontal nude, "David." After the Renaissance the male nude vanished again, returning in the mid-19th century with the advent of photography, an invention that snatched artistic expression from the controlling grip of the ruling class and handed it to the people. However, it wasn't until the 1960s that male and female nudity became a revolutionary act.

"Nudity is a problem for Americans. It disrupts our social exchange."–Eric Fischl, painter and sculptor.

In February 1970 in the *Berkeley Tribe*, a longhaired J. "Fuck" Poland, of the Sexual Freedom League, appeared in a photograph by Jean Raisler, sitting cross-legged on the floor, full-frontal nude, genitals exposed.

Nudity became a political statement several years earlier. In October 1967, a *Berkeley Barb* headline read: "More Nude-Ins for SF State." Two students, Adam Feldman and Patricia Vawter, were arrested and charged with indecent exposure at their nude-in at San Francisco State College. Phil Garlington, student body president, and 191 students signed a petition asking John Summerskill, college prexy, to "use your influence to get the charges dropped." The couple's attorney Larry Minkoff argued that nudity wasn't lewd or indecent. After all, there were nude statues in some federal buildings. The *Berkeley Barb* noted that the couple's action "fits into a wave of unofficial, unconnected nude-ins so far this year in Golden Gate Park, starting with free beachers dancing nude at the great Be-In." Nudity on San Francisco beaches and in parks became a political issue.

The full-frontal male nude raised the ire of the older men of the establishment more than their female counterparts. The men of the establishment did not want their privates tossed into the public arena. Wilhelm von Gloeden was a pioneer in nude photography, with his pastoral studies of relaxed Sicilian boys. Robert Aldrich, in his book *The Seduction of the Mediterranean: Writing, Art, and Homosexual Fantasy*, quotes from Curzio Malaparte's 1949 novel *The Skin*: "The true emblem of Italy is not the tricolor but the sexual organs, the male sexual organs. The patriotism of the Italian people is all there. Honour, morals, the Catholic religion, the cult of the family–all are there, in our sexual organs, which are worthy of our ancient and glorious traditions of civilization."

In the 1950s and 1960s "beefcake" magazines revived interest in the classic poses of the Greeks and Romans, men in posing pouches throwing discus and javelin. While the physique magazines were a study in homoeroticism, the hippies shucked their clothes as a revolutionary act. In April 1968, *Hair: The American Tribal Love-Rock Musical* opened on Broadway. With lyrics by James Rado and Gerome Ragni, music by Galt MacDermot, the musical focuses on a tribe of New York anti-Vietnam War draft resistors. The most controversial aspect of *Hair* was the attitude toward drugs and free love, most shocking of all, a nude scene lasting twenty-seconds. In Scott Miller's book, *Rebels With Applause: Broadway's Groundbreaking Musicals*, the author wrote:

> "Nudity was a big part of the hippie culture, both as a rejection of the sexual repression of their parents and also as a statement about naturalism, spirituality, honesty, openness, and freedom. The naked body was beautiful, something to be celebrated and appreciated, not scorned and hidden. They saw their bodies and their sexuality as gifts, not as 'dirty' things.'"

In the *New York Times*, Clive Barnes wrote: "At one point–in what is later affectionately referred to as 'the nude scene'–a number of men and women … are seen totally nude and full, as it were, face. … Homosexuality is not frowned upon–one boy announces that he is in love with Mick

Jagger, in terms unusually frank." Another shocking element of *Hair* was the tribe singing *Sodomy* at a fake Roman Catholic mass. The song is a list of sexual acts condemned by the church, including pederasty, a prod at the proclivities of some priests:

Sodomy
Fellatio
Cunnilingus
Pederasty

Father, why do these words sound so nasty?

Masturbation can be fun
Join the holy orgy
Kama Sutra
Everyone!

Another play that challenged sexual norms was *Che!* written by Lennox Raphael, a black Trinadadian playwright, poet and journalist. In March 1969, Da Latimer reviewed the play in the *East Village Other*. He wrote:

"This was a mistake. I got comestains [sic] all over it. ... it's clear that this revolutionary extravaganza was deeply inspired by the notorious photo of Che's corpse on a table being ogled by necrophiliac Bolivian generals. Have you ever been assaulted by a necrophiliac Bolivian general? ... It must have been ever so prurient for Che, lying there with his eyes and fly open, the innocence of his cause now eternally consecrated, like a marble nymph in Forest Lawn. You can see him in Lennox's play, being fondled and murdered by the President of the ... of the what? There's a question for you."

Two weeks later, Robert Gover, in the *Los Angeles Free Press*, wrote that he and his wife flew to New York to see *Che!* Gover wrote:

"New Left notables who were on hand–Jerry Rubin, Paul Krassner, Ed Sanders, NBC and CBS 'staffers,' the fire department sent 'inspectors,' the police department sent armed and dangerous 'Guardians,' and the rest of the audience was a costume party, the We's and They's of America today dressed in the symbols of the various we-they-ness.
    "Two of the play's four main characters–the president and Mr. Mayfang–arrived in a limousine. The President wore only a stars and stripes top hat and red, white and blue sash–the Emperor striding naked through his throngs–and Mr. Mayfang, played by a stern-faced chick, wore a silver lame jumpsuit, hung with a plexiglass dildo. The pig guardians stared. Hard. Their billyclubs dangling, forgotten, as the President's cock bounced jauntily on his bare thighs. ... the simulated shoving of cocks into mouths, pussies and assholes, and the spectacle of the Nun humping everything it pleased her Jesus-loving clit to

hump. For Che, the character, is constantly on the make. He'll be fucker or fuckee, it doesn't matter to him, as long as the fuck happens. ... By the play's end, Che has fucked and sucked his way into becoming the utterly fascinating love-object of the President ... "

Gover wrote that the play was "unbusted" that night, but a few days later, "after a large number of Gotham's 'Goodguys' had a turn at Peeping it," the play was raided and closed down.

In the March 5, 1970, *Village Voice,* Jonathan Black reported on the trial of the five performers, playwright, and lighting man of *Che!,* all convicted of obscenity and public lewdness:

"The defendants were acquitted of the crimes of consensual sodomy and conspiracy. Five of the convicted were given unconditional discharges; the remaining three–producer Ed Wode, playwright Lennox Raphael, and actor Larry Berkowitz, who played Che–were given 60-day jail terms, or alternatively, fines of up to $1000."

Rock musicians also jumped on the nudity bandwagon. In Atlanta's *Great Speckled Bird,* the Allman Brothers promoted their first album by posing full frontal nude standing in a stream. Another rock 'n' roll moment of public nudity occurred March 1, 1969, at the Dinner Key Auditorium in Miami, FL., when Jim Morrison, lead singer with the Doors, allegedly exposed himself in front of 12,000 people. According to *Dallas Notes*:

"Morrison attempted to incite a riot by announcing, 'There are no laws! There are no rules!' ... Morrison then unzipped his famous leather pants and let several thousand teenage chicks see what that bulge really looks like. He jacked off, reportedly to climax, and split in a limousine before the pigs could decide what to do."

The *Los Angeles Free Press* reported on the charges against Morrison:

"Gross lewdness, lewdly and lasciviously exposing his penis, simulating masturbation, simulating oral copulation, exposing his penis in a vulgar or indecent manner with the intent to be observed, profane and vulgar language such as: 'You're a bunch of fucking idiots'; 'Don't you want to see my cock?'; 'Grab your fucking friend and love him'; and the use of intoxicating liquor and drugs."

The *Daily Planet* reported on the court case: " ... Judge Murray Goodman is up for re-election, fighting for his political life, and using Jim Morrison as his pre-planned ticket to cash in on the radio, television and newspaper publicity that generates around a man like the Door's lead singer." The paper goes on to call Gov. Claude Kirk "an asshole," and says the witnesses are bogus:

> "Robert Jennings, a six foot, nine inch, red-headed freak, took the stand and told the jury he saw it all. He saw Morrison drinking. He saw Morrison put his hands inside his tight bellbottoms and play with himself. He saw Morrison get down on his knees in an attempt to simulate oral copulation on the lead guitar player. He saw Morrison whip it out and stroke it right there in front of God and everyone … he saw it all … so he says. Robert Jennings, when he is not being a puppet witness, spends his time working for Dade County. He is an employee of the prosecutor's office. He works for the same pigs who put Morrison on trial."

On September 20, 1970, a jury found Jim Morrison guilty on the misdemeanor charges of indecent exposure and profanity, and not guilty on the felony charge and the misdemeanor for drunkenness. He was released on a $50,000 bond and on October 30, 1970 he was sentenced to six months of hard labor, a $500 fine for public exposure and sixty days of hard labor for profanity. The sentences would run concurrently. An appeal was filed, but Jim Morrison died in Paris, France, on July 3, 1971 before it came to trial.

Two years earlier, another alleged homosexual revolutionary was arrested. In April 1968, in the *Great Speckled Bird,* a headline read, "Longhair Convicted":

> "Roman authorities, acting on information from a paid informer, have arrested the leader of a dissident group of pacifists. Jesus Christ, of no fixed address, was brought before Magistrate Pontius Pilate and bound over for trial. He was arrested in the company of several suspected homosexuals while loitering in an olive grove near Jerusalem. The Romans state that their attention was drawn to Christ when he was observed kissing another man under a tree."

In 1968 John Lennon and Yoko Ono released *Unfinished Music No.1: Two Virgins.* The front cover depicted the couple naked and facing the camera, on the back, they're facing away from the camera. *News from Nowhere*, a paper out of DeKalb, IL, reported that Chicago police had busted Head Imports, a hippie store owned by George Sells. The bust came after a complaint from a "Little Old Lady." There may or may not have been a "Little Old Lady," but it was Sgt. James Zarno of Chicago's Red Squad, who instigated the bust. The Red Squad was a Chicago police surveillance and information gathering team that focused on radical groups, including the Gay Liberation Front. *News from Nowhere* published a conversation that occurred after the arrest, first reported by Mike Royko in the *Chicago Daily News*. While in the presence of City Attorney Arthur Mooradian, an unnamed vice detective, and storeowner George Sells, Zarno said:

"What the hippies want is to get by with something like this and the next thing they will be undressing and walking around naked on Wells Street. ... Who in the hell would want a picture like that, with this Lennon standing there, showing his private organs? That Japanese girl–she's nothing to look at. Lennon must be soft in the head."

4

THE TWILIGHT WORLD OF THE HOMOSEXUAL

After the repression of the 1950s, the 1960s saw an increase in mainstream press exposés of villainous cartoonish homosexuals skulking around in their shadowy world. Though limited, the gay press tried to redress the balance. However, it was the underground press that brought the emerging radical gay movement to a wider readership. After the Student Homophile League formed at New York's Columbia College, the first signs of a Gay Generation Gap appeared between the stodgy Mattachine-style gay groups and the burgeoning counterculture.

"Once I had a secret love/That lived within the heart of me/All too soon my secret love/Became impatient to be free. … Now I shout it from the highest hills/Even told the golden daffodils/At last my heart's an open door/And my secret love's no secret anymore."—Secret Love by Doris Day (music by Sammy Fain/lyrics by Paul Francis Webster)

After its release in 1953, the song, *Secret Love*, from the film *Calamity Jane*, became a favorite in smoky gay bars, crooned by groups of inebriated men huddled around a piano. At the time, all love for homosexuals was a "secret love." The 1960s saw the media turn up the dimmer switch on the twilight world of the homosexual. Amidst articles in the mainstream press about raids and perverts, as well as salacious pieces on homosexuals in *Life* and *Time* magazines, the underground press started a serious public forum on sexuality.

Los Angeles' *Open City* was published by radical journalist John Bryan. Robert J. Glessing, in his book *The Underground Press in America,* said Bryan "had a penchant for all aspects of sexual freedom" and "an obsession with sex." At its peak, *Open City* sold 35,000 copies. In February 1968, in *Open City*, Corbet Grenshaw wrote "What Homosexuals Want," an article about gay publications: "'Underground' implies non-establishment, minority, liberal. There have for years been many different kinds of underground presses. … One of the most prolific underground circuits has been the 'Gay Underground Press.'" Grenshaw lists fourteen gay organizations, individuals, businesses, publishing rights-oriented papers or magazines in the US, including *Vector* (Society for Individual Rights, San Francisco); the *Ladder* (Daughters of Bilitis) national magazine; *Drum* (Homosexual Law Reform Society); the *LA Advocate* (Independent); *One* (One, Inc.); *Pursuit & Symposium* (James Kepner); and *Tangents* (Tangent). Grenshaw wrote that homosexual publications "suffer from undernourishment through lack of news, non-cooperation, and few newsgatherers." The combined circulation of these gay papers is unknown, but it's unlikely it added up to the sales of one successful underground paper. The *Berkeley Tribe* alone sold 53,000 copies a week, the *Los Angeles Free Press* over 100,000, Chicago's *Seed* 35,000, and smaller publications like the *Ann Arbor Argus* sold 14,000. In his book *The Paper Revolutionaries*, Laurence Leamer wrote that circulation of papers by members of the Underground Press Syndicate was 1,500,000. At their peak, the estimated readership of US underground papers was 18,000,000.

Grenshaw cited attempts to publish other homosexual papers:

"Cruise News, a low brow paper fell after a valiant stand. *Magpie,* just recently sprang up in Burbank, but it's a gay bar syndicated bi-monthly listing the cute bartenders, and what Bette Davis movie is playing at what bar. There is talk, and some day it may come off, of forming a Homo-Press Syndicate to later connect with the Underground Press Syndicate."

In January 1966, *Time* magazine published "The Homosexual in America." The article reads like an anthropological study:

"The late Dr. Edmund Bergler found certain traits present in all homosexuals, including inner depression and guilt, irrational jealousy and a megalomaniac conviction that homosexual trends are universal. Though Bergler conceded that homosexuals are not responsible for their inner conflicts, he found that these conflicts 'sap so much of their inner energy that the shell is a mixture of superciliousness, fake aggression and whimpering. Like all psychic masochists, they are subservient when confronted by a stronger person, merciless when in power, unscrupulous about trampling on a weaker person.'"

In comparison, in *Open City*, Grenshaw listed the more serious type of articles appearing in gay, and gay-friendly, papers:

"'Psychiatry and the Law … A Tangent's Report' (*Tangents*). 'Hippies Invade Perry's Advance Seminar' (*Prosperos Newsletter*. Prosperos is not a homosexual organization). 'Doctors Discuss Sex' (*One, Inc.*), 'Mother, Dad, Please Listen (*Mattachine Midwest*), 'Notes From the Underground: The Generation Gap (The *Ladder: A Lesbian Review*)."

The Prosperos, a group named after the magician in William Shakespeare's *The Tempest*, was co-founded by Thane Walker and Phez Kahlil (real name Richard James Featheringill) in Florida in 1956, before moving to Los Angeles in the 1960s. The Prosperos adopted a program of spiritual education; a cosmic cocktail of mysticism, psychology, astrology, and an acceptance of homosexuality, bisexuality, and androgyny. The group's mission statement stated: "The Prosperos is a non-profit religio-educational institution devoted to research, study and education in the New Frontiers of the heart, the mind and the spirit." The founders of Prosperos were devotees of Russian philosopher and spiritual teacher George Gurdjieff, as were many gays and lesbians over the previous decades, including Margaret Anderson and Jane Heap, the lesbian editors of Chicago's *Little Review*. The beliefs of the group are explained in "On Sexuality," an article in the November 9, 1969 issue of the *Prosperos Newsletter*:

"Sexuality is energy. And energy, in all its forms, is intelligence or consciousness. Sexuality is a factor of consciousness that can be turned to any creative endeavor. … Which brings us to the Sexual Revolution. So-called. Because, in light of sexuality as consciousness, it isn't a revolution at all, but an evolution–a greater opening-up of man's awareness of himself as a creative force."

For the first time, a public debate on sexuality was occurring outside of American Medical Association and American Psychiatric Association conferences. Discussion was taking place in colleges and universities, in student newspapers, and in the underground press. In October 1969, *Walrus,* produced by University of Illinois at Urbana–Champaign students, published "The Failure of Sexual Reform" by the controversial Austrian radical psychoanalyst Wilhelm Reich, with the following introduction:

"Western sexual taboos and mores are not entirely the results of a capricious unconscious. They are used by society to control people and channel them into desired activities. Sexual repression is thus an integral part of an authoritarian society. This chapter from *The Sexual Revolution* (1936) by Wilhem Reich has great relevance for America as it enters the 1970s."

Radical student gay activism began at New York's Columbia University on April 19, 1967, when the Student Homophile League (SHL) was issued a charter. Stephen Donaldson (real name Robert Anthony Martin, Jr.), an openly bisexual student, formed SHL in the fall of 1965. In *Gay Power: An American Revolution*, author David Eisenbach writes that in August 1965, Donaldson asked a social worker to call the dean's office to ask if Columbia would register a known homosexual. The administration responded by saying, "He would be allowed to register, on condition that he undergo psychotherapy and not attempt to seduce other students." In response, Donaldson formed SHL. On April 27, 1967, an article about the newly chartered organization appeared in the *Columbia Spectator,* the student paper, prompting a supportive editorial and a debate that played out on the letters page. After sending out press releases, Donaldson was interviewed by gay rights supporter Murray Schumach of the *New York Times*. On May 3, 1967, a front-page headline read "Columbia Charters Homosexual Group." In the piece Schumach wrote:

"The chairman, who used the pseudonym Stephen Donaldson, said in a telephone interview last night that the organization had been formed because 'we wanted to get the academic community to support equal rights for homosexuals.' ... In its declaration of principles, the league lists 13 points, including ... [that] 'the homosexual is being unjustly, inhumanely and savagely discriminated against by large segments of American society.'"

On May 12, 1967, *Time* also reported on SHL, who stated they were not a social group, but purely educational. Their aim was to fight for the right of homosexuals "to live and to work with his fellow man as an equal." Organizers of the League remained anonymous, because, as one anon reasoned, "We would be losing jobs for the rest of our lives." *Time* wrote:

"Columbia's administrators took a bemused but coolly legalistic stance toward the new group. The University Committee on Student Organizations at first denied the league recognition, since it refused to name its organizers. The dozen interested students then shrewdly enlisted eight officers of other campus organizations, all presumably heterosexual, to sign as sponsors, under a university rule that their names need not be made public. The committee then decided that it had no legal reason not to grant the group official status."

Time went on to say that other students appeared tolerant of the organization, with one sophomore commenting: "As long as they don't bother the rest of us, it's O.K." However, anonymity may have proven problematic, as some students were posing the question: "How do you treat them equally when you don't know who they are?"

The Gay Generation Gap widened when an established gay rights group objected to the publicity given to these young SHL upstarts. In *Gay Power*, David Eisenbach writes that Dick Leitsch, president of the Mattachine Society of New York (MSNY), objected to the media attention and, with the unanimous support of the board, contacted Frank Hogan, a Manhattan District Attorney and Member of the Columbia Board of Trustees, to advise him on how to undermine the Student Homophile League. Leitsch wrote:

> "The man using the pseudonym Stephen Donaldson is known to me and to the Mattachine Society as an irresponsible, publicity-seeking member of an extremist political group. We have grave doubts as to his sincerity in his stated aim as helping homosexuals, and feel that he may be, instead, a bigoted extremist, interested upon wrecking the homophile movement."

The publicity from Columbia's SHL caused a ripple. A similar group formed at Cornell University, followed by others around the country. The Cornell chapter was founded in March 1968 in response to an article about Columbia's SHL in the *Cornell Daily Sun*. *Scimitar*, an underground paper out of Ithaca, NY, claimed you could purchase the paper from "assorted degenerates roaming the streets." In the November 1, 1968 issue, Jearld Moldenhauer, president of Cornell SHL, wrote "Homophile on Record." He explained the group's aims:

> "The Student Homophile League, which is made up of homosexuals and heterosexuals, directs itself to three levels of concern: to encourage a reconsideration of societal myths which influence the ego structure typical of American citizenry; to voice our protest against those social institutions which discriminate against homosexuals; and to be of service to the homosexual in achieving a healthy self-concept."

On October 27, 1968, Charles Thorp, a student at San Francisco State University, addressed the "Symposium on the Life Style of the Homosexual." The event was sponsored by the Glide Foundation, affiliated with Glide Memorial Church, the pro-gay church that formed the Council on Religion and the Homosexual. One audience member, Thane Walker of the Prosperos, published the young student's speech, in a nine-page booklet, *What It's Like to be a Teenage Homosexual*. In the tract, Thorp argued that established groups like the Society for Individual Rights were campaigning for changes in the law that would only benefit those, twenty-one and over. Thorp asked, "Where does that leave the 20, 18 or 16 year old?" He had a point. Tensions between cops and gay teens in San Francisco's "Meat Rack" Tenderloin district were reaching a boiling point. Back in 1965, under the wing of Glide Memorial Church, Adrian Ravarour and Billy Garrison founded Vanguard, a gay youth organization. Ravarour was inspired by Jean-Jacques Rousseau's 1762 treatise *The Social Contract*, Thomas Payne's *Rights of Man,* the Bill of Rights, and Martin Luther King. Vanguard started a publication of the same name, though it started out as *V* and focused on drug problems. The editor used the pseudonym Jean-Paul Maurat, after the murdered radical journalist and politician during the French Revolution, whose eulogy was read by the sexual libertine, Donatien Alphonse François, Marquis de Sade. Clearly, these street kids were well read.

In the November 1966 issue of *V,* an editorial is titled: "Why Drugs in the Tenderloin?" The author answers with three reasons: "A) Rebellion; B) Escape; and C) Profit." Under "Escape" he wrote:

"The people who use drugs for escape are usually homosexuals, ex-convicts, and members of various racial and physical minority groups. Society rejects, damns, humiliates and generally makes them miserable. They attempt to escape the harsh realities of being condemned by society for being 'different' by the use of drugs. … In my own case, as in most cases of the escape variety, fear is the main motivating factor. The fear of non-acceptance by the controlling society. I'm gay, when I realized this at the age of 13, it scared me. My parents had been Victorian in their sex attitudes and only here and there did I hear veiled references to 'fags' and 'queers'; usually accompanied by a wish to kill all of them or similar punishment. Where could I go? I went to drugs."

In 1967 *Vanguard* joined the Underground Press Syndicate and published intelligent, well-written articles and poetry, often with a historical slant. In the September issue an editorial "Critique" notes the growing rift between established groups like SIR and an emerging gay youth movement aligned with militant civil rights groups, anti-Vietnam war protests, and also self-awareness, personal growth, and spiritual wellness:

"Thus far, the homosexual mass movement has maintained a discreet veneer. Indeed, most of the individuals involved seem to prefer a supplicant's role instead of reveling in each other's individuality. The overall intention is to pursue conformity to the Plastic Inevitable, etc. We suspect that progress for the movement involves repairing legislation and opening public opinion, but the most central issue is the expansion of each of us as total people.
   "Therefore, several dissident elements of the homophile community are deciding to publicly acclaim their dissatisfaction with this futile search for anonymity or 'acceptance' and to proclaim their personal freedom. By its very nature, the *Vanguard* hopes to remain near the spearhead of this probing dissatisfaction.
   "Obviously, dear reader, it is not our contention that all homosexuals are liberal. Indeed, some of society's most conservative bigots are cocksuckers. Let us assure you, however, there are many who are aware, turned-on people. We

do feel that the homosexual group–as a minority faction–has inherent similarity to other oppressed minorities and a collective interest in other minority rights activities. It behooves especially the more flagrant, outrageous homosexuals, and those who don't have any hangups about it to consistently become involved in the pursuit of individual rights not only for their immediate needs but also for the personal freedom of others."

Jean-Paul Marat was interviewed in the *Paper*, out of East Lansing, MI. Laurence Tate's's article begins with a quote from Jean-Paul Marat, the French revolutionary: "The important thing is to pull yourself up by your own hair, to turn yourself inside out and see the whole world with fresh eyes."

The *Paper* described San Francisco's Tenderloin as a triangular district in the heart of the city's downtown area:

"The business is prostitution (male and female), drug peddling, robbery, assault, and (as one church-sponsored study so admirably put it) 'other misbehavior.' It looks the part: It's bleak agglomeration of hamburger stands, cheap hotels, pornography shops, straight and gay bars, and what-have-you–splashed over at night with a conflagration of neon–can depress you even before you notice the people.

"It is estimated that up to a thousand young men and women between the ages of twelve and twenty-five live and/or work in the Tenderloin as prostitutes, pimps, jackrollers, and pill pushers."

The *Paper* reported that in the summer of 1966, street kids formed Vanguard and made the news when they picketed a Tenderloin café that discriminated against them. The café was Compton's, and the ensuing "riot" is often cited as being the first open confrontation between gays and the police in the United States. Although, in May 1959, street hustlers and drag queens clashed with LAPD at Cooper's Donuts, when John Rechy, author of *City of Night,* was arrested. A similar incident occurred in 1960 at a restaurant in Chicago. The *Paper*'s Laurence Tate, who sat in on a Vanguard meeting, gave a fascinating insight into the modus operandi of the gay youth group. He describes Jean-Paul Marat as "thin and pale, with black wavy hair piled on his head, his cheeks were reddish, his lips thick and babyish." On the subject of Compton's, Marat spoke of physical violence and verbal abuse from the management and the Pinkerton's Special Police Officers who patrolled there. A leaflet handed out at the picket read:

"WE PROTEST the endless profit adults are making off youth in the central city.

"WE PROTEST the unstopped and seeming unstoppable flow of pills which afflicts the area only those who are WILLFULLY BLIND can overlook.

"WE PROTEST police harassment of youth in the area when the big time speculators seem to work openly and receive NO ATTENTION.

"WE PROTEST and deplore the fact that the 'city fathers' sit about idly while this ugly situation grows worse.

"WE PROTEST being called 'queer,' 'pillhead' and being placed in the position of being outlaws and parasites when we are offered no alternatives to this existence in our society.

"WE ASK how youth can be relegates to this extreme degradation in a country which claims to be 'moral.'

"WE DEMAND justice and immediate corrections of the fact that most of the money made in this area is made by the EXPLOITATION of youth by so-called NORMAL adults who make a fast buck off situations everyone calls DEGENERATE, PERVERTED and SICK.

"VANGUARD PLEDGES that its youth will provide the help and concern adults seem unable to muster."

Marat explained:

"I've been on and off the streets for six years now. When I first got in town I was stopped by the police seventeen times in three days. The last time I got a dislocated jaw. That sort of thing happens all the time. ... I want to help these kids. I know them. ... They know they're gay. Anyway, it's tough for them to get a job. Most of them are dropouts. A lot of them are runaways. A lot have police records. Me for example, I could get a job tomorrow if I hadn't ... got into some trouble in Los Angeles ... Some of them are hair fairies, very effeminate. Some have other-than-honorable discharges from the service. A lot of them have drug habits. ... We find that no one has room for us in their society, therefore we must work together to form our own society to meet our OWN needs. ... We are willing to work with interested groups, but who can be more trusted and relied upon than ourselves."

Membership of Vanguard was between 50-100. At the meeting Laurence Tate of the *Paper* attended, neat rows of chairs were set up, and a crowd "drifted into the room." Sitting behind a long table were Vanguard's four officers. Tate described the gathering:

"There were perhaps forty or fifty people in the room; about ten were standing in the shadow by the far wall. Though there were more than enough chairs. The standees were all young, boys and girls alike in Levis and thin, cheap-looking jackets. Most of the boys wore tight T-shirts; most of the girls had on too much makeup. Near me sat a plump boy, all in tight-fitting black with a green scarf at his neck; I say 'boy,' but he had long upswept hair and a feminine face, so I was quite honesty never sure. Toward the back a very young sandy-haired girl in a rawhide jacket sat and chewed her nails; her mascara was so thick it reminded me of shoe polish. Various adults were mixed with the kids; several ministers; a priest; a well-dressed Negro man; his wife, and three small children; a dowdy semi Bohemian middle-aged couple; a few solitary men. ... The meeting got on to Old Business. The vice-president, a blond clean-cut type in a sweater and tie, got up and explained that Compton's had agreed to end discrimination, more or less. The kids would not be specifically harassed, but, if they lingered an hour over a cup of coffee or invited non-paying friends to the tables, they would be–well, pushing their luck."

After the meeting ended, chairs were folded and those who stayed for the dance had their hand stamped, "Not For Sale." A DJ set up a turntable and speaker on a table, then the lights were turned off and a blue spotlight turned on. Couples moved through the "blue shadowy light like tropical fish":

"A man in high heels, a red dress, and an orange wig was dancing with Vanguard's treasurer. Two middle aged women were doing a graceful waltz; one had very short hair and wore pants and a man's shirt; the other, in a cocktail dress, looked impeccably suburban, and, it occurred to me, rather like the mother of a friend of mine. Two oriental boys of perhaps thirteen or fourteen were doing a slow rock, staring glassily at each other. ... Several couples clustered in the center of the floor. A tall boy was dancing with a man with bouffant hair, lots of make-up, and large false breasts. Two young heterosexual couples ... were joking with each other, comparing dance steps; isolated from the rest, they looked as if they belonged at a high-school hop in some barny old gymnasium."

Not all young heterosexual radicals in the 1960s were aware of the campaign for homosexual rights, although articles on the subject began to appear in the underground press in 1967. On August 1, 1967, in the *Washington Free Press*, Frank Speltz ventured forth into a DC "gay ghetto" and wrote, "The World of Washington Homophiles." The article begins:

"I'm prejudiced–against homosexuals. So are you. Admit it. When two men walk past you in the street hand in hand, something grabs you in the guts and you suddenly feel very uncomfortable. Why? Why should love between two human beings turn you off? Or don't you think them capable of love as you know it?"

Here are some of Speltz' observations:

——— "Both the police and Mattachine Society estimate the homosexual population of Washington at a quarter of a million. ... Next to Negroes, homosexuals are America's largest minority–15 million, to be approximate. So every tenth person you pass on the street has a life style and emotional makeup entirely different from yours."
——— "All over Washington there are communities of homosexuals, living together for the same reason hippies or radicals do: economy, camaraderie, security. I visited a 'ghetto' community, remarkably well integrated racially,

where about twelve homosexuals live. I was received with openness and infinite patience as I blurted out all those 'do Negros tan in the sun?' questions: 'do you sleep with each other much?' 'Where do you buy your dresses?' 'Why don't you change your sex if you don't like it?' ... It turned out that all of us 'straight' people wonder the same things about homosexuals, because all of us have the same sexual fantasies and stereotypes."

—— "There are about fifteen Washington gay bars. ... The mecca for homosexual activity, curiously enough, is the same area in which servicemen and travelers gather--13th Street and New York Avenue, N.W. There are three gay bars on the block there. Denizens of the area have a very logical explanation of why that area is the all night meeting ground for homosexuals, travelers and servicemen: homosexuals thrive on numerous social contacts, and accept the fact that most liaisons are by their nature temporary; travelers seek out friendly (and at home often forbidden) companionship of a temporary and anonymous nature; servicemen, because of their pent-up sexual needs and segregated lives, have learned that other men can gratify these needs. Two interesting facts add light to this phenomenon: it is estimated by one sociologist that nearly fifty percent of the country's homosexuals are (or were) Roman Catholics, whose strong emphasis on segregated (by sex) education, sexual guilt (masturbation, contraception, homosexuality are all considered sins), and authoritarianism would explain this fact. Also a surprising number (again nearly half) have served in the armed forces, where some said they had discovered their homosexuality."

—— "I asked every homosexual I talked with whether he considered himself a hippie, what he thought of hippies, and whether hippies were homosexuals of a new order. The answers were surprisingly similar: hippies reflect the culmination of a modern rejection of a dependency on sexual-role-playing. Consequently virile, heterosexual men actually prefer to wear their hair long and to wear gay clothes. But they do not, as a group, alter their sexual roles—men still prefer women, and vice versa. LSD and marijuana are as popular among homosexuals as among hippies, probably because both groups are very intensely creative, having let go of outmoded taboos and accepted new pursuits."

Much of Speltz' article focused on drag queens, cross-dressing, and the difference between "High Drag," "Medium Drag," and "Low Drag." This prompted a letter from "A homosexual (But you'd never know)":

"Dear Editor.
"In an article on homosexuals ... your writer gives the impression that all, or most, homosexuals 'change' their sex by dressing up in women's clothing, etc. While I appreciate the sympathetic tone with which he wrote about homosexuals, it is unfortunate that his article will perpetuate the myth of the effeminate queer. Fact is that the vast majority of homosexuals never wear women's clothes and never have any desire to do so. Most homosexuals look like 'normal' men and they seek partners who also look and act normal. It is understandable, however, that your author is unable to make contact with this

type of homosexual, because their concern for anonymity is very great. This same concern prevents me from signing my name."

While the underground press championed the gay cause, some of its readers were still "evolving" on the issue. In September, 1967, in a letter to the *East Village Other,* about an upcoming TV program titled "Custer," about US Army Lt. Col. George Armstrong Custer, who died at the Battle of the Little Bighorn in 1876, Brother Don wrote: "Who the fuck made this cat into a hero is beyond me. If we look back into history we shall find the honorable Mr. Custer was an egotistical, butchering fag."

5

SADOMASOCHISM

Sadomasochism comes out of the closet in the arts with Andy Warhol's Velvet Underground, Kenneth Anger's *Scorpio Rising*, Mick Jagger's "faggy little leather boys," and articles in *Life* magazine and Los Angeles' underground paper, *Open City*.

"All universal moral principles are idle fancies."–Marquis de Sade.

In the spring of 1967, an ad in Chicago's *Seed* read: "Custom Leather–sandals, capes, belts, bags" from a store called Leather Fetish, 1545 N. Wells, in the hippie/gay neighborhood. Prior to the 1960s, fetish, leather, and sadomasochism, were "perversions" shrouded in secrecy, but the counterculture dragged S&M out of dank dungeons and into the sunlight for public scrutiny. In 1963, Michael Leigh's book, *The Velvet Underground*, detailed outlaw sexual behavior, husband and wife swapping, orgies, homosexuality, sadism, and masochism. Two years later Lou Reed, John Cale, Sterling Morrison, and Maureen Tucker formed the Andy Warhol Factory-affiliated New York rock band the Velvet Underground. One of their early songs was *Venus in Furs*:

Kiss the boot of shiny, shiny leather
Shiny leather in the dark
Tongue of thongs, the belt that does await you
Strike, dear mistress, and cure his heart

Severin, Severin, speak so slightly
Severin, down on your bended knee
Taste the whip, in love not given lightly
Taste the whip, now plead for me.

Venus in Furs was inspired by Leopold von Sacher-Masoch's novel of the same name. In the story, Severin von Kusiemski is infatuated by Wanda von Dunajew, and wants to be her slave. He asks her to degrade and humiliate him, which she does, though she loses respect for him in the process. Sacher-Masoch is the great-great-uncle of British singer and actress Marianne Faithfull, whose famous boyfriend, Mick Jagger, starred in the film *Performance*, singing the title song *Memo From Turner*.

I remember you in Hemlock Road in nineteen fifty-six.
You're a faggy little leather boy with a smaller piece of stick.
You're a lashing, smashing hunk of man
Your sweat shines sweet and strong.
Your organ's working perfectly, but there's a part that's not screwed on.

One aspect of the homosexual subculture that fascinated heterosexuals was the S&M leather scene. Homophile organizations, who campaigned for gay rights by focusing on the similarities between heterosexuals and homosexuals, probably squirmed when they read Paul Welch's 1964 article "Homosexuality in America" in *Life* magazine:

"On another far-out fringe of the 'gay' world are the so-called S&M bars ('S' for sadism and 'M' for masochism). One of the most dramatic examples is in the warehouse district of San Francisco. Outside the entrance stand a few brightly polished motorcycles, including an occasional lavender model. Inside the bar, the accent is on leather and sadistic symbolism. The walls are covered with murals of masculine-looking men in black leather jackets. ... A cluster of tennis shoes–favorite footwear for many homosexuals with feminine traits–dangles from the ceiling. Behind it a derisive sign reads 'Down with sneakers!'
"'This is the antifeminine side of homosexuality,' says Bill Rudquy, part owner of the bar. 'We throw out anybody who is too swishy. If one is going to be homosexual, why have anything to do with women of either sex? We don't go for the giddy kids?'"

In October 1967, gay Chris Allen wrote about leather bars in *Open City*, saying there were "five or six gay leather bars in Los Angeles and about five more semi-leather." Allen's article is illustrated with a Tom of Finland drawing of two muscular leathermen. Allen described leather bars as "crude," with "no furniture, a couple of stools, jukebox, pool table, game machines, and sawdust on the floor." The jukebox played loud C&W and soul music, the clientele included cowboys, "queer Marlboro men," and a "cross-fertilization between the two fetishes." The décor consisted of "chains, torture instruments, male pictures, posters, announcements and other gay trinkets, the place looks like an 'in den.'" In the bathroom, graffiti read: "8 ½ inches," "S wants M," "Bill's really a dyke" and "Reagan is Ayn Rand in drag." Allen's piece continued:

"Not all leather or motorcycle queens are S&M (sadists and/or masochists). Much of the façade they present is just that–fetish and façade. In fact, there's a hell of a lot of nelly faggot under all that denim and leather. But S&M there is– the chains worn on the right shoulder, arm or ankle indicate the masochist, as does an earring in the right ear. A left earring singles out the sadist. ... There is a heavy accent on showing a 'basket'–revealing the outlines of the genitals (and ass) under tight pants. Bare chests, tight tee shirts, tattoos–but always masculine sex symbols and images. Each body has been dressed carefully according to the wearer's need and the type of partner he wishes to attract. The results are–too-often ludicrous. The leather queen trips out on the feel, the sight, the sound, taste and smell of this black hide; from leather underwear to leather sheets. ... The bizarre practitioners–the pissed-on, shat-on, come–on, waiting for that one-in-a-thousand consenting adult."

At "last call" when the lights go up:

"A lot of queens quickly flee at this sudden exposure, but those who no longer care linger, pressing their hopes, perhaps a popper in their motorcycle jacket ... making sure that so-and-so sees him caress his basket ... idle conversation to that guy they were afraid to talk to all night. He's too drunk to give a damn. Then, at the last stroke, out they wander into the smokeless, quiet fresh air of early morning. They stand around, watching where each is headed–one last look at Him–that leather-draped ass as it settles into the cycle seat. The Harley's roar up, the VW's putt off, and the weary bartenders sweep up the debris in the silence, picking up half-empty bottles in the nicotine-leather scented stale air. Into 'The City of Night' the gay ones have gone, carefully scrutinizing each male pedestrian they pass ... maybe he's the one ... and he's looking, too ... going home. Tomorrow morning ... oh, shit. Damn. A good blow job–anything. There's always masturbation."

Kenneth Anger's underground film *Scorpio Rising* also contributed to the interest in gay bikers. The movie stars Bruce Byron as Scorpio, and explores the occult, biker subculture, Catholicism, Nazism, and the hero worship of James Dean and Marlon Brando. There is no dialogue but the film has a soundtrack of 1950s singers like Ricky Nelson, the Angels, the Crystals, Bobby Vinton, Elvis Presley and Ray Charles. In May 1967, Greg Barrios reviewed *Scorpio Rising* in *Rag*, a paper out of Austin, TX. He described a biker lying on a bed reading a newspaper. On the wall behind him was a bulletin board "replete with photos, magazines, clippings and other memorabilia (including a dishonorable discharge from the Marine Corps)." The biker is smoking. He stubs out his cigarette in an ashtray, near a photo of James Dean, known in Hollywood as "The Human Ashtray," after his rumored fetish for having cigarettes stubbed out on his chest. Barrios wrote:

"In retrospect, the sociological elements seem a bit heavy-handed. ... Also, the homoerotic elements seem overstated, with multiple images of males posing in inviting gestures. But this seems more of a stylistic device that emphasizes the narcissistic vanity of certain cyclists as well as the way cyclists may appear to other males (especially homophiles)."

The September 1967 Chicago *Seed* review read:

"Kenneth Anger may be a faggot, but he retains his maleness. The first time I saw *Scorpio Rising* I felt an adolescent excitement with the sound of revving hogs, the heavy if ambiguous masculinity: at Aardvark [underground movie theater] it was mostly hilarious: heavy boots waddling interminably, somehow conveying the self-conscious image of the wearer; lighting a match in his teeth and burning himself as Brando possibly did, learning to do it from *The Wild Ones*; pissing in his helmet before an altar, and staring at the golden-red reflections, you wonder if he'll drink it. The whole mystique of the motorcycle cult is here: homosexuality, Nazism, paradoxically the Christ-imitation (spiritual power), the hard sex of gleaming chrome and leather, dissipated in masturbatory vibrations on the road. Mounted warriors of some esoteric ideal, the last knights."

In an interview with Shelly Burton in Detroit's *Fifth Estate*, Kenneth Anger described the Vietnam War as "the Establishment's way of masturbating young boys violence." And on the subject of America: "It will never be anything but a lonely sad land, crying out in the wilderness. Its culture will not take root because it is dancing on the graves of Indian nations it has robbed, raped and plundered. Their magic is stronger than the white man's, and we are paying a terrible price for our sacrilege."

6

TROUBLE WITH THE LAW

As gay writers came out of the closet and wrote for the underground press, a more accurate picture of the lives of homosexuals began to emerge. It became clear to the "straight' readers that the entrapment of gays in public restrooms by policeman exposing their genitals and raids on gay bars were commonplace. These accounts of gay harassment mirrored the harassment of African-Americans in the US, and workers, and students worldwide.

_____

"A cop sleeps inside each one of us. We must kill him. Drive the cop out of your head."–Graffiti during the French riots of 1968.

_____

As time went by, less "straight" reporters ventured into the "gay ghetto," and more homosexual writers took to the typewriter and wrote articles for the underground press. On September 27, 1967, in *Open City,* Bob Garcia wrote "Cops Hassle Hustlers," about homosexual prostitution in Los Angeles. The following week hippie gay activist Morris Kight responded with "The Truth About Gay Scene." In his article, Kight described the police as "the last vestige of the puritan tradition on which America was founded, [who] feel that they are the last moral force in the nation." Kight continued: "Capt. [Charles W.] Crumley of our Hollywood precinct stated in Mr. Garcia's article that the vice detail 'are not encouraged to use provocative gestures to lure the homosexual. Would that this were true!" Kight goes on to describe the clothes worn by police agents provocateurs:

"White jeans-tight, white tennis shoes with blue trim, colored polo shirts (green, orange, red and cocoa are preferred) and a sexy leer. ... These people are called 'studbusters.' ... One of Crumley's men, Officer Reno, is alleged to make a daily round of Griffiths Park's Gay Row ... feeling himself through his pants. If no luck he goes down to the Broadway Department Store in Hollywood where, in the John, he stands by the hour exposing himself, sometimes with an erection and always with a lonely, wanted, needed, love-me leer. Almost any comment to him is interpreted as a 'lewd' proposal, and out come the silver cufflinks."

Kight claimed Los Angeles police entrapment methods were reported accurately three years earlier in Paul Welch's 1964 *Life* magazine article, "Homosexuality in America." Welch wrote that while there was no law against being a homosexual, there were laws against specific sex acts. In California, it was illegal to solicit someone in a public place to engage in a lewd act. Those found guilty were registered as sex offenders, along with rapists and child molesters. Welch wrote in 1964:

"Inspector James Fisk says that the 3,069 arrests for homosexual offenses made in Los Angeles last year represent merely a 'token number' of those that should have been made. 'We're barely touching the surface of the problem,' Fisk says. 'The pervert is no longer as secretive as he was. He's aggressive and his aggressiveness is getting worse because of more homosexual activity.' ... In their unrelenting crackdown on homosexuals the Los Angeles police use two approaches: one is an effort to deter homosexual activity in public, and the other is an arrest effort. The first includes patrolling, in uniform, rest rooms and other known loitering places. ... Then the police go the rounds of the 'gay' bars to make their presence felt. To arrest homosexuals the police have an undercover operation in which officers dressed to look like homosexuals–tight pants, sneakers, sweaters or jackets–prowl the streets and bars. The officers are instructed never to make an overt advance: they can only provide an opportunity for the homosexual to proposition them."

In the same issue of *Open City*, under "Gay Advice," it's reported that Crumley and a Sgt. Alexander had recently met with leaders of the homophile community. The meeting was held in the home of Jerry Joachim, head of Personal Rights in Defense and Education (PRIDE). Fifteen leaders from nine Los Angeles groups attended: The Council on Religion and the Homophile, Daughters of Bilitis, Los Angeles and Long Beach branches of the National League for Social Understanding, Omega Delta Nu, One Inc., PRIDE, Pursuit and Symposium, Tangents, and Zeta Tau Iota. Also present were a representative of the Student Homophile League of New York City, and a member of San Francisco's Society for Individual Rights. *The Los Angeles Free Press* wrote of the meeting:

"Differences in point of view are not dispelled in a few hours of talk, but the Captain's exposition certainly displayed his in-depth interest in the intimate intricacies of the homophile predicament. In attempting to distinguish the friendly gesture from the lewd, the worldly vice man noted, 'when the hand lingers there (on the 'butt' of a drinking buddy') over a sort of a lengthy period of time it's no longer a salutation. He might reach clear up underneath and sort of not pat him on the rear, but pat him on the front in reverse.'"

When asked who made the complaints that lead to gay bars being raided, Crumley let slip that City Councilman Paul H. Lamport was the primary source. Lamport spent 1967 harassing homosexuals and hippies. In June 1967, in the *Los Angeles Times*, Lamport accused city departments of having a secret program to "welcome an invasion of 100,000 hippies" and proposed a resolution that would order the departments to "cease and desist" from giving "dissident non-conformist groups" special consideration. It was defeated, but the following year, a resolution passed, "designed to keep hippies from annoying and molesting people on Hollywood streets."

As a result of gay groups meeting with the cops, Jerry Joachim wrote in *Open City*:

"PRIDE is asking you to think about something: your conduct. It must be above reproach in public places. ... We are going to ask you not to cruise in public parks. This presents an intolerable situation for the LAPD, and rightly so. ... We are asking you particularly to boycott Griffith Park. Show the LAPD that we can keep our word–obey the law."

A more complete transcript of the meeting was published in the October 18 issue of *Open City* and the October issue of the Los Angeles *Advocate*. The *Advocate* was first published in September 1967 as a PRIDE newsletter, started by Richard Mitch (under the name "Dick Michaels") and Bill Rau ("Bill Rand"). The periodical was inspired by a January 1, 1967, police raid on two gay bars, the Black Cat Tavern, 3909 Sunset Blvd., and New Faces, 4001 Sunset Blvd. The Black Cat opened in November 1966. On New Year's Eve that year, it was raided by police. When customers kissed at the stroke of midnight, undercover cops started beating them. Thirteen patrons and three bartenders were arrested. The celebratory "kiss" led to two of the arrested men being listed as sex offenders. The raid caused a riot, during which cops attacked New Faces, knocking the woman owner to the ground and beating two bartenders unconscious. One required surgery to remove his ruptured spleen, but he was subsequently charged with assaulting a police officer. A few days later 200 people attended a protest, organized by PRIDE, the largest gay demonstration to take place before the Stonewall Riots.

At the PRIDE meeting between gays and cops, most of the organizations in attendance were older, established homophile groups. However, there was a new generation of militant gays emerging in the underground. In January 1968, a letter from Sam Richman was published in *Open City*.

"I know of no word that brings as much fear to the average homosexual … no word more fearful than COP. … Captain Crumley of the Hollywood Police Station came to meet with the LA homophile (a nice word for homosexual) organizations. So historic was this meeting in this wasteland that San Francisco sent a representative.

"And what happened? … They don't harass–the cops I mean. They don't entrap. Their plainclothesmen don't wear tight pants. They don't raid gay bars. They don't lie on the stand in court. They investigate all legitimate complaints. Naughty officers who might say the wrong thing in a solicitation are quickly retrained.

"Yeah. Uh-huh. Tell it to the thousands of homosexuals arrested in this area. … Where is the homosexual today? If I may borrow an analogy, the Mexican-American may be where the Negro was a couple of years ago, but the homosexual is back in '48 or '49. Nowhere. There may be a difference in what makes a homosexual a minority, but the same handcuff goes on his or her wrists that clamp the flower child. But the homosexual is a unique minority. He belongs to a nebulous group–there are no distinguishing characteristics. … The trouble is, there aren't enough homosexuals willing to stand up and say, 'MAN, I've had it with you.'"

One gay man who stood up to the Hollywood police was John W. who wrote an account of his entrapment and arrest in *Open City*. One night John left the Los Feliz Theater and was driving home alone, when three guys in a Volkswagen pulled up alongside him. The driver was making odd gestures, holding up three, then four fingers. Intrigued, John lowered the window and the driver engaged him in conversation. The driver said the other two in the car were a couple, but maybe he would like a foursome. The driver asked John what he was into. John said he was tired and on his way home. "Are you a cop?" asked John. The driver replied by asking him the same question. John said, "Somebody told me recently that it is the law now that if you ask a cop if he was one, he had to tell you." The driver replied, "Yeah, I heard that too. I think it's true." John: "Are you a cop?" Driver: "No, I'm not. Are you?" John asked: "Do you like sixty-nine?" Driver: "Yeah, I dig that." Then a second guy climbed out of the Volkswagen and John was arrested. Second cop to driver: "What did you get?" Driver: "He said he liked to sixty-nine."

John W. fought the case:

"The trial early this year went smoothly. My lawyer, Sheldon Andelson, asked the vice officer questions based on the dialogue between me and the cop and made it quite clear that the cop was lying. When I testified, I was frank and open and did not pretend to be naïve. I told it as it was, and the Judge believed me. He dismissed the case for 'lack of evidence!' Unfortunately, he didn't call it what it was: Entrapment."

Andelson defended many gay victims of entrapment and bar raids in the 1950s and 1960s. A multi-millionaire, patron of the arts, founder and chairman of the West Hollywood based Bank of Los Angeles, Andelson was a major fund-raiser for politicians like Sen. Edward Kennedy, and former Vice-President Walter Mondale. He remained in the closet until the 1970s, and died of AIDS in 1987 aged 56.

In February 1968, the *Los Angeles Free Press* reported that in Laguna Beach, CA, councilmen were waging war on gay bars, after deciding homosexuals on the beaches offended tourists:

"Behind the Orange Curtain–The City Fathers of Laguna Beach are currently bending every effort to make Gay Boys unwelcome in that exciting little community. At stake in the battles now going on is the fate of two of the remaining gay watering spots in Laguna, the Sea Horse and Dante's."

A "queer contention," argued Joan Martin of the ACLU, as a large number of Laguna's tourists were gay. "This has been going on since 1965," said Martin. "My client, the respected owner of the Sea Horse, brought in clippings dating that far back on this witch hunt." The police and Alcoholic Beverage Control (ABC) used decoy vice cops in Bermuda shorts and tennis shoes to revoke the license of the Barefoot and close down Dante's. They were less successful at the Sea Horse where, in spite of the undercover cops, there hadn't been an arrest for three years. The *Los Angeles Free Press* continued:

"Using a different tactic the ABC stepped in and began revocation proceedings against the owner, a woman with three children to support from the bar. ABC charged that she was running a 'disorderly bar' because a female customer (heterosexual) told off-color jokes. They also contended that sing-a-longs were off-color. Words to popular songs were changed such as 'Cruising down the river ... ' to 'Cruising down Laguna.'
"To further their arguments, some of the six ABC officers who testified said they had been groped. There was no proof, however, as one officer's buddy did not see the alleged groping, and the groper walked away before he could be arrested. The officers admitted that they had allowed themselves to be groped. Their final argument was that this kind of bar was keeping the public from enjoying the place. Mrs. Martin wondered who the public is. One afternoon, there were about 80 people in the 22'x25' bar."

Martin compared the police tactics to the "Spanish Inquisition" and "witch hunts of the past." "If they start closing bars because customers swear or tell dirty jokes ... all the bars in Southern California would be closed. All the homosexuals want is a place of their own where they won't bother anyone."

In July 1968, *Open City* published "Anatomy of a Raid" by Dick Michaels, from a story told to him by David S. The story was about the Yukon, a Los Angeles gay bar on Beverley Boulevard. Michaels wrote:

"The Yukon's greatest asset was its manager and regular bartender, Tommy. He was a blond, good looking young man with a nice body and an infectiously happy personality. ... Tommy had been running the bar since it opened some six months earlier. He worked hard to build up the business and was proud of how much he had accomplished in that time."

The Yukon was a small bar and Tommy was careful when it came to illegal activity, including enforcing the no-touching rule. A handshake was acceptable, but in some bars a friendly slap on the back was not. Not that the law mattered, because vice cops just made things up. The raid occurred on a Friday night in March. David S. was at the bar with his lover, Larry. Michaels continued:

"At one point about 12.30 a.m. Tommy was passing by and stopped to talk to me. After we talked a few minutes, I saw that he wasn't paying attention. He was looking over my shoulder toward the door. I turned and saw several uniformed policemen coming in. Two plainclothesmen were with them. One of them, whom we later referred to as Hooknose, yanked the jukebox cord and ordered the lights turned up. ... Hooknose announced, 'We're going to make a few arrests. Just stay where you are. Anyone who runs will be shot.'"

Hooknose randomly tapped twelve customers on the shoulder, including David S. and Tommy, saying, "You're arrested." At the station, fingerprints and mugshots were taken, then a cop told David S. "See that boy in the blue shirt?" David knew the guy in question, he had known him for years, but never had sex with him. "You humped him," said the cop. Davis S. told *Open City*: "That's pretty much the way it went for each one. Lee was accused of groping someone sitting next to him, and that guy was charged with rubbing legs with Lee."

The young, predominantly "straight" readers of the underground press were, for the first time, reading first-hand accounts of the harassment of homosexuals at the hands of an abusive police force. The pages of underground newspapers were filled with stories of police brutality.

In the first few months of 1968 alone African-Americans had numerous run-ins with abusive police. On February 8, three students were killed and twenty-eight wounded at South Carolina State College in Orangeburg. On April 6, Bobby Hutton, the treasurer of the Black Panthers was gunned down by Oakland cops. On March 6, 200 black marchers were attacked with tear gas in Social Circle, GA. In June 1968, Detroit's black community newspaper, *Inner City Voice*, featured the headline, "Racist Cops Beat Black Mother." While the mainstream media ignored stories, or sided with the police and the "Establishment," the underground press was relentless in their coverage of police brutality. The stories continued, "Police Abuse Prisoner" in Milwaukee's *Kaleidoscope*, "Police Resume Haight Raids" in *Rolling Stone*, "Cops Cripple Yippies" in *Pterodactyl*, and in *Fifth Estate*, "Police Riot at N.Y. Yip-In." In March 1968, in a *Seed* article about the "Orangeburg Massacre," Carl Bloice reported in his "Notes From a Black Reporter in Orangeburg": "Suddenly with no warning, no order to disperse or shots in the air, the patrolmen opened fire with high gauge double shot guns on students milling around." In Western Michigan University's *Western Activist*, Joe Ellin wrote "U.S. Police State": "At the University of Wisconsin and at Brooklyn College recently anti-war demonstrations were broken up with excessive and unnecessary violence. The American Civil Liberties Union charged 'brutal police action,' and 'unnecessary police violence' in the two cases." Ellin quotes from the ACLU bulletin #23131, dated Dec. 26, 1967, about the Wisconsin protest, when the school Administration called police to a non-violent rally against Dow Chemical Co., the makers of napalm: "The apparently unprovoked, indiscriminate and free use of clubs by Madison police (most of whom had removed their police identification badges from their uniforms) against unarmed civilians ... is probably the most flagrant case of police brutality in the last 25 years in this community."

Underground newspapers began publishing names, photographs, and sometimes addresses, of "guilty" cops. In the summer of 1968, *Buffalo Chip*, out of Omaha, NE, published photographs of two patrol cops, Richard L. Gilliam and Duane G. Pavel, under the headline: "CAUTION THE FOLLOWING POLICE OFFICERS ARE KNOWN RACISTS. THEY ARE ARMED AND EXTREMELY DANGEROUS TO BLACK PEOPLE." As a result of their coverage of police brutality the underground press was raided and harassed. In New York's *Rat*, Peter Novak of the *Washington Free Press* reported how on the night of Martin Luther King's assassination, he and Craig Scott, of Liberation News Service, were arrested while talking to three black citizens. Police ignored their press passes. Their offense was "never exactly stated." Arresting Officer "D.C. police badge #1627" was heard to say: "We're gonna get every nigger and long-haired son-of-a-bitch."

Police brutality was not limited to the US, as worldwide students and workers protested repressive governments. In the underground press, the police were depicted as a volatile, undisciplined, sadistic army of thugs, the thin blue line between the will of the people and progress. Worldwide, police responded to dissent with state-sanctioned beatings, shootings, executions, and massacres. In 1968 this image of police solidified. In Generalísimo Francisco Franco's fascist regime, Spanish students at the University of Madrid protested police brutality against those demanding democracy, trade unions, worker rights, and education reform. The Prague Spring in Czechoslovakia ended with the USSR invasion in August. In West Germany students protested former Nazis teaching in universities. In Italy students battled police in the Sapienza University of Rome. In Poland students at Warsaw University protested the government banning *Dziady*, the 1824 play by Adam Mickiewicz, because it was "anti-Soviet." An anti-Vietnam war protest outside the US embassy in London ended with eighty-six injured and 200 arrested. Japanese students protested American military bases in Japan because of the Vietnam War. And Military Police in Brazil killed high school student Edson Luís de Lima Souto at a protest demanding cheaper meals for low-income students.

Serving as a template to global revolutionaries were the events in France in May 1968 with the student and proletariat uprising. It began when students occupied the Sorbonne University of Paris and were attacked and beaten by police. On May 6, the national student union, the Union Nationale des Étudiants de France (UNEF), along with university teachers, marched in protest against police brutality, leading to street battles. At the time, French President Charles de Gaulle ruled over a strictly regulated country: women were forbidden from wearing pants to work, married women needed their husband's permission to open a bank account, homosexuality was a crime, it was legal to fire factory workers on the spot, and the one TV news channel was controlled by the government. The police takeover of the Sorbonne led to the formation of Front homosexuel d'action revolutionnaire in 1971, the French Gay Liberation Front. A poster pasted on a wall at the Sorbonne in May 1968 read "Comité d'action pédérastique révolutionnaire." The group held meetings at the École Nationale Supérieure des Beaux-Arts in Paris. Front homosexuel d'action revolutionnaire, started by lesbians, invited men to join in 1971. The organization was co-founded by Communist writer Guy Hocquenghem, a veteran of the May 1968 student rebellion and author of the book *Homosexual Desire*. His co-founder was Communist writer and eco-feminist Françoise d'Eaubonne. Other early members of Front homosexuel d'action revolutionnaire included feminist writer Christine Delphy, who co-founded the feminist magazine *Nouvelles questions féministes* with Simone de Beauvoir in 1977; Daniel Guérin, the bisexual French anarcho-communist author, and painter and surrealist photographer Yves Hernot.

One early action taken by the group was to zap Ménie Gregoire's radio show, an episode called "L'homosexualité, ce douloureux problem," where she discussed homosexuality with religious leaders and doctors. The short manifesto of the Front homosexuel d'action revolutionnaire was published in the leftist newspaper *Tout! Ce Que Nous Voulons*, edited by Jean Paul Sartre, the French existentialist, playwright, and author. The manifesto read:

"Manifeste des 343 salopes

"Nous sommes plus de 343 salopes
Nous nous sommes faits enculer par des Arabes
Nous en sommes fiers et nous recommencerons."

Translated:

"Manifesto of the 343 sluts

We are more than 343 sluts
We have been buggered by Arabs
We are proud of it and we will do it again."

On July 1, 1968, Herbert Marcuse, the German philosopher, sociologist, and political theorist, contributed "Impressions of the French Revolution" to Palo Alto's *Midpeninsula Observer*, an article about the police takeover of the Sorbonne:

"For a reason nobody actually understands, since the demonstration was perfectly peaceful, the rector of the university, apparently on the suggestion of the Minister of the Interior, asked for the police to clear the courtyard. The police appeared and invaded the Sorbonne for the first time in the history of this university.

"This was indeed historical novelty. European universities are immune against the police. The police are not supposed to enter the universities and that is one of the age-old traditions which is actually adhered to in France and other countries. It was the first time in history that the police intervened and by force cleared the courtyard, with several hundred students injured."

In July 1968 in the *Georgia Straight, Vancouver Free Press*, reporter and gay activist, Allen Young, wrote "Rebellion in Berkeley" which began: "Berkeley has had a rebellion, the first off-campus white rebellion America has known in recent years." The trouble started on June 28, one year before the Stonewall Riots. The uprising began with a rally in solidarity with French students and workers, and was sponsored by the Young Socialist Alliance, and the Youth Division of the Socialist Workers Party. Since no permit was issued, the city declared the rally illegal and ordered the crowd to disperse. Police fired tear gas into the crowd, and among cries of "Up

Against the Wall Motherfucker," the protestors scattered, some building barricades and others setting fires. Molotov cocktails, firebombs, and bricks were thrown. The fighting continued the following night, and the city called for a curfew. Windows were broken. Over 100 were arrested. In "Berkeley Burns" in the *Los Angeles Free Press*, Lenny the Red and Black wrote: "The cops were hassling us just like we were niggers."

In the *Berkeley Barb*, G.K. wrote:

"Now we whites know what it means to be black. ... Thousands of bay area TV viewers saw it for themselves on Channel 5. In an absolute macabre setting, a gang of cops dash into the murky gloom of The Forum coffee house, swinging their cubs.

"Screams come forth, a body is dragged out and dumped on the sidewalk like a heap of garbage and the cops walk off without looking back as a sobbing girl covers the youth with her body.

"The street youth apparently called the cops insulting names. It never occurred to the police to arrest him. Just beat the shit out of him and leave him on the sidewalk bleeding and dazed. None of the cops wore their badges."

While students and police battled in the streets, individual cops took it upon themselves to rid their own backyard of undesirables. In April 1968, Hickory Kid at *Dallas Notes* wrote that at Southern Methodist University, "Campus Cops Peek Under Toilet Doors for Homosexuals at ... Fondlin' Library":

"The SMU Security Patrol is playing out a drama in the Fondren Library that has all of the mystery of the old movie *Phantom of the Opera*. There are furtive figures slipping into little-used passages and narrow escapes. What is all the mystery about? Some dope fiend attempting to make a buy? Perhaps an assassination plot against President Tate? No. It is just the fact that the number one hangout for homosexuals on the campus today is the men's room in the basement of the Student Center."

According to the Hickory Kid, cop Grady "Cheyenne" Newton took it upon himself to "clean-up" the campus of homosexuals. In two months he picked up over sixty men and between the 16th and 21st March, the "Toilet Patrol" entrapped nineteen more. For the benefit of "straight" readers, Hickory Kid explains how to detect a toilet used by homosexuals:

"The first sign that there may be a 'problem' in any public restroom is that numbers of men will loiter around it for considerable periods of time. ... Another clue to look for is whether there are holes cut in the walls separating the stalls. The walls in the Fondren Library toilets are made of marble but have been nicely pierced by a hole approximately two and a half inches in diameter. This hole allows homosexual relations between parties without them ever having to leave their stalls."

Hickory Kid explains the latest tactic of the urinal cops:

"On the weekend of March 22, the bottom four inches of the toilet door was cut off. This allows the Toilet Patrol to observe the feet of any sex fiend lurking in the toilet stalls. ... A clever trap set, no doubt, by good old Grady. So if you see a big fat cop on his knees looking under the toilet door don't be alarmed. It's 'T-Man Grady.'"

In October 1968, the New Orleans paper *Ungarbled Word* reported on a raid on Club Stand-In, a gay establishment in the French Quarter. Twelve men were arrested, in addition to four members of the band, and the owner:

"In the process of checking the club out, the vice heard music from the back room. They inquired and were told that the purchase of a $2.00 drink would admit them. They paid up and entered the room, where they saw men dancing in 'intimate' fashion. The vice then showed their I.D.'s and busted everybody. The men were charged with 'obscenity by dancing intimately with members of their own sex.' The band was charged with 'vagrancy by loitering,' and the owner was charged with 'keeping a disorderly place and employing minors in an alcoholic outlet.'"

The article is followed by a COMMENT:

"All accounts that this reporter obtained from concerned parties indicate that the vice handled the bust fairly and politely; too bad the men who make the laws don't do the same. Harassment of homosexuals is an old story in the United States. Aside from unfair laws and the constitutionally unfounded legislation, harassment takes the form of ostracization by the public. The local *Greyface Press,* in their account of the arrests, made a point of listing the names, ages, and addresses of those twelve men who were neither guilty of harming anyone, disturbing the peace, nor inflicting their views on the public. If this doesn't constitute harassment, what does?"

In September 1968, a letter from "Paul" appeared in Detroit's *Fifth Estate*:

"I am a homosexual, and on a recent Saturday night me and another guy were walking around Milwaukee Ave., between Woodward and Cass. The Pigs told us to leave the sidewalk and not to come back. Knowing our full rights we kept on walking. We were dragged into the pig car. And told if we ever came back to a 'public street,' we would spend the night in the Pig Pen! Also be fined. Well they let us go, and I wish to say one Pig said 'homosexuality is illegal,' why then do the gay bars still stay open? Or is it because they pay the Pigs to keep them open? I think the cops are wrong! I am going back to this street, with other friends, I would like to know if you could give me the name of a person to call if the Pigs get them, also, money and shit for my getting out? Please help."

7

CLAMPDOWN ON ALTERNATIVE LIFESTYLES

From the late 19th century Spirit Fruit Society to the late 20th century psychedelic world of San Francisco's Haight Ashbury, the "Establishment" has never taken kindly to Utopian communities, alternative religions or sexual societies. In the late-1960s one of the greatest fears was the bending of gender identity, the sissyfication of America's youth–wearing long hair, beads, robes and talking about love. The first aim of the 'Establishment' was to stop the virus of free thought from spreading, by suppressing the arts, the underground press, and all other forms of unregulated communication. Their first targets were poets like Allen Ginsberg and Lenore Kandel, and banning films like Andy Warhol's *Chelsea Girls*.

———————

"We haven't seen the end of what happened in the Haight. Actually, we're seeing a backlash from it now, forty years later, which confirms how powerful it really was. The dark minions who can't abide natural buoyance or the notion of self-generated enlightenment never tire of trying to stamp out the fire we got started there, but that won't happen."–Grateful Dead's Bob Weir in his preface to Charles Perry's book, *Haight Ashbury*.

———————

The 1960s saw a rebirth of Utopian societies. Many young homosexuals migrated to hippie neighborhoods in large cities. There they experimented with communitarian Utopias and found new ways of living, politically, spiritually, and sexually.

The first wave of Utopian communities in the 19th century reached a peak in the 1920s. One early group that advocated "sexual alternatives" was the Oneida Community, started in 1848 by John Humphrey Noyes. The group practiced "free love." Every man was married to every woman and vice versa. In Charles Nordhoff's book *The Communistic Societies of the United States*, the author wrote:

> "'Complex marriage' means, in their practice: that, within the limits of the community membership, any man and woman may and do freely cohabit, having first gained each other's consent, not by private conversation or courtship, but through the intervention of some third person or persons; that they strongly discourage, as an evidence of sinful selfishness, what they call 'exclusive and idolatrous attachment' of two persons for each other."

The Shakers, a communistic religious sect, was founded in England by Ann Lee in 1747, and moved to America in 1774. The Shakers practiced a "sexual alternative," celibacy and abstinence. One Utopian group that accepted homosexuality was the Spirit Fruit Society. The group started in the 1890s in Lisbon, OH, later moved to Ingleside, IL, ending its days in Soquel, CA. The founder, Jacob Beilhart, rejected the concept of personal property, and taught that happiness is achieved through selflessness, by following your conscience, and taking responsibility for one's own actions. Members of the Spirit Fruit Society lived and worked together, shared property, were free to choose their sexual partners, including those of the same gender. Not surprisingly, the Spirit Fruit Society was hounded by both the press and the authorities. In the 13 June, 1904, *Chicago Tribune,* a headline read, "Stop 'Spirit Fruit' Meeting":

> "The meeting of the 'spirit fruit' society at 681 West Lake street was stopped yesterday afternoon, and the hall was ordered closed by Police Lieut. John T. O'Hara. With a fireman he had inspected the place, and declared it violated the building law. Honore J. Jaxon, a member of the society and lessee of the hall, was arrested. … More than 300 persons were in the hall, and Jacob Beilhart was expounding the 'spirit fruit' doctrine when the order came to close."

The Spirit Fruit Society continued long after the death of its founder, who succumbed to peritonitis on November 24, 1908. The *Chicago Tribune* wrote that he was "mourned by 8,000 followers." His obituary includes the statement: "Although frequent charges of scandal in connection with his colony were made by outsiders, the members expressed the utmost confidence and affection for their leader, and neither he nor they made any open attempt to refute the accusations."

In the 1960s a similar fear and loathing of "alternative societies and sexualities," was present. The police crackdown in neighborhoods like Haight Ashbury in San Francisco, Greenwich Village in New York, Old

Town in Chicago, and Piedmont Park in Atlanta–each with a large gay population–was ruthless. In November 1966, *Rag*, out of Austin, TX, reputedly the first underground newspaper in the South, reported that the Psychedelic Shop, "San Francisco's mind-expansion central" in Haight Ashbury, was raided on two consecutive days. The police confiscated *The Love Book*, a small volume of poetry by Lenore Kandel, which police claimed could "excite vicious or lewd thoughts or acts." The cover depicted a young Buddha and "beautiful maiden" in intimate embrace, but it was the poem, *To Fuck With Love* that raised the ire of the authorities. Store clerk Allen Cohen and co-owner Jay Thelin were arrested for "knowingly possessing obscene matter with the intent to sell." Cohen was also editor of the *Oracle*, an underground paper, and Thelin, its publisher. Witnesses to the raid said the police detained ten customers for half an hour, lined them up against a wall, frisked them, and took names and other information. "How these actions related to the charges of obscenity," wrote the *Rag*, "the cops did not explain."

The Love Book was also confiscated at San Francisco's City Lights Bookstore, where Ron Muszalski was arrested. In the spring 1994 issue of *Argonaut*, the Journal of San Francisco's Museum and Historical Society, Jeffrey M. Burns wrote "Lenore Kandel: Historical Essay," in which he named police inspectors Sol Wiener and Peter Maloney, as organizers of the raid on both stores. Ten years earlier, City Lights was charged with obscenity for publishing Allen Ginsberg's *Howl*. Ginsberg's line, "The asshole is holy" didn't sit well with the status quo. Tame by comparison, *The Love Book* offended by using "four-letter words" and depicting Gods in coitus:

> "I kiss your shoulder and it reeks of lust
> the lust of hermaphroditic deities doing
> inconceivable things to each other and
> SCREAMING DELIGHT over the entire
> universe and beyond … "

During the protracted court case, District Attorney Frank Shaw accused Lenore Kandel of attempting to "condition us into a new type of morality." Kandel responded by telling Shaw he was "beautiful." After ten hours of deliberation, the jury found the defendants guilty, concluding that the book was obscene and had "no redeeming social value." In 1971 the verdict was overturned. Negative publicity caused book sales to soar. Kandel thanked the police by donating one percent of the profits to the Police Retirement Association.

Kandel's counterculture résumé was impressive. Jack Kerouac used her as inspiration for Romana Swartz "a big Rumanian monster beauty," in his novel *Big Sur*. She was with Allen Ginsberg on January 14, 1967 at the Human Be-In in San Francisco's Golden Gate Park, where she read from *The Love Book*. She read a poem at the Band's 1976 "Last Waltz" concert at the Winterland Ballroom in San Francisco. Kandel also appears in Kenneth Anger's 1969 underground film *Invocation of My Demon Brother*, with convicted killer and "Manson Family" member Bobby Beausoleil as Lucifer.

In the spring of 1967, a warm-up to the Summer of Love, articles appeared in the underground press like Jeff Jassen's "Slug-Happy Cops Wreak Havoc in the Haight" in the *Berkeley Barb*, and other stories like, "Tells How Haight Cops Exploit Hips." In the first issue of Chicago's *Seed* a headline reads: "Free Wells St. Liberate Old Town; Police Trained by Former SS Officers?" The article begins: "Wells Streeters. Teeny boppers, hippies, beatniks, and even straights are being bugged and harassed, even arrested, with increasing frequency." Old town alternative businesses advertised in the psychedelic *Seed*: underground films were shown every Monday at the Aardvark Cinémathèque at Second City, 1846 N. Wells; Leather Fetish at 1545 N. Wells for custom made sandals, capes, belts, bags; the Witches Haven Coffeehouse and Sanctuary at Ogden and Sedgwick; and the Gallimaufry fashion workshop at 206 W. North Ave. There were also several gay bars, like the Inner Circle, 1842 N. Wells St., owned by Claudia Murphy, and gay-friendly folk music dives like the Yellow Unicorn, 868 N. State St., owned by George Ramsey, described by Milwaukee's *Kaleidoscope* as "a show all by himself." Around Clark and Division Sts., there were still a few gay bars left from its heyday as a gay nightlife center in the 1940s and 1950s, and three El stops north were three notorious Mafia-run female impersonation bars: the Chesterfield 2831 N. Clark St., the Annex 2863 N. Clark St., and the Orange Cockatoo 2850 N. Clark St.

The ragbag of anarchic notions, Eastern philosophies, rock music and drugs that made up the hippie ideology, not only baffled society at large, but also the traditional Left, who saw "potheads" as counter-revolutionaries. A hippie Be-In or Love-In was more Gandhi planting seeds than Trotsky storming the barricades. In April 1967 Conrade Averitt, in the *Washington Free Press*, reported on a Human Be-In:

"What occurred in Washington ... at P Street Beach was a phenomenon for Peace and Civil Rights groups to contemplate. 2000 turned-on-to-love 'hippies' showed up for a Human BE-IN. ... This group of supposed acid freaks, pot-heads, a-politicos, drop-outs, escapists, hummed among themselves a day of LOVE. ... 2000 beings humming to themselves all day with the blowing of konk shells, kazoos, stroking of strings, the constant caressing of bells by the movement of wind and bodies, clapping of hands, dancing, rushing the crowd with squeals of laughter. ... And with them, the paranoid world of the cop. They parked their cars on the grass and milled among the crowd. They must have been a bit puzzled."

The *Seed* reported a tribal gathering of 5,000 hippies for a Love-In on Detroit's Belle Isle Park on the Detroit River. The event was organized–if that's the right word–by John Sinclair, head of the commune Trans-Love Energies and on the Committee to Legalize Marijuana. Sinclair later managed the anarchist rock band MC5, and was a leader in the White Panthers. Those who attended the Love-In wore "flowing robes, capes and diffraction discs. Others painted their hands and/or faces with strange magic symbols or words of peace and love."

Sheil Salasnek struggled to describe the event in Detroit's *Fifth Estate*:

> "It is impossible to do justice to it because so many things were going on at once. ... A stranger hands you a painted Easter egg and waits to share it with you. Someone else sets up cases of oranges and tomatoes and offers them to everyone passing by. A woman in a pure white nun's habit with a diffraction grid on her forehead is handing out slices of kosher salami, and a grey-haired old man is handing out balloons. ... Two young girls are picking dandelions and placing them under the windshield wiper of the WXYZ station wagon while the occupants of the car are out asking the hippies what their movement is all about and whether there is any social significance to love-ins."

The *Seed* reported on Chicago's first Tribal Be-In at North Avenue Beach. On May 14, 1967, 2,000 hippies welcomed the sun and listened to bands like Yellow Brick Road, the Griffith Harter Union and Little Boy Blues: "By mid-morning, the promise of a beautiful gathering was clearly made: balloons, kites, and flowers dotted the length of the beach, worried police unaware that they were needlessly concerned, drifted through the scattered groups, bracing themselves for whatever it was they felt would come." In Chicago, smaller Be-Ins and Love-Ins took place, like one organized by students at the University of Illinois, Chicago Circle, on May 26 on the grass at Halsted and Polk Sts.

In the spring of 1967 gay classified ads appeared in a couple of underground papers: In the *Berkeley Barb*: "SF Man desires meeting other men interested in male clothing fetishes," and "Shy, gay almost hippy 33 would like to meet same." Or in the *Los Angeles Free Press*: "Young man would like to extend his (alas!) tiny circle of intelligent, sensitive aware male friends under 30 years old. Eventually room mating possible," and "Male exec. 35 educated, cultured, sophisticated, social, attractive, interested in 25-35 serious sincere honest gentleman, no phonies or effeminate types." The summer of love was gay-inclusive, at least in the pages of West Coast underground newspapers.

On October 21, 1967, on an anti-Vietnam War march on the Pentagon, a clean-cut George Edgerly Harris III, Jr., wearing a turtleneck sweater, was photographed sliding flowers into the gun barrels of the Military Police.

Harris later reinvented himself as Hibiscus, a female impersonator and leader of the psychedelic gay liberation theater collective, the Cockettes. This band of drag misfits performed regular shows at the Palace Theater in San Francisco, like *Journey to the Center of Uranus*, starring Divine, who sings, "If there's a crab on Uranus you know you've been loved," while dressed as The Crab Queen.

With men growing their hair long and painting their faces, handing out flowers to policemen at Be-Ins, wearing beads and bells, robes and kaftans, the mainstream media obsessed on the sissyfication of a generation of men. In August 1967, Valerie Walker wrote "Hair Piece" for the *Seed*, about machismo and the fading line between masculine and feminine:

"Everyone's heard of the attitude, deep enough in some to be a sickness, of machismo. Machismo, in case you'd spent the last twenty years in a closet, is Spanish for–just what DOES the word mean? The definition is nebulous; the connotations are male, masculine, tough, hung, a big, BIG man. Brando in *The Wild Ones*, early Elvis–they were muy macho. ... Pubic beards really bugged the squares in the 1950s. But now–all these boys with Long Hair on their HEADS! Beards at least were a proof of masculinity, even though tainted with the aura of Fidelismo; but Jeez, these kids, ya can't tell the boys from the girls ... Lovely longhairs–they aren't afraid to say to Hell With Machismo we wear beads and earrings and long hair and we still get the chicks! And we know what to do when we get them, too."

Walker assures women that unisex fashions for men may be anti-machismo, but there was nothing homosexual about it. Heterosexuality still ruled. Also in the *Seed*, a letter from "Just a Woman" mourned the loss of the old gender roles:

"Whatever happened to the time when men felt it was their duty to protect their women from harsh and ugly things. Have those days vanished forever? ...Pity for the men of the world who don't know the feeling of male pride that comes with putting his hands over his woman's ears to shut out words of harsh ugliness. Women who are the vessels of life ... women who nurture the young and inspire the old, why have you sacrificed the rightful respect that should be paid to you? Why do you trade your dignity for some glib conversation and some faggot's idea of a chic pants suit?"

In 1967 underground movies and movie theaters fell victim to censorship. In October, Richard Benner in the *Los Angeles Free Press* wrote, "Vice Guerillas Bust Film, Keep Isla Vista Minds Pure." Benner reported that Santa Barbara's DA David Minier, Sgt. Joel Honey and special investigator, Michael Serio, raided the Magic Lantern Art Theater and confiscated avant-garde filmmaker Andrew Noren's *Change of Heart*. The film, described as "a somber study of the death of the senses," depicts a man and woman naked, sometimes embracing. The secrecy of the raid was compromised by a leak from the DA's office. When the police arrived, they were met by a hundred residents protesting censorship. In the *Isla Vista Argo* under the headline, "Magic Lantern 'Smut' Bust," is a photograph of protestors carrying signs: "War Is the Only Obscenity," "Obscenity is a Crime Without a Victim" and "End State Control of the Creative Arts." In January 1968, the *Gazette Citizen* wrote: "Judge Arden T. Jensen of Solvang, sitting in the Santa Barbara-Goleta court, declared the movie obscene with 'no redeeming value.' He suggested the predominant theme of the film was 'Filthy Sex.'"

Andy Warhol's hit underground film *Chelsea Girls*, a Bacchanalian, hedonistic view of the world, was showing in selected theaters. An ad for the film in the *Berkeley Barb*, quoting from the mainstream *Los Angeles Examiner*, read:

"THEY–Homosexuals, Sadists, Masochists, Narcissists, transvestites, dope addicts–do strange things.

"Their world is macabre. They wear leather jackets and leather miniskirts. They wear papal robes. Sometimes they wear nothing. They carry whips and chains. They play bizarre games. They have weird, lethargic orgies. They speak unprintable words. They hit one another and scream at one another and make love to one another. And they give one another injections of something—in their arms, in their naked backsides, sometimes just jabbing the needle through tight-fitting seats of wide-belted levis [sic]. It's a vision of hell … like baring the acid-seared soul of underground America."

In Chicago, the twelve reels of film that made up *The Chelsea Girls* were seized by police in a raid on the Town Theater, 322 W. Armitage, in the heart of the hippie/gay neighborhood. The *Chicago Tribune* reported that Detectives John Cello and Edward Rifkin entered the theater with a search warrant and confiscated the film. No one was arrested but a warrant was issued for Anthony Ariola, the film projectionist. The *Seed* wrote:

"As all of Chicago's newspaper critics have panned *The Chelsea Girls* of Andy Warhol, a different viewpoint needs to be reported. Few viewers are anything more than confused and bored by this film, because they have no point of reference in their experience from which to identify with the homosexuals and drug users of the Chelsea, a hotel in Greenwich Village. The lives of the people are completely alien to the average man, and apparently he finds no interest in them. … The films which cater to today's taste almost invariably involve violence to women. How much more obscene they are than the straightforward homosexuality of the 'Pope!' … We have been so dulled by gross titillation that many of us can no longer feel the reality of sexual tension that exists in the muddle of limbs on the boss homosexual's bed, as his pretty boys eat fruit and play skin games, their talk terribly mindless."

Terry Clifford's review in the *Chicago Tribune* read:

"Warhol enables the viewer to indulge in a kind of simultaneous Peeping-Tom-ism as he focuses (occasionally) on a group of lesbians, homosexuals, junkies, pill-pushers, sadists, masochists, and plain old narcissists, wearily watching them banter and bicker and express such sentiments as 'shaddup.' ... A shoddily-made film which can out-gross the best of them, *The Chelsea Girls* a great deal of the time is distorted by a soundtrack that sounds like the inside of a three-minute car wash–which probably is a blessing, since much of the dialog is puerile and petulant, ranging from 8th-Grade Snicker to College Rank. It's evident, however, that the crudest four-letter word to Andy Warhol is 'edit.'"

In 1966 Andy Warhol and his band of sex and drug radicals, like transsexuals Holly Woodlawn, Jackie Curtis, Candy Darling, and other assorted Superstars, began a series of multimedia shows in a Polish ballroom on St. Marks Place in New York's East Village. Entitled "The Exploding Plastic Inevitable," they featured the music of Lou Reed, Nico and the Velvet Underground. The East Village had become a mecca for artists and musicians, in an area with an eclectic mix of intellectual, gay, hippie, Latin, African American, and old European. In 1967, Walter Bowart wrote, "Good Bye Groovy Tuesday, Memorial Day Debacle" in the *East Village Other*: "On Memorial Day, May 30, several thousand neighbors of the Lower East Side watched a clear cut incident of police brutality, where the police attacked passive 'hippies,' hospitalizing three, and roughly handling a pregnant woman; arresting 36 others, over-acting on a simple noise 'complaint.'"

Local hippies had been targeted before. A week earlier cops raided a commune on East 11th St. on six occasions, resulting in several arrests. Each case was thrown out of court because "in plain English, the charges were phony." The hippies in Tomkins Square Park on the Lower East Side were chanting Hare Krishna. They were waiting for a rock concert to start. The New East Village Association had obtained permits for a series of summer concerts in the park. When someone complained about the noise, police arrived and stopped "a negro girl" from drumming on her congas. This was followed by paddy wagons and thirty cops attacking the hippies with billy clubs, a pregnant woman was dragged away by her feet. The crowd soon swelled to thousands, aided by local radio reports. The incident reminded locals of the "Beatnik Riots" in Washington Square six years earlier, when police used the same tactics.

The *Village Voice* reported that on April 9, 1961, several hundred musicians gathered in Washington Square Park, to sing folk songs, a Sunday ritual. However, on this day, the New York Police Department came to evict them, after Park Commissioner Newbold Morris banned music from

Washington Square. The *Village Voice* wrote:

"The demonstration turned into a knockdown-drag-out, with police using what many termed 'brutal methods' in dispersing a crowd of hundreds of singers. Fights broke out, 10 demonstrators were arrested, and at least 20 others including police were injured. … Harold 'Doe' Humes, 34 year old novelist and central figure of the recent fight against the Police Cabaret Bureau, climbed up on a lamp post. 'Since when are guitar players more dangerous than the hysterical cops who push them around' he shouted."

Dave Van Ronk, the bearish, anarcho-Marxist folk singer, wrote in *The Mayor of MacDougal Street: A Memoir*:

"The regular get-togethers had actually started somewhere in the 1940s when a few friends took to meeting in the park for loose song sessions. These had grown until the police began taking notice and there were all sorts of arguments, leading eventually to an inner core of musicians arranging to get regular permits. Naturally, a lot of us despised the idea of needing an official permit, but it did have one advantage: the rule was that everyone was allowed to sing and play from two until five as long as they had no drums, and that kept out the bongo players."

Van Ronk, a heterosexual compatriot of Villagers Bob Dylan, Tom Paxton, Phil Ochs, and Joni Mitchell, was snatched by the police, dragged into the Stonewall Inn, beaten, jailed, and charged with felony assault on a police officer, during the Stonewall Riots in June 1969.

It soon became clear that "Flower Children" were an easy target for police and their billy clubs. As Frank Zappa pointed out in the song, *Who Needs the Peace Corps?* on his Mothers of Invention album *We're Only in it for the Money*:

First I'll buy some beads
And then perhaps a leather band
To go around my head
Some feathers and bells
And a book of Indian lore
I will ask the Chamber Of Commerce
How to get to Haight Street
And smoke an awful lot of dope
I will wander around barefoot
I will have a psychedelic gleam in my eye at all times
I will love everyone
I will love the police as they kick the shit out of me on the street.

The New Left was highly suspicious of hippies, free love, drugs,

Eastern, or any, religion, and especially homosexuality. In November 1967, "Hippies on the East Village and the Revolution" was published in Chicago's *New Left Notes*, the official paper of the Students for a Democratic Society (SDS). The article reports on the invasion of hippies into the East Village, and its impact on working class residents there. A" Negro" told the anonymous author: "'Man you writing an article about them scabrous motherf's, be sure to tell how they STINK!' … a white girl, who maintains herself at a fairly high social level, said, 'This is just a passing thing. These kids will all go home to Mama. They have no fire in them-this isn't a movement!'" The article goes on to tell the story of two girls who fled to the Village to become hippies because of "guilt for the white race, etc." "One quickly got pregnant and had a Negro baby, later gave it up, and returned to Boston. The other had a number of affairs with hippy boys but soon learned after much struggle that she was an invert. Last seen she was THAT way."

The New Left publications kept all-things-homosexual at arms' length. Gay author, activist, and SDS member, Allen Young, told the author of this book: "A gay presence [in SDS] … you have to be kidding. There were NO openly gay people active in the New Left prior to Stonewall. Plenty of closeted gays like myself and we didn't know each other, maybe suspected a bit … "

The Summer of Love lasted just one summer. By the fall of 1967 the Utopian hippie dream in Haight Ashbury was over. An influx of runaways, tourists, and bad drugs flooded the neighborhood, destroying the organic nature of the movement. In October the *Seed* wrote about the Death of Hippie celebration: "A funeral procession carried Hippiedom in a coffin, in which were thrown all the beads, posters, and excess hair of the 'image'; the coffin was burned in the Panhandle after being exorcised."

The Age of Aquarius was over.

8

UNDERGROUND PRESS SYNDICATE

The "Establishment" harassment of the underground press was relentless, victims of the House Un-American Activities Committee, police raids, and beatings. The Underground Press Syndicate was founded to share articles and other information, enabling gay news published in large cities like San Francisco to be re-published and read by isolated LGBTs in small towns across the nation.

"Whoever controls the media, the images, controls the culture."–Allen Ginsberg.

In November 1967 in *Middle Earth*, an underground paper out of Iowa City, Marshall Bloom wrote that Rep. Joe Pool (D-TX) described the underground press as "smutty" and written by "gutter journalists" for a readership of "potential degenerates." Bloom reports that Pool, a member of the House Un-American Activities Committee (HUAC), had called for a "preliminary investigation into the underground press." Pool was up for re-election and chose as a major platform, the closing-down of Dallas newspaper, *Notes From the Underground*, which had been recently banned from the Southern Methodist University (SMU) campus. In January 1968, *Fifth Estate* reported that J.D. Arnold, an SMU student, was suspended for selling *Notes From the Underground* and "members of the paper's staff who are also SMU students have retreated into anonymity in the pages of *Notes*." The HUAC investigation was announced during Pool's speech to the Conservative Party of the Yale Political Union, in which he said:

"These smut sheets are today's Molotov cocktails, thrown at respectability and decency in our nation. ... [The papers] capitalize on the innocence and confusion of the very young. ... [the] more obscene and dirty their newspapers are, the more they will attract the irresponsible readers whom they want to enlist in their crusade to destroy this country."

Countering the argument, Thane Gower Ritalin wrote in the *Seed*:

"Is it not absurd for newspapers, other communications media, teachers, preachers, and politicians to harangue against the supposed 'dirtiness' of a few unwashed Hippies when those same organizations and individuals have allowed the conversion of our atmosphere into stinking, eye-stinging poison; the pollution of lakes and streams into garbage-and disease-laden graveyards for birds and fish; the disintegration of countless neighborhoods into rat and pain-infested slums; and the conversion of the airwaves into channels for the massive distribution of bilge and trash?"

The Underground Press Syndicate (UPS) was formed in mid-1966 by five papers, the *East Village Other*, the *Los Angeles Free Press*, the *Berkeley Barb*, the *Paper* (East Lansing, MI) and *Fifth Estate* (Detroit). The *San Francisco Oracle*, the *Rag* and the Mendocino, CA, psychedelic publication, the *Illustrated Paper*, all signed on soon afterwards. This budding network of publications grew to 271 by 1971. The first meeting was held in March 1967 at the home of Walter Bowart, the editor of the *San Francisco Oracle* in Stinson Beach, CA. The meeting was "chaotic," "largely symbolic," and "amorphous." A headline in the May 15 *Fifth Estate* read: "Underground Press Has Tribal Meeting." The article went on to say:

"There was one who attended the conference who was not a member of the UPS, but who told of ancient prophesies written in cave petroglyphs and confirmed by many visions; that one was Rolling Thunder, an emissary from the Shoshone and Hopi nations, who told the conference how 'after the gourd of ashes fell from the sky, it was written that man would enter a time of great trial.'"

Rolling Thunder claimed hippies were reincarnated Native Americans, "long-haired gypsies." Important decisions made at the gathering were that UPS members could freely reprint content from other papers, they would share subscriptions, and publish a list of UPS members.

News, articles, cartoons, and artwork were disseminated, so a paper in Iowa could reprint a first-hand account of a riot in Los Angeles, an article about Black Panthers in North Carolina, or news about homosexuals. For the first time, homosexuals in small towns were reading and seeing positive images of themselves, through dozens of papers on sale in headshops, sold at protests, passed around at music festivals, or carried in backpacks across country by a transient population. While the mainstream press treated homosexuals as oddities and sex perverts, classified ads and gay news were appearing in the underground press, with headlines like, "Gay Marine to Get Aid," and "Gay Vote Scramble" in the *Berkeley Barb,* or in *Fifth Estate,* "End Anti-Sex Law," or *Open City,* "A Homosexual Views the Draft."

In a July 1967 issue of *Provo,* a bi-weekly out of Los Angeles, a headline read, "The Underground and the Establishment":

> "A lovely new network of underground communications media has appeared and ideas are flowing more freely than ever within the conscious community. The speed with which the underground is growing can be seen in the proliferation of these vehicles of expression. According to the *Paper.* 'Total circulation of UPS papers is estimated at 264,000.' The *Paper* found 33 underground papers in existence by June 1, 1967. A count of underground papers made on July 3, 1967 finds 46 claiming the rights of membership in the underground press syndicate, and no doubt there are more than that."

9

HOMOSEXUALS AND THE DRAFT

In California, the mainstream press was accused of cherry-picking what news they deemed suitable for its readers. A scandal involving Gov. Ronald Reagan's allegedly gay staff and a tape-recording of an eight-man sex orgy were ignored. Also overlooked were aspects of the protests against the Vietnam War, like servicemen holding up signs supporting protestors who stopped a troop train. While singers and writers like Phil Ochs and Tuli Kupferberg suggested feigning homosexuality to dodge the draft, some homosexuals campaigned for inclusion into the military.

"When I was in the military, they gave me a medal for killing two men and a discharge for loving one."–Inscription on Tech. Sgt. Leonard Matlovich's gravestone.

Toward the end of 1967 a scandal broke after syndicated columnist, Drew Pearson, wrote an article about California Governor Ronald Reagan's personal staff being infiltrated by homosexuals. "Is Ronnie Gay?" ran the headline on the front page of *Open City*. The sub-heading read: "Press in California Blacks Out Column":

"Last week California's newspapers and television stations carried endless debates engendered by a Drew Pearson column which charged Governor Ronald Reagan's personal staff contained a number of homosexuals.

"Reagan angrily denied the charge. Pearson appeared in Los Angeles and challenged the actor-governor to a lie test which Ronnie declined to take. The feud boiled on with the entire nation watching.

"It is curious to note that, despite the furor, not one single California newspaper which normally runs the Drew Pearson column ever printed the text of what Drew Pearson had written about Reagan. We feel this strange omission should be rectified and below print the full Drew Pearson column. ... We'd like to note that *Open City* couldn't give less of a damn whether or not Ronnie Baby has homosexuals on his staff. (We rather agree with Robert Scheer who noted [in *Open City*] last week that 'I'm alarmed about Reagan, but not because he has two homos on his staff. I think it'd be a better staff with 50 faggots.')

"We are even pleasantly amused by some of the rumor that is now going around that Ronnie himself is a bit gay. (He might be a bit more human were it so). What really bothers us, though, is the suppression of columns like the Pearson column, the cloak of silence which 'respectable' newspaper publishers throw over politicians they favor in high office, all the while loudly proclaiming that 'we have a free press in this country which presents all sides of the news.' Bullshit."

Pearson, who back in the 1950s had a hand in outing Sen. Joseph McCarthy (See the author's *Chicago Whispers: A History of LGBT Chicago Before Stonewall*), begins: "The most interesting speculation among political leaders in this key state is whether the magic charm of Gov. Ronald Reagan can survive the discovery that a homosexual ring has been operating in his office." Pearson goes on to say that Arthur Van Croft, a former Los Angeles police detective, now in charge of Reagan's travel security, produced a tape recording of a sex orgy at a cabin near Lake Tahoe, rented by two Reagan staffers.

According to Pearson:

"Eight men were involved. They included two members of Reagan's staff, one athletic advisor on youth activities who has since gone on leave for the fall season, one man who's managing the mayorality [sic] campaign of Harold Hobbs, GOP candidate for mayor of San Francisco; and two sons of a California state senator. ... Reagan, though given this evidence last winter, did not move to clean up his office until last August when certain members of his staff were abruptly dropped. No explanation of the reasons for their departure was given. ... It will be very interesting to note what effect the incident has on the Governor's zooming chances to be the President of the United States."

At least one reader chastised *Open City* for publishing Pearson's column, which they deemed homophobic. In a January 1968 letter to the editor, James Cotton wrote:

"I can't agree with your having printed Pearson's vicious garbage. ... I think that since the matter of whether or not homosexuals worked for the Governor has no bearing on their fitness or his, and since Pearson's cry of 'Shame!' is merely pandering to the worst prejudices of our dying Mom-and-Apple-Pie syndrome in the U.S., it was way out of keeping for a paper like *Open City* to give it space. ... There is plenty to criticize Reagan for, God knows. He is plainly unfit for the Governorship of this (or any) state. And we are all shaken up by the idea that the American public, beside itself with frustration at the bloodthirsty imbecilities of LBJ, might vote Ronnie into the White House. But surely whether or not he is a homosexual has nothing to do with the case."

The mainstream press regularly suppressed news. The underground papers covered protests against the Vietnam War from their inception. Two articles on the cover of the August 13, 1965 first issue of the *Berkeley Barb*, "Peace Action: GI's Cheer; Trainmen Jeer" by Bob Randolph, and "August 12 ... Black Day For Berkeley" by R.R. (possibly the same author) deal with anti-Vietnam War protestors attempting to stop a twenty-car troop train at the Santa Fe stations in Berkeley and Oakland. In "Peace Action" Randolph wrote:

"It is not often that American citizens attempt to stop troop trains with their cargo of GI's headed overseas, this time to South Vietnam. Not since 1916 has such opposition to U.S. war moves existed. It was big news, yet the commercial press ignored the most revealing part of the story—the crudely lettered signs in the window of one of the trains, put there by some of the troops on board. 'I don't want to go,' said one of them. Others said, 'Lucky civilians,' and 'Keep up the good work, we're with you.'"

In 1965 over 200,000 US troops were sent to Vietnam for "Operation Rolling Thunder," bombing raids of North Vietnam which continued for three years. That year, Phil Ochs recorded his anti-war song, *Draft Dodger Rag*, instructing young men how to avoid serving in Vietnam. The how-to of possible deferments includes epilepsy, flower and bug allergies, multiple drug addictions, and homosexuality:

Sarge, I'm only eighteen, I got a ruptured spleen
And I always carry a purse
I got eyes like a bat, and my feet are flat
My asthma's getting worse

Consider my career, my sweetheart dear
My poor old invalid aunt
Besides, I ain't no fool, and I'm goin' to school
And I'm workin' in a defense plant.

Tuli Kupferberg, a member of New York rock band the Fugs, along with author Robert Bashlow, wrote *1001 Ways to Beat the Draft*. The list includes:

"93) Take your boyfriend with you when you get called and insist that you will not serve unless you can sleep with him at night; 112) Give the psychiatrist your standard three-minute lecture in favor of bisexuality, being sure to mention again and again that animals do it; 123) Conspire with a known homosexual in the Soviet embassy in Ankara; 135) Offer the psychiatrist $2.00 if he will allow you to perform an unnatural act on his person; 152) Tell the psychiatrist to spread his cheeks because you suspect him of hiding marijuana there; 514) Go Gay; 629) Go to Times Square, find a few dozen bugger mates and get a prolapsed rectum; 630) Crawl in backwards while sucking off Allen Ginsberg; 746) Write your Congressman that a member of your local draft board is a faggot and tried to seduce you and when you refused to go along he classified you 1-A. Include carbon copies of indignant letters you have sent to the *New York Times*, the *New York Daily News*, the FBI, and Selective Service headquarters in Washington, none of which have even bothered to reply. Tell the Congressman that you feel he is your last resort, and if he doesn't answer your letter immediately you are going to picket his home."

In May 1968 in the *Seed*, an anonymous writer reviewed the book *How to Stay Out of the Army: A Guide to Your Rights Under the Draft Law* by African-American civil rights lawyer Conrad Lynn. The reviewer wrote: "None of these books will provide a magic method of beating the draft because there are no solutions. Possessing a very obscene tattoo or being gay come about as close as you can get to magic."

Spokane's *Natural* published the anonymously written, "Homosexuals and the Armed Forces," which stated:

"It is well understood today that the limp-wristed swish that symbolizes male homosexuality in popular humor is the exception rather than the rule. The jockey-est of the jock-straps in our athletic programs, the burliest of the barrel-chested professional wrestlers and the bravest and best of our armed forces personnel are quite often 'homophiles.' It is to be expected, I think, that homophiles would seek out societies comprised exclusively of their own sex.

"Sexually segregated institutions always have a high incidence of homosexual activity for the self-evident reason. The military provides such a society for the homophile individual who has outgrown boy's schools (or girl's schools) and wishes to avoid the dishonor and accompanying inconvenience of prisons and mental institutions.

"Homophiles are hung-up heavier than the rest of us with the sadist-masochist thing that serves as a psychological premise for the soldier's ethic, the entelechy of which is warfare."

One spoof depicting the absurdity of the US Armed Forces' ban on homosexuals came in 1969 with the movie *Gay Deceivers*. The film follows Danny Devlin (played by Kevin Coughlin) and Elliot Crane (Lawrence P. Casey) who escape the draft by pretending to be gay. When they are put under military surveillance, they try to blend in with the gay residents of their apartment building, while still dating girls. The twist ending, is that when caught they're still not inducted, because the Army investigators are gay and keeping heterosexuals out of the military. In the *Celluloid Closet*, Vito Russo wrote:

"The saving grace of [The Gay Deceivers] is the comic performance of Michael Greer as Malcolm, the landlord. Greer not only wrote his own role as a flamboyant queen (complete with Bette Davis imitations) but apparently rewrote the screenplay in places, making it 'funnier and less homophobic than was intended' wherever he could. 'It was also one of the few films,' said Greer, 'in which the gays didn't end in suicide or insanity.' It was a good example of gay humor used in an oppressive situation. Malcolm was a stereotype with a sense of pride."

In 1967, at Riverside Church in New York City, Martin Luther King delivered his "Beyond Vietnam: A Time To Break Silence" address to the Clergy and Laymen Concerned about Vietnam. On the subject of the draft he said:

"As we counsel young men concerning military service, we must clarify for them our nation's role in Vietnam and challenge them with the alternative of conscientious objection. I am pleased to say that this is a path now chosen by more than seventy students at my own alma mater, Morehouse College, and I recommend it to all who find the American course in Vietnam a dishonorable and unjust one. Moreover, I would encourage all ministers of draft age to give up their ministerial exemptions and seek status as conscientious objectors. These are the times for real choices and not false ones. We are at the moment when our lives must be placed on the line if our nation is to survive its own folly. Every man of humane convictions must decide on the protest that best suits his convictions, but we must all protest."

King argued the conflict in Vietnam was a civil war, nothing to do with the US, that African-Americans were sent there to fight for freedoms they did not have at home. The Black Panthers also opposed the war, though they preached "revolution," believing King's non-violent civil rights campaign had failed. Some disagreed with both King and the Black Panthers, like Bayard Rustin, the gay Quaker, pacifist, and advisor to King. Rustin had been a conscientious objector during World War II. On February 17, 1944, he was found guilty of resisting the draft and sentenced to three years in prison. Two decades later he was the deputy director of the 1963 March on Washington for Jobs and Freedom. On the Vietnam War he sided with moderates, like the National Association for the Advancement of Colored People (NAACP) and the National Urban League (NUL), who believed change was only possible by lobbying congressman. Rustin counseled against listening to radical African-American voices, like

Julius Lester of the Student Non-Violent Coordinating Committee (SNCC), who wrote in *New South Student: Newsletter of the Southern Student Organizing Committee*:

"To resist is to make the President afraid to leave the White House because he will be spat upon wherever he goes to tell his lies, because his limousine will find the streets filled with tacks and thousands of people who will surge around it, smashing the windows and rocking the car until it is turned on its side. Have we forgotten? The man is a murderer."

Or Bobby Seale, co-founder of the Black Panthers, who told the *Berkeley Barb*: "If I find a white cop in my community brutalizing one of my people, I'm going to kill him."

While some homosexuals protested the Vietnam War, others campaigned against their exclusion from military service. In 1966, David Sanford wrote "Boxed In," about gays and the draft, in the *New Republic*:

"Many homosexuals do serve in the military, and without scandal. But they must dissemble, hide their sexual tastes from draft boards and in pre-induction screening. The last of 70 items on the medical history form prospective draftees must fill out when they report for physicals reads, 'Have you ever had or have you now … homosexual tendencies?' If a homosexual checks the 'no' box, he violates a federal law and risks a fine and imprisonment. If he checks 'yes,' he is disqualified and he may be permanently handicapped in getting or holding a job."

In the May 1966 issue of Chicago's *Mattachine Midwest Newsletter*, a piece entitled "A Moral Dilemma" stated:

"Personal prejudice is one thing. But when popular ignorance becomes embodied into law and policy that summarily and without regard to individual merit affects millions of citizens the course is clear. Honorable men protest. Legislation regarding homosexuals is hodgepodge law based on widely and responsibly disputed myths. The target example is the draft."

The "Moral Dilemma" was explained in the *Chicago Sun-Times* in April 1970, with a question answered in "The Draft Counselor," a twice-weekly column telling young men about their rights under the draft:

Question: "I am a homosexual. I hold an II-S student deferment now. Are you rejected for being a homosexual? Is there any way in which you are tested?"

Answer: "The Army's medical standards list 'overt homosexuality' as a cause for rejection. Your local board may classify you I-Y or IV-F if you are rejected, depending on what the physicians at the examining station recommend.

"To obtain a physical deferment you must submit a letter from a psychologist or psychiatrist describing your condition, outlining its history, and detailing how it would interfere with your functioning in the military. If you have had psychological treatment, this should be indicated."

The author goes on to warn the questioner that government agencies, prospective employers and schools, will have access to this information. If you admit you're gay, you could be denied work and an education in the future. The author continued:

"You should also consider carefully whether, by in effect having yourself 'certified' as a homosexual, you may be reinforcing tendencies which are not truly permanent. Some men are able to reach a bisexual or even heterosexual adjustment through therapy. Whether you want to do this is your own decision, of course.

"For these reasons, you should fully discuss your situation with a psychiatrist or psychologist before he writes a letter. You are also advised to contact an experienced draft counselor to see whether you may be eligible for some other deferment that would cause fewer potential complications."

On March 18, 1966 the Committee to Fight Exclusion of Homosexuals from the Armed Forces, a group based in Los Angeles, issued a statement:

"General [Lewis B.] Hershey has frequently declared that there is a dangerous shortage of eligible men to serve in the armed forces.

"YET ... More than 17 million men and women who are morally and physically qualified to fight for their country are denied this right simply because they are homosexual.

"FURTHER: EVADERS OF MILITARY SERVICE are making widespread use of the anti-homosexual rule to escape the draft by falsely claiming to be homosexual.

"Millions of homosexual men and women have served with honor as soldiers, sailors, airmen and marines in the wars of our country, past and present. BUT –

"Many thousands of these have been dishonorably discharged after loyal service for no other reason than being discovered to be homosexual.

"Write to the President, and to your congressman, to protest this waste of needed manpower and the unjustified denial of the right of a loyal citizen to serve his country in war; and close this loophole for draft evaders. End the rule which excludes a man or woman from military service for the sole reason of homosexuality."

A headline on the cover of the May 20 1966 *Berkeley Barb* reads "Homosexuals Rally For Equal Draft":

"'The Homosexual's Response to the Draft Call—a Moral Dilemma' will be the focus of a rally planned by the Committee to Fight Exclusion of Homosexuals from the Armed Forces, 2 p.m. Saturday, May 21st at the Federal Building in San Francisco. ... The demonstration will be a part of a national protest on Armed Forces Day. ... Public demonstrations planned in other cities are: picketing of the White House and the Pentagon in Washington D.C., a motorcade and distribution of leaflets to the public and at local military installations in Los Angeles, Town Hall meetings in Philadelphia and New York City. Other cities where National Protest Day will be observed include Sacramento, Kansas City and Chicago."

In Los Angeles, the mainstream press ignored their protest, only the *Los Angeles Free Press* and the gay *Tangents* covered it. In the May *Tangents*, Don Slater described the fifteen-car, twenty-mile route, motorcade protest:

"'Oi veh!' burst forth a tiny woman, clutching herself in disbelief at the corner of Wilshire Blvd. and Fairfax Ave. 'This we don't need. My son is already a homosexual.' Angeltown pedestrians and motorists, who, up to that moment were convinced they had 'seen everything,' were witnessing their first gay motorcade. Sponsored by the Los Angeles Committee to Fight Exclusion of Homosexuals From the Armed Forces, the caravan of cars had just swung into the heart of Los Angeles' Jewish community, and, with two-thirds of the over-long itinerary completed and with only the Hollywood District to go, riders and drivers in the motorcade were beginning to welcome the prospect of completing the adventure without incident."

Traveling in the motorcade were the Rev. Alex Smith of the First Methodist Church, Carma Scott from the Prosperos, Professor Vern Bullough and his wife (Bonnie), and the Rev. Philip Cain of the American Eastern Orthodox Church. In Washington DC, members of the local Mattachine Society picketed the White House, then twenty protestors, led by Dr. Franklin Kameny, marched to the Pentagon. In Philadelphia, 10,000 leaflets were handed out at the city's Navy Yards, and 40-50 people protested at the Federal Building Plaza in San Francisco.

In the September 1966 issue of New York's *Realist*, the take on homosexuals in the military included two pages of Mort Gerberg cartoons under the title "The Fag Battalion." At the top of the first page, a news item reports on the Committee to Fight Exclusion of Homosexuals from the Armed Forces and their assertion that seventeen million US homosexuals were eager to fight for their country. The Gerberg cartoons depict stereotypical, swishy, pursed lipped, long-lashed, military personnel. One shows two soldiers holding hands. The caption reads, "I hope we take some prisoners. I'd love to see if it's true what they say about Oriental men." Another cartoon shows a soldier reprimanded by his superior–"Burnhill, how many times have I told you not to lubricate your rifle with K-Y Jelly." Still another cartoon features a soldier digging, "I adore digging foxholes, it's so anal." They continued in the same vein over two pages.

In a "Letter from a Homosexual," John L. Timmins, Secretary of Mattachine Society, NY, responded:

"I cannot help but wonder why the *Realist* seems to be anti-homosexual. ... I found the 'Fag Battalion' to be as obnoxious to me as I do 'The Committee to Fight the Exclusion of Homosexuals from the Armed Forces.' We at the Mattachine are aware of the activities of this very small group of people, and we have received a great deal of undeserved criticism from their activities. I would like to take this opportunity to point out that we are not only non-related groups, but that MSNY vigorously oppose the war in Vietnam, whereas others in our group favor it. Since the goal of this Society, and the homophile movement, is to procure the legal rights denied the homosexual by law and to educate the public in regard to homosexuality, we refuse to mix issues by engaging in foreign policy. ... Not only did we not participate in their leafleting campaign, but we heartily disapproved of it, because it splits the homosexual community into pro-war and anti-war factions."

Beneath Timmins' response is an Editor's Note: "Fighting the exclusion of homosexuals from the armed forces would certainly qualify as a civil rights activity; if that form of discrimination is ever remedied, then those homosexuals who don't want to be drafted will no longer be able to exploit their deviation rather than face the consequences of conscientious objection."

Timmins' letter was followed by a "Letter from a Heterosexual," from Warren Simpson, Dept. of Sociology, University of Alabama: "I understand that homosexuals held a nationwide demonstration in protest of the armed services policy of excluding their ranks from military employ. Wouldn't it be a gas if they composed some sort of fight song, possibly The Ballad of the Pink Berets."

In October 1967 in *Open City*, was the piece "A Homosexual Views the Draft" by out-gay writer Chris Allen. The article is a jumble of politics, sexual innuendo, and stereotypes. He starts with an anti-war statement: "Should I, or should any member of ANY minority in this country kowtow to the whims and wishes of the Establishment? Hell, no. In Vietnam we're already killing proportionately more black people than WASPS in those clap-filled rice paddies." On the "Moral Dilemma," Allen added:

"It's a hell of a decision for a lot of homosexuals, whether to check the box or not. On the one hand, there is the threat of death in combat and involvement in wanton killing. Perhaps worse, there is the threat of life in Big Brother's military lap. On the other hand comes public disgrace and economic confinement. ... Of course ... in time of war, all able-bodied men are fair game for lecherous old Uncle Sam. I guess it doesn't matter if John Doe sucks off his buddy in the trench then, as long as he kills his quota of women, kids and Commie bastards."

Allen suggests the reason for rejecting "fairies" was not their inability to kill, but something far more sinister:

"No, they're scared the commies (Vietcong women? THRUSH agents? CIA dropouts?) will blackmail his ass for precious government secrets like 'Who was the real Walter Jenkins?' 'Who killed Jack Kennedy?' 'How do we plan to put a mouse on the moon?' They're scared that homosexuals will undermine the morals of the guys in uniform. Believe me, them that wants to go down will anyway–whether it's at the S.F. Embracadero 'Y' or in Saigon. ... A hell of a lot of fairies–and I'd venture to say most of them-don't want to go the basic training route 'cause that's not their scene. A lot of them are cowards–chickenshit, I believe the term is. And their health couldn't take it. It's my opinion that the Mattachine Society's recent stand of petitioning the U.S. government to let queers in the armed forces is a ridiculous 'safe bet.' They know the military won't take them, and it makes a damned good arguing point to show up the Feds as refusing to let the queers die for their country."

If the military did allow gays, Allen wrote, "they'd get the S&M's ... and the rest of the homosexuals would quickly develop a heart condition, or the vapors. ... As for me, it's not my bag. I'd crack up the first week."

In March 1968, "Gay Army Life" was published in the *Fifth Estate*:

"Both homosexuals and the U.S. Army desire young men, so the Defense Department has quietly instructed induction centers to enlist homosexuals, provided they are not the 'obvious type.' ... According to the Committee to Fight Exclusion of Homosexuals from the Armed Forces, there are documented cases of homosexuals being accepted for military duty, by declaring the men in question were not homosexuals because of a lack of sufficient proof. Legally, the Committee states these men should not be forced to produce evidence they are not homosexuals; a simple declaration should be all that is required. Furthermore, if the military is willing to accept homosexuals, they should do so openly instead of covertly ignoring their own regulations."

Similar reports in the *Berkeley Barb* and the *San Diego Free Door* suggested "more than a dozen practicing homosexuals have been re-classified since the first of the year."

10

LEADING UP TO CHICAGO'S PERFECT STORM

In 1961 Illinois became the first state in the US to decriminalize homosexuality, though someone forgot to tell the Chicago Police Department. In 1968, with the upcoming Democratic National Convention (DNC), Mayor Richard J. Daley set about cleaning up the city of gay bars and other undesirable elements. After the Martin Luther King assassination and subsequent riots, the covert actions of Chicago's "Red Squad" raised tensions around the hippie/gay neighborhood of Old Town, the location where the DNC "Police Riots" began.

"The issue of civil rights was too much for the establishment to handle. One of the chapters of history that's least studied by historians is the 300 to 500 riots in the U.S. between 1965 and 1970."–Tom Hayden.

Carl Sandburg's Chicago, "Hog Butcher for the World ... Stormy, husky, brawling, City of the Big Shoulders" lived up to its name in the summer of 1968, when violence erupted at the Democratic National Convention. The Chicago *Seed* utilized Sandburg's "Hog Butcher for the World" line to describe the city's notoriously corrupt police force. In many ways, Chicago hadn't untangled itself from the 1920s Prohibition-era web of politicians, cops, and mobsters. While Chicago was haunted by the ghosts of its shady past, the state of Illinois was ahead of its time. In 1961 Illinois became the first state in the US to decriminalize homosexuality. The Illinois Criminal Code of 1961 arrived with little fanfare and was ignored by the mainstream press, with the exception of the *Chicago Sun-Times*. On

December 21, 1961, a headline was buried on page 43: "'New Criminal Code In Effect Jan. 1." The article went on to say: "The code, signed by Gov. [Otto] Kerner July 28 after passage by the General Assembly, reflects new outlook on philosophy and morality." The San Francisco-based *Mattachine Review* wrote: "The Illinois Revised Criminal Code … has apparently by omission, silence and implication, repealed the sodomy law." An item in the lesbian newsletter, the *Ladder,* read:

> "While the homophile movement has long expounded the need to change our sex laws to this effect, now that it has happened I can't help wondering if there will be any appreciable difference in attitude of law enforcement regarding the homosexual. The legality of homosexual practices in private will not bring social approval; nor will there be an abatement by law enforcement officers in their drive against gay bars or apparent homosexual activity in public."

The *Ladder* was right to be skeptical of the police. In fact, the raids on Chicago gay bars, bathhouses, and even private parties, increased throughout the 1960s. Richard J. Daley was Mayor of Chicago from 1955-76. By 1968 he had the city sewn up. Daley was the third in a succession of bullish Irish Mayors, following Edward J. Kelly 1933-1947 and Martin H. Kennelly 1947-1955. Kelly banned Lillian Hellman's lesbian play *The Children's Hour.* He also closed down lesbian bars, Twelve-Thirty Club and Roselle Inn, also the K-9 drag bar. Though rumored to be gay himself, Kennelly ordered the closing of many gay clubs on Chicago's North Side.

After Martin Luther King Jr. was assassinated April 4, 1968, riots erupted across the US. In Chicago they stretched twenty-eight-blocks of West Madison St., affecting Roosevelt Rd., the Austin and Lawndale neighborhoods on the West Side, and Woodlawn on the South Side. The next day, Daley imposed a curfew, closed the streets to traffic, and halted the sale of guns. Some 10,500 police, 6,700 Illinois National Guards, and 5,000 US Army troops poured into the area. The Mayor issued an order to "shoot to kill any arsonist or anyone with a Molotov cocktail in his hand, because they're potential murderers, and to shoot to maim or cripple anyone looting."

The police had been the enemy of the civil rights movement for years. In Los Angeles, the Watts Riots began August 11, 1965, when a routine traffic stop of Marquette Frye, a 21 year-old African-American, erupted into a six day battle, during which there were thirty-four deaths, 1,032 injuries, 3,438 arrests, and over $40 million in property damage. In August 1965, the *Los Angeles Free Press* published "Malpractice by Police Trigger to Watts Riots" which described the events:

> "Black and white patrol cars, with red lights on and sirens screaming, only incensed the gathering crowds and provided easy targets for gangs of roving

youths and young adults. Almost every police vehicle was dented and crumpled as the officers ran into the crowds, striking at the bystanders while the culprits almost always ran back into dark alleyways and yards into which the police were afraid to go."

In March 1966 Bayard Rustin wrote "The Watts" in *Commentary*, a magazine of Jewish culture:

"The riots in the Watts section of Los Angeles … [was] viewed by many of the rioters themselves as their 'manifesto,' the uprising of the Watts Negroes brought out in the open, as no other aspect of the Negro protest has done, the despair and hatred that continue to brew in the Northern ghettoes despite the civil-rights legislation of recent years and the advent of 'the war on poverty.' … The whole point of the outbreak in Watts was that it marked the first major rebellion of Negroes against their own masochism and was carried on with the express purpose of asserting that they would no longer quietly submit to the deprivation of slum life."

One year after the Watts Riots, the Charleston, SC, *News and Courier* wrote:

"The first anniversary of the Watts riots was marked Saturday by a summer festival as gay as a Mardi Gras. … Nearly 2,000 persons, both Negro and white, were on hand for the opening of the festival Friday. … The place to make the scene Friday night was the Watts Happening Coffee House, where an adaptation of Jean Genet's play *The Blacks* was performed. The adaptation was entitled *Licorice.*"

Jean Genet, the French author, playwright, homosexual, thief, and outspoken supporter of the Black Panthers, published *The Blacks: A Clown Show* in 1958. Genet also included specific instructions on how it should be performed:

"This play, written, I repeat, by a white man, is intended for a white audience, but if, which is unlikely, it is ever performed before a black audience, then a white person, male or female, should be invited every evening. The organizer of the show should welcome him formally, dress him in ceremonial costume and lead him to his seat, preferably in the first row of the orchestra. The actors will play for him. A spotlight should be focused upon this symbolic white throughout the performance. But what if no white person accepted? Then let white masks be distributed to the black spectators as they enter the theater. And if the blacks refuse the masks, then let a dummy be used."

In the years prior to the 1968 Democratic National Convention in Chicago, issue after issue of underground newspapers published stories of police brutality. "Control the Cops," read the front-page headline of a December 1966 *Berkeley Barb*. In October 1967 Tom W. Smith in the *Rag* wrote, "Oakland Police Brutality Plants Seeds of White Revolution." The *Midpeninsula Observer* ran a story, "Fairmont Demonstrators Are Brutally Attacked." In the first issue of *Seed*, in April 1967, a headline read: "150 Police Raid Women for Peace." Chicago Women for Peace held a fundraiser at the home of Dr. Arnold Abrams, an associate professor at De Paul University, to raise money to send members to the April 15th Peace March in New York City. After police overpowered Dr. Abrams, nineteen women were arrested and charged with resisting arrest or aggravated assault. Dr. Abrams was charged with selling liquor without a license. A neighbor counted twenty-one squad cars and four paddy wagons. "As those arrested were being taken away," wrote the *Seed*, "a policeman stopped one photographer saying, 'Don't take my picture I don't want anything to do with this.'"

Police harassment of dissident groups in Chicago meant the 1968 National Democratic Convention was a riot waiting to happen. The Chicago Police Department's Subversive Activities Unit, known as the "Red Squad," was a covert police intelligence-gathering group that infiltrated political and social groups perceived to be radical. Chicago's Red Squad dated back to the Haymarket Riot of 1866, when it was formed by a coalition of business owners and Police Captain Michael J. Schaack. Together, they spread lies, wild rumors, and conspiracy theories, which they used to justify a campaign against anarchists, immigrants, and labor unions. Tactics used by the group included bribing witnesses, surveillance, and intimidation. In the 1960s the Chicago Red Squad gathered information on groups like the American Civil Liberties Union, National Association for the Advancement of Colored People, National Lawyers Guild, the Black Panthers, Youth International Party (YIPPIES), Students for a Democratic Society, and later Operation PUSH, Women's Liberation and Gay Liberation Fronts.

In Chicago's *Kaleidoscope* March 14, 1969, an article appeared about the *Chicago Journalism Review* obtaining a confidential Red Squad dossier on A.A. Raynor, an elected Chicago alderman. It's an example of intelligence collected by the Red Squad leading up to the 1968 Democratic National Convention:

"He is a successful businessman and one of the first independent black politicians to make a dent in the Democratic machine. His activities and statements are closely watched by ... the 'Red Squad.' ... Part of the Red Squad's confidential dossier on Rayner and an organization in which he is active, Veteran's for Peace, was obtained by the *Chicago Journalism Review*. It describes the South Side alderman this way: 'Rayner now believes that the black people will rise and a revolution will ensue. He also believes that if the black people do not get their 'just due' at the Democratic National Convention there will definitely be trouble."

In Mayor Daley's enthusiasm to clean up the city for the Convention, he sent police to raid and close down gay bars. One bar was the Trip. In *Chicago Whispers: A History of LGBT Chicago Before Stonewall*, this author wrote:

"On September 8 1967 Dean T. Kolberg and Ralf L. Johnston opened the elegant Trip restaurant and bar at 27 E. Ohio St. The Trip was raided twice. First on January 28, 1968 when police arrested fourteen men, eight charged with public indecency, the rest with being employees of a disorderly house. Ralla Klepak, who defended hundreds of cases involving gay men, was attorney for the defense. On March 29 in Jury Court the charges were dismissed because the police entered the bar illegally, by impersonating members of the club after illegally obtaining cards. Two months later the bar was raided again and plainclothes officers arrested an employee and a patron."

It was an open secret that cops were shaking down gay bars. Jim Bailey explained how "Police Harass Gay Bars" in the December 1968 issue of Chicago's *Second City*:

"One of the most lucrative sources of illegal gain for Chicago policemen is extortion of owners of bars which cater to homosexuals. One trick policemen use is to advise the gay bar proprietor that he needs a larger front window so that passers-by can see inside. For $800 this requirement can be waived. ... Sometimes a policeman will hire a minor, give him false identification papers, and have him enter a gay bar to order a drink. Then the policeman comes in and just by coincidence the first person he checks for identification is the plant. If a minor is caught in a gay bar the owner can be arrested and charged with running a disorderly house. ... Liquor licenses are expensive in Chicago: $1000 a year for a permit to operate a bar until 2:00 in the morning and $2000 for a 4:00 A.M. (5:00 A.M. on Fridays and Saturdays) permit. The licenses are obtained from the liquor commissioner, who incidentally is also the mayor of Chicago. If the bar owner is arrested he can usually pay the policeman $300 and nothing more happens. ... Police officers even have falsely claimed that they have been propositioned in bars. Actually some vice cops probably have propositioned the customers themselves because a few officers have been dismissed from the police for being homosexuals."

There was little homosexual content in the early issues of the *Seed*, but in January 1968, gay classified ads appeared in Chicago's *Kaleidoscope*: "GAY GIRL, 19, desires older partner, 20-30. Write Anita c/o P. Pope 7007 N. Sheridan. Serious only."

Old Town was Chicago's "Haight Ashbury," with headshops, coffee shops, and music venues, like Solidarity Books, "purveyors of anarchist, IWW, revolutionary socialist, surrealist, psychedelic and fantasy books, pamphlets and periodicals," and Headland, for "Brass Hookah's, pouches, etc." Some were skeptical of the political commitment of Old Town hippies.

In September 1967 an unsigned letter in the *Seed* claimed hippies lacked humor, after the writer had tried to order an "I'm Leary of Acid" button in a store. He thought the play on words might elicit a smile from the "longhair with the granny glasses" behind the counter:

> "Not a bit. He grimly accepted my order. I left the shop with much the same feeling that I have when I shop at Marshall Field's. Point is, they're a grim bunch, these kids. They tend to become a kind of burlesque of the establishment, in much the same way that homosexuals, who adopt a super-feminine façade, become a kind of bizarre burlesque of their female antagonists. Ultimately, the hippie charade (in terms of their costume and manners) may turn out to be as pathetic and absurd as the homosexual in drag. When the summer is over, I suspect that most of them will go home and get their haircuts and wash their feet and go back to school, the ones that survive their adventures with dangerous drugs and cautious experiments in civil disobedience may write some interesting essays on 'What I did on my summer vacation.'"

Lysergic acid diethylamide (LSD) officially arrived in Chicago in the fall of 1966, when "acid guru" Dr. Timothy Leary visited. Bruce Schmiechen, in the *Rag*, out of Austin, TX, wasn't impressed: "Tim Leary came to Chicago recently with his new religion. Billing himself as a member of 'one of the oldest professions,' he gave little more intimation of the actual properties of LSD than a priest would tell of a wine high in discussing communion." Schmiechen also criticized Leary's $1,000 speaking fee. It's not surprising tough-talking blue-collar Chicagoans didn't fully embrace Leary's up-in-the-clouds California spirituality. The city's history of hardcore labor activism and bone-chilling winters, erased whimsical notions of a blowing-bubbles-in-the-park "Turn on, tune in, drop out," lifestyle. An editorial in the *Seed* suggested the Windy City may be "too hostile and unfriendly, or the cultural soil too barren, to support [the hippie culture]." In October Larry Reynolds wrote in the *Seed* that, "Chicago is an angry jungle of hard-faced hippies."

11

THE YIPPIES ARE COMING

As early as 1966, pre-YIPPIE Jerry Rubin wrote of his dream to build a coalition of one-issue organizations to jointly fight for the freedom of all oppressed peoples. However, this motley collection of disparate groups under the umbrella of the New Left couldn't agree on anything. Out of this mess, a group of frustrated artists and writers formed the Youth International Party (YIPPIES) preaching an anarchist-Dada philosophy of revolution and free love. The YIPPIE Festival of Life at the 1968 Democratic National Convention in Chicago turned into a "Pig Riot," and young people, many of them gay, left the city bruised, battered, and hell-bent on overthrowing the "Establishment."

"Revolution is not something fixed in ideology, nor is it something fashioned to a particular decade. It is a perpetual process embedded in the human spirit."–Abbie Hoffman.

In January 1966, a young Jerry Rubin wrote the following "Statement of Intent" in the *Berkeley Barb*, where he envisioned a coalition of radical groups:

"The Bay Area is a radical's dream. Oakland is a city teeming with unrest, exploitation and potential new social forces. The potential coalition includes a mass radical student base, a liberal middle class, and the large Negro ghettos. These forces must now combine issues–ranging from poverty, slums, racial discrimination, to the war in Vietnam to the QUALITY of life in America–and offer new politics in the Bay Area. ... Are we ready to move from single-issue orientation to multi-issue radicalism?"

In a July, 1967 *Rag*, Arthur Varbrough explained the origins of New Politics:

"The National Conference on New Politics [NCNP] grew from a meeting of liberals and radicals at Santa Barbara, California, in August 1965. The meeting resulted from discontent and anger at the failures in problem-solving in our society and abroad, the 1964 elections, and the escalation of the Vietnamese War."

The NCNP published a "heritage of failures" in the following statement:

- Failure to aid societies seeking overdue revolutionary change.
- Failure to work effectively for world peace and disarmament through the U.N. and other world organizations.
- Failure effectively to guarantee equal rights to all our citizens.
- Failure to wage an effective fight against the unequal distribution of wealth, the oppression of the poor, and the decay of our cities.
- Failure to mobilize our affluent citizenry to aid the suffering and starving people throughout the world, and
- Failure to protect the freedom of ideas and to extend the means for their free expression.

One year prior to the 1968 Democratic National Convention, the NCNP met in Chicago's Palmer House Hotel for "New Politics –'68 and Beyond." In New York's *Win*, Martin Jezer wrote:

"In the grand ballroom of this posh house of hospitality, 2,000 delegates from 372 organizations sought to build a unified radical movement and decide whether New Politics should run a third ticket in the 1968 Presidential election, form a permanent third party, or concentrate on local community organizing to build a radical base at the grass roots."

In the *Berkeley Barb*, Marvin Garson wrote, "What Happened in Chicago-An Analysis: The Whites: A Clown Show" in which he described the NCNP: "A play staged by blacks for their own edification, using white actors. As the converse of Genet's play, its logical title would be *The Whites: A Clown Show*." Garson noted the problems started early on:

"A Black Caucus was meeting somewhere in the hotel, and whites weren't allowed in. Rumors began floating around that the whole Black Caucus, or part of it, had moved to a separate convention on the South Side, or was about to. A 'Black Support Caucus' of whites was formed to find out what the hell the blacks were doing."

The convention opened with Martin Luther King's keynote speech to an audience of 5,000 people, mostly white. The whites cheered, while young blacks made a point of not applauding. In his speech, King acknowledged losing the support of young blacks, as they aligned themselves with the revolutionary Socialist Black Panther Party. Martin Jezar in *Win* described King as "anathema to most blacks" and "the hero of the more moderate and politically-oriented whites at the convention." Jezar added that outside the hotel, the Blackstone Rangers, a Chicago street gang, played drums and chanted, "Kill Whitey, Kill Whitey." On the second day the convention fell into "black" and "white" factions, and the Black Caucus issued an ultimatum: "Either accept our 13-point resolution without amendment or we split." The resolution demanded fifty percent of black people on all committees, condemned the "imperialistic Zionist war," leading to cries of anti-Semitism, and demanded "total and unquestionable support of all wars of national liberation." Cynthia Edelman in the *Seed* wrote that one of the demands was a pledge to subdue the "'savage and beastly' character of whites." She also noted that "black speakers were invariably flanked by tall, African-robed guards, as though they feared other panelists might attack" and that H. Rap Brown, the National Chairman of the Student Nonviolent Coordinating Committee (SNCC) refused to speak to whites, his second in command, James Forman spoke for him. The Black Caucus 13-point resolution was approved. James Retherford in "What's Left After Chicago?" in Bloomington, IN's *Spectator*, described the conference as being attended by "black nationalists, SNCC officials, Communists, SDS organizers, Trots, Maoists, anarchists, Nihilists, hippies and fatcats," and that "house detectives at Chicago's Palmer House Hotel traveled through corridors in platoons." He added that, "a number of delegates broke into the Palmer House swimming pool for a post-midnight skinny-dip."

Homosexuality was not on the agenda at the NCNP gathering, though the decriminalization of homosexuality was voted on under "sex laws." A "Summary of NCNP Resolutions" was published in the *Seed*:

- Vietnam: Immediate withdrawal of all troops other than Vietnamese.
- Latin America: NCNP support revolutionary activity in Venezuela, Bolivia, Guatemala, Brazil, Argentina, Peru and Colombia.
- South Africa: Boycott American companies which profit from slave labor e.g. General Motors.
- Spanish-America: Restoration of 1848 Treaty of Guadalupe-Hidalgo, guaranteeing their land to those of Mexican descent.
- Appalachia: Put an end to strip mining which despoils the land. Place welfare programs in the hands of the people. Stop harassment of local organizing groups.

- Sex: No laws except against forcible rape and child molestations. Polygamy and group marriage recognized.
- Drugs: Scientific evaluation. Drug addiction an illness, not a crime. Legalize marijuana. All now imprisoned for drug use, freed.
- Nonviolence: "Pain, destruction and bitterness follow the use of violence ... civil resistance and creative disorder have greater power to achieve the changes desired ... "
- Civil Liberties: Abolition of HUAC. CIA open to public inspection. FBI case spying on citizens, concentrate on organized crime and enforcing civil rights.
- Draft: Abolition of the draft; presently, encouragement of open resistance.

No homosexual groups attended the NCNP, because there was no radical gay movement at the time. Militant gay activism came after the Democratic National Convention in Chicago. However, there were signs of it in universities. The *New York Times* published "Wayne University Destroys Files Protested by Students" on May 5, 1967: "Wayne University announced today, after a 24-hour student protest against the maintenance of files on alleged homosexuals and 'psychos,' that the files had been destroyed." Howard Rubenstein, a student activist, discovered secret files kept on homosexuals, "both convicted and alleged," in the school's public safety department. He also discovered a "psycho file." William Kearst, the University's president, denied knowledge of the files, but school officials later admitted the files were kept by a previous administration.

Early reports of a Youth International Party (YIPPIE) event in Chicago came in January 1968. The *Seed* wrote:

"A group of 25 artists, writers, and musicians have agreed to participate in the founding of the Youth International Party, or YIP today. YIP will stage a massive Youth Festival this August in Chicago which may just coincide with the Democratic National Convention-although the two are, of course, entirely unrelated. The initial founders are as follows:

"StuAlbertElliottBlinderMarshallBloomBreadandPuppetTheatreLenChandler ShirleyClarkeCountryJoeandtheFishBobFassTheFugsBarbaraGarsonMarvinGar sonPeteGessnerAllenGinsbergWaltGundyArloGuthrieAbbieHoffmanAllenKat zmanPaulKrassnerSharonKrebsKeithLampeRaymondMungoTomNewmanPhil OchsBobOckeneSueOrrinThePageantPlayersJerryRubin.

"STATEMENT FROM YIP

"Join us in Chicago in August for an international festival of youth, music, and theatre. Rise up and abandon the creeping meatball! Come all you rebels, youth spirits, rock minstrels, truth seekers, peacock-freaks, poets, barricade-jumpers, dancers, lovers, and artists! ... The life of the American spirit is being torn asunder by the forces of violence, decay, and the napalm-cancer fiend. We demand the politics of ecstasy! We are the delicate spores of a new fierceness that will change America."

American Dream, out of Tempe, AZ, as well as other underground papers across the nation, published Jerry Rubin's, "The Year of the YIPPEES," in which he outlines plans for the Chicago YIP "Festival of Life." Rubin wrote that the music will be free. He claimed to have lined-up: "Country Joe and the Fish, the Fugs, Arlo Guthrie, Phil Ochs, and the United States of America." Once the YIPPIE invasion had been announced, the Chicago police stepped up their harassment of gay bars, underground newspapers, Black Panthers, leftist groups, head shops, and alternative music venues. In late February, Sunshine Seymour, "Wardrobe Mistress" at the *Seed,* was picked up by plainclothes police and charged with being a runaway, even though her mother confirmed she wasn't. In the same issue, the *Seed* wrote that their printer, Merrill Printing Co., had written to them, stating: "The policy of our new owners is such that they do not want to print the *Seed.*" The new owner of Merrill was the owner of the *Chicago Tribune.* Seattle's *Helix,* published "An Open Letter to Mayor Daley," from *Seed* editor Abraham Peck in response to an incident on April 25, when cops searched seventy people and arrested twenty, during a raid on a meeting of the Youth International Party at 2121 N. Clark St. Eighteen YIPs were charged with disorderly conduct, one with resisting arrest, and one with drug possession.

Two days later, Chicago cops beat unarmed peace demonstrators at an anti-Vietnam War rally at the Civic Center. In the *Seed,* G wrote:

"Suddenly someone broke ranks, his feet burning a path west on Washington, away from the crowd and the pursuing police. The hunt was on. The cops finally had a chance to do their thing. ... The cops blocked off an alley containing their brothers billyclubbing this white kid until he was a mess of red knobs and globs. ... Around the corner, back on Dearborn, I paused among a knot of girls giving first aid to a blood-soaked face whose forehead had been split. ... Whitey could learn from his oppressed black brothers about sticking together in hard times. In time this will come. For every man beaten, twenty-five will be affected. They will return. The war is on."

In early April, after rioting and looting occurred following the assassination of Martin Luther King, Mayor Richard J. Daley set a curfew of 10:30 p.m. for those under eighteen. It was this ordinance that cops used to close down a May 20 concert and fundraiser for the Free City Survival Committee (aka. YIPPIES) at the Electric Theater at 4812 N. Clark St. New York's *Rat* reported that 1500 hippies were dancing in the strobe lights when ten cops walked in and told Alan Russo, the club's owner and YIPPIE supporter, they were checking for curfew violations. They ordered the music stopped, but the band, the 43rd Street Snipers, continued playing, so the cops destroyed their equipment. Russo was arrested, as were many others. Twenty-five squad cars, five paddy wagons, and two mail trucks were waiting outside. Known YIPPIES were selected for a beating.

A similar benefit a month earlier escaped the attention of the police. The concert was to raise funds for the *Seed* and the YIP's "Festival of Light." It was also the venue for a backroom YIPPIE meeting. In his book, *Chicago '68*, David Farber writes:

"From Lake Villa, the YIPPIES went to Chicago to coordinate things with a local group of 'hippie leaders' and to try to get all the permits or whatever they needed from the city to make everything legal and hassle free. Jerry Rubin had gotten this particular ball rolling several weeks earlier when they'd flown into Chicago and met with several of the locals, talking up YIPPIE and laying the groundwork for a working relationship. The night of March 25 marked the first time the local hippies, who were supposed to be in the process of becoming the local YIPPIES, and the New York YIPPIES met as a group.

"They met backstage at the Cheetah Club, in Uptown, where a benefit was going on for the nascent YIPS and the *Seed*, Chicago's relatively new underground newspaper and headquarters for many of the local YIPPIES. ... During and after the benefit, the New York YIPPIES discussed sites for the Festival of Light with locals, including Valerie Walker, Al Rosenfield, and John Tuttle, and then drafted the permit application. Both the locals and the New Yorkers signed the application. The joint signatures were a strategic move aimed at offsetting cries of 'outside agitators.' The permit requested the use of Grant Park, Chicago's main lakefront park, located just east of the Loop and, at the time, the hotels in which the delegates would be staying. The permit went on to explain that the festival would be the 'nation's biggest music festival' and that the YIPPIES wanted to sleep in the park and have the city provide sanitation facilities and health department aid in setting up kitchens in the park."

In the *Seed,* Steve wrote:

"Next morning at nine, sunny and warming up for a gorgeous day-crowds of reporters in the *Seed* office; Mike Royko with his Mickey Mouse watch (YES!) and the *Washington Post* guy [the New York Yippies had a *Post* reporter with them], all them Yippies in tow, including one I hadn't met before, Jim Fouratt. Paul Krassner, Jerry Rubin and Abbie Hoffman conferring on the exact working of the official request for Grant Park, which I had the honor of typing (how come everybody in the world thinks that typing skill is a function of the X chromosome?); then off in Colin's truck to the Park District Commissioner's office. ... At the Park District, Soldier Field: we freaky types get our pictures took descending from the truck, then an interview with Channel 7 out on the grass (Jim Fouratt chanting 'yippie! yippie! yippie' the whole time, all of us cracking up laughing every three seconds or so) ... "

After handing the application in at the Park District, the YIP's moved on to the Mayor's office, where they were met by "an obviously frightened guard" who told the YIPPIES that "hizzoner" was in Council Chambers. The YIPPIES then encountered "a little old man" who shared this exchange with Jerry Rubin:

> L.O.M: "Three of you can go up to the tenth floor, where an aide to Mayor Daley will see you. Who are your leaders?"
> YIPPIES, in unison: "We don't have any leaders."
> J.R: "All we want to do is present this petition."
> L.O.M: "Three of you can go up to the tenth floor, where an aide to Mayor Daley will see you. Who are your leaders?"
>
> (Repeat three times before L.O.M. retires from the field)"

The YIPPIES and pressmen took the elevators to the tenth floor where they presented their petition to a Mayor's aide, "wrapped in a picture of a naked lady (Jim Fouratt's contribution to good intergovernmental relations)." Fouratt was a gay hippie, a YIPPIE, and later a participant in the Stonewall Riots and leader in the Gay Liberation Front. At YIPPIE meetings, Fouratt often broke into song, singing lyrics like "Bullshit, this is all bullshit. You are going to dance with a dead lady, the Democratic Party." In the August 7, 1967 *New York Times*, Stephen Golden reported on a "Be-Out," Fouratt and a gathering of hippies protesting gentrification in Greenwich Village. At the time, Fouratt was a Digger, a radical San Francisco-based anarcho-community group, who believed money should be abolished. The Diggers supplied the needy in the Village with free food, medical care, transport, temporary housing, and also organized rock concerts. The Diggers took their name from a band of Protestant agrarian communists, founded in Britain by Gerrard Winstanley in 1649. The *New York Times* described the 1960s New York incarnation as, "one of a dozen or so sociological, or extended, families in the East Village. The hippies have discarded all ties with a biological family and extended families are the only ties."

Fouratt owned a mimeograph machine and printed daily political bulletins, which he distributed in the East Village. The "Be-Out" involved sitting on the sidewalk chanting "Hare Krishna," then holding hands in the middle of the street, blocking traffic. When tourists began taking photographs, Fouratt and the Diggers responded by peering back at them through plastic binoculars. Finally, the Diggers surrounded a new Oldsmobile and clapped, chanted, polished the headlights, wiped the hood and windshields, much to the amusement of the two occupants. The Diggers dispersed when residents pelted them with eggs and a full bottle of bourbon.

In Abbie Hoffman's 1980 book, *Soon to be a Major Motion Picture*, he describes Jim Fouratt as a "gay blond-on-blond cherub, off Broadway actor

[who] tried to make the street sing":

"The original flower child, Jim played the perfect innocent, constantly popping up in the middle of violent chaos with a surprised 'what me?' look on his face. When we caused problems for the Newark police by smuggling truckloads of food and equipment into the black ghetto riots, Jim managed to upset the cops so much they pistol-whipped him in the can. Once late for a meeting, Jim ran through the streets, bumped into a policeman hard enough so the ice cream in his cone swan dived onto the cop's jacket. He got busted for assaulting an officer with an ice cream cone. Pure Fouratt. I had many a vision of Jim's alabaster body, topped by Peter Frampton-like ringlets, hanging blood-spattered from a corner streetlight. Indeed, I had come to think of 'Fouratt' as a special act of courage. Last time I saw Jim was '71-ish at some close-out antiwar rally. He was giving a speech dressed as a woman. 'You don't know freedom,' he proclaimed to the crowd, 'unless you've put on a dress.'"

Thanks to the YIPPIES publicity campaign, a flimflam of theatrical bravura that owed more to Dada than Marxism, they came under close police scrutiny. In *Pterodactyl*, out of Grinnell, IA, Barry Ancona gave a first-hand account of a raid in the early hours of March 23, 1968 on a YIP-In, on the upper level of Grand Central Station in New York. There were three thousand people there when the police attacked, and Ancona wrote that Don McNeill, a reporter for *Village Voice* was hurled through a glass door, receiving five stitches to his head, even though his press credentials were pinned to his coat. In Detroit's *Fifth Estate*, Frischberg-Jezer-Bloom wrote:

"At about 12:45 a.m. fifty tactical patrol force policemen charged into the main terminal from an adjacent waiting room, nightsticks flailing, beating and knocking over YIPPIES and some commuters, they led a flying wedge into the crowd. ... Many persons were dragged from the terminal by their hair."

The article ends: "Far from the media's image of innocent babes who would come flocking home when the shit went down, New York Hippies, too, are standing their ground as the battle lines with the cops become drawn."

In April, *Le Chronic*, out of Roxbury, MA, published "Chicago: Festival of Life & Death" by Harvey Wasserman:

"Chicago is many things, but one thing it will never be, this summer or any other, is a picnic. To begin with, the City is not New York, with a long tradition of liberalism and a spirit of tolerance emerging from its international atmosphere, nor is it San Francisco with a history of Upton Sinclair and a well-deserved reputation for at least knowing how to enjoy itself. Chicago is perhaps the prototype American city. It has its huge black ghettos, its filthy air, its isolated exclusive suburbs, its unchallengeable city machine. ... Many of the immigrants came fleeing the Russians, and every year the city holds a 'captive nations' parade, peopled largely by Eastern Europeans and Baltic refugees. Not surprisingly, these people are more than unsympathetic to left-wing causes—they are downright hostile."

Lee Webb in the *Washington Free Press* criticized the "YIPPEES" tactics of "provocation and confrontation," preferring peace and love: "So let's keep the YIPPEE carnival a rock band and flower concert and forget the tactics that will get 12 year old flower children and us all impaled on bayonets."

One gay man with a low opinion of YIPPIES was Jann Wenner, editor of *Rolling Stone*, who questioned their credibility in a blistering attack on the cover of the May 11, 1968 issue:

"A self-appointed coterie of political 'radicals' without a legitimate constituency has formed itself into a 'Youth International Party,' opened up offices in New York City and begun a blitzkrieg campaign to organize a 'hip' protest at the 1968 Democratic National Convention in Chicago during August. Their techniques are as old fashioned as those of any city-boss politician, as up to date as the cleverest Madison Avenue 'media buyer' and as brassy as any show biz promotion man. It looks like a shuck. … The YIP Party has manipulated the media into making them a reality, and they must now manipulate the potent symbol of music, they must get the rock and roll figures if any substantial number of people are going to turn up. Nobody is going to go to Chicago in the middle of summer to hear Jerry Rubin deliver one of his endless speeches, but they will go if it is going to be a music festival, if it's going to be like Monterey. But the whole thing has been set up to be totally unlike Monterey. The YIP party has made a great deal of what celebrities have 'pledged' to come. Those four or five are symbolized by the Fugs, Timothy Leary and Phil Ochs: one is an old-style group with little popularity and little place in the new music; another is a 'name brand' leader who wore out his welcome when he tried to become a leader and has now lost his relevance; and another is an old political protest singer who has changed his clothes, his hair, his record company and his instruments but is still an old political protest singer."

Wenner predicted a bloodbath in Chicago. The first issue of *Rolling Stone* was published November 9, 1967, a for-profit lifestyle, rock and roll, hip culture, magazine, and not a part of the underground. Abe Peck, the editor of *Seed*, in his book *Uncovering the Sixties: the Life and Times of the Underground Press*, described Wenner and his mentor, Ralph Gleason, as having "a general disbelief in American politics" yet "not really enchanted anymore with radical politics." According to Robert Draper, in his book *Rolling Stone Magazine: The Uncensored History*, Wenner eventually tuned in to what was happening:

"A year later *Rolling Stone* pivoted distinctly to the left. The magazine's April 5,

1969, issue investigated a popular theme: 'American Revolution 1969.' … Most conspicuous about that issue, however, was the oddly reluctant tone in Jann Wenner's lead editorial. As if a gun was being pressed against his temple, he wrote, 'Like it or not, we have reached a point in the social, cultural, intellectual and artistic history of the United States where we are all going to be affected by politics. … These new politics are about to become a part of our daily lives, and willingly, or not, we are in it."

In the first eight months of 1968, many incidents, local, national, and global, all reported in the underground press, created the volatile mood leading up to the Perfect Storm that was the 1968 Democratic National Convention. On January 5 pediatrician Dr. Benjamin Spock, William Sloan Coffin, chaplain of Yale University, novelist Mitchell Goodman, student Michael Ferber, and activist Marcus Raskin were indicted in Boston on charges of conspiracy to encourage violations of the draft laws. The war in Asia was threatening to spread, when on January 23 North Korean patrol boats captured the USS Pueblo, a Navy intelligence spy ship. Later in the month the North Vietnamese launched the Tet offensive. In February, General Nguyen Ngoc Loan, a South Vietnamese security official, was filmed executing a Viet Cong prisoner. Also, the US casualty toll for a single week in Vietnam was 543 Americans dead and 2547 wounded. In March, Antonin Novotny, the President of Czechoslovakia, resigned. In April Martin Luther King Jr. was assassinated. Two days later Bobby Hutton, treasurer of the Black Panthers, was shot and killed by Oakland Police. On April 23, an occupation of the administration building at Columbia University ended when police violently removed protestors, arresting 628. May saw "Bloody Monday" in France, when police battled 5,000 students. Also in May, Student Non-Violent Coordinating Committee militant Rap Brown was found guilty of carrying a gun while under indictment and sentenced to five years. That June, in a loft in New York City, Andy Warhol was shot by Valerie Solanis. Three days later Sirhan Sirhan assassinated Senator Robert Kennedy. In July, Abbie Hoffman's "The Yippies Are Going to Chicago" was published in the *Realist*. In August the Republicans nominated Richard Nixon to be their presidential candidate. Also in August, the Soviet Union invaded Czechoslovakia with over 200,000 Warsaw pact troops, putting an end to the "Prague Spring." And on August 26th Mayor J. Daley opened the 1968 Democratic National Convention in Chicago.

While Chicago braced itself for the YIPPIE invasion, tensions between the city's youth and police were at an all-time high. One incident occurred in Lake View, a budding gay neighborhood "protected and served" by Cmdr. John Fahey at the Town Hall Police District where gay men were constantly harassed by the cops. Things came to a head on June 4 when nineteen-year-old Ronald Nelson was fatally shot in the back by police officer Richard L. Nuccio. Nelson was allegedly a street hustler, who some say was gay, bi, or straight gay-for-pay. The shooting occurred after Benjamin Citron, owner of Franksville Drive-In hot dog joint, called police to complain about rowdy youths in his parking lot. Police officers Richard L. Nuccio and Kenneth Hyatt arrived and questioned nineteen-year-old Steve Austill, a friend of Nelson's. (Some reports say Ronald Rothmund, another cop, was present). Citron pointed to Nelson, and told police: "He's the one!" Nelson ran down an alley. Officer Hyatt yelled, "Stop him! Stop him!" Officer Nuccio dropped to one knee, aimed and shot Nelson in the back. One witness, an off-duty private in the Army, said Nuccio grabbed Nelson by the arm and dragged him thirty feet into the alley. When Austill got to his friend's body, Nuccio was laughing, "I shot the punk in the ass." The cops refused to call an ambulance. Nelson was thrown into a paddy wagon and died at the hospital. Nuccio's version was that while absconding, Nelson threw a knife at him and he shot in self-defense, a story contradicted by Noel Kitchen, a sailor stationed at Great Lakes Naval Training Center, and a dozen other witnesses. After a cursory investigation, the shooting was ruled "justifiable." Meanwhile, anger in the community reached fever pitch. On July 11 citizens at a board meeting of the Lake View Citizen's Council (LVCC) recommended Nuccio be indicted for murder. Outraged mothers voiced concern about their children's safety, but Town Hall cops closed ranks and harassed witnesses. San Francisco's *Movement*, wrote:

"Another [youth] was stopped at a red light. When it turned green, he was pulled over, and arrested for going through a red light. He spent the weekend in jail, without being allowed a phone call. This same youth was pulled over, for no reason, on his way to the LVCC board meeting. On seeing the leaflets about the meeting in his car, the cop said, 'In my book, that's illegal. You better not say anything tonight about the Nelson thing. If I find you alone one night, you're going to be dead in an alley too.' ... The cop who arrested him was Nuccio's cousin."

Nuccio didn't see the inside of a jail cell until May 15, 1973, five years after he shot Ronald Nelson in the back. Ralla Klepak, lawyer for the Nelson family, had also represented Dean T. Kolberg and Ralf L. Johnston, owners of the Trip gay bar, closed down earlier in the year during Daley's cleanup of the city. While shuttered, Mattachine Midwest used the three-story restaurant and bar to host the North American Conference of Homophile Organizations (NACHO), an umbrella group for homophile organizations. NACHO was founded in 1966, inspired by *Life* and *Time* exposés of the homosexual lifestyle, and founded to present a united and respectable homosexual face to the general public. In his book *Gay Power: An American Revolution*, David Eisenbach writes that one NACHO founder,

Foster Gunnison, Jr. was concerned the homophile movement would be taken over by "fringe elements, beatniks, and other professional non-conformists." NACHO was plagued by differences of opinion from the outset. Some groups, like the Daughters of Bilitis (DOB), refused to give up their autonomy, wary that men couldn't understand the needs of lesbians. DOB president Rita LaPorte compared NACHO and DOB to husband and wife, arguing that men dissipated women's energy in a marriage, and lesbians would suffer the same fate at the hands of a male-dominated NACHO. From August 11-18, 1968, representatives from twenty-six gay rights groups, among them Shirley Willer, a past president of the DOB, Larry Littlejohn, president of the Society for Individual Rights, Barbara Gittings of New York DOB, and Frank Kameny of Washington, DC Mattachine. The conference was contentious, with DOB pulling out altogether, but NACHO is remembered for Frank Kameny adopting the slogan "Gay is Good," inspired by the African-American "Black is Beautiful." NACHO 1968 adopted a Homosexual Bill of Rights. The *New York Times* reported that NACHO delegates recommended sending questionnaires to those seeking political office, forcing them to take a public stand on homosexuality. In the *New Republic* a sidebar on the NACHO conference was added to an article about street battles at the DNC convention. It read:

> "It had been rumored that the YIPPIES would hold a 'Homosexuals for Humphrey' rally in Chicago. The 'homophiles' claim to be fifteen million strong, and argue that no politician can turn up his nose at that many votes. Unlike other minority groups, the homosexuals have few defenders. One college professor recently traced the nation's ills to an undercurrent of 'hippies, homos and hooligans.' While medicine and psychiatry continue trying to unravel the complexities behind homosexuals' inverted lives, they are stalked and caged by vice cops who perch on toilet seats to peer through peepholes."

The NACHO conference in Chicago was covered by several underground publications, including San Francisco's *Haight Ashbury Maverick*, Los Angeles' *Open City*, and *Black Panther*, the latter under the headline "Bill of Rights for Homos." Chicago's *Kaleidoscope* published the Homosexual Bill of Rights in full:

> 1) Private consensual sex acts between persons over the age of consent shall not be an offense.
> 2) Solicitation for any sexual act shall not be an offense except upon the filing of a complaint by the aggravated party, not a police officer or agent.
> 3) A person's sexual orientation or practice shall not be a factor in the granting or renewing of federal security clearances, visas and the granting of citizenship.
> 4) Service in and discharge from the armed forces and eligibility for veteran's

benefits shall be without reference to homosexuality.

5) A person's sexual orientation or practice shall not affect his eligibility for employment with federal, state or local governments, or private employers.

AREA OF IMMEDIATE REFORM

1) Police and other government agents shall cease the practice of enticement and entrapment of homosexuals.

2) Police shall desist from notifying the employers of those arrested for homosexual offenses.

3) Neither the police department nor any other government agency shall keep files solely for the purpose of identifying homosexuals.

4) The practice of harassing bars and other establishments and of revoking their licenses because they cater to homosexuals shall cease.

5) The practice of reviewing less-than-honorable military discharges, granted for homosexual orientation or practice, shall be established, with the goal of upgrading such discharges into fully honorable.

6) The registration of sex offenders shall not be required.

7) City ordinances involving sexual matters shall be rescinded and these matters left to state legislatures.

8) Conviction for homosexual offenses shall not be the basis for prohibiting issuance of professional or any other license nor for the revocation of these licenses.

9) No questions regarding sexual orientation or practice shall appear on application forms, personal data sheets or in personal interviews.

10) No government agency shall use the classification of homosexuality as an alleged illness to limit the freedom, rights, or privileges of any homosexual."

A fuller account in the *Haight Ashbury Maverick* added:

"The Conference proclaimed July 4, National Demonstration Day and set up a Sex Enlightenment Week during the month of May. It commended the American Civil Liberties Union for its statement on homosexuality and the City of New York for employing homosexuals in the city government. It expressed 'sharp disappointment' with Canadian Prime Minister Pierre Eliot Trudeau for following the British rather than the Continental pattern of homosexual law reform; protested laws which exclude and deport homosexual aliens from the United States; called for an objective approach to homosexuality in courses on sex education; encouraged repeal of state laws against homosexual acts and protested the denial to homophile organizations of space in newspapers and other media for legitimate organizational advertising.

"The twenty-six organizations in the North American Conference are subdivided into three regional conferences in East, Midwest, and West. Houston was the chosen site of the 1969 conference. The officers elected were: Mark Jeffers, young president of Kansas City's Phoenix Society; as chairman; Doug Sanders, a Vancouver lawyer noted for his work with draft refuges in Canada; and, as secretary, Stephen Donaldson, 22 year old Columbia University junior who founded the Student Homophile League, as treasurer."

A month after NACHO, Texas-based African-American magazine *Sepia* published "The Homosexual Fights Back" which began:

"The police cars jockey into position under cover of darkness. Inside the meeting hall, several 'pedestrians' begin to converge on the meeting place. No, this isn't Russia, and this isn't Russian secret police about to pounce on some freedom lovers in one of the satellite countries. This is, or rather was, a routine police raid on a gathering place for American homosexuals whose only 'crime' is in being 'different.' But this scene is changing fast. The homosexual, formerly hounded by the police as an animal, is standing up and fighting."

The final days leading up to the Convention were tense, as anti-Vietnam War protestors flooded into the city. In the early hours of August 22, four days before the Convention, in the hippie/gay neighborhood of Old Town, Native American Dean Johnson, a seventeen-year old from Sioux Falls, SD, was shot and killed by Officer John Manley, a notorious figure in the gay community. Manley built a career out of entrapping gay men in public urinals. Manley and Officer Frank Szwedo stopped Johnson for a curfew violation, but the teen allegedly pulled a .32 revolver on them. When the gun misfired, Manley shot Johnson dead. "Hippie Killed by Policemen in Old Town," read the headline in the *Chicago Tribune*, in an article that described Johnson as "dressed as a hippie with long hair and beads." Johnson was in Chicago to protest the Vietnam War. The shooting occurred at North and Wells Sts., a few blocks from Lincoln Park, the epicenter of the first night of riots. In the *Seed* office, Abbie Hoffman, enraged by the shooting, said, "Don't let them kill no more people. We've got to stop them killing our people." In his book *Chicago '68*, David Farber describes the memorial service organized by *Seed* staffers:

"In Lincoln Park, to a small crowd of longhairs, SDSers, partying motorcycle gang members, and a host of security agents and mass media representatives [Lower East Side SDS member Tom] Neuman announced that Dean Johnson 'died of pig poisoning. ... We're suffering from pig and media poisoning.'"

The first confrontation between anti-war protestors and police started at 11:00 p.m. the night before the Convention opened, when 3,000 peaceniks were herded out of Lincoln Park and onto the intersection of Clark and Wells Sts., including poet Allen Ginsberg. In October, Lawrence Lipton, author of *The Holy Barbarians* and *The Erotic Revolution*, wrote "Allen Ginsberg in Chicago," published in the *Los Angeles Free Press* and *Georgia Straight: Vancouver Free Press*:

"I was in Lincoln Park, on my way to join Allen who was chanting the Om, that I sustained my injuries at the hands of the Chicago Cops. Not until a few days later were we able to meet for dinner and conversation. He had undergone tear gas attacks three times but he insisted on coming to visit me."

Lipton and Ginsberg walked to a nearby restaurant:

"We went back to the dining room and asked for a table. The owner took one look at us and told us all the tables had been reserved. There were vacant tables all around us. There was counter service, so, taking the proprietor at his word we sat down, but the girl came over and told us that 'the boss won't let me wait on you.' We got up and left. One of the patrons, a young man, followed us out and expressed his sympathy. He knew perfectly well what had happened and was chagrined about it."

Lipton and Ginsberg settled on a Chinese restaurant across the street, where the Chinese-American waitress "dug poetry" and "asked for our autographs." Lipton noted he once had a similar experience in Chicago, with author Richard Wright:

"In the company of a black author I was a white nigger so far as the bigoted restaurateur was concerned. ... This time, with Allen, the social stigma was hair and, of course, our dress. It could have happened at any time in Chicago ... but it was worse than usual because of the police state terror in Chicago. To insist on one's civil rights on such an occasion would only have brought the police down on us and we had both had enough of Mayor Daley's Gestapo. It would have been like a German Jew in Hitler's Germany calling in the Storm Troopers to protect his civil rights. That is to say, naïve, if not downright suicidal."

Lipton, in his *Los Angeles Free Press* post-Convention analysis, reported on how the police forced hotels to evict YIPPIES and reporters of the underground press:

"My room reservation, at the Lincoln Hotel across from Lincoln Park, which has been confirmed only the night before, was already canceled when I arrived with my baggage in the morning. The desk clerk denied having any reservation. Ed Sanders [poet and member of the Fugs rock band] is here ... with his wife and his little girl and he stands at this moment in danger of eviction. This is the kind of pillar to post hassle that is being imposed on everybody connected with the underground press or is known to be friendly with the YIPPIE Festival of Life. ... Keith Lampe, handling press for the Youth International Party, and David Lewis Stein, YIPPIE Ambassador at Large ... have also been evicted from the Lincoln Hotel, under pressure from plainclothesmen who are doing the undercover cloak and dagger work of local and federal Gestapo. At this minute Allen Ginsberg is still living at the Lincoln Hotel."

Ironically, in the basement of the Lincoln Hotel was the notorious Lincoln Baths, a gay bathhouse going back to at least the 1940s. The Lincoln Baths were raided regularly, most famously on June 13, 1964, when thirty-three men were arrested and again on March 5, 1966, when thirty-two ended up in court.

The 1968 National Democratic Convention was marred by street battles between police and protestors. The YIPPIE protest may not have been the musical "Festival of Life" that Jerry Rubin predicted, but it served to highlight the vast chasm between the youth of America chanting "The Whole World is Watching," and the "Establishment," protected by a rabid out-of-control police force, unleashed by Mayor Richard J. Daley. "The police are not here to create disorder, they're here to preserve disorder," announced Daley, in a Freudian slip. What shocked the media covering the Convention was the disregard for freedom of the press. Nobody was surprised when a bullet, fired from a police car, shattered the storefront window of the *Seed* office, but Dan Rather of *CBS News* being punched in the stomach on camera was a different story. Veteran newsman Mike Wallace was also roughed-up on the Convention floor, Walter Cronkite talked about police "thugs" on TV, and on NBC's *Today Show*, the host, Hugh Downs, called the Chicago police "pigs."

Daniel Walker, Vice President of the Chicago Crime Commission, was appointed to head the Chicago Study Team to investigate violent clashes between police and protestors. In December, 1968, *Rights in Conflict: "The Chicago Police Riot"* was published. The "Walker Report" acknowledged that while protesters deliberately provoked police, the police responded with uncritical violence. Walker named it "The Police Riot," though as early August 30, Atlanta's *Great Speckled Bird* named it as such. The Report noted that though police officers committed criminal acts, none were arrested, or even disciplined. Identifying them was a problem, as during the riots, many removed their nametags and badges. The first reporter attacked was Lawrence Green of the *Chicago Daily News*, who was pushed to the ground. When he yelled "Press! Press! Press!" he was clubbed in the back and told, "Fuck your press cards." Frederick DeVan, a photographer from *Life* magazine, had his cameras broken. Winston S. Churchill II, grandson of Britain's World War II Prime Minister, was knocked to the ground while reporting for the *London Evening Standard*. Other reporters beaten were from *Newsweek, Time, Chicago Sun-Times*, CBS, NBC-TV, *Paris Match, Manhattan Tribune, Business Week, Washington Post, Chicago's American, New York Times*, and *Chicago Tribune*. In all, forty-nine newspersons were roughed-up by police: forty-three were hit, three were maced, and three were arrested; twenty-two were reporters, twenty-three photographers, and four members of TV crews; in ten of the incidents, photographic equipment was deliberately destroyed.

In December, Seattle's *Helix*, reported that Marvin Garson, editor of the counterculture tabloid, the *San Francisco Express Times,* served twenty days in jail for his part in the protests. In an email to this author, Leo Laurence, who covered the Convention for KGO Radio, wrote:

"I was beginning the long process of coming out of the closet at the Convention, and I had some great experiences as a Gay man. The horror of Chicago during the Convention definitely changed my views of the police. I went to the Convention as a conservative Republican. When I returned to San Francisco, I radically changed and became a Gay militant."

12

AFTER THE "PIG RIOT"

After the "Pig Riot," gay writers Jean Genet and William Burroughs, both in Chicago for the Democratic National Convention, wrote about their experiences in *Esquire* magazine. The Convention radicalized peace loving hippies into a ragbag army of revolutionaries, the consensus being that attempting to influence politicians was pointless. The underground papers now supported the use of violence against the police, some instructing their readers how to use guns. This, however, lead to an increase in raids on the underground press.

"Nothing Wrong with America That a Good Erection Won't Cure."–David Mairowitz in the November 15, 1968, issue of *Other Scenes*.

After the tear gas cleared from the 1968 Democratic National Convention, the mainstream press was divided on what happened, while the underground press was resolute in its condemnation. An article on the cover of Atlanta's *Great Speckled Bird* began: "America has turned its Convention City into an armed camp against her own people. The 'democratic process' is dead. ... We, the youth of America, in the tens of thousands, come here in our justified anger and are met at gunpoint." "CZECHAGO U.S.A." ran the headline in the *Berkeley Barb*, and Detroit's

Fifth Estate published "2,3 Many Chicago's":

> "Chicago and the Democratic Convention were the end of a fantasy trip. The last illusion that social change could be brought about through popular pressure on the Democratic Party was shattered beneath the clubs of Daley's pigs and the manipulations of the Humphrey political machine."

In the September issue, Chicago's *Mattachine Midwest Newsletter* joined the chorus of outrage:

> " … the whole world saw the hatred and violence of which Chicago police are capable, whether one's sympathies are with the demonstrators or not, the police tactics during the week of the convention … belong in a history of Nazi Germany. … Anyone within reach of a TV set during the convention saw billy clubs being flailed wildly at everyone within reach. … The cops had gone berserk. To our surprise, many of the gay community were present in Lincoln and Grant parks, collecting signatures on our petitions and observing police and demonstrators. They confirm that the police action was entirely out of line with any 'provocation' (which in most instances amounted to name-calling in reply to police name-calling)."

In the *Los Angeles Free Press*, Lawrence Lipton wrote that three writers, Jean Genet, William Burroughs and Richard Seaver, were staying at the Sheraton Hotel for $40 a night paid for by *Esquire* magazine. He described the taping of a radio interview: "Jean Genet, speaking in French, interpreted by Allen [Ginsberg], is saying that 'if police can carry guns, and the army carry grenades in and around the convention hall he cannot understand why anyone should be molested by the police because of his strange clothes and hair-do." Lipton only told half the story. *Esquire* hired four writers to cover the Convention: Terry Southern, Jean Genet, William Burroughs, and John Sack. Richard Seaver, the American translator, editor, and publisher, was also there, to translate Genet's article into English. Seaver was an anti-censorship campaigner and championed the work of D.H. Lawrence, Jack Kerouac, and the Marquis de Sade. Also in the group was gay John Berendt, *Esquire* editor, and later author of the award-winning *Garden of Good and Evil*. Terry Southern, author, essayist, and screenwriter, had been active in the Greenwich Village beat-poet scene and later co-wrote the screenplays for *Dr. Strangelove*, *Easy Rider*, and *The Magic Christian*. Reporter John Sack was a war correspondent, sent to document the Convention from the police point of view. The first article to appear in the November 1968 *Esquire* was Terry Southern's "Groovin' in Chi," in which he described meeting the other writers:

> "Six p.m. Rendezvous of our hard-hitting little press team–Jean Jack Genet,

Willy Bill Burroughs, and yours truly as anchor man, trying to lend a modicum of stability to the group. Also on hand, Esky editor young John Berendt–his job: straighten these weirdos. And K.F.S. ("Keep Flying Speed!"). We met in this queer little Downstairs Lounge, one of several bars in our hotel, the Chicago-Sheraton–and John Berendt was quick to charge us with our respective assignments: 'You Jean Jack Genet, on the alert for all manner of criminality and perversion in high places! You, Big Bill Burroughs, let your keen and experienced eye discern any sign of sense derangement through the use of drugs by these delegates, the nominees, and officials of every station! Now then, you, T. Southern, on double alert for all manner of absurdity at the convention."

On the first night, the *Esquire* press team set out for Lincoln Park to find Allen Ginsberg. Southern wrote: "We found Allen, seated in the center of a group of fifty or so, doing his thing, which in this case was the 'Om.'"
After police warned protestors to exit the park:

"We sat down with the others, and joined the Oming, which especially delighted Genet; we stayed there for maybe half an hour, while the circle grew steadily larger, and the 'final warnings' were repeated. It was now nearing midnight. Burroughs looked at his watch, and with that unerring awareness of which he is capable, muttered, 'They're coming.' At that instant, the banks of searchlights blazed up on the armored van which was already moving toward us. Fanned out on each side of the van were about a thousand police."

The *Esquire* press team took refuge in Allen Ginsberg's room at the Lincoln Hotel. In Genet's essay, "The Members of the Assembly," he wrote:

" … my eyes are burning from the gas: a medic pours water into them, and the water spills over me down to my feet. In short, in their blundering clumsiness, the Americans have tried to burn me and a few minutes later to drown me. … And what of the convention? And democracy? … We leave the hotel: another azure policeman–or beautiful girl in drag–holding his billy club in his hand the way, exactly the way, I hold a black American's member–escorts us to our car and opens the door for us: there can be no mistake about it: we are White."

Genet begins his *Esquire* article: "Chicago reminds me of an animal which curiously is trying to climb on top of itself." Of the Lincoln Park episode he referenced Dean Johnson, the seventeen-year old shot and killed by Officer John Manley:

"An American Indian, carrying a furled green flag, explains to us that it will be taken tomorrow to the airport when Senator McCarthy is scheduled to arrive and speak. Unfurled, the flag bears upon its green background the painted image of a seventeen year old boy–some say he was Indian, others black–killed two days before by the Chicago police."

Genet had this to say regarding the Chicago police:

"The thighs are very beautiful beneath the blue cloth, thick and muscular. It all must be hard. This policeman is also a boxer, a wrestler. His legs are long, and perhaps, as you approach his member, you would find a furry nest of long, tight, curly hair. That is all I can see–and I must say it fascinates me–that and his boots, but I can guess that these superb thighs extend on up into an imposing member and a muscled torso, made even firmer every day by his police training in the cops' gymnasium. Higher up, into his arms and hands which must know how to put a black man or a thief out of action. ... but the thighs have parted slightly, and through the crack which extends from the knees to the too-heavy member, I can see ... the whole panorama of the Democratic Convention with its star-spangled banners, its star-spangled prattle, its star-spangled dresses, its star-spangled undress, its star-spangled songs, its star-spangled fields, its star-spangled candidates, in short the whole ostentatious parade ... "

William Burroughs, in "The Coming of the Purple Better One," wrote:

"I have described the Chicago police as left over from 1910 and in a sense this is true. Daley and his nightstick authority date back to turn-of-the-century ward politics. There are anachronisms and they know it. This I think accounts for the shocking ferocity of their behavior. Jean Genet, who has considerable police experience, says he never saw such expressions before on allegedly human faces."

Not everyone approved of the *Esquire* articles. Barbara Kingston in the *MidPeninsula Observer*, a leftist paper out of Palo Alto, CA, accused *Esquire* of castrating Chicago "to fit the world of potency-through-products" like Seagram's, Ballantine's, Revlon, Pontiac, and other advertisers. Kingston admits that *Esquire*'s reportage team of Genet, Southern, Burroughs and Sack, are all good writers, but "the result was confusion" Kingston wrote:

"*Esquire* decided to see Chicago as an isolated event, with no causes and no consequences. The curtain went up on Sunday and came down on Thursday. *Esquire* paid attention only to what happened in those five days. It didn't want its readers to think about Vietnam or machine politics. ... *Esquire* called [the writers] 'black humorists.' ... Burroughs and Genet don't write funny books. Genet was in prison and wrote about holy fags. Burroughs was a junkie for fifteen years."

Kingston accused Burroughs of "taking refuge in fantasy." It seems she expected left wing political tracts from two creative writers and was oblivious to the revolutionary content of *Naked Lunch*, or *Our Lady of the Flowers*. Genet, at least, was political in his support of the Black Panthers. In March 1970, Genet was in Los Angeles protesting police persecution of the Black Panther Party, where he described the mainstream press as "cowardly and bought off." Sue Marshall in the *Los Angeles Free Press* wrote that the press conference, with Raymond "Masai" Hewitt, Minister of Education for the Black Panther Party, was poorly attended. With Judy Oranger of *Ramparts* magazine as interpreter, Genet said: "White Americans have been violent to blacks for over 200 years. How do you expect the Panthers to react? Violence begins on the blacks in America." Genet predicted this was "the eve of the downfall of the United States," adding, "rather than a military failure, it will be a liberation movement from within."

The Chicago "Pig Riot" radicalized thousands of formerly pacifist, flower power, Gandhi followers, turning them into a ragbag army of Marxists and Anarchists. After the Democratic National Convention, underground newspapers published photographs of longhaired hippie revolutionaries, under headlines like "Kill the Pigs." The *Black Panther* published a photograph of Huey Newton sitting in a wicker peacock chair, a spear in one hand, and a shotgun in the other. In November 1968, Canada's *Georgia Strait: Vancouver Free Press* had a naked woman holding a rifle on the cover. In February 1969 the cover of Detroit's *Fifth Estate* depicted a collection of handguns and the word "NOW!" In March 1970, the cover of *Berkeley Tribe* depicted eight full-frontal naked men holding rifles, under the headline "Freakin' Fag Revolution." Two months later the Madison *Kaleidoscope* openly advocated the killing of police. A headline on the cover read, "Take Up the Gun," and an article inside taught readers how to buy a used weapon. Under "Nice guns to have around," it begins: "PISTOLS: The 38 special revolver is the standard handgun on both sides of the revolution. By using standard caliber weapons, brothers and sisters will be able to supply shells that fit your piece, and valuable ammunition can be liberated from the 'pigs.'" In September 1970, *Ain't I a Woman*, an Iowa City lesbian feminist paper, had a drawing of a gun-toting woman on the cover, and under the headline "Miss Craig's Face-Saving Exercises," instructions on how to load and fire a weapon.

However, not everyone advocated gun violence. In April 1969 in the Milwaukee *Kaleidoscope*, James Sorcic suggested questioning the cops' manhood:

"The main thing to keep in mind when dealing with the police is to take every opportunity to confront them, and make them feel as small and worthless as possible. For example, give up the idea of calling them 'pigs.' This only adds to their fantasy of being virile. Hit them with ego-crushers like: motorcycle faggot, blue sissy, or a fucking coward with a gun hanging down between their legs. Take advantage of their low mentality every chance you get. Use four syllable words, and laugh in their faces when they ask you what it means. Attack their sexuality. Treat them all like faggots or child-molesters. Try anything or everything to break their spirit. Forget that shit about them being 'human beings' because they're not."

One gay San Francisco reporter at the Democratic National Convention was Leo Laurence. Josh Sides, in his book *Erotic City: Sexual Revolutions and the Making of San Francisco*, wrote:

"Back in San Francisco, Laurence easily found work as a reporter for KGO Radio and a writer for the *Berkeley Barb*, where he reported on the antiwar and sexual freedom movements. While he was covering the activities of the SFL [Sexual Freedom League], he began to think seriously about coming out. Until then, his pieces on sexual freedom and homosexuality had been published under the pseudonym Gary Patterson. But in the summer of 1968, Laurence became 'radicalized.' On his way back to California from a trip to Indiana, he stopped in Chicago for the Democratic National Convention. 'It was a war zone,' he recalled of that infamous convention, 'and it is what turned me from a conservative Republican to a Leftist democrat. I was never the same.'"

One pre-radicalization event covered by "Gary Patterson" in the *Berkeley Barb* was a gay dance in San Francisco. He wrote: "'Everybody is having a gay time,' a tall young slim blond boy said as he danced about with his partner, Johnny, at the '*Berkeley Barb* Want Ad' dance." The dance was organized by the Society for Individual Rights (SIR), and held at the group's community center at 83 Sixth Street. At the time, SIR was the largest gay organization in the United States with almost one thousand members. The party celebrated the gay "Want Ads" in *the Berkeley Barb*:

"Every weekend SIR has gay dances with different motifs, such as this one called want ads. Beautiful things happen at them. ... Music filled the room. Moving to the dance floor [two] fellows – one blond and tall, the other a darker Italian with long flowing hair–started dancing. Soon the room was filled with fellows swinging to the beat. In public, the gay community isn't permitted the privilege of showing love or affection to each other by society's customs and laws. But inside the private SIR Community Center, gay males and females are relaxed and happy. Or maybe just plain gay."

After the Convention, Patterson returned to San Francisco and wrote "Straight Scribe Gets Bent" in the *Berkeley Barb*:

"Chicago was a turning point for the world, for the revolution, and for me. I went to Chicago as a straight reporter for the establishment's 'Working Press.' I came back changed, committed, and delighted. ... The story I expected to cover was on the convention floor. But once there, all I saw was disgusting, all I heard was monotonous, and all I felt was sickening. I decided … to hell with all the crap in this convention hall, I'm going for the story downtown."

Patterson was tear-gassed three times as he marched up Chicago's Michigan Avenue, arm in arm with comedian and political activist, Dick Gregory. On the day of his departure, Patterson was impressed by a variation of Jim Morrison's Doors song "Five to One" scrawled onto the sidewalk: "The Old get Older. The Young get stronger, May take a week, may take longer. They got the gas, we got the numbers. We gonna win. Yeah! We're taking over.'" Patterson's new radical gay politics surfaced in the *Berkeley Barb* the following week. In a bid for the US Senate, conservative Republican, Max Rafferty, wrote to SIR saying, "I will oppose any change in the present law against homosexuality except to make them more severe." Patterson wrote: "That one sentence has mobilized the homophile community throughout California in an unprecedented campaign to defeat Rafferty's bid for the U. S. Senate." SIR reprinted Rafferty's statement and mailed it to over 10,000 gay people "from the Oregon border to the Mexican line." It was circulated in gay bars, baths and clubs. Patterson ended his article: "The gay crowd is fighting mad at Rafferty, and anybody who's been in a bitch fight with a queen knows how fierce they can be. Rafferty's in for trouble." Max Rafferty lost the election to Democrat Alan Cranston. This wasn't the first time San Francisco's SIR took an interest in a political campaign. A year earlier "Gay Vote Scramble" in the *Berkeley Barb* referred to an article in SIR's *Vector* newsletter, which began:

> "Want to know why John Burton lost the last election in San Francisco?
> "A partial answer at least appeared in last month's *Vector* ... [who] charged Burton with having neglected the homophile vote. … Judging by the overwhelming number of ads by SF politicos in the current October issue [of *Vector*], some politicians have become educated. The ads urge the election of Newsom, Ertola, Cheacy, Connor, Stern and Riordan, for supervisor. A good-sized ad seeks the election of Johnson for Sheriff. Bill Billings seeks the vote for Mayor."

Democrat Assemblyman, John L. Burton, who was running for State Senator, lost to Milton Marks.

In the fall of 1968, gay underground press reporters began "coming out," and documenting their lives in newspapers aimed at a heterosexual audience. Ron Kurtis, in San Diego's *Teaspoon Door* and Los Angeles' *Open City* offered "straights" a glimpse into the homosexual world:

> "The homosexual is in the most delicate possible position. The vast majority of us genuinely want to find a lasting relationship, just as do the heterosexuals.

And, like everyone else, we must meet many, many people before we find someone with whom we are compatible enough with to establish a stable relationship. The problem is—where is such a meeting possible? The church certainly is not welcoming us with open arms! Griffith Park, while terribly tantalizing to some homosexuals, is neither attractive nor justifiable to most of us. What may be obtained in the public baths is certainly not a situation which might ultimately reach a marital status. For most of us the gay bar is the only current answer."

The following week, Kurtis continued with "Why Homosexuals Trick":

"Why is the homosexual so often promiscuous? A few simple reasons are obvious. He lacks restricting matrimonial ties. And since he lacks the approval of church or government, and anything he does is basically 'wrong' from the start and he's committing a crime merely by giving way to his sexual inclination, then why does it matter if he fucks one man or half a dozen?"

Harassment of gays was rampant nationwide. In October 1968, New Orleans' *Ungarbled Word* reported on a raid in the French Quarter where Municipal Vice Cops busted twelve men for obscenity, four members of the band, and the club's owner:

"While checking out Club Stand-In on the corner of Conti and Burgundy, the vice cops heard music coming from a back room. On enquiring, they were told if they bought a $2.00 drink they could go in, which they do, only to find men dancing together in 'intimate fashion.' The cops showed their ID and busted everyone, and charged them with 'obscenity by dancing intimately with members of the same sex,' and the band was charged with 'vagrancy by loitering' the owner with 'keeping a disorderly place and employing minors in an alcoholic beverage outlet.'"

An editorial COMMENT read:

"The local Greyface Press, in their account of the arrests, made a point of listing the names, ages, and addresses of these twelve men who were neither guilty of harming anyone, disturbing the peace, nor inflicting their views on the public. If this doesn't constitute harassment, what does?"

In *Open City*, Sam Winston wrote "Be Gay AND Hip," about homosexuals in the 'hippie scene," describing the rift between "hip" and conservative gays. In it, he suggests the Stampede bar on Santa Monica Blvd., for "you long-haired Americans who prefer the same sex." He added:

"If you've wondered why homosexuals have not flocked to the underground, it's probably because most of the underground is based on the left part of the political spectrum, and homosexuals come in all ideological colors. Try telling a Conservative Republican homosexual he should support Eldridge Cleaver. What is cool, though, is that the underground feels 'whatever-turns-you-on' is OK and the people in the underground can concentrate on being human beings. Too many homosexuals consider themselves homosexuals first and humans secondly."

Winston's naming of Eldridge Cleaver was unfortunate as the black writer and political activist was virulently anti-homosexual. In San Francisco's *Ramparts* magazine June 1966, Cleaver wrote, "Notes on a Native Son," a damning essay on the work of African-American gay author James Baldwin. Cleaver wrote: "There is in James Baldwin the most grueling, agonizing, total hatred of the blacks, particularly of himself, and the most shameful, fanatical, fawning, sycophantic love of the whites that one can find in any black American writer of note in our time." Cleaver criticized the use of cosmetics to bleach the skin, and "nose thinning and lip-clipping operations," calling it "the racial death-wish of American Negroes." He continued:

"It seems that many Negro homosexuals, acquiescing in this racial death wish, are outraged and frustrated because in their sickness they are unable to have a baby by a white man. ... This racial death wish is the driving force in James Baldwin. ... Homosexuality is a sickness, just as much as baby-rape or wanting to become head of General Motors."

Cleaver wasn't the only black homophobic writer. In his 1966 book, *Home: Social Essays*, LeRoi Jones (later Amira Baraka), in his virulently anti-gay essay, "American Sexual Reference," wrote:

"Most American white men are trained to be fags. For this reason it is no wonder their faces are weak and blank, left without the hurt that reality makes—anytime. That red flush, those silk blue faggot eyes. So white women become men-things, a weird combination, sucking the male juices to build a navel orange, which is themselves."

The difference between Cleaver and Jones's homophobia, is that Cleaver was "straight," whereas Jones was homosexual. In the book, *Amira Baraka: The Politics and Art of a Black Intellectual*, African-American author Jerry Gafio Watts writes:

"Jones's endorsement of the rape of white women and his homophobic attacks on white men were part of his broader strategy to bury his own homosexual past under black sexual exotica and sexist venom. He knew that popular knowledge of his homosexuality would have undermined the credibility of his militant voice. By becoming publicly known as a hater of homosexuals, Jones tried to defuse any claims that might surface linking him with his homosexual past."

After the "Pig Riot" at the Democratic National Convention in Chicago the rhetoric in the underground press and from leaders in the "Movement" became violent and confrontational. The *Los Angeles Free Press* reported on Eldridge Cleaver speaking to students in the Edwin Pauley Memorial Basketball Pavilion on the UCLA campus. On the subject of California's governor: "I say Ronald Reagan is a punk, a sissy and a coward. I challenge him to a dual to the death right now. He can choose his weapons. He can choose a baseball bat, a knife, a gun or a marshmallow. I will beat him to death with a marshmallow, cause he's a punk."

The fall of 1968 saw a crackdown on underground newspapers. Prior to his election as the 37th President of the United States, Richard Nixon came out in favor of a federal anti-smut law. The underground press, with its nudity, profanity, and openness to sexual experimentation, was targeted. The "Establishment" used "obscenity" as an excuse to stifle political dissent. Typical of the raids, were those on October 30 and November 15 on *Dallas Notes*, reported in the *Great Speckled Bird*:

"Detectives from the Vice Squad of the Dallas Police Department raided the office of *Dallas Notes* ... with a search warrant allowing them to seize 'pornography.' The cops carted off two tons of alleged pornography–all the back issues of *Dallas Notes* and all other underground papers in the office–in two flat back trucks brought for that purpose."

Three staff members were booked for "possession of pornography." The article in the *Great Speckled Bird* continued:

"The police also confiscated three typewriters, cameras, lenses, and other darkroom equipment, graphic arts equipment, over $100 in checks, approximately $30 in cash, bookkeeping records, subscription lists, and all other material which might be used to publish a newspaper. They also seized many political books and posters. (Is Chairman Mao pornographic?)"

At the police station, the publisher, Stoney Burns, admitted kidnapping the Lindbergh baby, which probably didn't help his situation. In spite of the arrests, the paper survived.

In December Thorne Dreyer wrote, "Law Harasses Underground Papers," in New York's *Guardian*. The article is a catalogue of government repression. Atlanta's *Great Speckled Bird* was forced to print out-of-state, after the DeKalb Parents League called the paper obscene. *Kudzu*, out of Jackson, MS, had salesmen arrested and staff beaten by deputy sheriffs. Philadelphia's *Distant Drummer* had salesmen arrested. Milwaukee enacted a "no-nipple" law to censor *Kaleidoscope*. The staff were arrested and charged with obscenity, the editor, John Kois, had his car firebombed. John Bryan, editor of *Open City* in Los Angeles was convicted of obscenity. Christian Eaby, editor of Philadelphia's *Lancaster Free Press* also faced obscenity charges. New York's *Rat* had to find a new office after the FBI visited their landlord and he doubled their rent. *Rag* in Austin, TX, was unable to find office space, after police visited potential landlords. *Orpheus* in Arizona was turned down by twenty-five printers. Bruce Dancis, editor of *First Issue* in Ithaca, NY, and Jim Retherford of the Bloomington, IN *Spectator* were both convicted of resisting the draft. And Pete Rothchild, editor of St. Louis' *Xanadu*, John Mathieson, of Minneapolis' *Raisin Bread*, Tony Seed, editor of the *Canadian Free Press*, and John Sinclair of Detroit's *Sun* and *Fifth Estate* were all busted for dope.

13

THIRD SEX IN THE THEATER AND MOVIES

In 1968, plays and Hollywood movies depicted homosexuals as jealous, possessive, maudlin drunks, worthy of a modicum of sympathy. However, while the good citizens of Jackson, MS, closed down the lesbian movie *The Fox*, and in Atlanta, the Fulton County Court Solicitor General confiscated Andy Warhol's *Lonesome Cowboys*, Los Angeles hosted the first Homosexual Film Festival.

"For better or for worse we're undergoing a flurry of films about homosexuals. Mostly it's for the worse-the films have taught us little about homosexuals, less about ourselves. Unless, of course, we're all voyeurs when it comes to perversion." – Paul Schrader, in his review of *The Sergeant* in the *Los Angeles Free Press.*

In Chicago, the *Seed* was financed by ads from hippie-oriented businesses, like the Underground Theater at Armitage and Clark St. One ad read: "An exciting new policy of the Beat-Off-Beat in Far Out flicks by today's angry young filmmakers. Midwest Premiere of *Guns of the Trees* ... two young couples explore life and love in our Mod, Mod world, with 'With-It' verse by Allen Ginsberg." The movie, directed by Jonas Mekas, was made in 1961, and features dropouts like beatniks, from a pre-Vietnam War and LSD era of sputniks and the Bay of Pigs, when tortured souls wrote poetry, chain-smoked, and starved in filthy garrets. Ginsberg is on the soundtrack, reading his poems *America* and *Money* from the *Howl* collection.

The "Establishment" ruled Hollywood and mainstream filmmaking, but "way out" films by underground filmmakers were a threat to the status quo. In August 1968, the *North Carolina Anvil* reported the seizure of *Flaming Creatures*, a 1963 film directed by Jack Smith. The film, considered a masterpiece of avant-garde filmmaking, contains an amusing discussion about oral sex, an orgy of topless women and, most shocking of all, exposed male genitalia. Cinema Inc., a Raleigh film society, was charged with obscenity, after Charles William Holland, one of the group's members, complained to the police after seeing *Flaming Creatures* at the Raleigh Little Theater. After complaining, Holland, accompanied by Det. J.L. Stoudenmire and Det. Larry Barbour, attended the film at a second showing, when it was seized. The *North Carolina Anvil* wrote:

"Maj. Robert E. Goodwin, chief of the Investigative Division of the Raleigh Police Department, and City Court Solicitor Henry V. Barnette Jr. viewed the film. … Goodwin said, 'I wouldn't want any members of my family and certainly no minors to see this film. As for art, it depends on what you call art. Everything is art up to a point. There is art in woodworking. This is not art in my opinion. It is nature in the raw.'"

In the summer of 1969, the *Great Speckled Bird* wrote: "The monsoon season has come to Atlanta." The headline referenced an anti-smut campaign started by Hinton McAuliffe, Fulton County Court Solicitor General. Targets included a magazine publisher, the Ansley Mall Mini-Cinema and the Central Adult Theater. At the Mini-Cinema, McAuliffe confiscated Andy Warhol's *Lonesome Cowboys*. The *Great Speckled Bird* wrote:

"Initially the witch hunt seemed directed at the city's homosexuals, who were recently driven out of Piedmont Park by, among other expedients, the use of photography. The raid on *Lonesome Cowboys* was precipitated when 'a representative of the Citizens for Decent Literature was in Atlanta on business and came by and paid us a visit and told us what this movie was about,' according to McAuliffe. And so the crusaders expected the Mini-Cinema to be full of homosexuals. Was the movie busted for 'obscenity' or for its subject matter (homosexuality)? As I remember, the explicit lovemaking was all heterosexual."

Los Angeles was a different story. In December 1967 an ad appeared in the *Los Angeles Free Press* for a double feature at the Park Theatre, 710 S. Alvarado, for *Homosexuality in Men and Women* and *The Hole*. The former film was described as, "The British clinical report that blows the lid off all the phony statistics. … Many doctors and police authorities believe that every

6th man is homosexual." The latter film is "A Taut-Bone-Bare Throbber!" that "Out-Genet's Genet!"

In July 1968 an ad in the *Los Angeles Free Press* read: "LA's First Homosexual Film Festival Breaks Every Attendance Record!" The festival included Shirley Clarke's *Portrait of Jason, a Male Hustler*, an interview with African-American gay hustler, Jason Holiday (real name Aaron Payne), filmed in Clarke's apartment in New York's Chelsea Hotel. In the opening scene, Holiday is holding a copy of the *East Village Other* underground newspaper. Shirley Clarke was a co-founder of the YIPPIES. In March 1969 a review of *Portrait of Jason* by gay writer Miller Francis Jr. appeared in the *Great Speckled Bird*. (He also wrote under Francis Miller Jr.) In the review, Francis alludes to the Berdache, boys-raised-as-girls, in the Native American tribes:

> "For all its 'gutter realism,' its film-in-the-making 'documentary' quality, *Portrait* is actually an exploration into the world of social myth. It is easy to say that Jason is a male whore, a hustler, a female impersonator, a black queen, but to say that and no more is to overlook Jason's most significant role, the 20th century Western civilization version of the 'shaman.' An institutionalized form of homosexuality and transvestism found not only in the ancient world but in many nonliterate cultures of the modern world up to the present day, the shaman is a social position adopted by men who take on the role of women defined by their culture (dress, mannerisms, job, life style, etc.), but in addition they are looked upon as soothsayers, oracles, magicians, dream-interpreters. The transvestism results from an evidently universally held belief that women are more closely in tune with the world of the psyche, the transvestite the ideal medium between the two worlds."

In many ways 1968 was the year homosexuality came out of the closet in movies, books, music, and theatre. On June 28, 1968 one year before the Stonewall Riots, *Time* magazine published "Where the Boys Are," which begins by quoting a transvestite in Federico Fellini's film *La Dolce Vita*, who says, "By 1970 the entire world will be homosexual." *Time* wrote: "Looking at some recent American films, the moviegoer might be inclined to believe that the prognosis is already coming true. Hollywood has suddenly discovered homosexuality, and the 'third sex' is making a determined bid for first place at the box office."

None of the mainstream 1968 movies painted a rosy picture of homosexuals. THE GOOD NEWS: The dandified sissies of the 1920s and 1930s, and the psychosexual monsters of the 1940s and 1950s, were mostly OUT. THE BAD NEWS: IN were sad pathetic gin-soaked emotional cripples, tragic victims of circumstances, worthy of a modicum of sympathy, but who get their comeuppance in the end. THE GOOD NEWS: This crop of movies with crapulent homosexuals prompted more debate on the subject of sexual variance in the underground press. Gay stereotypes were challenged in reviews and letters to the editor. In an article in the February 23, 1969 *New York Times*, the pseudonymous Ronald Forsythe asked "Why Can't 'We' Live Happily Ever After, Too," a plea for more positive images of homosexuals in the arts:

> "Much like the American Negro of 20-30 years ago who saw himself on stage and screen-and read about himself in novels-as Black Joe or Prissy or Shoe Shine Boy, the American homosexual has a complaint: He does not believe his life must end in tragedy and would like to see a change in his image reflected in the entertainment he pays to see and the books he buys to read. Like any minority group, he, too, would like his 'Place in the Sun.' He has been striving for it in life by seeking the revocation of laws that harass him unjustly; he would like also to achieve it in the creative worlds of the novel, plays, films, music, art, and television."

In *Boom!*, a disastrous adaptation of Tennessee Williams' *The Milk Train Doesn't Stop Here Anymore*, Elizabeth Taylor and Richard Burton are typecast as drunks. The movie tagline was, "She outlived six rich men!" Taylor plays Flora "Sissy" Goforth, a dying millionaire and Burton, Chris Flanders, a poet nicknamed the Angel of Death, who eyes her jewels. Noel Coward plays the homosexual Witch of Capri–a gossipy fag to Goforth's hag. Homosexual characters turned up everywhere, including a dead one in *The Detective,* starring Frank Sinatra, Lee Remick, and Jaqueline Bisset. Sinatra is New York police detective Joe Leland, who investigates the murder of the homosexual son of a department-store magnate. Leland is told by his boss to wrap up the case quickly. In New York's *Rat*, the reviewer wrote:

> "Joe comes through; he nabs a pathetic, deranged homosexual, weasels a confession, sends the poor fellow to the electric chair. … When Joe discovers that the homosexual was actually innocent of the murder, he resigns saying that 'There are things worth fighting for, but I can't fight them within the department.'"

Rat quotes from the movie, when a girl describes the murdered homosexual: "He was gay. But he was civilized." Leland said of the girl, "That girl is nineteen years old. She's a pusher, an addict and a whore. The streets are full of hundreds of kids just like her, all going the same route, all part of the Great Society."

Another gay-themed movie that year was *The Fox*, about a lesbian couple living in the country, whose relationship falls apart over a man. The handsome young "fox" who threatens the lesbian love affair is sailor Paul Grenfel (Keir Dullea). In Palo Alto's *Midpeninsular Observer*, Nancy Moss wrote:

"Ellen March (Anne Heywood) and a fox which has been threatening their chickens on an isolated Canadian farm she runs with her lover, Jill Banford (Sandy Dennis) face each other across a frozen snowy expanse. The fox's nose twitches and its eyes stare unblinking. ... From beginning to end this is a gauche and heavy-handed film. The script is awkward, without a word in common with the original story by D.H. Lawrence. There is also an air of unreality which isn't dispelled even by the rather pleasant and messy setting. It is difficult to believe, for instance, that the masculine half of a lesbian couple is likely to wear eye-liner and lipstick, especially on a Canadian chicken farm."

Kudzu, a newspaper offering "Subterranean News from the Heart of Ole Dixie," out of Jackson, MS, reported in November 1968 that *The Fox* had been banned by "the combined forces of (1) the Jackson City Government, (2) the Jackson Federation of Women's Clubs, and 3) the people of Jackson who support all that happens by their silent lives." The article continued: "Negative actions generally spring from fear, and the fear in this case seems to be homosexuality. All the clap-trap about 'obscene,' 'dirty' etc. is simply another way of saying forbidden, for we try to forbid that which we fear."

The trouble started when the manager and projectionist of the Paramount Theatre were arrested for showing *The Fox*. *Kudzu* wrote:

"The action was taken on the advice of a group of ladies ('obviously communist dupes') from the Jackson Federation of Women's Clubs, as part of a citywide conspiracy instigated by Mayor Thompson and his band of terrorists, whose express purpose is to hide the truth about life from the people of the city of Jackson. ... Now, the Jackson Federation of Women's Clubs is an organization that excludes men. Overtones of lesbianism, eh? ... Ladies, your psycho-sexual hang-ups are showing."

Kudzu also published the comments of Jimmy Ward, editor of the mainstream *Jackson Daily News*:

"Regarding the controversy over banning the movie *The Fox* at a downtown theatre; I have not seen the film; I do not plan to see it, do not wish to see same. All reviews by responsible critics I have read describe the movie as a sack of trash featuring the love affair between two women, a practice known in medical circles–as well as by the general adult public–as lesbianism, decidedly another form of sexual queerism. Few mature persons would want to view sordidness of that nature unless afforded the facilities to take a shower before, during and immediately after the show, but theatres aren't equipped with functional appliances such as showers."

Underneath *Kudzu* commented: "Mr. Ward, if you need to shower after thinking about a movie on homosexuals, if you get that sexually excited, we suggest that you see a psychiatrist, or can the crap and go enjoy the movie!"

On April 14, 1968, Mart Crowley's play *The Boys in the Band* opened off Broadway at New York's Theater Four, where it ran for over one thousand performances. On April 18, the *New York Free Press* published John Lahr's review. Lahr, the son of Bert Lahr, *The Wizard of Oz* star, later wrote *Prick Up Your Ears*, a biography of British gay playwright Joe Orton, *Dame Edna Everage and the Rise of Western Civilization: Backstage with Barry Humphries*, and edited *The Diaries of Joe Orton*. In his *Boys in the Band* review, Lahr wrote:

"Homosexual theater is a strange alloy of bravura and despair, an experience fascinated with its own facades, which vacillates between a longing to be embraced and an intentional outrageousness opting for that most tepid of affections-astonishment. In the wide spectrum of homosexual spectacle, the body becomes a fulcrum of play, the obsession which brings comfort and sometimes guilt. 'There's one thing about masturbation,' says one of the gay characters in *The Boys in the Band*. 'You certainly don't have to look your best.' There is, in that line, hilarity, sadness and talent. ... The important question about homosexual theater is not the irrational disgust of a public, chained to its Puritan repressiveness like a dog to its vomit, but whether it can ultimately offer anything substantial to the stage."

A year later when *The Boys in the Band* was staged at the Committee Theater in San Francisco, two very different post-Stonewall reviews appeared in the *Berkeley Barb*. One, by Bob Hayes, revels in the "swish camp" of the past. Hayes wrote:

"It's a tough play, and despite the lack of masculinity indicated in the plot, took balls to produce effectively. ... The whole thing is about ... well, it's about faggots, that's what, faggots. Fruity, fairy swishy limp wrist homosexuals at a birthday party they gave for one of their own. ... It's generally good entertainment and if you dig fast, bitchy, Eve Arden lines all over the place, it's worth seeing. If it had been done 10 years ago, however, 'The Boys' would have been taken offstage one by one-carried away, if you will, and crucified."

The other review by Rt. Rev. Michael Francis Itkin, of the Moorish Orthodox Church of America, views the play through the lens of a new radical political awareness:

"Now before saying anything else on the subject, I am (against my better judgment) forced to admit that the production of *Boys in the Band* is very good theatre. ... But having said that, I am faced with several very serious questions. Can one truly separate aesthetics and entertainment from the social impact of a work of art? Does *Boys in the Band* help in the acceptance of the homosexual minority by society and does it work towards an alleviation of the oppression of the Gay or, rather, does it reinforce stereotypes and, as such, aid and abet in the continuance of oppression. Should it have been produced at all? ... Perhaps the biggest objection to *Boys in the Band* is that it will be, for many in 'straight' society, the sole depiction they receive of the Homosexual. It's a depiction which can only reinforce such stereotypes concerning the Homosexual as 'immoral, vice-ridden, sick, aberrated, deviant.'"

In 1970, gay writer David Senn, reviewed *The Boys in the Band* for Chicago's *Seed*:

"During the production of Mart Crowley's play, *The Boys in the Band*, the 'nellie' character, Emory, describes his efforts on his senior prom decorations, ending his monologue with a whisper, 'Oh, Mary, it takes a fairy to make something pretty.' Somebody in our audience shouted, 'Amen.' After everyone finished laughing, my roommate leaned over and whispered in my ear, 'Oh, Mary, it takes a fairy to say something stupid like that.' The 'amen' that echoed in the theater attests to an image of the homosexual that is both false and self-deceiving. No matter how many writers, playwrights, artists, musicians, interior decorators or beauticians are practicing homosexuals ... they are not all intelligent, cultured, gifted and more tolerant than heterosexuals. In the world of art, moreover, there is an equal number of 'straights' who are capable of producing objects of beauty. Philip Roth is no less an artist because he is not 'gay' nor is Christopher Isherwood a genius because he doesn't like 'pussy.' The tagline that seems to add a patina of respectability to any work is no longer 'the play's the thing' or 'the novel works,' but rather 'the author's gay.' ... Mary, it may take a fairy to produce a beautiful work, but that doesn't mean every fairy is a Truman Capote."

Another play about homosexuals was Charles Dyer's *Staircase*, which opened on Broadway January 10, 1968. The play is about the relationship between Harry C. Leeds and Charles Dyer (the author used his own name and an anagram of his name for the characters), an elderly gay couple who owns a barbershop in the East End of London. The play focuses on one drunken night, after Charles, in drag, propositions a police officer in a pub called the Adam's Apple. The play was adapted into a movie starring Rex Harrison and Richard Burton. Miller Francis Jr. reviewed the film in the *Great Speckled Bird*:

"Beware!–Staircase is about as abysmal a movie as you'll ever see. Nothing speaks well for this film. The too visible framework behind it is another play, Edward Albee's *Who's Afraid of Virginia Woolf?* There are two characters who have built up a psychic equilibrium based on verbal violence. Like the famous symbiotic marriage of George and Martha, Richard Burton and Rex Harrison have learned to thrive on their cutting and slashing; and both of them respect the limits and boundaries beyond which mutual agreement does not allow them to go. During the film, of course, they do overstep these boundaries, and the balance is upset. Harrison brings in a young hustler for revenge just as Martha seduces the young college teacher to get back at her husband. The 'telegram' announcing the death of their imaginary son is present in *Staircase* in the form of a summons ordering Harrison to appear in court to stand trial for appearing in drag at a bar and propositioning a young man."

Francis ended his critique with:

"It is becoming more and more clear that a serious film about homosexuality that challenges us out of our preconceptions cannot be made until it can cast a Mick Jagger and a Terence Stamp as happy lovers and show their nude love-making scenes. Until then I guess we will be deluged with subsequent versions of *The Sergeant, The Gay Deceivers,* and *Staircase.*"

In May 1968, Richard A. Ogar interviewed Flawless Sabrina (real name Jack Doroshow) for the *Berkeley Barb.* Sabrina was the promoter of the 1967 Miss Camp All-America drag contest featured in *The Queen,* a documentary about a beauty pageant in New York City. Ogar described Doroshaw as, "a good-looking, business-like man of 27, delicate but not what I would call faggy." Doroshaw claims to have written a drag novel *The Twelfth of Never,* and a cookbook, *Flawless Sabrina's Cooking Guide for Single Fellows or No One Can See You When You Are Alone in the Kitchen.* Ogar spoke with Sabrina and Harlow, his protégée, the winner of the pageant. "If either of these men is 'sick,' they don't provide any clues," wrote Ogar, "Each is frank, witty, extremely likeable. In fact, they seem to be two of the LEAST uptight people I've met in some time. I made no secret of the fact that I dig them."

In the interview, Sabrina disassociates herself from "The Gayety" (gay community), suggesting drag queens "identify with straight life." Sabrina's theory goes that because a man paints his face, he wants to look like a girl and pick up men as a real girl would pick up a man:

"In the typical arrangement between two males, each wants the other male to be more of a man than he is, because that's part of what a homosexual male is about. What kind of fantasy is THAT? A wants B to be more of a man than he is, and B wants A to be more of a man than HE is. And by the same token, each wants to be less of a man than the other so the other can be more of a man than he is. Man, that's a lot of work! With the paint queen, at least, you have the precedent in straight life. SOME precedent in straight life. But you have no precedent for the other gay relationships."

In New York's *Rat,* Leon Gussow wrote about the documentary:

"*The Queen* is an unusual documentary that records the Miss American Camp Beauty Pageant and the preparations leading up to it. The Pageant drew drag queens from all over the country to New York City's Town Hall, where they modeled evening gowns and bathing suits, and did chorus numbers to such songs as *It's a Grand Old Flag.* ... One of the more striking aspects of the drag queens' personalities is their constant fussiover [sic] the minutiae of gay grooming. They are continually worrying lest their wigs or make-up not be exactly right, and the fine points of homosexual attire provide an inexhaustible topic of conversation. By taking the various details associated with modern femininity, disassociating them from the pretense of heterosexual allure, and exaggerating them outrageously, the drag queens demonstrate exactly how ridiculous and degraded is the Madison Avenue-inspired image of woman at the present time."

In 1968, filmmaker John Waters wrote "Silver Screen," a movie column in the *Baltimore Free Press*. At the time Waters had made three films, *Hag in a Black Leather Jacket, Roman Candles*, and *Eat Your Makeup*. On *The Queen*, Waters wrote: "The Queen, which has been widely and favorably reviewed, is, as the ads claim, 'a stone cold gas.' ... Miss Crystal from Manhattan, the loser who walks off the stage seconds before the winner is announced, especially captures the bitchy, tinsely, glamorous ... world of the transvestite."

In Detroit's *Fifth Estate,* Dennis Raymond wrote:

"Despite its subject, *The Queen* is anything but shocking and sensational, but then neither is it patronizing and mocking. Where one might feel scorn, disgust, repulsion, one is moved to understanding, compassion, and, above all, humor. ... When they get together, their humor is simply inspired. One asks another about his draft board: 'Did you tell them you were homosexual?' 'No,' is the reply, 'They told me.'"

In Atlanta's *Great Speckled Bird*, gay reporter Miller Francis Jr. wrote:

"We've all been indoctrinated with the belief that the homosexual subculture is termed 'gay' ironically, that its inhabitants are laughing on the outside, crying on the inside. Actually the reverse is true. Homosexuals, outside the private parties, the gay bar, the drag ball etc. live in a totally hostile world, one which is not merely anti-homosexual but anti-sexual. The word 'gay' accurately describes the mood which reigns wherever homosexuals can meet and enjoy each other's company without the real degradation, that of pretense. The paddy wagon and the billy club (not to mention universal moral revulsion and censure) are never far away."

Francis ends with:

"If you are not gay and you see *The Queen*, your experience will
illuminate some of the darkness of life in America; it will show you things–
about yourself and the country in which you live–that you probably never
would have seen otherwise. And, after all, isn't that one of the functions of film

and drugs and sex and revolution–to take us where we think we were not able to go, but where we need, desperately, to be."

In *The Paper Revolutionaries: The Rise of the Underground Press*, Laurence Leamer calls Miller, "the most articulate of the cultural radicals. [He] maneuvers the symbols of cultural radicalism with the subtlety and sureness of Marx working with the tools of economic determinism." In March 1969, in the *Great Speckled Bird*, Miller reviewed *The Sergeant*, a mainstream film about unrequited love, starring Rod Steiger as a lovesick and jealous homosexual US Army officer. Miller wrote:

"Aside from Steiger, *The Sergeant* is really quite a mess–in fact it is such a mess, it almost winds up being an interesting film, largely because of its failures. This bitter tale of a lonely, repressed army hero (Rod Steiger) stuck away in a European nowhere land and his frustrated attempts to establish a relationship with a young all-American-type soldier in his command (John Phillip Law) is so thoroughly botched that the film seems to want to go in opposite directions at once. As a result, it goes nowhere."

Also in the *Great Speckled Bird*, Dianne Pellman slammed *The Killing of Sister George*:

"The Killing of Sister George is not a good movie. It is a boring one that sees lesbians with quotation marks around them and seeks to exploit the public curiosity for private profit. ... Primarily the movie concerns Sister George's being written out of her part after four years as reigning queen of her soap opera and the consequent disintegration of her life with Alice. ... All of this climaxes in the now famous scene when Alice is seduced by Mercy Crawford, typical executive woman seen as bitch. This is the scene where Alice exposes her breasts, Mercy arches her eyebrows and the music throbs on and on. How I wish I could tell you it was erotic. How I wish. But believe me two hours of boredom is not worth two minutes of nipple nibbling–at least not the way they do it here. ... What touches us about homosexuals is not how different they are from us, but how similar. Showing us a gay bar and a bit of s and m cheapens a movie when you have no other point than to sensationalize."

Not everyone agreed with Pellman's heterosexual take on *The Killing of Sister George*. In a letter to the editor, Richard L. Stevens wrote:

"The recent review by Diane Pellman of *The Killing of Sister George* forgets every tenet of journalistic expertise as well as revolutionary insight you have tutored us on. I would have assumed, after your 'black about black' and 'girls about girls' the *Bird* would have only a lesbian write her impressions of *Sister George*. It is now very obvious it was needed. Mrs. Pellman demonstrated absolutely no insight as to the interpersonal conflict and emotional activity present and excellently portrayed in *Sister George*. ... Her review demonstrated no insight into the life of a homosexual and reeked of a paternalism and condescending attitude. The words used by Mrs. Pellman reminded me of a 'white liberal' in the early 60's talking about the poor beat upon Nee-grow! never recognizing the implicit racism in his voice. ... *Sister George* portrays some of life, real honest-to-goodness life. It is the love of people for someone whom they admire for her professional ability. It is the pain of being thrust into a lonely world without anyone to cry with. It is the ecstatic joy of a routine of Lowell and Hardy [sic] in a crowded Dyke bar. It is the prejudice of business in forgetting the feelings of those which make it work. It is the rivalry for the love of someone who is young. It is the fright of one who has lost another and now must face a heartless battle of sex for instant pleasure. This movie is life in real proportions but it takes more than watching and sitting on your ass to absorb. ... This film must be fused into your experience of life and you must become a character you are viewing."

In February 1969, Paul Eberle wrote in the *Los Angeles Free Press*, that filmmaker Robert Aldrich had filed legal action against the *Los Angeles Times* for censoring advertising for *The Killing of Sister George*. Eberle wrote:

"Aldrich describes the *Times*'s censoring of his advertising as 'arbitrary and capricious.' ... The ad contained a line drawing, a simple caricature of a nude woman showing a breast and buttocks. The *Times* removed the breast and the crack of her ass. ... 'I guess they thought it was better to have a half-ass than a whole ass,' Aldrich said with some bewilderment, when asked why he thought the *Times* had done that. There was also the phrase 'consenting adults' in the ad copy. The *Times* insisted upon deleting the word 'consenting.' You figure it out."

14

THE "PIG RIOT" TO THE "STONEWALL RIOT."

After the Chicago "Police Riot," Leo Laurence returned to San Francisco and co-founded the radical Committee For Homosexual Freedom, inspired by the Black Panthers, and concerned itself with non-gay causes by joining the picket lines at San Francisco State College and the Delano Grape Strike. It was a time when the underground press began publishing homosexual news stories about police rape, gays losing their jobs, shootings, and harassment in public parks by cops and vigilante groups.

"If we ever hope to win our battle, we must fight.First, we must unshackle ourselves from fear, for it alone is our omnipresent enemy."–Del Shearer, president of DOB/Chicago in a letter to the *Ladder* April 1961.

After the 1968 Democratic National Convention in Chicago, young people's distrust of the police intensified. The cops were the thin blue line separating old men who started the Vietnam War and young men expected to fight it for them. The seed of gay militancy was planted in Chicago in the summer of 1968, took root in San Francisco in early 1969, and blossomed at New York's Stonewall Inn that June.

Signs of radical gay liberation began after the *Berkeley Barb* published "Homos to Vote." San Francisco's Society for Individual Rights (SIR) was holding elections for the position of editor of *Vector*, their monthly magazine. The post was "hotly contested by two candidates with deeply divergent outlooks." Guy Straight, a publisher of male physique magazines, stated that *Vector* should be on sale in "smut shops." The other candidate, Leo Laurence, thought "self-respect" was more important and aimed to "upgrade the magazine" with better writers, political articles, turning it into a gay *Life* or *Look*. "Sixty nine is going to be a gay year," Laurence told the *Berkeley Barb*:

"We want to make political changes from Nixon on down. We want to declare war on public ignorance of homosexuality. ... San Francisco is the gay capital of the country, many here don't feel guilty. But in other communities a lot of gay life exists underground. People are still afraid."

Laurence became the editor of *Vector* in February, in a 2-1 victory. He told the *Berkeley Barb*:

"When the black man became proud, he became more militant. That same power is starting to hit the homosexual movement in the Bay Area. ... There's unbelievable new interest in SIR and the homosexual movement, especially among people in their 20s, from emancipated teenagers to college graduates."

In January 1969, New York's *Guardian* published a story on a strike at San Francisco State college, started by the Black Student Union (BSU) and Third World Liberation Front (TWLF) demanding autonomous cultural studies. President of SF State College, Samuel Ichiye Hayakawa, responded by ordering all "rallies, parades, be-ins, hootenannies, hoedowns, shivarees," banned from campus. Hayakawa had the support of California Governor Ronald Reagan, who promised to keep the college open "at the point of a bayonet." The following week's *Guardian* reported that Dr. Carleton Goodlet, publisher of the *San Francisco Sun Reporter*, a "Negro" paper opposed to the Vietnam war, joined the picket, along with the Community Strike Support Coalition, and "a contingent of white liberals from Marin County."

Detroit's *Fifth Estate* detailed the origins of the strike:

"Robert Smith was, before all this nasty mess, the president of the college. A good sort of starry-eyed liberal, he met a demand by the BSU to set up a department of Black Studies. He somehow neglected to supply funds or faculty. Black students, not being as backward as white liberals might think, took careful note of the discrepancy. In alliance with the TWLF, they demanded that any non-white student seeking admission to SF State be automatically admitted. California junior colleges already do admit all comers. If that wasn't enough, a part-time English instructor and student, George Murray, found a third job: Minister of Education of the Black Panther Party. On October 28, 1968, Murray announced a strike at a BSU rally. He coincidentally advised nonwhite students to carry guns for self-defense."

The following month homosexuals joined the SF State College picket line. The *Berkeley Barb* wrote: "In an expression of solidarity the third sex joined the Third World this week." The Rev. Ray Broshears, a spokesman for the Ad Hoc Homophile Committee for the Student Strike, told the *Berkeley Barb*, "It's about time we spoke out and stopped being closet queens." He added that the cops were already "uptight" about an article, "Telling It Like It Is: State College From A Homosexual Perspective," by Morgan Pinney in *Vector*. The piece suggested gays join the picket line. Pinney wrote: "We are a minority which knows blatant discrimination. ... We may hide behind various straight, respectable facades ... But isn't it better to stand as a man, speaking for our rights (even while the police clubs are falling) than live in the shadows as 'queers?'" Broshears claimed police were already retaliating against the alliance between gays and African-Americans. "More and more boys and drag queens are being picked up and charged with male prostitution. The cops say we are on the side of the 'commies.'"

Prior to moving to San Francisco, the Rev. Ray Broshears, a Pentecostal Evangelist, lived in New Orleans, roommate and lover of David Ferrie, a suspect in the John F. Kennedy assassination. On September 13, 1968, the *Los Angeles Free Press* reported that Broshears had been questioned by New Orleans District Attorney Jim Garrison who, a year earlier, launched an investigation into JFK's assassination, after receiving tips from Jack Martin, a private investigator. Martin named David Ferrie, a pilot, as a co-conspirator. Ferrie died in 1967 under suspicious circumstances. As a result, Ferrie's friend, Clay LaVerne Shaw, known in New Orleans gay circles as "Clay Bertrand," was arrested and tried in 1969. He was acquitted. According to the *Los Angeles Free Press,* the Kennedy connection came to light when Broshears appeared on the Stan Bohrman *Tempo 1* TV show, where he said that David Ferrie admitted his involvement in the assassination plot. Broshears claimed that Ferrie and Lee Harvey Oswald were both bisexual CIA agents. After relocating to San Francisco in 1968, Broshears reinvented himself as a radical gay activist. Later, in 1973, he founded the Lavender Panthers, a vigilante group. In an article in *Time* magazine, a photograph depicts the Rev. Raymond Broshears, in clerical collar, on a sidewalk holding a rifle, accompanied by two longhaired gay Lavender Panthers. The photograph also appears in the August 1, 1973 issue of the *Advocate*.

Tales of police sexually abusing gay men were common on the gay-grapevine but were rarely reported for fear of reprisals. Articles about LGBT rape never appeared in the mainstream press, a fact which underlines the importance of underground newspapers. On April 3, 1969, *Distant Drummer* wrote about Joseph Riley, a black gay man raped by two cops. Riley was a cross-dresser. A year earlier two cops forced their way into his apartment. "At first, they wanted oral sex," Riley told *Distant Drummer*, "and then it turned out one of them was a sadist. He smeared hand lotion all over a candle, and he said he was going to stick it up my rectum." The cops told Riley he would be expected to pay them $20 every time they crossed his path. The following day Riley filed a complaint with the Human Relations Commission (HRC), but Clarence Farmer, head of the HRC, "lost" the complaint and kept the story out of the press. *Distant Drummer* pointed to a conspiracy between the Police Department, the DA's office, the news media and HRC. Two years later, Riley was awarded $9,000 in damages.

In California, homosexual acts were illegal. One of the few pro-gay elected officials was African-American Assemblyman Willie Brown. In March 1969, Leo Laurence, in the *Berkeley Barb*, interviewed Brown about his "consent law," designed to decriminalize sodomy. Brown said: "I'm not going to let them ... use the stupid excuse that the 'political climate' isn't right for people to be sexually free. ... We, the people, demanding sexual rights for everyone, hetero and homo, must set the timetables. And, the time is NOW!" The Consenting Adult Sex Bill passed in 1975, was signed into law by Governor Jerry Brown, and became effective January 1, 1976.

The "Generation Gap" between young militant gays and older "Establishment" gays became clear in March 1969 when Leo Laurence told the *Berkeley Barb*: "Society has made us perverts for too goddamn long. ... It's time for a change—right now." In a *Vector* editorial, Laurence called for an end to the status quo, blaming "society at large," and complacent gay organizations. He described gay groups as, "Timid, uptight conservative, and afraid to act for the good of the whole community." Laurence told the *Berkeley Barb*:

> "I fully expect up-tight members and officers of SIR [Society for Individual Rights] to try and stop me as editor. ... But I promise *Vector* is going to be honest in its reporting, even if it makes our middle class homosexuals mad. ... If the uptightness of the present leaders breaks the revolution ... then they must go. ... None of the established groups like SIR, Tavern Guild, and the gay bars are eager for change. Once the revolution comes there'll be no need for such groups." Laurence urged gay groups to join with other militant causes like the Black Panthers, the Resistance, and anti-war groups. Such alliances would help when "common causes arise."

A photograph alongside the article is of Leo Laurence embracing another man. The caption reads: "GAY EDITOR SHOWS WHAT HE MEANS." The other man was activist and writer, Gale Whittington.

A week later the *Berkeley Barb* reported that Laurence was asked to resign his editorship of *Vector*. "It didn't take long for the gay editor to find out older homos didn't dig what he was putting down," wrote the *Berkeley Barb*.

Members of SIR objected to talk of "gay revolution" and had asked Laurence to resign. He refused. In the same issue of the *Berkeley Barb*, was the headline: "Gay Rebel Gets Shafted by Uptight Boss." The "rebel" was Gale Whittington, fired as an accounting clerk at the States Lines Steamship Company, after the photo of him embracing Laurence in the *Berkeley Barb* was published. M.B. Brochen, Whittington's supervisor, responded, "The case is closed, and I don't want to discuss it further."

Laurence told the *Berkeley Barb*:

> "We are organizing a campaign that will show the States Lines, or any other employer, that they don't indiscriminately fire homosexuals who are good employees, and get away with it. ... The social revolution that is sweeping the country has given new pride to the Blacks and is now giving fire to homosexuals. ... The revolution is going to hit companies like States Steamship Lines until it hurts. We are demanding that they immediately re-hire Gale Whittington. If they don't, militant homosexuals will show that company what Gay Power really means. ... The public has a big surprise coming this year if they think they can push homosexuals around and get away with it."

On April 11, the *Berkeley Barb* published, "Homo Revolt Blasting Off On Two Fronts." The piece began: "The Homosexual Revolution of '69 started this week in San Francisco as militant homosexuals made war on both gay and straight Establishments." After the SIR board stripped Laurence of the *Vector* editorship, he lashed out in the *Berkeley Barb*:

> "*Vector* was beginning to show our gay leadership for what it really is: a bunch of middle-class, up-tight, bitchy old queens. ... The SIR leadership and Tavern Guild couldn't take the heat, so they decided to hang me. ... Getting kicked out as *Vector* Editor by the Gay Establishment is a victory for the homosexual revolution. SIR leadership is damned worried because militant revolutionary homosexuals like myself and other members of the new COMMITEE FOR HOMOSEXUAL FREEDOM are on the attack."

The Committee For Homosexual Freedom was co-founded by Leo Laurence and Gale Whittington. The group's first action was to picket the States Lines Steamship Company. On the first day about fifty "guys, gals and sympathizers" turned up. *The Berkeley Barb* wrote: "There were mostly young people, a few in business suits, two Indians, one man with a baby, and even a pet monkey. It was difficult to tell who was gay and who was straight." Laurence told the *Berkeley Barb*:

> "Our revolution is quite different than the blood baths hitting college campuses. ... Our militancy is in our openness, our pride in gayness, rather than the violence that some associate with militancy. Homosexuals are not a hostile bunch, yet, I feel our sexual revolution is helping everyone by removing

guilt, concealment, double-lives, and hypocrisy from our lives."

In his essay, "My Soul Vanished from Sight: A California Saga of Gay Liberation," in the book *Out of the Closets: Voices of Gay Liberation*, (edited by Karla Jay and Allen Young,) Konstantin Berlandt recalled the picket line:

"We formed a small circle on the sidewalk below the skyscrapers. A thousand straight people in suits and nylons passing by, some not looking; young businessmen concertedly talking to each other and avoiding the pickets like we were trees in pots; some disapproving, reading the signs, frowning, looking at us, frowning and disgusted; some friendly, smiling, glad to see us in front again today."

Two gay men embracing in a newspaper was shocking, but in the April 18 *Berkeley Barb*, another barrier was broken. That issue included a photograph of the wedding of Ronald Hummer, stripped to the waist and wearing white Levis, his "bride" Chuck Mardin, in white satin and carrying a bouquet of carnations. The copy explained:

"A kiss seals the marriage of two men who celebrated the union with a Hawaiian wedding at the Aloha Club in Hayward. ... The double-ring ceremony had all the significant symbols of any wedding: flowers, gowns, wedding march, exchange of vows, a forgetful groom and a super-wise nervous bride. The only difference was that they were male. ... 'It's the life they chose, and I think it's wonderful,' said the stepmother of the groom ... 'of course, it would be better if the churches let these gay kids get married in the church, but I don't think that's far off.'"

In an unprecedented move, the April 25 issue of *Berkeley Barb* contained an entire page of gay related news. "Gay Strike Turns Grim," a report on the ongoing action against States Steamship Company, stating that among the gay militants are veterans from other battles: "i.e. Stanford Sit-In, SFSC Strike, Anti-Draft groups, and veterans of the Yippy fight in Chicago last year." The *Berkeley Barb* interviewed protestors like Charles Thorp, who said:

"Homosexuals are stepping out of their ghetto-bars and double lives and into the power struggle. We must be freed from the chains of fear and death that have now repressed all but our sexual organs. ... We will take our freedom. ... We will burn our faces with tears and cover our hands in blood, but we will get our freedom as homosexuals. We will fight until our bodies no longer give blood, 'til we no longer exist, or until we can freely grow to our capacities without intervention by this murderous society."

Anti-draft campaigner Carl Wittman, told the *Berkeley Barb*: "It's a question now of a fight for survival, not just a fight for our rights." Michael Cooke, expelled from the University of Texas eight years earlier for a soapbox speech on homosexuality, commented as well: "Fear and intimidation have ruled the gay world for 2000 years. The only legacy this has brought me is the feeling I have precious little to lose. The time is ripe for some militancy." The "Pink Panthers" strike spread to the Los Angeles offices of the States Steamship Company as well. The Los Angeles picket was led by the Rev. Troy Perry, founder of the Metropolitan Community Church, a Christian ministry affirming LGBT's. Perry told the *Berkeley Barb*:

"We had over 200 people that crowded around the picket line amazed at the courage of our people. ... The attitude of the kids here ... is that it's time we do something to show Los Angeles that we're not going to stand idly by anymore and watch our gay community get pushed around."

On the same *Berkeley Barb* page was the headline: "Killer Cops at Large." The piece explained: "Murder charges will be filed against two Berkeley pigs involved in the death of Frank Bartley." On April 17, thirty-three-year old Bartley, a gay man, was fatally shot in the head by Officer Weiker Kline in Aquatic Park. Kline and his partner Officer Frank Reynolds were 'sex police,' known for their entrapment methods. One enticed homosexuals into committing sex offenses while the other moved in to arrest. Kline claimed he shot Bartley accidentally during a struggle. Commenting on the "accident," Leo Laurence said:

"Berkeley gays had better wake up before it's too late. The uptight middle class gay establishment will talk about Frank Bartley's murder in the bars, but they won't get off their dead asses and DO something about it. ... If the gays don't stop being too scared to act, they are going to get shot and killed. And Berkeley proved it this week. I call the shooting of Frank Bartley an official murder. ... All gays have got to join the revolution and take a stronger stand."

A month earlier Howard Efland, a gay man in Los Angeles had been dragged from the Dover Hotel and beaten to death on the sidewalk by police. In February 1970, in the *San Diego Free Door,* Don Jackson wrote about plans for a memorial service, and explained what happened:

"David Mase, former manager of the Dover, reports, 'L.A.P.D. Officers Lemuel L. Chancey and Richard F. Halligan frequented the hotel. They would brazenly enter over the protest of the hotel employees. The officers would wander around the halls, trying doors. When they found a door open, one would enter the room and play with his dick, hoping to entice the hotel guest. At the first sign of interest, the cop in the room would signal his colleague waiting in the hall to come in and make an arrest.' Mase testified that hotel guests were frequently beaten by the pigs. ... In spite of clear cut evidence of

1st degree murder, the coroner's jury returned a verdict of 'excusable homicide."

In San Francisco, the Committee for Homosexual Freedom (CHF) supported another non-gay cause, the Delano Grape Strike, led by the United Farm Workers (UFW) against low-paying grape growers in California. The strike began September 8, 1965, and for five years was a cause célèbre. The union and their supporters organized consumer boycotts and marches. In May 1969, on International Grape Boycott Day, 150 people picketed Safeway supermarkets. The *Berkeley Barb* published a photograph of picketers, including two gay men holding hands. Another San Francisco protest, organized by CHF, was outside Tower Records, following the firing of clerk, Frank Denaro for being gay. During the picket, the protestors were attacked by a group of school age thugs, but Father Bob Richards, a Catholic priest, stepped in and calmed the situation. Later, when an unmarked squad car arrived "carrying four leather-jacketed pigs," Rev. Richards, in clerical garb, asked to see a cop's badge and was told, "Don't mouth off when we pass by or I'm going to do one of two things. I'm either going to smash your face in, or lock you up." In June, a *Berkeley Barb* headline read: "Record Dealer Bows to Gays, Rehires Clerk." Leo Laurence told the paper:

> "For the first time in the history of the gay movement, militant, non-violent tactics have been used to win a major victory. ... The gay establishment has been trying for years to do what we have done in two weeks. They have gotten some fair employment pledges, but the gay establishment has never gotten someone's job back."

Before gay newspapers, the location of homosexual bars and bathhouses was passed word of mouth, as were "cruising" areas like restrooms in public parks. In the 1960s public parks became venues for political rallies, or Love-Ins, like the Chicago Flower Children celebration of the Summer Solstice in Grant Park in 1967. In September 1968, Boston's *Old Mole* reported on a dispute over the use of Boston Common by a New York Lower East Side anarchist group, Up Against the Wall Motherfucker. The Common was a gathering place for East Coast hippies, until the police moved in and hundreds were arrested. In the ensuing battle, a Marine and an airman were stabbed. Up Against the Wall Motherfucker took their name from a poem by the anti-gay homosexual black poet LeRoi Jones, quoted by Jerry Gafio Watts in his book *Amira Baraka: The Politics and Art of a Black Intellectual*: "All the stores will open if you will say the magic words. The magic words are: Up against the wall motherfucker this is a stick up! ... We must make our own World man, our own world, and we can not do this unless the white man is dead. Let's get together and kill him my man."

In May, Atlanta's *Great Speckled Bird* published a story about crime in Piedmont Park and the hippie/gay neighborhood: "The question of collective self-defense has been raised again after a shotgun shooting of eight people in a Waffle House. ... Other incidents in recent weeks have included a stabbing, several near fights, threats, and a reported increase of harassment of homosexuals in Piedmont Park." Two weeks later the *Great Speckled Bird* published, "The Park Belongs to the People" by Howard Romaine. In the piece, Romaine wrote: "'We in the 5th Ward need help,' Ald. Everett Millican told the Atlanta Board of Aldermen ... 'We get everything dumped on us–homosexuals, sex deviates and others using the parks all hours of the night." Other problems in the area, according to Millican, were a rash of fires, hippies, noise from rock bands in Piedmont Park, and massage parlors. Millican and his colleague, Alderman George Cotsakis, proposed an ordinance regulating noise levels and banning parking after 11:30 p.m.

In the same issue of the *Great Speckled Bird,* an ad read:

"ATTENTION ALL GOOD PEOPLE: George Cotsakis and G. Everett Millican, two alderman 'representing' the Fifth Ward, are trying to drive us out of town, i.e. they want to apply the final solution to all of us 'hippies, homosexuals, sex deviates, etc.' who use Piedmont Park. They are starting their evil campaign by trying to outlaw rock music in the park. If you would like to tell these senile men where it's at, you can reach them at: Cotsakis, 150 Ottley Drive, NE, 873 4401 (business), 219 Little John Trail, NE, 8744768 (residence); Millican, 500 Bishop Street, NW, 351 50741 (business), 2520 Peachtree Road, NW, NW, Apt. 302. 237 6569 (residence). Tell it like it is."

Not everyone appreciated putting gays and hippies in the same sentence. On June 9 on the "Letters" page, Jose Himmler II wrote:

"Hey, why put us with the sex perverts and homos? We aren't like them man, we're totally different, we've got a thing going that really leaves them behind. Not that I'm saying they're all wrong-everybody should do his thing the way he wants-but *Bird* it sure is Hell on recruitment. Hey *Bird*, give us an article or something on us and the homos. Show it like it is baby, but don't mess our minds up with this 'Hell yeah,' business. We don't go for it man."

There were additional park problems in Queens, New York City, where vigilantes cut down fifteen dogwood trees, eleven London planes, and other foliage, in an area off Grand Central Parkway at 78th Avenue in Kew Gardens, a "rendezvous for homosexuals." In the *New York Times* locals admitted forming a "vigilante committee" to "harass the homosexuals," by cutting down the area used for their clandestine trysts. Later it was revealed that after complaints about the tree-cutters, a squad car turned up, two cops spoke to the vigilantes, and then left them to cut down more trees. In New York City's leftist *Guardian*, John Gabree wrote:

"Joan Luxemburg of Flushing has complained in a letter to Mayor John Lindsay and other city officials that she stopped a police car (No 1176) just outside the park that evening to report seeing vandals. She said the police told her that neighborhood residents 'were doing a job which the police were not able to do to the satisfaction of the community.'"

15

THE STONEWALL UPRISING

By June 28, 1969, the night the Stonewall Inn was raided, Greenwich Village and the surrounding area was already a tinderbox. Police harassment of hippies and minorities was so prevalent in the area that even a squirrel running up a tree caused a riot. Militant gay activism had started with Leo Laurence's Committee For Homosexual Freedom in San Francisco, but Stonewall gave it somewhere to hang its hat.

"GAY PROHIBITION CORRUPT$ COP$ FEED$ MAFIA."–Graffiti at the Stonewall Inn.

Dozens of underground newspapers were on sale in New York stores like Ed Sanders' Peace Eye Bookstore on East Tenth Street on the Lower East Side, and Craig Rodwell's gay Oscar Wilde Memorial Bookshop, in Greenwich Village. In these papers, with their psychedelic graphics, nudity, profanity, sometimes brilliant/other times atrociously written articles, that gays met through classified ads, learned the extent of cop abuse nationwide, and discovered that, in San Francisco at least, a radical gay movement was emerging, led by Leo Laurence and the Committee for Homosexual Freedom.

In New York City, on April 21, 1966, Craig Rodwell, John Timmins, and Dick Leitsch, accompanied by four reporters and a photographer, staged a "Sip-In," reported in the *New York Times* and *Village Voice*. The three Mattachine members were protesting a State Liquor Authority (SLA) regulation, allowing bar owners to refuse service to homosexuals. The protest was sparked by the appearance of a sign in the Ukrainian-American Village Restaurant in Greenwich Village that read: "If You're Gay, Stay Away." When the protestors arrived the restaurant was closed, someone had tipped off the owners. Lucy Komisar in the *Village Voice* wrote that she could see the handwritten antigay sign through the window, next to others reading "No Credit," "No Dancing," and "No Spitting on the Floor."

In an article headlined "3 Deviates Invite Exclusion By Bars" the *New York Times* noted that after failing to enter the restaurant, the group went to the Howard Johnson restaurant at Avenue of the Americas and Eighth St., where Leitsch read a statement to the manager:

"We, the undersigned, are homosexuals. We believe that a place of public accommodation has an obligation to serve an orderly person, and that we are entitled to service as long as we are orderly. We therefore ask to be served on your premises. Should you refuse to serve us, we will be obligated to file a complaint against you with the State Liquor Authority."

According to the *New York Times*, the manager, Emile Varela, "doubled with laughter." The *Village Voice* said Varela asked, "How do I know you are homosexuals?" After laughing, he added:

"Why shouldn't they be served a drink? They look like perfect gentlemen to me. I drink. Who knows if I'm a homosexual or not? It's pretty ridiculous that anybody should determine what anybody's sex life is. I think there's plenty of lawmakers whose sex life I could challenge–and they drink too. I don't think the government has any right to question any man's sex life. If the government does, I think there ought to be a few marches."

Varela turned to the waiter and said, "Bring the boys a drink."

The group was also served at the Waikiki, a Polynesian-themed bar, a block away, where the manager, who called himself Mr. Urban, told the *Village Voice*: "Certainly, I serve anybody as long as he doesn't annoy anybody." Finally they tried Julius', well known as a closeted gay bar. The manager refused to serve them. The Mattachine Society filed a complaint with the City Commission on Human Rights and the State Liquor Authority dropped their discriminatory regulation in March 1967. However, this didn't stop the harassment, or the negative articles in the *New York Times*. In March 1967, the State Liquor Authority revoked the license of Tony Pastor's Inc. in Greenwich Village, for "permitting the licensed premises to become disorderly in that it permitted homosexuals, degenerates and undesirables to be on the license premises in an offensive and indecent manner." Again, in November 1967, the *New York Times* reported the closing down of two private gay clubs, Two Penny Civic Association, Ltd., 36 East 30th Street and El Baron Club, 74-02 Eliot Ave., Middle Village. A club official told the *Times*: "The clubs have been set up so that our members may sit around and talk, enjoy a drink and meet socially. They have no cabaret licenses, so there is no dancing, and they do not sell liquor. In most you have to have a membership card to get in."

It was no secret the Mafia owned, or had investments in, many of the seventy-three bars, restaurants, and clubs frequented by homosexuals in New York City. In November 1967, Charles Grutzner in the *New York Times*, reported: "The Mafia is selling off some of its concealed investments in bars catering to homosexuals and is reinvesting the money in private clubs that are immune from routine police inspection and State Liquor Authority control." Grutzner described the police raid on the two clubs: "At 36 East 30th Street, police found about 350 men and women on separate floors of the four-story building run as a club under the name Two Penny Civic Association, Ltd. ... At El Baron Club there were 200 persons when the police issued a summons." Grutzner went on to say that because of increased tolerance of homosexuals, legitimate businessmen, "who had previously shunned that field as too risky and socially repugnant," are breaking the Mafia monopoly by investing in gay bars.

In August 1968, Thorne Dreyer wrote an article in the *Washington Free Press* describing a small-scale riot on New York's Lower East Side and the bad blood between police and citizens. Dreyer described a brawl in an upscale Italian bar, after young Puerto Ricans walked in. The bar was subsequently firebombed, followed by two nights of rioting. Dreyer wrote:

"People don't riot because of inflammatory incidents. They riot because they're pissed off and they're just looking for an excuse. On the east side they rioted because they hate cops and because cops are a symbol for all the unnamable frustration that comes from living in a tight ugly ghetto. Because the people don't have anything to call their own, and if they can't even control their own streets that's a pretty sad state of affairs. And besides, those Tactical Police Force cops with the shiny white helmets and the itchy trigger fingers are pretty ugly mothers. ... Monday and Tuesday night the cops were everywhere and everywhere bottles were thrown at them. Some street barricades sprang up, some fires were started, some store windows were smashed. Several times cops fired the guns over the buildings; at least once they fired into a hallway where people had just run. ... The press reported the incidents, as they always do, in racial terms. It was Puerto Ricans that rioted, said the [*New York*] *Times*. No mention of blacks and hippie/poor whites. Well, let me tell you, it was citizens that rioted."

Another example of volatile relations between police and citizens occurred in September 1968. In Palo Alto's *Peninsula Observer*, Bruce Detwiler wrote: "Squirrel Starts Riot 'Liberate the Trees!" Seventeen-year-old John Angel was a familiar figure with his pet squirrel Tripper in Greenwich Village's Washington Square Park. This particular day a Frisbee scared Tripper and the squirrel bolted up an elm tree. Angel climbed up after him. "Predictably," wrote Detwiler, "John was violating a tree-climbing ordinance. ... Needless to say the police could have been understanding, but they weren't." Police from the Tactical Patrol Force (TPF) arrived. Angel refused to leave the tree without his pet, so a seventy-five foot ladder truck from the fire department and paddy wagons rolled up. Eventually, Angel climbed down, was cuffed and taken away. Detwiler wrote: "For people under 30 the cops were very easy to dislike at this point. 'Why don't you help him get his goddamned squirrel,' someone shouted. The spectacle had drawn a considerable throng of onlookers, and the mood was getting hostile." As Angel was driven away, "a ripple of righteous indignation rippled across the park." More people climbed up the tree. The TPF gathered around the elm "like a pack of hungry dogs around a treed cat." When the cops dragged a man named Gonzales from the tree and started beating him, the crowd turned hostile. Detwiler wrote:

"Amoeba-like, the angry masses pushed in on the cops and Gonzales and proceeded to swallow them up. A shower of cans and bottles hit a paddy wagon as it was attempting to leave, preventing it. Then the cops started brandishing their clubs and the blood started to flow. Litter baskets were ablaze and park benches dismembered. One cop was hit in the face with a beer can. Another was dragged from his horse and roughed up. It was reported that another one broke his leg. ... There was a lot of ugliness on both sides and by 11 p.m. when things had finally quieted down again, 22 people were in jail–charged with disorderly conduct, harassment, inciting a riot, and reckless endangerment–and five cops were in the hospital."

On February 6, 1969, the *New York Times* reported a police crackdown, "on drunks, homosexuals, loiterers and other undesirables in the Times Square area. Then, in April, Claudia Dreifus wrote "Smut Control" in the *East Village Other*:

"There are two kinds of men who make their bread by pimping porn: the sleazy old men who run the Times Square bookstores, and the politicians who, for lack of anything intelligent to say, make 'smut' a campaign issue. John Murphy, a Staten Island Congressman running for Mayor in the Democratic Primary made some highly amusing headlines as a result of a recent moralistic tour of the Times Square area. A movie-star handsome man, he attributes the moral decay of New York City to the deliberate negligence of John V. Lindsay. 'The smut wasn't so widespread when Mayor Wagner was at City Hall,' the Staten Island legislator complained. Murphy says that porn can be purchased even in the most respectable of neighborhoods and that prostitution and homosexuality are being practiced openly. ... As for the non-linear forms of immorality, the Congressman offered an all-American approach to the problems of homosexuality and prostitution. 'We have to legislate stiffer penalties and really ENFORCE them. Girls have to be rounded up and their pimps worked over.' ... As for his remarks about homosexuals, it was clear that he was not soliciting the gay vote."

Fanning the flames of anti-police sentiment was the book *Police Power: Police Abuses in New York City* by Paul Chevigny, published shortly before the Stonewall Riots. A review by Joan Goulianos *in Rat Subterranean News* began:

"The extent of police power in America is becoming increasingly visible as more white middle class people are being arrested. This does not mean that there is more police power, but only that white middle class people still expect and get better attention from the courts and the media. Ghetto people, black people, radicals, and so-called 'outcasts' have always known the range of the police. ... Although the motivation for police abuse is not always clear at first, Chevigny has found that in nearly all cases, the motivation turns out to be an act which the police interpret as defiant. This act may be something as seemingly harmless as a remark about a policeman's action or an attempt to note down his badge number. The police tend to identify certain groups as defiant. Addicts, bums, homosexuals, prostitutes, represent a corruption of the social order and the police are prone to carry out illegal searches and arrests-usually with very few repercussions because these groups generally are powerless and the society condones periodic 'clean-ups.'"

One of these "periodic cleanups" led to the raid on the Stonewall Inn. On June 1, 1969 the New York State Liquor Authority (SLA) decided unlicensed bars had to apply for licenses, mostly those who catered to minorities like Gays, Hispanics or Blacks. The Stonewall Inn, 53 Christopher St., was an after hours private club for members only with a membership fee of $3 for the evening. The bar consisted of two large rooms and was known to be a fire risk. Three years earlier the previous bar on the site had burned out, and the new owner, "Fat Tony" Lauria, a capo in the Genovese crime family, painted the charred walls with black paint and opened for business to gay hipsters, hustlers, drag queens, and underage runaways. As Dick Leitsch, Executive Director of the Mattachine Society of New York, explained in a letter to the *Village Voice*:

"The real point of the matter is the fact that the SLA will not grant licenses to gay bars, and they will use any technicality under the law (and there are thousands of them) to refuse a license. Applicants for licenses are asked, point blank, if they intend to use the premises to serve homosexuals, or will permit homosexuals to 'congregate' on the premises. Those who say 'yes' won't get a license. If they lie and get their license, they are still closed on the grounds that 'homosexuals were permitted to congregate on the premises and conduct themselves in an unlawful manner.' ... The point is that the SLA wages a vendetta against gay bars, and no bar has a chance of staying in business without paying off and engaging in other illegalities. This effectively keeps most decent businessmen out of the business and leaves the field wide open to underworld elements and businessmen who will make a quick buck and get out of the business."

The lesbian publication the *Ladder* claimed the going rate for a New York liquor license ranged from $10,000 to $30,000. Prior to the Stonewall Riots, several gay bars were closed down, including the Sewer, the Checkerboard, and the Tele-Star, all raided when few customers were present. The *New York Daily News* estimated two hundred people were in the Stonewall when it was raided. The raid came at a time when things were looking up for gays in New York. On May 5, the city's Civil Service Commission announced that homosexuality was no longer a bar to applying for certain jobs under its authority. However, this didn't extend to the police and fire departments, a firewall of bigotry and political influence. The Stonewall Inn was first raided on June 24, 1969. In an article in the *East Village Other*, Ronnie Di Brienza, shared his thoughts on the raid:

"Basically, I am not gay, but I am not straight either. I must consider myself a freak. My close associations are with people who are among the minorities. ... Homosexuality ... is a reality and not just a passing thing. The establishment and their elite Gestapo, the pigs, have been running things too long. First you had the Negro riots a few years back, which woke up white cats like myself to the fact that, though I am white, I am just as much considered a nigger as the black man is. From those early battles came the more intense militant organizations, who like myself are sick and tired of being niggers and want to become real and human. We have reached the end of the bottom of the oppressed minority barrel. The gay people are the last people anyone suspected would violently demonstrate for equal rights. Well, let me tell you baby, you just don't fuck with the gays anymore. They too, have turned the other cheek once too often.

"On Tuesday night, June 25, [it was June 24] the Stonewall Inn on Christopher Street was raided by the brave, stick-swinging pigs. The Stonewall has more or less become a gay institution in the Village, and has survived as such for the past three years or so. All of a sudden, however, the pigs decided to start playing political games on the fags, because when did you see a fag fight back? It used to be that a fag was happy to get slapped and chased home, as long as they didn't have to have their names splashed onto a court record.

Now, times are a changing.' Tuesday night was the last night for bullshit."

Di Brienza goes on to say for the next two nights, "grumbling could be heard among the limp-wristed set."

Presumably the first raid failed to achieve the desired result, because Det. Inspector Charles Smyth and Det. Seymour Pine returned with eight plainclothes police officers, including two women, at 1.20 a.m. on June 28. Employees were arrested first. Howard Smith, in "Full Moon Over Stonewall" in the *Village Voice*, described the police criteria for who was and who wasn't arrested: "It was explained to me that generally men dressed as men, even if wearing extensive make up, are always released; men dressed as women are sometimes arrested; and 'men' fully dressed as women, but who upon inspection by a policewoman prove to have undergone the sex-change operation, are always let go." It was a hot night with a full moon. Some gays may have been out for a late night cocktail after seeing Andy Warhol's *Lonesome Cowboys* at the 55th Street Playhouse, or *The Killing of Sister George* at the Waverly, 6th Ave. at 3rd St. Or theatrical productions like *When Queens Collide* presented by Trocadero Co. at Millennium Film Workshop, 46 Great Jones St., or Oscar Wilde's *Salome* at West Side Actors, 252 W. 81st St. At the Stonewall the customers were taken out one by one and either released or bundled into a paddy wagon. Di Brienza in *East Village Other* wrote:

> "So into the Stonewall goes Inspector Smyth, Inspector Pine, four fuzz and two policewomen (God knows what the hell policewomen wanted to do there), and the bust was on. The pigs proceeded to bust all the employees of the establishment, and some fags, too, for good measure. Poof, it starts. The fags have gone revolutionary. A crowd was waiting outside, possibly five hundred in all. Every time someone was released from the bar, cheers would go up along with 'Gay Power.'"

Another account of the raid by Anon in *Rat Subterranean News* was headlined: "Queen Power–Fags Against Pigs":

> "About 1.30 Saturday morning, I happened along Sheridan Sq. with a friend looking for a beer when we saw a crowd gathered outside the Stonewall, a famed gay bar. We walked over to see what was happening. About 3-400 guys were jammed in around a police car in front of the door, taunting several pigs in plainclothes guarding the entrance. 'They raided the joint, the fucking bastards,' a couple of guys told us. 'Why?' we asked. 'Operating without a liquor license.' 'Shit, man, they's out like always to chase down and give us a good fuck. They aint got nothin' else to do during the summer,' a hip spade was shouting."

The crowd jeered, booed, and shouted "Up against the wall, faggots!"

and "Beat it off, pigs!" *Rat Subterranean News* reported one man in a dark red T-shirt shouted, "Nobody's going to fuck around with me. I aint going to take this shit," as he danced in and out of the crowd. Anon continued:

"They began shouting for different people that they knew were being held. 'We want Tommy, the blond drag queen.' Shouts went up. Pennies ricocheted off the van, a beer can hit the door. Suddenly Tommy appeared in a blond wig, etc. and walked coolly out the door. Shouts and screaming. 'We want Tommy.' Tommy, not held by the pigs, smiled and suddenly took off into the crowd to the left. The pigs were really flustered. Many went running after Tommy who took off in a taxi."

Lucien Truscott IV in the *Village Voice* wrote:

"Cheers would go up as favorites would emerge from the door, strike a pose, and swish by the detective with a 'Hello there, fella!' The stars were in their element. Wrists were limp, hair was primped, and reactions to the applause were classic. 'I gave them the gay power bit, and they loved it, girls.' 'Have you seen Maxine?' 'Where is my wife–I told her not to go far.'"

Three drag queens were thrown into the paddy wagon, then a scuffle broke out as an individual refused to go willingly; most say it was a butch lesbian, possibly Marilyn Fowler, the only woman arrested that night. *Rat Subterranean News* claimed it was a man: "5 or 6 cops guarding the van tried to subdue him with little success. Several guys tried to help free him. Unguarded, 3 or 4 of those in the van appeared then quickly disappeared into the crowd." The paddy wagon was pummeled and kicked as it drove away. The crowd surged forward and Pine and his detectives retreated and barricaded themselves into the Stonewall. Anon in *Rat Subterranean News* continued:

"Then a can or stone cracked a window. Soon pandemonium broke loose. Cans, bottles, rocks, trashcans, finally a parking meter crashed the windows and doors. Cheers went up. A sort of wooden wall blocking out the front plate glass windows was forced down. Then with the parking meter a ram, in went the door. The cops inside were scared shitless, dodging projectiles and flying glass. The orgy was taking place. Vengeance vented against the source of repression– gay bars, busts, kids victimized and exploited by the mafia and cops. Strangely, no one spoke in the crowd or tried to direct the insurrection. Everyone's heads were in the same place."

The *Village Voice* offices were half a block from the Stonewall, so it wasn't surprising they had two reporters on the scene. The July 3 issue had two front-page stories on the raid: "Full Moon Over Stonewall" by Howard Smith and "Gay Power Comes To Sheridan Square" by Lucien Truscott IV.

By a stroke of luck, Smith became trapped with the police inside the bar, while Truscott IV was on the outside. Smith wrote: "The turning point came when the police had difficulty keeping a dyke in a patrol car. Three times she slid out and tried to walk away. The last time a cop bodily heaved her in. The crowd shrieked, 'Police brutality!'" As the cops retreated into the bar, Pine asked Smith, "You want to come in? … You're probably safer." Inside, windows smashed and the walls and floor shook under a hail of bricks and debris. The door was battered down with a parking meter and a salvo of projectiles flew into the bar. Officer Gilbert Weisman was hit in the eye. This riled the cops and as they tried to shut the door Det. Inspector Smyth was hit in the head by a beer can. Smith continued:

> "Pine, a man of about 40 and smallish build, gathers himself, leaps out into the melee, and grabs someone around the waist, pulling him downward and back into the doorway. They fall. Pine regains hold and drags the elected protestor inside by the hair. The door slams again. Angry cops converge on the guy, releasing their anger on this sample from the mob. Pine is saying, 'I saw him throwing somethin'' and the guy unfortunately is giving some sass, snidely admits to throwing 'only a few coins.' The cop who was cut is incensed, yells something like, 'So you're the one who hit me!' And while the other cops help, he slaps the prisoner five or six times very hard and finishes with a punch to the mouth. They handcuff the guy as he almost passes out."

The beaten man was "straight" Brooklyn-born folk singer David Van Ronk, arrested for felonious assault of a police officer. Patrolman Gilbert Weisman suffered a lacerated right eye and scratched cornea. According to Truscott's account, it took three cops to take down the bearish Van Ronk. It was two days before the singer's thirty-third birthday and he had been in the nearby Lion's Head, a hard-drinking watering hole for writers, when the trouble started. Van Ronk, singing in Greenwich Village coffee houses since 1956, was a mentor to Bob Dylan, passionate in his political beliefs, and a member of the Trotskyist American Committee for the Fourth International. When the door of the Stonewall was battered in a second time, cops turned a fire hose onto the crowd, but it produced only a weak stream of water. Truscott IV wrote: "Several kids took the opportunity to cavort in the spray, and their momentary glee served to stave off what was rapidly becoming a full-scale attack." Anon in *Rat Subterranean News* wrote: "The pigs carried futility to the extreme and turned the fire hose on the mob through the door. Jeers, derision. Some shouted to 'grab it, grab his cock.'"

Smith in the *Village Voice*:

> "A door over to the side almost gives. One cop shouts, 'Get away from there or I'll shoot!' It stops shaking. The front door is completely open. One of the big

plywood windows gives, and it seems inevitable that the mob will pour in. A kind of tribal adrenaline rush bolsters all of us; they all take out and check pistols. I see both police women doing the same, and the danger becomes even more real. Pine places a few men on each side of the corridor leading away from the entrance. They aim unwavering at the door. One detective arms himself in addition with a sawed off baseball bat he has found. I hear 'We'll shoot the first motherfucker that comes through the door.'"

A trashcan filled with paper was set on fire and shoved through the window. Smith wrote that Pine aimed his gun at the perpetrator but didn't fire: "The sound of sirens coincides with the whoosh of flames where the lighter fluid was thrown. Later, Pine tells me he didn't shoot because he had heard the sirens in time and felt no need to kill someone if help was arriving. It was that close." The cops doused the trashcan with the fire hose and the crowd dispersed after the Tactical Patrol Force arrived. The rioting continued until Wednesday night with running street battles, police beatings, and guerilla tactics like bottles thrown from rooftops. In the *Ladder* it was noted that at a July 9 meeting of the Mattachine Society of New York, a young man said police were still plucking gays off the street and beating them in police cars. A letter from Kevan Liscoe in the *Village Voice* wondered if the New York's TPF had received "courses in sadism by one of Chicago's finest."

A week later, Walter Troy Spenser wrote "Too Much My Dear" in the *Village Voice*:

"The fags, obviously, in this case are the victims of some sort of clash between the police and whoever the people are who operate the Stonewall. (It also seems like unfairly bad timing for them, knocked out of both indoor sports at the Stonewall and outdoor recreation with all those up-in-arms Kew Gardens vigilantes harassing them out of their park. After all, my dear, if they aren't safe in Queens, what is the value of the name? Maybe the city or state should set aside something like a bird sanctuary for them). ... An interesting sidelight to the Stonewall demonstrations ... is the bizarre alliance between the Stonewall Queens, the Stonewall heavies, and street people against the cops."

In the same issue of *Village Voice* is a letter signed by Leo Skir, Robert Cobuzio, Kirk Lindsay, George King, and John Kane which read: "As Jewish, Spanish-Welsh-Irish, Italian, black members of the American homosexual community, we find the use of words like 'fag' and 'faggot' as offensive as 'kike,' 'spick,' 'mick,' 'wop.' 'nigger.'"

New York's gay paper *Come Out!* wrote:

"The *Village Voice* and its writers have once again shown where their heads are really at, during this past summer of 'Gay Power.' They've consistently demonstrated their contempt of the Gay Community in their coverage of the long overdue rebellion of another oppressed minority. Their handling of the first Gay Riots in history read like a copy of the *New York Daily News*. Instead of being concerned about the civil rights of the Gay minority they were preoccupied with the uptight establishment's reactions to the riots. Their demeaning use of derogatory terms for homosexuals and lesbians was a pure demonstration of anti-humanistic liberal sentiment."

The mainstream media coverage of the Stonewall Riots was predictable. The *New York Daily News* was blatantly homophobic, though amusing to read in retrospect. Jerry Lisker headlined his article, "Homo Nest Raided, Queen Bees Are Stinging Mad," which began:

"She sat there with her legs crossed, the lashes of her mascara-coated eyes beating like the wings of a hummingbird. She was angry. She was so upset she hadn't bothered to shave. A day old stubble was beginning to push through the pancake makeup. She was a he. A queen of Christopher Street. Last weekend the queens had turned commandos and stood bra strap to bra strap against an invasion of the helmeted Tactical Patrol Force."

Other highlights include:

" … Queen Power reared its bleached blonde head in revolt. New York City experienced its first homosexual riot. 'We may have lost the battle, sweets, but the war is far from over,' lisped an unofficial lady-in-waiting from the court of the Queens. 'We've had all we can take from the Gestapo,' the spokesman, or spokeswoman, continued. 'We're putting our foot down once and for all.' The foot wore a spiked heel."

And:

"The crowd began to get out of hand, eye witnesses said. Then, without warning, Queen Power exploded with all the fury of a gay atomic bomb. Queens, princesses and ladies-in-waiting began hurling anything they could get their polished, manicured fingernails on. Bobby pins, compacts, curlers, lipstick tubes and other femme fatale missiles were flying in the direction of the cops. The war was on. The lilies of the valley had become carnivorous jungle plants." The article ends: "The police are sure of one thing. They haven't heard the last from the Girls of Christopher Street."

The *New York Times* coverage on June 29 and 30, was less florid:

"Heavy police reinforcements cleared the Sheridan Square area of Greenwich Village again yesterday morning when large crowds of young men, angered by a police raid on an inn frequented by homosexuals, swept through the area. Tactical Police Force units assigned to the East Village poured into the area about 2:15 A.M. after units from the Charles Street station house were unable to control the crowd of about 400 youths some of whom were throwing bottles and lighting small fires. Their arms linked, a row of helmeted policemen stretching across the width of the street made several sweeps up and down Christopher Street between the Avenue of Americas and Seventh Avenue South. The crowd retreated before them, but many groups fled into the numerous small side streets and reformed behind police lines."

Leo Laurence wrote "Gays Hit NY Cops" which ran in the *Berkeley Barb* and the *San Diego Free Door*:

"Homosexuals took to the street in New York City last weekend and joined the revolution. A two-day battle resulted after New York Pigs busted a popular gay bar, the Stonewall Inn in Greenwich Village. … Ironically, it was a chick who gave the rallying cry to fight. Pigs were loading her into the wagon when she shouted to a big crowd of bystanders: 'Why don't you do something?' … Meanwhile, pigs inside the bar were raising hell. Reports from the scene say they looted a juke box, cigarette machine, telephone money, the safe cash, register and tips."

Laurence quoted a first-hand account from J. Marks, co-author of the book, *Rock and Other Four Letter Words*, with photographer Linda Eastman, later Mrs. (Paul) McCartney. Marks' account read:

"I saw a taxi make the mistake of turning into the street when an enormous roar came from about 400 people. … They attacked the cab, banging in the sides, and parading on the hood and top. The cabbie got out and began messing up a few kids and about fifteen jumped him. Meanwhile, about 15 others were trying to let the passengers get to freedom. A city bus ran through the street, but the mass of people wouldn't let it through. They created a thunderous sound beating on the sides of the bus before passing it through. Police came and the crowd pulled away for a moment, then they descended onto the prowl car. They first knocked off the red flashing light. Then they started shaking the squad car sideways as if to tip it over. At that point, an enormous group of TPF (Tactical Patrol Force) arrived with helmets and started marching in a line and swept the crowd back. The kids formed a chorus line opposite the helmeted police line and started singing and dancing. The TPF advanced again and scattered them."

Marks told Laurence, "The gay community in New York City has been inspired by your homosexual liberation stories in the *Barb*."

In his analysis of Stonewall in New York's *Guardian*, John Gabree wrote:

"Activism has clearly sprung up in the homosexual community. As outlaws, they have been subjected to the same radicalizing influence of the police as other street people and minorities. A standing one-liner all week was 'I've become a left deviationist.'

"A generation gap seems to exist for homosexuals as it does for other minorities. Last week it was the younger ones who seemed most determined not to hide and who were going to get their rights, by force if necessary. 'We have to fight back," said one.

"Many seem to be developing a sophisticated understanding of U.S. Society's motive in suppressing them. 'We strike at the family,' one told the *Guardian*, 'and we undermine all the bullshit about virility that keeps most men in line.' The vision of an army of aggressive militant homosexuals should give the rulers of New York something to think about."

In Canada, Montreal's *Logos* wrote:

"Gay power lost that round to the local vigilante group and their chainsaws ... But about two weeks later trouble erupted again-this time in the city itself, as the latently homosexual NYPD once again decided to wipe out the psycho-sociological phenomenon of flaming homosexuality by arresting transvestites at the Stonewall in Sheridan Square. ... Retaliation to the arrests ranged from fires and barricades to gay cheerleaders chanting: 'We are the Stonewall girls/We wear our hair in curls/We have no underwear/We show our pubic hair!' Will Madison Avenue cash in on 'Gay Power'? Only your hairdresser knows for sure!"

In 2004, in New York's *Downtown Express*, Lincoln Anderson interviewed eighty-four-year-old Deputy Inspector Seymour Pine, who apologized for the Stonewall raid, confirming the police were homophobic: "There was no question about that ... but they had no idea about what gay people were about." He claimed the raid was not about gays, but the Mafia. The profits from Stonewall and other New York gay bars padded the coffers of Genovese crime boss Matthew "Matty the Horse" Ianniello, kingpin of Times Square smut. Pine recalled receiving a tip that the Stonewall was involved in a stolen European bonds scam. "If we could close them down, we'd see what would happen to the bonds that were surfacing," he said. On the night of the raid two policewomen were in the bar posing as lesbians, and two male cops. They were looking for illegal activity like dope sales. Pine and his partner Charles Smyth were across the street awaiting a signal. No signal came. "It got to the point that either they were in trouble or they had forgotten what they were supposed to do." So Pine and Smyth entered the bar, expecting the clientele to do as they were told but Pine said, "They were acting differently. ... When we entered, they weren't going to go." Pine described being trapped in the bar: "It was very scary. ... If someone pulled a trigger, we were dead–because they would've just run over us. In the end, a policewoman climbed through a rear vent and ran to the local firehouse to phone the Sixth precinct for help."

16

THE AFTERMATH: JULY TO DECEMBER 1969

Even before the Stonewall Riots there were rumblings of gay militancy in Minneapolis with Fight Repression of Erotic Expression, a group inspired by Leo Laurence and the Committee for Homosexual Freedom. However, it was in New York that the Gay Liberation Front (GLF) was founded to fight Capitalism, the "root cause of all oppression of homosexuals." Articles about gays and Marxism began to appear in the underground press, in places like Ann Arbor, MI, and Spokane, WA. GLF may have adopted the "Left" and its myriad causes, but the "Left" had not adopted gay rights. In late 1969 the GLF paper *Come Out!* was published, then hijacked by gay revolutionaries after the first issue.

———————

"It was one of the few historical dates I can think of that had tremendous repercussions on people's intimate lives. For example, before Stonewall I went to a straight shrink and I wanted to be straight, but after Stonewall I went to a gay shrink to learn how to be a 'good gay.' There are so many people who can look back at that one event and say that it really changed their lives and for the better. So many days with political meanings have had ghastly consequences, like Bastille Day for instance. But Stonewall can only be seen as a positive experience."–Edmund White.

———————

In his book, *Stonewall*, Martin Duberman writes that after the second night of rioting, Craig Rodwell, owner of the Oscar Wilde Memorial Bookstore, composed a flyer: "THE MAFIA AND COPS OUT OF GAY BARS" predicted the riots would "go down in history." In it, Rodwell accused police of "colluding with the Mafia" to stop gays from opening "decent gay bars with a healthy social atmosphere (as opposed to the hell-hole atmosphere of places typified by the Stonewall).'" Coming from Chicago, Rodwell was all too familiar with the tangled web of Mafia, cops, and gay bars. In the flyer he called for a boycott of Mafia-owned bars.

In the *Berkeley Tribe*, a breakaway paper from the *Berkeley Barb*, Leo Laurence wrote:

> "The Mafia buys the pigs with payoffs, but not so the 'movement.' New York City gay militants are fighting both. ... The Mafia fearing the revolution? Maybe. ... Twenty one persons were arrested in the NYC gay riots. Surprisingly, the most daring defiance to the pigs' riot clubs came from the effeminate 'queens.' Like one Puerto Rican who shouted at a big bull pig: 'How'd you like a big Spanish dick up your little Irish ass?' That freaked the pig so much he hesitated swinging for just a split second and the 'queen' split. A large group of gay kids were being rushed by two young pigs in another incident. Someone shouted: 'Let's grab the pigs, rip off their clothes, and screw them both!' They too freaked and retreated fast with their pig tails between their legs."

On July 10, Bill Wingell published "Great to be Gay: A Time for Holding Hands," in Philadelphia's *Distant Drummer*. "Sporting 'Gay is Good' buttons and carrying placards with such slogans as 'End Sexual Fascism,' a group of East Coast homosexuals held its fifth annual 'equal rights' demonstration on July 4th outside Independence Hall." The "Annual Reminder" began on July 4 1965, was organized by East Coast Homophile Organizations (ECHO), as a picket to remind Americans that homosexuals are denied the right of "life, liberty, and the pursuit of happiness" as prescribed in the US Declaration of Independence. In 1965 thirty-nine people attended, men wearing jacket and ties, the women dresses. The last "Reminder" was in 1969, a few days after the Stonewall Riots. Wingell estimated fifty protestors, and "[Lieutenant] George Fencl and his Civil Disobedience squad" were out in strength. The picket was peaceful. "In fact," Wingell wrote, "the only dispute of the day arose between marchers themselves."

Wingell's piece continued:

> "As this reporter was talking to several demonstration leaders, who were in their late 30s and '40s, one breathless young man came running up to tell them that two girls had been ordered not to hold hands while marching. The demonstration organizers said they backed that order. 'There is a time and a place for holding hands,' advised Barbara Gittings, 37, of Philadelphia. 'On the picket line–no.' The young man, who identified himself as Craig Rodwell, 28, chairman of New York's Homophile Youth Movement in Neighborhoods (HYMN), was upset. 'Our message is that homosexual love is good. Holding

hands is not inappropriate,' he insisted. 'If you don't change, you're going to be left behind,' Rodwell told the demonstration leaders. To this reporter he added: 'There's a generation gap among homosexuals too.'"

Rodwell and his lover, Fred Sergeant, continued walking hand-in-hand, as did two lesbian couples. Reaction from the public was mixed, but Leonard Evolov, a passerby, said: "Let them march by all means if they want to. Society is so far from accepting this behavior it's quite difficult to speak rationally about it ... But the mere fact that these people are surfacing is an advancement."

On July 10 the *San Diego Free Door* published a call-to-arms from Solar Plexus:

"How long will it take San Diego gays to realize that we are fighting for our lives? As long as the fascist pigs can step on you, they are happy. Are you? Do you approve of police harassment in the bars? Do you like to hide your personal life from people in order to gain employment or housing? Do you approve of fat-assed capitalist pigs who aren't even gay, becoming wealthy by owning and operating gay bars, because you, being gay, couldn't get a permit to run a place of business, let alone get a liquor license? Do you like state and federal laws which determine the careers open to you? Do you like the fact that no profession is open to you if you are honest about yourself–no matter how dedicated you may be to helping the sick, or giving legal aid to the underdog? Would you like a police record for doing what is natural for you, in your home, between consenting adults? Are you a masochist? Baby, you must be!

"You are sitting in your darling Establishment home, with only the 'proper' friends, with a good job, the proper clothing–hiding from the real world in your Plastic-Fantastic Society composed of frauds and phonies, knowing the truth about yourself but never daring to speak it openly. You might have to miss a payment on your Cadillac if you were honest, right? Or how about your 'beautiful' home? What if the neighbors found out? And you have the guts to complain about persecution of the homosexual? What are you doing to help?"

An article entitled "Minneapolis Movement" in the *Berkeley Tribe*, states that the "Homosexual Revolution" was being taught at the Free University in Minneapolis by two former students, founding members of Fight Repression of Erotic Expression (FREE). In a letter to Leo Laurence at the *Berkeley Tribe*, Steve Irig and Koreen Phelps, wrote: "Militant gays here in Minneapolis have been following your struggle for sexual freedom, and we really dig it." The *Berkeley Tribe* noted that the *Minneapolis Daily*, the campus newspaper, wrote that FREE was based on Leo Laurence's philosophy that Gay Power was "a revolutionary movement paralleling Black Power" and "One should not hide the fact that one is homosexual." On November 5, 1993, Scott Paulsen interviewed Koreen Phelps for the Twin Cities Gay and Lesbian Community Oral History Project at the Minnesota Historical

Society. Phelps described meeting Steve Irig:

"He was really far-out. He would find his jewelry on the street. He'd pick up little pieces of tin or metal things or whatever and he'd string and wear this stuff. He'd walk around and wear this big black cape with a red silk lining and he was flamboyant and very creative. He always thought that we shouldn't have streetlights because it interfered with nature, and you couldn't see the stars. ... That was his opinion. He was really a free spirit guy, long hair and the whole thing. ... I don't know how we came out [to each other]. ... We just seemed to like each other. We just sat and talked to each other and things seemed to come out then, we started talking about how would a person meet someone else like ourselves."

Out of their friendship came FREE. Marcus in the *Berkeley Tribe* reported on "Gayrevs" (Gay Revolutionaries) FREE sponsoring a booth at the University's Welcome Week festivities, where they distributed 6,000 leaflets. Other activities of the Minneapolis group included "weekly picnics (another alternative to the bloodsucking bars) and sensitivity sessions." Stephen Irig commented on the organization's Welcome Week booth: "A good percentage of new students and many older ones are gay or closet case types ... we want to prove to them that they are not sick, not immoral or otherwise perverted ... that they are good and beautiful people."

The Gay Liberation Front (GLF) was founded in New York City soon after the Stonewall Uprising, and GLF "came out" to the underground press August 12 in *Rat Subterranean News*, reprinted in the *Great Speckled Bird*, *Walrus*, out of Champaign, IL, among others, when members laid out their radical agenda:

Q: "What is the Gay Liberation Front?"

A: "We are a revolutionary homosexual group of men and women formed with the realization that complete sexual freedom for all people cannot come about unless existing social institutions are abolished. We reject society's attempt to impose sexual roles and definitions of our nature. We are stepping outside these roles and simplistic myths. We are going to be who we are. At the same time, we are creating new social forms and relations, that is, relations based upon brotherhood, cooperation, human love, and uninhibited sexuality. Babylon has forced us to commit ourselves to one thing ... revolution."

Q: "What makes you revolutionaries?"

A: "We formed after the recent pig bust of the Stonewall. ... We've come to realize that our frustrations and feelings of oppression are real. The society has fucked with us ... within our families, on our jobs, in our education, in the streets, in our bedrooms; in short, it has shit all over us. We, like everyone else, are treated as commodities. We're told what to feel, what to think, what to be

... all for the needs of a money-making machine that has successfully packaged us into antagonistic groups, keeping us divided by racism, sex, and other fears. We identify ourselves with all the oppressed: the Vietnamese struggle, the third world, the blacks, the workers ... all those oppressed by this rotten, dirty, vile, fucked-up capitalist conspiracy."

Q. "Can you pinpoint the oppression as it specifically relates to homosexuals?"

A. "Up until now the traditional homosexual has been forced to attempt to live two separate existences which precludes his being able to live fully in either. Through a system of taboos and institutionalized repressions, society has controlled and manipulated (and in our case denied) sexual expression. The socialization process of the society is nothing but a phony morality impressed upon us by church, media, psychiatry, and education which tells us that if we're not married heterosexuals producers and pacified workers and soldiers that we are sick degenerate outcasts. We expose the institution of marriage as one of the most insidious and basic sustainers of the system. The family is the microcosm of oppression. A male worker is given the illusion of participating in the power of the ruling class through economic control of his children and through the relation he has with his wife as a sexual object and household slave."

Q. "What does the GLF intend to do?"

A. "We are relating the militancy generated by the bar bust and by increasing pig harassment to a program that allows homosexuals and sexually liberated persons to confront themselves and society through encounter groups, demonstrations, dances, a newspaper, and by just being ourselves on the street. The program will create revolution of mind and body as we all confront the opposition."

Q. "Why do you identify with the revolution when homosexuals are oppressed in other revolutionary cultures?"

A. "We feel in this respect that previous revolutions have failed, for any revolution that does not deal with the liberation of the total human being is incomplete."

Q. "Who is the enemy?"

A. "Certainly the system, but this system does not exist apart from people. Our aggressiveness is in terms of asserting our identity and reaching out to our brothers and sisters. Our program is a program for free love for all, but in a system that denies people that right, we intend to defend ourselves from the violence that is being brought down upon us. Until publication of the newspaper, Come Out!, we will have a newsletter. ... Join us!"

While New York gays started GLF, in San Francisco, Leo Laurence and the Committee for Homosexual Freedom (CHF) formed alliances with other groups in the "Movement," including the Black Panthers. In the *Berkeley Tribe*, Laurence wrote: "Gays Get Panther OK." The CHF asked the Panthers if they could hand out leaflets at a rally in Bobby Hutton Park. Laurence wrote: "A Panther official who OK'd distribution of our leaflets on the Homosexual Revolution said: 'Our Board of Control hasn't endorsed this, but we're for anyone who wants freedom, so go ahead.'" In a later *Berkeley Tribe* article, Laurence revealed the statement handed out at the Panther rally was drafted with the help of Stu Albert, the very straight co-founder of the YIPPIES. The CHF also joined anti-Vietnam war protests.

In the November 25, 1969 issue of New York's *Corpus 'The Main Body,'* Dr. Leo Louis Martello wrote that on August 9 the Gay Liberation Front joined the Nagasaki-Hiroshima Peace Parade "carrying lavender banners featuring their name and on each side the symbols for man and woman." One banner read: "THE THIRD SEX SUPPORTS THE THIRD WORLD STRUGGLE." Martello was an Italian American author, gay rights activist, founder of the Witches Against Defamation League, and practitioner of the Strega Tradition, a form of neo-pagan witchcraft, inspired by his Sicilian heritage. He authored many books, including *Weird Ways of Witchcraft*, *Understanding the Tarot*, and *Witchcraft, the Old Religion*.

In August, Michigan's *Ann Arbor Argus* wrote about CHF's newsletter helping "radical gay heads to fight capitalism, the root cause of all oppression of homosexuals in America." Later in the month, the *Spokane Natural* published "Homosexuality and Capitalism: Why Don't They Like Us?" by Michael Cooke:

> "As a Marxist, I see all of recorded history to the present as motivated primarily by the class struggle, which is a necessary and fundamental feature of all private property systems. The division of man into classes arose along with private holdings in land and the institutions of marriage and family with the introduction of agriculture in man's pre-history. It is primarily because we do not fit readily into a family structure, the basic unit in private property systems, that we are judged untrustworthy … and expendable."

In the *Berkeley Tribe*, gay militant Konstantin Berlandt wrote, "Been Down So Long, it Looks Like Up to Me," retitled "On Gay Liberation" in the *Great Speckled Bird*. The piece is an account of running gay liberation workshops at the "straight" United States Student Press Association (USSPA) convention in Al Paso, TX. Berlandt wrote that his resolution urging the USSPA to support the gay liberation movement got no signatures. "People weren't interested," wrote Berlandt. "People were more concerned with other things, people were afraid to put their names down on a blank sheet of paper supporting homosexuals." In his essay in Karla

Jay and Allen Young's 1972 book *Out of the Closets: Voices of Gay Liberation,* Berlandt addressed the birth of his activism:

"I read about gay liberation in the old *Berkeley Barb*, a picket line at States Lines Steamship Company where Gale Whittington had been fired from his job for his picture appearing in the *Barb* hugging Leo Laurence in an article on the gay revolution. A friend asked me if I wouldn't write an article on gay liberation for the *Daily Cal* to help a group get started in Berkeley. I went to a Committee for Homosexual Freedom meeting to interview Leo Laurence, sat in on a meeting and joined the picket line at States Lines the following Wednesday."

After GLF New York formed, one of their first targets was the *Village Voice*. In September, Claudia Dreifus wrote "Gay Power Comes to the Village Voice" in the *East Village Other*, accusing the *Village Voice* of dismissing Stonewall as "faggot grumblings due mostly to Judy Garland's death." Dreifus wrote:

"Rather than fight ludicrous laws banning homosexuality, the homophile has sat back and passively accepted his role as society's outcast. But on June 28th of this year, something happened that was astoundingly different. When a contingent of police began raiding the Stonewall Inn, a popular gay spot in the West Village, the gay folk shocked the world: They rioted."

On Inspector Pine, Dreifus wrote: "[Pine] beat the holy shit out of Lennox Raphael after busting him on dozens of counts of 'consensual sodomy' and 'public lewdness,' in connection with his play *Che!*' Dreifus then targeted the *Village Voice*'s Howard Smith, author of "Full Moon Over Stonewall," saying his prose was "liberally laced with the word 'faggot'–the gay equivalent of 'nigger.'" When GLF tried to place an ad for a dance in the *Village Voice*, they were told to remove the word homosexual from their copy. Thirty GLF members responded by picketing the *Village Voice* offices. A delegation met with Ed Fancher, the publisher, and soon afterwards, Lois Hart, a GLF activist appeared and said: "We won, they've agreed to take our ad and never again to use the word 'faggot.'"

On the West Coast, the *Berkley Barb* reported that Gale Whittington, of the Committee for Homosexual Freedom, spoke at a rally of 2,000 in Sproul Plaza, Berkeley, during the University of California's "disorientation week." The event launched the "Gay Guerillas," whose objective was to encourage closeted gays to come out:

"The gay guerillas plan to tour University campuses with infiltration teams, in order to liberate homosexuals. An encounter group is currently being formed at San Francisco College for dynamic, dialogue, and confrontation, to activate homosexuals to join the exodus from the closet and to gain acceptance by straights. To this end, they intend to align themselves with other militant causes."

The *Berkeley Barb* noted gay liberation was "experiencing a rapid growth." Although only twenty people attended a meeting the previous month, 300 turned up for a 'Come Out' party on October 17 at their headquarters in Berkeley. While militant gay liberation and consciousness-raising was on the rise in New York, Minneapolis, and the West Coast, other states lagged behind. In the monthly *Aquarian*, out of Temple Terrace, FL, Maria Mrazek wrote "In Defense of the 'Gay World'":

"It is generally thought that homosexuals are made early in life within the family group, encouraged either by an overly-protective mother or by failure to identify with a masculine father image. The instigator is propinquity, not hereditary. The female homosexual also flourishes in a home where the father is homosexual or overbearingly aggressive. In many cases puritanical parents condition their sons to beware of sexual love as something dirty or evil; since girls are to be feared, boys seem less dangerous as love objects. Without meaning to, many parents contribute to their children's homosexuality. ... While you needn't love homosexuals, you can at least open your minds enough to admit that they do exist, and that it is not such a rarity anymore. And while you needn't encourage it, don't punish or penalize others for their beliefs."

Clearly the underground press was "evolving" on gay issues. In *Rag*, out of Austin, TX, an anonymous author claimed the city's VD problem was made worse by people refusing to admit that homosexuality existed. The article focused on "straights" acquiring VD from homosexuals:

"The first point to be made is that this article should interest more people than just those who engage in homosexual activity. This is because the homosexual community (if that term makes any sense, which I doubt) is not something that is isolated and off somewhere in a corner. Rare is the man who confines his sexual activity to members of his own sex. Many such men have a girlfriend (or several of them). Many are married, such that when they go out to commit an abominable Crime against Nature not to be mentioned among Christians, they commit adultery as well. ... This complicates the matter of trying to control the spread of VD. ... Catching venereal disease from homosexual contacts is a frequent occurrence, but that fact is sadly not recognized by many authorities who should recognize it."

By late October a Berkeley chapter of GLF had formed and, along with the Committee for Homosexual Freedom and Gay Guerilla's, picketed the *San Francisco Examiner*, handing out leaflets that read: "Society has a new nigger." The word "nigger" had been used in this context before, as in Jerry Farber's "The Student As Nigger," published in the *Rag* in 1967, the *Great*

Speckled Bird in 1968, and others, and Gayle Rubin's "Woman As Nigger," (Parts I & II) in Michigan's *Ann Arbor Argus* in 1968, and later Naomi Weisstein's "Woman As Nigger," in Chicago's *Second City* in 1970. The *San Francisco Examiner* protest was in response to an article written by Robert Patterson that labeled homosexuals "queers," "deviates" and "sick," and gay bars, "traps" where homosexuals "gather for their sick, sad revels." The protest did not go without incident. After *San Francisco Examiner* staff dropped bags of purple printers ink out the windows, the protestors used it to make footprints on the sidewalk and handprints on the building. That's when police moved in and arrested the "Gay Fifteen," including Leo Laurence. In the *Berkley Tribe*, Laurence wrote: "That's when the pigs panicked and called in their 'heavies,' the Tac Squad." A fuller account of the arrests was published in the *Berkeley Barb* and *San Diego Free Door*, which claimed thirteen were arrested. The first arrested was Steven McClave, "the Abbie Hoffman of the Gay Liberation Movement." The piece reads:

> "A squad of police exited [a van] and burst into the crowd, seizing McClave. A tug-of-war followed when his fellow demonstrators held him to prevent arrest. Suddenly the cops struck wildly at heads and with special incentive, at crotches with their three foot long nite sticks. When McClave was finally thrown into the paddy wagon, he screamed to the Pig: 'Kill a queer for Christ.'"

The next arrest was Karen Hurrick, who was maced, knocked to the ground, beaten, then thrown into a paddy wagon. Darwin Dias had a dental plate knocked out and was kicked in the stomach. Michael Carboni suffered a broken rib. Two hours later the remaining protestors staged a sit-in at the office of Mayor Joseph Alioto, where three more were arrested. As a result of the protest at the *San Francisco Examiner*, Laurence was fired from his job as radio news editor at KGO radio. Robert Patterson, who wrote the offensive article, was fired from the *San Francisco Examiner* two years later after fabricating a series of six reports about his visit to China, when he hadn't even bought a visa.

In December, Don Jackson wrote in the *Berkeley Barb*, about a day of picketing: The day started at Union Square, where two-hundred protested the harassment of gays; continued to the Airline Terminal to picket Delta Airlines, after they refused to board a man wearing a Gay Pride button; then to a hustler bar called the Trap, which GLF called a "Walk in Closet"; and finally the Tom Cat Theater, showing "cock swinging" films, to protest the exploitation of gays. Jackson wrote: "Many of the pickets wore 'T' shirts emblazoned with the 'Purple Hand,' which has become the symbol of the Gay Liberation movement." The "Purple Hand" came from the handprints protestors left on the walls of the *San Francisco Examiner* building.

After KGO radio fired Laurence, KFOG-FM came under scrutiny for an editorial accusing homosexuals of frequenting San Francisco's theater district, bringing with them "the inevitable associates of gamblers, thieves, pickpockets, dope pushers, and narcotic addicts." The CHF planned to picket, but KFOG-FM caved in and agreed to allow the gay militants to state their opposition to the editorial on air. Meanwhile, GLF joined other radicals supporting strikers at the Oakland GE plant. Although, Konstantin Berlandt was quoted in the *Berkeley Tribe*, as being told by strike organizers: "Don't say who you are. ... Just say you're a radical, but don't say you are Gay Liberation." Also, the gay trio of GLF, CHF, and the Gay Guerillas, picketed the Seventh Annual Beaux Arts Ball at the Merchandise Mart in San Francisco. Leo Laurence wrote in the *Berkley Tribe*: "Halloween and New Year's Eve have historically been the only times of the year the pigs permit the hundreds of 'Drag Queens' in San Francisco to come out of their closets and into the streets without getting busted." The protestors felt the drags "should have the right to do their thing; not just twice a year, but every day; not just at a drag ball, but at work, school, church and on the streets." The protest was against the "Gay Establishment" sponsors of the Beaux Arts Ball, the Tavern Guild, a group of business owners operating over one hundred "Gay Ghetto Bars and restaurants in the Bay Area."

Though it was not taken seriously, the rapid rise of GLF did not go unnoticed in the mainstream press. On October 31, *Time* magazine published, "The Homosexual in America," an insulting and unflattering expose of gay life, which included the following:

"Though they still seem fairly bizarre to most Americans, homosexuals have never been so visible, vocal, or closely scrutinized by research. They throw public parties, frequent exclusively 'gay' bars (70 in San Francisco alone), and figure sympathetically as the subjects of books, plays and films. Encouraged by the national climate of openness about sex of all kinds and spirit of protest, male and female inverts have been organizing to claim civil rights for themselves as an aggrieved minority."

And:

"Nor is it necessary for a homosexual to join a homophile organization to enjoy a full social life: Homosexuals are often the parlor darlings of wealthy ladies ('fag hags'). Marriage in these circles can involve a homosexual and a busy career woman who coolly take the vows of companionship—and so that they can pool their incomes and tax benefits for a glittering round of entertaining."

And:

"Discrimination aside, what about the more indirect propagation of homosexual points of view? Homosexual taste can fall into a particular kind of self-indulgence as the homosexual revenges himself on a hostile world by writing grotesque exaggerations of straight customs, concentrates on superficial stylistic furbelows or develops a 'campy' fetish for old movies."

In November, several members of the "Movement" "came out" and discussed their homosexuality in *Win*, the magazine of the War Resistors League (WRL), which had an older readership. The cover headline read: "My homosexual needs have made me a nigger." The line is from an essay in the issue by Paul Goodman, "Memoirs of an Ancient Activist." Goodman was a novelist, playwright, poet, and psychotherapist. Born in 1911, he was an anarchist who embraced the New Left of the late 1960s. Goodman wrote:

"In general, in America, being a queer nigger is economically and professionally less disadvantageous than being a black nigger, except in the areas like government service, where there is considerable fear and furtiveness. ... I have been fired three times because of my queer behavior or my claim to the right of it and these are the only times I have been fired. I was fired from the University of Chicago ... and from Black Mountain College."

Another *Win* article was "Notes for a More Coherent Article," by David McReynolds, a paid staff member of the WRL. McReynolds' article described the ramifications of "coming out" to your boss, especially in the established "Left":

"Months ago, before this issue of *Win* was being discussed and before the 'Gay Power' street action in the Village and before the trees were cut down in Queens, I had decided, for reasons that remain as mysterious to me as the seasons, that I had to make public the fact that I am homosexual. ... The kids could not care less, either about any personal statements I might make or about this issue of *Win*. They are neither more nor less homosexual than I recall them 20 years ago, they are just far less hung up about the matter. But tolerant as the kids may be, they do not pay my salary at WRL and they do not, by and large, send in the extra contributions needed to keep *Win* going. The money comes from an older generation. Do I have the right, as a staff member of WRL and an associate of *Win*, to threaten the public image of one of America's oldest and largest pacifist groups, or make the raising of funds more difficult for WRL and *Win*, by a 'personal honesty' of this kind? Am I not imposing upon the WRL and *Win* a burden that it would be better I did not impose?"

A third *Win* article, "The New Homosexual and His Movement," by Bob Martin, chairman of NACHO Youth Committee, and national chairman of the Student Homophile League at Columbia University, stated:

"The overwhelming majority of those who practice homosexuality can do so while maintaining a flawless public image of unimpeachable heterosexuality. These are the people who run businesses, command soldiers, ran for public office, and play football by day, making love in their own way by night. Traditionally, the homosexual has been a social conservative, for traditionally every homosexual who could do so led a double life. He spent half his time building up an image of respectability and perfect straightness to compensate for the dangers of his love life. He 'passed,' and in so doing sought to pay the utmost homage to a society of whose acceptance he was never sure. In trying to be more Catholic than the Pope, he denied his unique heritage as a homosexual, the inheritor of a tradition going back to the dawn of time. Moreover, in accepting middle-class heterosexual values of repression, guilt, and inhumanity he was in essential contradiction to his own nature as a sexual non-conformist. Yet here, in coloring himself like a chameleon to the standards around him, he sought safety. ... Today ... there is a 'new homosexual' at large in this country. Long since liberated in Europe and elsewhere, he is just now beginning to unlock the chains of fear left over from the anti-homosexual witchhunts of Joseph McCarthy. He is standing up, he is claiming what is his by right, and he is at long last, taking pride in himself both as an individual and as a member of a minority group in rebellion."

In November, Don Jackson, in the *Berkeley Barb,* wrote: "Gay Liberation Peace March," about four hundred gay people marching to Golden Gate Park. The gay contingent was organized by Berkeley GLF and CHF; with Los Angeles GLF and GLF from San Jose State College also represented. The protestors marched behind a banner reading, "Homosexuals Against the War," and chanted, "Say it clear, say it loud, we're Gay and we're proud" and, to the dismay of passers-by, "Suck Cock to beat the draft." In addition, the group handed out pamphlets and a poem that ended, "Beautiful Vietnamese man. Let's suck and fuck. Let's not kill each other anymore." The peace march was the subject of an article by the Rt. Rev. Michal Francis Itkin in the December 5 *Berkeley Barb*. In it, he noted a "division in our ranks." At the rally after the march, when Black Panther Chief of Staff David Hilliard spoke, a split occurred in the gay contingent, with pacifists like Itkin shouting him down with "Peace, Now," and others saluting with a clenched fist. Itkin wrote:

> "It is obvious that those of us who hold to the principals of revolutionary nonviolence and the building of a community of love on decentralist lines, could not, in any way support David Hilliard when, under the pretense of speaking for peace he called for violence, when under the pretense of speaking for peace he spoke against the peace movement ... when under the pretense of speaking for peace he attempted to have the anthem of his political party (vanguard or not) imposed on us as the anthem of the entire Movement that day. We cannot see that violence, in any man's hand, is any less violent."

After the rally in Golden Gate Park, Hilliard was arrested for saying:

"Fuck Nixon, that motherfucker ... we'll kill him." Hilliard already faced charges of attempted murder after a Panther-Police gun battle that killed Bobby Hutton in April 1968. The *Berkeley Barb* wrote that the Black Students Union & the Chicano Students Union of Merritt College held a rally in support of David Hilliard. Panther Chief Roland Young, a DJ fired from KSAN for urging his listeners to send Nixon a telegram repeating Hilliard's remarks at the rally, ended his speech with "Fuck Nixon, that Motherfucker. Fuck him in the ass."

In November, *Walrus*, out of Champaign, IL, interviewed Aubrey Bailey, a member of CHF, who compared the rise of gay militancy to that of Black Power:

"In the past most homosexuals have been apolitical, and suddenly quite a number of young ones have become quite militant. I think there's a close parallel [as] that in the black community. It used to be that most black people although they were often very much oppressed were apolitical or in fact, fairly conservative. Suddenly, I think more and more a larger number of homosexuals will be actively promoting revolution of one sort or another, preferably non-violent revolution."

On November 1st and 2nd, the Eastern Region Conference of Homophile Organizations met in Philadelphia and gave birth to what is now called the Gay Pride Parade. According to Boston's *Broadside and the Free Press*, "the radicals took the homophile movement along some new, uncharted paths." The piece continued:

"Most significant, perhaps, was the resolution (passed 54-6), urging homosexuals to take part in the November 15 anti-war march on Washington. The group avoided a firm stand on the issue of the war, however. Liberals and moderates held sway on the basis of their view that the movement must not involve itself in 'extraneous issues.'"

The delegates also voted to declare "a new gay holiday," the Christopher Street Liberation Day, held the last Saturday in June to remember the Stonewall Uprising.

In 1969, the sodomy law in Texas was challenged. (At the time, Illinois was the only state where homosexuality was legal.) Alvin Buchanan, a gay man, was arrested on sodomy charges in a public restroom, entrapped by undercover cops. After being sentenced to two five-year concurrent jail terms, Buchanan filed a lawsuit against Dallas police, claiming they violated his rights under the 1st, 4th, 5th, 6th, 9th, and 14th Amendments to the US Constitution. In November 1969, *Dallas Notes,* under the headline, "Court May Okay Cocksucking," reported that Michael C. Gibson and his wife,

Jannet, had joined Buchanan in the lawsuit. The heterosexual couple said they feared arrest, as the law banned oral and anal sex for both homosexuals and heterosexuals. A panel of three federal judges, Irving Goldberg, Sarah T. Hughes and William M. Taylor Jr., struck down the Texas sodomy law in 1970, but a year later the US Supreme Court upheld it. In 1973 the Texas Legislature rewrote the state's sodomy law to exclude heterosexuals, leaving "homosexual sodomy" a crime with a $500 fine and up to one year in jail. "Homosexual sodomy" remained illegal in Texas until 2003.

In California, homosexuality stayed illegal until 1976. On November 15, 1969, over one hundred members of the "Gay Establishment" turned up to protest the state's anti-gay sodomy laws. The Rev. Troy Perry led the march, sponsored by the Committee for Homosexual Law Reform. Don Jackson was dismissive, describing the speeches as "Auntie Tom" in the *Berkeley Barb*:

> "At the state building, a pulpit and chairs had been set up at the top of the stairway for the dignitaries. The followers sat on the steps. The rally which followed had the hallmarks of a patriotic-religious meeting, complete with the pledge of allegiance, a few prayers, and patriotic and religious songs."

In New York, on November 14, 1969, GLF published *Come Out!* "A NEWSPAPER BY AND FOR THE GAY COMMUNITY." The front page read: "COME OUT FOR FREEDOM! COME OUT NOW! POWER TO THE PEOPLE! GAY POWER TO GAY PEOPLE! COME OUT OF THE CLOSET BEFORE THE DOOR IS NAILED SHUT! ... OUR FRIENDLY NEIGHBORHOOD TAVERN IS A MAFIOSO-ON-THE-JOB TRAINING SCHOOL FOR DUM-DUM HOODS."

The paper boldly predicted: "COME OUT! will hasten the day when it becomes not only passé, but actual political suicide to speak of further repression of the homosexual."

In *Voices of Revolution: The Dissident Press in America*," Rodger Steitmatter wrote:

> "Come Out! was the printed voice of the Gay Liberation Front, born in New York City a month after Stonewall and quickly spreading across the country. The organization was composed of young men and lesbians whose revolutionary vigor had been inflamed by U.S. involvement in Vietnam, becoming to the Gay and Lesbian Liberation Movement what the Black Panthers had become to the Civil Rights Movement. The leftists demanded not only gay rights but the complete overthrow of American Society."

In *Old Mole*, out of Boston, Dotty LeMieux wrote, "Gay Liberation-a Straight View," in which she welcomed the publication of *Come Out!*: "With tears in my eyes, I read the first truly believable and unprovoked articles by men reflecting respect for the women's movement." In the first issue of *Come Out!*, the *Village Voice* came in for a drubbing, as did Joel Fabricant, the heterosexual owner of *Gay Power*, *Kiss*, and the *East Village Other*. *Come Out!* wrote: "It has been the sad plight of the homosexual in our society to be the victim of the money-hungry opportunist: the mafia bar owner, the blackmailer, the sticky-fingered rough trade. A recent and deplorable perverting of the gay movement for profits can be found in the bi-weekly *Gay Power*." *Come Out!* goes on to accuse Fabricant of attacking "homosexuals by name in print," endorsing mafia-run bars, and including pornography. In *Gay Press, Gay Power*, editor Tracy Baim quotes *Come Out!* staff member John Lauritsen:

"At the next meeting of the Gay Liberation Front (GLF) following publication of [the first] issue, members of the 'June 28 cell' announced that they had taken over *Come Out!*–allegedly in order to rescue it. *Come Out!* staff were strongly opposed to the move, but we were caught off guard. Marty Robinson called the act outright theft, and was so furious that he had to be physically restrained by his friends. Unfortunately, at this point GLF had no structure, and voting was prohibited (everything had to be by 'consensus'), so we were unable to thwart the expropriators. This unpleasant episode was one of the most important reasons that Marty Robinson, Jim Owles and Arthur Evans later split from GLF, in order to found the more orderly Gay Activists Alliance (GAA). At any rate, new people took over *Come Out!*, and I and most of the original staff members were out in the cold."

In *Gay Power* Dr. Leo Martello published his opinion on the coup:

"Certain gay militants have set themselves up as moral guardians: They have attacked both *Gay Power* newspaper as 'exploitative' and *Gay* newspaper as 'establishment.' They have 'suggested' in strong terms that all writers connected with the former resign without offering anything in return. The 'good of the cause' (their cause) requires sacrificial victims, and further, the victim's consent. Some of the most vociferous opponents to both newspapers are also the same ones who stole another gay community publication [*Come Out!*], paid for by the parent organization's treasury, and this theft was aided and abetted by the 'silent majority' of members who said nothing, did nothing. This same group [June 28 cell] tried to pass a 'censure' ruling on *Gay Power*. 'Censure' of course is just one step from 'censor.' Strange that none of them thought to 'censure' themselves for their own amoral actions. Disguised as altruism, sugarcoated as 'higher consciousness,' masked as morality, denigrated as 'capitalistic' and 'exploitative' these homosexual humbugs hope to hide their power lust. Instead of concentrating their energies on producing a better product they vent their spleen on all competitors."

While the New York GLF fractured, barely four months after it formed, over 1,000 people turned up for the West Coast Gay Liberation Conference, a five-day event organized by Dunbar Aiken and Carl Whittman. In an interview with the *Berkeley Barb*, Gale Whittington remarked: "Militant homosexuals often attacked more conservative organizations like SIR (Society for Individual Rights) in San Francisco and MCC (Metropolitan Community Church) in Los Angeles during 1969 as being 'counter-revolutionary.' But those attacks seem to be disappearing."

Jim Kepner, activist and reporter for the 'Establishment-oriented" *Advocate* told the *Berkeley Barb*:

"I really didn't expect to enjoy this. I expected a bad show. Most of the reports on Gay Liberation reaching Los Angeles emphasize the friction between the militants and the conservatives. ... But, it wasn't a hate trip I found. One of the problems of being older (Kepner has a few gray hairs) is keeping up with the changes in the movement. My first reaction to the New York City gay riots last spring was typically middle class, with horror for the broken windows and property damage, but now I feel proud that homosexuals are finally doing something."

In the last days of the decade, the *Berkeley Tribe* published Carl Wittman's "Refugees From Amerika: a Gay Perspective," a lengthy article on where the gay movement stands. The piece was also published as "Gay Power: A Manifesto" in Madison's *Kaleidoscope*. Wittman wrote:

"San Francisco is a refugee camp for homosexuals. We have fled here from every part of the nation, and like refugees elsewhere, we came not because it's so great here, but because it was so bad there. By the tens of thousands, we fled small towns where to be ourselves would endanger our jobs and any hope of a decent life; we have fled from blackmailing cops, from families who disowned or 'tolerated' us; we have been drummed out of the armed services, thrown out of schools, fired from jobs, beaten by punks and policemen. And we have formed a ghetto for protection."

On lesbians, Wittman wrote:

"It's been a male-dominated society for too long, and that has warped both men and women. So gay women are going to see things differently from gay men; they are going to feel put down as women, too. Their liberation is tied up with both gay liberation and women's liberation. ... We look forward to the emergence of a lesbian liberation voice."

17

WOMEN'S LIBERATION IN THE UNDERGROUND PRESS

The Women's Liberation Front was born at the Students for a Democratic Society 1967 National Convention in Ann Arbor, when women questioned their role as dishwashing typists in the radical movement. A few months later a Women's Lib group formed in Chicago, then others nationwide. One of the first direct actions was to protest the Miss America Contest in Atlantic City, followed by the Miss Ann Arbor Pageant and North Carolina's Miss Durham Contest. Like GLF, Women's Lib identified themselves as revolutionaries.

———————

"The man over there says women need to be helped into carriages and lifted over ditches, and to have the best place everywhere. Nobody ever helps me into carriages or over puddles, or gives me the best place—and ain't I a woman?

"Look at my arm! I have ploughed and planted and gathered into barns and no man could head me—ain't I a woman? I could work as much and eat as much as a man— when I could get it—and bear the lash as well! And ain't I a woman?

"I have born thirteen children and seen most of 'em sold into slavery and when I cried out with my mother's grief none but Jesus heard me—and ain't I a woman." – Sojourner Truth 1851 on the cover of *Ain't I a Woman*.

———————

In January 1966, *Time* magazine, in "The Homosexual in America," wrote that lesbianism was caused by a fear of men, and was "far less visible but, according to many experts, no less widespread than male homosexuality." Lesbians were certainly "less visible" in the early years of the 1960s underground press. Occasionally a classified ad appeared, like in April 1968 in the *San Diego Free Door*: "BI & GAY GIRLS. If interested in organizing a social club write POB 458, Cardiff-by-the-sea. Tell us about yourself, hobbies, interest; whether bi or gay, married or single, and your ideas on what a club should offer-hobby show, theater party, etc." Or in Chicago's *Kaleidoscope*: "GAY GIRL, 19, desires older partner, 20-30. Write Anita c/o P. Pope 7007 N. Sheridan. Serious only."

Nobody used the word "lesbian."

In January 1966, *New Left Notes*, the newspaper of Students for a Democratic Society (SDS), published "December Conference Impressions" about an SDS conference in Champaign-Urbana, IL:

"For the first time at an SDS conference women came together to talk about problems of women as an oppressed underclass. Movement men unaware of the problems of women should reflect that in most ERAP [Economic Research and Action] projects, in many 'radical' marriages, and in the National Office, women frequently get relegated to 'female' types of work–dish washing, cooking, cleaning, clerical work etc."

In July 1967, Jack A. Smith wrote "SDS Sets Out On Radical Path" for the *Guardian*, about SDS women at the 1967 National Convention in Ann Arbor, MI:

"One of the most interesting and controversial resolutions, entitled, 'Statement from the Women's Liberation Workshop,' failed to gain convention approval but probably stimulated greater thought than any other proposal. Briefly, the young women who drew up the resolution defined the role of the American female, including the role of women in SDS, as one of colonial dependence and exploitation. The proposal contained a program advocating communal childcare centers, distribution of birth-control information and devices, legalized abortion and other modest measures. But the resolution must have touched a raw nerve in a surprisingly large number of males in the audience, many of whom began to act like children at a Saturday matinee when the women who sponsored the statement made reference to the existence of male chauvinism in SDS. Some of the men appeared particularly upset by a phrase in the document which called on women 'to help relieve our brothers of the burden of male chauvinism.' Moved by the hostility the proposal engendered, Jane Adams, Midwest organizer, told the male delegates: 'A lot of you guys are getting furious because for the first time in your life you have had to face your own attitudes about superiority.'"

The proposal of the SDS Women's Liberation Workshop was published in full in the July 10, 1967 issue of *New Left Notes*. In November, the paper reported that a Women's Liberation group was forming in Chicago and in its Preliminary Statement of Principles, it stated:

"Women must not make the same mistake as the blacks did at first of allowing others (whites in their case, men in ours) to define our issues, methods and goals. Only we can and must define the terms of our struggle. ... The liberation of women can not be divorced from the larger revolutionary struggle."

In February 1968, Evi Goldfield, in Ann Arbor's *Radicals in the Profession*, wrote:

"In Chicago we have the healthy beginnings of a Radical Women's movement which is growing quite rapidly. This summer a group of about ten women met regularly to discuss women's role in society and in the movement, women's oppression and liberation, etc. In the fall the group expanded, and there are now five local Radical Women's groups in the city."

However, it was the men *and* women of the Grinnell College, IA, Women's Liberation Front that staged the first protest. *Pterodactyl*, Grinnell's off-campus underground newspaper, published the resolution on women's liberation approved by the SDS in Ann Arbor. Two weeks later, *Rat* wrote that "ten women and ten men" from Grinnell protested Bruce Draper, *Playboy*'s campus representative, when he spoke at the college's sex education series. According to *Rolling Stone*, Draper's intent was to "intellectualize about tits-and-ass on the printed page," and explain "*Playboy* publisher Hugh Hefner's 'swinging' philosophy." The protestors sang *You've Got to Walk That Lonesome Valley*, while they stripped naked, one holding a sign that read, "Playmeat of the month." *Rat* wrote:

"Molly Malcolm, one of the co-sponsors of the protest, said they were attacking '*Playboy*'s distorted view of sexuality.' The group's printed statement said in part: '*Playboy* claims to espouse a philosophy that asserts the body is good and the body is beautiful, but *Playboy* demeans the human body. Pretending to appreciate and respect the beauty of the naked human form, *Playboy* in actuality stereotypes the body and commercializes on it."

Cassell Carpenter, a female staff writer at *Kudzu* wrote:

"As in other areas of the movement, the voice of the woman is rising against superficiality, exploitation and meaningless morality epitomized by the American ideal of plastic sexless 'beauty' and mindless sexless 'sex', commercialized and propagated by Madison Avenue, Hugh Hefner, and Bert Parks."

In August, Baltimore's *Peace and Freedom News* reported on a Women's Liberation group starting up in the city. A month later Detroit Women's Liberation joined other groups from New York, New Jersey, Florida, and Iowa, to protest the Miss America Contest in Atlantic City. In Detroit's *Fifth Estate*, Nancy Homer wrote that seventy women protested "the mindless boob symbol." Homer wrote:

"The women picketed, sang protest songs, presented a skit with a dummy representing 'the prostitute Miss America,' and passed out leaflets. The songs included *We Shall Not Be Used*, sung to *We Shall Not be Moved*, and *Aint She Sweet*.

Aint she sweet
Making profit off her meat
Beauty sells she's told so she's out pluggin' it
Aint she sweet.

In *Rat*, Robin Morgan wrote that one guerilla theater skit at the Miss America Contest, involved "the filling of the Freedom Trash Can with instruments of women-torture–bras, curlers, false eyelashes, steno pads, dishcloths, and issues of 'women's magazines.'" From the balcony, women unfurled a "Women's Liberation" banner, and shouted "No more Miss America." Some women were arrested: "Naomi Jaffee returned to her chair and quietly refused to leave, displaying her ticket, until she was wrenched away. Peggy Dobbins, already in custody, was meanwhile being given Indian burns by five cops–the fuzz have to get their jollies somehow." In March 1969, Beth Schneider in the *Ann Arbor Argus* reported on a protest at the Miss Ann Arbor Pageant, when thirty-five women sang and chanted before fifteen ushers escorted them out. The following month in the *North Carolina Anvil*, Elizabeth Tornquist wrote that Durham and Chapel Hill women's liberation groups protested the Miss Durham Beauty Pageant. The only coverage in the mainstream press appeared in the *Durham Herald*, who wrote: "None of the picketers were entering any beauty contests." Across the nation, the voices of Women's Liberation were heard in the underground press. In November 1968 in Atlanta's *Great Speckled Bird*, Judith Brown wrote:

"The consensus about the black still holds for the woman: (1) she is of inherently inferior and alien mentality, her mind being vague, bound by personal experience (scatterbrained or just plain dumb); (2) she is a happy person, and all she asks of life is a little attention, a regular sex life, new hats, dresses, and second-hand Cadillacs; (3) she does not join 'mixed' groups for the stated purposes but to be with men."

In December 1968 in the *Peninsula Observer*, Melody Kilian of the

Women's Caucus, Vancouver BC, wrote "A Strategy of Love: Sexual Guerillas," which looked at the "woman's issue" and the traditional roles of men and women:

> "The roles are so strong that in order to resist them we are going to have to become real sexual guerillas, or love guerillas. As soon as two people enter a publicly acknowledged long-term relationship almost all the other people around, and every institution and custom and value and norm of this society, begin to stereotype them into traditional husband-wife roles. The tide is almost irresistible. The awareness and intent of the two people involved almost doesn't matter. They are seen as each other's sexual property. Marx knew this and wrote about the abolition of marriage, but this whole area has not been seriously investigated by the Left."

Like GLF, Women's Lib described themselves as revolutionaries. In December 1968, Noel Ignatin wrote in *New Left Notes:* "Women's liberation as a revolutionary task leads us to two inescapable conclusions: (1) Women who desire equality must become revolutionaries. (2) All revolutionary organizations and all individuals, both male and female, who desire revolution must fight for the equality of women." In February 1969, San Francisco Women's Lib disrupted the KYA Bridal Fair at the Masonic Auditorium. The *Berkeley Barb* reported that women handed out leaflets explaining how society is "bombarded by the mass media with images of the pretty, sexy, passive, child-like vacuous woman," and how women who don't fit the image are "told to buy a new hair color or a new kitchen floor." In March, in *Fifth Estate*, Dena Clamage's article "Women's Liberation: the Only Path is Revolution," is illustrated with a drawing of a woman suckling a baby to her breast, while cradling a rifle in her lap. Clamage wrote:

> "It is not enough to say that women's liberation depends on being able to get an equal piece of the American apple pie. That pie is inedible. … a revolution is necessary in order to lay the base for the eradication of chauvinism and supremacy."

Women's Lib also aligned itself with the black movement, even co-opting the word "racism." In March 1968 in the *Ann Arbor Argus*, radical lesbian, later SM advocate, Gayle Rubin wrote "Woman As Nigger":

> "The basic premise of women's liberation is that women are an exploited class, like black people, but that unlike blacks, they are not marginal to our technocratic society. So that one might expect that social control of women is less slipshod and more subtle than that of black people. In other words, women suffer from some form of racism, as that word is currently used. Racism has come to refer, in the past year or so, to something enormously more complex than what it meant in the days of the first sit-ins. It refers to any dynamic

system of social, political, economic, and psychological pressures that tend to suppress a group whose members may be influenced by some form of biologically determined distinction, and whose suppression may be contrary to what would be expected by normal divisions of class."

Both GLF and Women's Lib challenged the "straight" male-dominated New Left. In *First Issue,* a radical paper out of Ithaca, NY, Henry Balser wrote:

"Some people are now questioning male chauvinism. And, of course, women are taking the lead. It started with a few women in the movement, mainly in SDS. They brought up the issues at the last national SDS convention, in Ann Arbor, Michigan. And since then, the women's liberation workshops have been set up in Chicago, at Queens College in New York, and elsewhere around the country. And they have challenged many of us of the so-called stronger sex to re-examine our attitudes."

In *Old Mole*, out of Cambridge, MA, Larry Crocker wrote:

"If you've been anywhere near the radical scene in the last year, you've probably heard the phrase, 'male chauvinism.'

"American girls are brought up to think of themselves as products. They spend endless hours worrying about the packaging of the product–clothes, cosmetics, hairstyling, the right sweet, but sexy, smile. Dating is a marketing operation. The girl barters her female product presence for entertainment, gifts, and suburban security. To get as good a price as possible, it is of the utmost importance that the merchandise be free of extraneous attributes such as independent interests, beliefs, politics, or even intelligence beyond what is required to be a reasonably entertaining dinner conversationalist. They just get in the way of the essential product–a docile female body, housekeeper, family-raiser, and low-key companion. The central thing for a girl to remember is that it's the man's trip–she's just along on it."

In November 1969, Milwaukee's *Kaleidoscope* included a Women's Liberation Special, in which Jennie Orvino wrote:

"The Kaleidoscope supplement on Women's Liberation will threaten you. You men may laugh with relief and say 'at least they've got it out of their systems and we don't have to hear them bitch anymore.' Or you may get angry and call us misguided, sick, castrating, bitter dikes. Women may think we DO have a point (they would have been out in their bloomers marching with the Suffragettes) but articles advocating masturbation and LESBIANISM, for god's sake, are going a bit too far. But for all the shock, the name-calling and the indignation the issue will bring down, one thing is clear. Women are getting it together."

Also featured in *Kaleidoscope*'s Women's Liberation Special is Anne Koedt's "Myth: Vaginal Orgasm," where the author, a founding member of New York Radical Feminists, muses on the redundancy of men:

"Men fear that they will become sexually expendable if the clitoral organ is substituted for the vaginal as the basic pleasure for women. Actually, this has a great deal of validity if one considers only the anatomy. ... Lesbian sexuality, in rubbing, one clitoris against the other, could make an excellent case, based on anatomical data, for the extinction of the male organ."

Another item in the women's issue of *Kaleidoscope* is a photograph of a male nude, a flag over his genitals, with the caption:

"'I never have enough,' says Jeremy Huck, our 22-year old, cinnamon-eyed playmate of the month. An accomplished rock musician and composer, Jeremy is currently working on a revolutionary opera celebrating the struggle of the Vietnamese people against American Imperialists. This well-hung six-footer has had a one-man exhibit of rubber sculpture at the Robert Fraser Gallery in London. He really grooves on MDA and his measurement is 9 inches."

In the Kaleidoscope women's issue, lesbians are represented by Del Martin and Phyllis Lyon, founders of the Daughters of Bilitis, who wrote "The Realities of Lesbianism," which states:

"A Lesbian is a woman who prefers another woman as a sexual partner; a woman who is drawn erotically to women rather than to men. This definition includes women who have never experienced overt sexual relations with a woman–the key word is 'prefers.' There is really no other valid way to define the Lesbian, for outside the sexual area she is as different in her actions, dress, status and behavior as anyone else. Just as there is no typical heterosexual woman, neither is there any typical Lesbian."

18

1970: A NEW DECADE

In the first six months of 1970 GLF groups sprang up in universities nationwide including cities like Tallahassee, Chicago, and Detroit. While mainstream newspapers suppressed stories about the harassment of LGBT's, articles in the underground press documented gay people being fired from jobs, entrapped in public restrooms, and arrested in bar raids. Some gay leaders predicted violent uprisings between gays and cops. While the Detroit GLF clashed with the Episcopal Church, other GLFs battled to hold dances, conferences and other gay events on campus property. Cracks began to appear in GLF when lesbians confronted gay men's chauvinism, and the "Generation Gap" widened at the West Coast Regional Homophile Conference.

"One cannot like an aspect of oneself which one always tries to conceal."–Albert Camus, in his play *Caligula*.

In early 1970 reports of new GLF groups began to appear in underground newspapers across the country. One formed in Tallahassee, FL, where Judy wrote in the city's *Amazing Grace*, that "large numbers of straight and gay brothers and sisters [were] working behind the scene and giving generously of their bread." At West Virginia University in Morgantown, the *Liberator* reported on "a small, but growing, group of gay students ... laying the groundwork for a gay organization." Don Jackson in the *San Diego Free Door* wrote about two upcoming GLF protests, one in Hollywood at Barney's Beanery, where a sign hung on the wall reading

"Fagots Stay Out," and another, a campus kiss-in at San Jose State College, where there were plans to hold gay Saturday night dances in the Student Union building. Jackson also reported on a raid, in Los Angeles, at the Society of Anubis Christmas Party:

"At the height of the merrymaking, eleven vice pigs surrounded the private clubhouse of the Society. They barged in without a warrant, shoving aside the security guard employed by the Society to watch the door. Everyone present was searched, hassled, I.D.'s checked, etc. Pig photographers rushed around the room to photograph all the guests. ... The bartender and one member were arrested on charges of conducting a business without a license and selling alcoholic beverages without a license."

The Society of Anubis (SOA) was a state-chartered, non-profit gay organization with 800 members.

Police departments around the country learned nothing from the Stonewall Riots. Certainly the police in Chicago, after garnering worldwide criticism for their actions at the 1968 Democratic National Convention, went about the business of harassing gays as usual. At 3:30 a.m. on September 8, 1969, Chicago police raided the Annex, a bar owned by Nick Dallesandro, a man ensnared in a web of organized crime. Again, on September 20, 1969, the Vice Control Division of the Chicago Police Department raided the 21 Club, 3042 W. Irving Park, where twelve men were arrested. In the October *Mattachine Midwest Newsletter*, Jim Bradford and William B. Kelley wrote that a week after the 21 Club raid, the Blue Pub was also hit and four men were taken away in a paddy wagon. This was followed on October 9 by a raid at the Alameda Club. In response to the raids, Jim Bradford, the Mattachine Midwest president, predicted: "THE NEW MILITANCY EMERGES." At the time of the raids, Chicago GLF formed at the University of Chicago. On October 3, 1969 Henry Weimhoff, a student at UC, placed an ad in the ROOMMATES WANTED section of *Maroon*, the student newspaper, that read: "2 Gay Students Wanted to Share 5 Rm Unfrn. Apt. (53rd & Harper) $52 & Utils. 955-7433. (Keep Trying)." The handful of students who answered the ad, collectively placed another ad in the *Maroon*: "GAY POWER IN 69-70 Anyone interested in joining the Hyde Park Homophile League write Box 69, c/o *Maroon*. Replies kept confidential." Two months later the group renamed itself the University of Chicago Gay Liberation Front (UCGLF). In January 1970, Dan Borroff wrote "Come Out" in the *Seed*: "Chicago's homosexual community can no longer endure subjugation by the underworld and an ignorant public which does not truly understand human sexual behavior."

In January 1970, the *Berkeley Barb* reported that the "militant Gay Liberation Front" was organizing nationwide protests against the ABC network, after they fired Leo Laurence from his job as a News Editor. The

Berkeley Barb wrote:

> "Laurence's writings were reprinted by the underground press worldwide, and
> were used to develop other radical homosexual organizations throughout the
> country. His radical politics, revolutionary writings, and strong union activities,
> apparently were too much for the ABC network."

The "nationwide" protests failed to materialize. In San Francisco's *Good
Times*, and Britain's *International Times*, John James wrote, "Gays Blow
Minds," about bystanders' opinion of protestors chanting "KGO: blow
blow, gay blow, good blow" and "suck cock and beat the draft" outside the
Golden Gate Avenue Studios of KGO/ABC Channel 7. One middle-aged
black man said, "There are the losers," another, "The word isn't gay or
homosexual, it's asshole."

Police arrested Steven Matthews and Pat Brown. In May, Don Jackson
in the *Berkeley Barb* wrote that Matthews and Brown demanded a jury of
their peers i.e. an all-gay jury. The judge declined. Jackson wrote:

> "Steve Runyon, of the S.F. riot pigs, aggressively swaggered into the court
> room, sat on the witness chair, jock-tripping pig style, with his legs spread wide,
> his head cocked arrogantly, and testified that he heard Matthews and Brown
> shouting 'Suck cock to beat the draft.'"

Laurence's case against ABC was heard in the offices of John Kagel,
the arbitrator. Much to Laurence's chagrin, the proceedings were closed to
the press. Jefferson Fuck Poland, reporting for the *Berkeley Barb*, slipped in
briefly but was asked to leave. Laurence wrote in the *Berkeley Tribe*:

> "The chief witness for the 'prosecution' was bossman [General Manager Ed]
> McLaughlin. ... Before, during, and after his testimony, he sucked on his cigar,
> moving it slowly in and out his mouth, in and out, in and out. If he handles a
> cock with the same finesse, he's a superb cock sucker."

A headline in the February 13, 1970 *Berkeley Tribe* read: "Leo Wins!"
Laurence's firing from ABC lead to an article in the *Berkeley Tribe,* in which
he interviewed Roland Young, KSAN's first black deejay, recently fired for
supporting the Black Panthers. Laurence asked Young about opposition to
the Gay Liberation Front within the Panthers. Young answered: "Some
oppose homosexual freedom 'cause they fear it will stop procreation and
end the species." Young pointed out he didn't agree with that statement.
Laurence told Young that while some blacks were concerned about the
anti-gay attitude of some Panthers, he had recently attended an all-night
vigil at the Panthers' headquarters in San Francisco, where he engaged
members on the subject of gay liberation: "'Right on!' came back the

answer every time, 'I'm for anybody who is after freedom and wants to rip off the fascists in this country,' was a typical Panther comment. Not once did I find hostility to the Gay Liberation movement from a Panther." Young suggested black homosexuals "create their own 'Gay Caucuses' within existing black organizations," or "push for black participation within the Gay Liberation organizations."

Firing an individual on the grounds of their homosexuality was commonplace. In the *Berkeley Tribe*, Gale Whittington reported the story of David Carpenter, a postal worker, fired for being gay. Carpenter explained to members of the Committee for Homosexual Freedom how "Big Brother" investigated his private life to determine his "moral competency." On November 3, 1969 he was verbally fired. On December 5 he received this official notice:

> "The investigation developed information which raised a question as to whether you meet the suitability requirements for employment in the competitive Federal service under the provisions of section 731.201 of the Civil Service regulations because of the unfitness evidenced by your conduct in living with a person of your sex, who is a homosexual and impersonates a female and representing yourself as living in a matrimonial relationship with this person."

Anger and frustration over bar raids, firings and police entrapment reached fever pitch. Don Jackson, in the *Los Angeles Free Press,* wrote that some gays, including Leo Laurence, predicted violent confrontations. Jackson quoted from a recent interview with Laurence in *Tangents*:

> "If the oppression of the homosexual is not stopped, if discrimination in employment, in government, is not stopped, if the hypocrisy taught in churches, the lies taught by the schools is not stopped–then this country is in danger, and there's a likelihood of having a violent revolution, where there will be fighting in the streets of every city across this country, where there will be sniping by hostile people. I'm opposed to violence. But if the government doesn't change, that's probably what will happen."

Jackson quoted Steven McClave, "a leader of the more aggressive faction of the Committee for Homosexual Freedom," who stated:

> "As homosexuals develop a group identity, so we prepare to meet violence with violence. We will provoke violence by exposing the latent aggressions directed against us. Such provocation will radicalize not only the gay community, but our aggressors as well–overt, hard-core bigotry is more successfully confronted than safe, liberal, discriminatory tolerance. Both left and right will be radicalized, reducing the great mainstream. We forsake even militant non-violence and embrace first a defensive militant violence."

In his article, Jackson sums up:

"There is unfortunately a growing hostility between gays and some heteros–particularly cops. A high degree of frustration among homosexuals is well established. The younger gay element has demonstrated its dissatisfaction with increasing encounters with the police in New York, San Francisco and Los Angeles. Melees have ensued involving numerous injuries and considerable property damage. ... Government officials should be alarmed over the potential violent uprising and act quickly to alleviate the conditions causing the dissatisfaction."

In the *Los Angeles Free Press*, Tony De Rosa suggested gay men "must get their balls back." De Rosa wrote:

"If force is needed to convince straights that we mean to be equal and free, then we must use force. The blacks and the students have discovered that years of peaceful protest doesn't change a thing, but a few well-placed bombs, riots and fires seem to act like a laxative on society's conscience."

In *Good Times*, Tiresias wrote about the schism between gay men and lesbians in San Francisco GLF:

"Gay Liberation is, for all practical purposes a male group. There are many reasons for the poor showing of females at Gay Liberation meetings. First of all, gay males seem to outnumber gay females in this society. Females in our society are given solid grounding to get married and have kids. ... Hence, many gay and bisexual women are forced by the society into heterosexual roles. In addition, the few women who do show up at Gay Liberation functions find male chauvinism is prevalent just as in straight society, with the additional factor that many gay men dislike, fear, and generally ignore women."

The University of Chicago Gay Liberation Front (UCGLF) went public on January 21, 1970 when members participated in a forty-five minute round table discussion on WHPK, 88.3 FM. The topics included, the oppression of the homosexual in society, the gay student on campus, and the formation of a militant gay organization. Two days later the first "zap" took place when nine UCGLF members attended a "straight" campus dance and danced with their partners. The reaction from "straights" was amusement. At the end of January, the *Maroon-Grey City Journal* published an article by Henry Weimhoff, UCGLF co-founder, entitled "The 'Problem' of Homosexuality" which begins:

"With the challenge to traditionally accepted mores and values of our society increasingly endemic, a new voice is heard, from the segment of the population labeled 'homosexual.' Who are they, these homosexuals, and what do they want? Human beings with the abilities and potentials of any other human beings, with a sexual orientation different from the majority, but in essence equally meaningful and valuable. Homosexuality is neither an affliction to be cured, nor a weakness to be resisted."

The next UCGLF zap was against Police Sgt. John Manley Jr., a notorious cop who, for years, lurked in restrooms, entrapping hundreds of gay men. In the *Mattachine Midwest Newsletter*, David Stienecker, the editor, penned a humorous piece suggesting Officer Manley might be "getting off" on the restroom arrests. In the next issue a photograph of Manley appeared with another warning about his nefarious activities. On February 7, 1970, Manley arrested Stienecker at his home and charged him with "criminal defamation." By all accounts, Manley was visibly shaken when Stienecker pleaded innocent and fought the charges. Jim Bradford, Mattachine Midwest president, told Chicago's *Second City*:

> "We try to alert both the homosexual community and police officials to over-zealous officers who twist the law for their own purposes. We can not let this act of repression do anything but redouble our own dedication to freeing this city's homosexuals from police abuses. Manley's contempt for freedom of the press and other constitutional guarantees should draw condemnation from all quarters."

On May 6, after three court appearances, Stienecker and Renee Hanover, his lesbian lawyer, turned up a fourth time to be told the case was dismissed, after, according to *Second City*, "the complainant failed to appear."

Skulking around in restrooms exposing their privates wasn't limited to Chicago police. In January 1970, the *Berkeley Barb* reported on the University of California campus cops: "Students for Gay Power were set to picket the University's Harmon Gym … in opposition to police participant observation entrapment of homosexuals in the gym's men's room." A petition demanded an end to the entrapment and funds saved "be used to protect women from rape on campus." According to Kenney Lundgren of Students for Gay Power, there had been forty arrests since the fall, and some "campus pigs," go as far as "getting into the act."

More cases of police brutality appeared in the underground press. Gale Whittington in the *Berkeley Tribe* wrote: "Four city policemen and two military policemen forced their way into the apartment of Arthur Ornales, a Mexican-American Gay, WITHOUT SEARCH WARRANTS AND WITHOUT PERMISSION." Ornales was questioned about an AWOL soldier, but claimed he didn't know him. That's when "pig" Lloyd Yeargain forced Ornales into the bathtub and beat him around the face and chest, "mumbling insults about his sexuality," and "IN FRONT OF

WITNESSES." The beating took place at the Hospitality House of San Francisco, a "refugee camp and crash pad for the lonely people of the Tenderloin." An investigation into the incident by GLF and the Committee for Homosexual Freedom found that pressure from the police lead to the story being ignored by the *San Francisco Chronicle*. This was nothing unusual. The *Berkeley Tribe* reported that lesbian activist Del Martin told *Vector* magazine: "Citizen's Alert has been trying for years to get publicity about police brutality and the papers have refused to touch it."

In the first few months of 1970, there were few lesbian voices appearing in the underground press. On February 13, 1970, Milwaukee's *Kaleidoscope* included a Gay Liberation Special with articles about GLF in Wisconsin, another written by a "Fag Hag," and "A Word to Our Gay Sisters," explaining the lack of lesbian articles:

> "The *Kaleidoscope* Gay Liberation Special is directed to and from the gay male point of view. For a number of reasons the gay female position is not taken up here. We realize that the situation of the gay woman is uniquely different from that of her gay brothers, and that we, as males, cannot presume to speak for her. In the absence of a lesbian voice, we have not presumed to do so. *Kaleidoscope* will continue to carry news of the Gay Liberation movement. Hopefully, there will be considerable gay female coverage in future issues."

At the First Unitarian Church of Los Angeles, twenty-two homosexual organizations met for the West Coast Regional Homophile Conference (WCRHC). In the *Berkeley Tribe*, Leo Laurence wrote that WCRHC, considered "Establishment" by GLF, voted to demand $90 billion dollars be paid to gays in reparations by the "Christian Churches of Amerikkka." Don Jackson in the *Los Angeles Free Press* added that GLF member Morris Kight tacked a bill for $90 billion on the door of First Congregational Church, because "The Congregational or Puritan Church is one of the most guilty." In the *Berkeley Tribe*, Laurence wrote that at WCRHC, the new GLF groups were "detested by some closet queen leaders," many of them upset by talk of violence and revolution. Marcus Overseth, editor of the gay publication, the *San Francisco Gay Free Press*, said: "To call ourselves part of the political revolution is cutting our heads off. To identify with the New Left is dangerous." Laurence ended his *Berkeley Tribe* article by writing about a private party held in the "hills of suburban L.A": "One formerly 'Gay Establishment' leader, handsome, about six feet tall, slim, smooth, and sexy, willingly was stripped and sucked regally. It was a voyeurist holiday. I get hard thinking about it." Douglas Key's report in the *Los Angeles Free Press* was less titillating, noting that standing ovations were given to GLF speakers, Morris Kight and Henry "Harry" Hay. *The Berkeley Barb* reported that Hay, chairman of Los Angeles GLF and founder of the Mattachine Society, said: "The Gay movement went on the wrong path, trying for middle-class respectability. ... The shoe never fit. The reappearance of the Gay Lib idea revives the community spirit and frees our lives from the heterosexual lifestyle."

Another standing ovation was given to Pvts. Antoinetta Garland and Sandy Hagen of the Women's Army Corps, both AWOL. These "brave and courageous martyrs" had publicly "come out" on radio and TV. Garland and Hagen, who had gone AWOL from bootcamp in Anniston, AL, were members of GLF and Women's Lib. Mother Boats, founder of the Psychedelic Venus Church, described as "a pantheistic nature religion, humanist hedonism, a religious pursuit of bodily pleasure through sex and marijuana," wrote in the *Berkeley Barb*:

> "Sandy and 'Tony' are female homosexuals. ... They oppose the war, ally themselves with the War Resistor's League and fellow escaped prisoners. They decided to leave the military because it degrades human persons, forbids sexual freedom, and devotes itself to bigotry and killing."

At WCRHC Garland said: "There are so many homosexuals who refuse to get involved ... it's time for us Women to get off our asses and stop letting men fight our battles for us." In July, a report in *Distant Drummer* read: "Because of Gay Liberation Front intervention, two WACs are receiving honorable discharges from the U.S. Army for homosexuality." After Garland and Hagen went AWOL, GLF acted as go-betweens, notifying the Pentagon and arranging a date and time for the women to give themselves up. However, when MPs and "assorted high brass" turned up to be greeted by reporters and TV cameras, they left without the WACs. A month later the women turned themselves in at Fort McClellan. Eventually they received honorable discharges.

Although GLF aligned itself with the New Left, turning out for union strikes and peace protests, the gesture was not reciprocated. In the *Berkeley Barb*, Don Burton wrote:

> "It pains me to see that most of the Movement is too uptight to honestly support Gay Liberation. I've heard all sorts of excuses, ranging from 'You're (Gay Lib) not together enough for us,' to 'Gay Lib just isn't where it's at.' Sometimes I hear 'Right on, Gay Lib!' or the feeble 'Keep it up, brothers,' yet I've seen very little active support from the majority of the Radical Community. ... The Panthers haven't supported us actively yet, but they HAVE rapped with us. They're getting their heads straight on it. ... Then Women's Liberation (not Gay Women's Lib). They're something else again. All I've seen and heard from them is hostility ... for everybody. They want to have nothing to do with Gay Lib, yet both groups are fighting the same oppressive Chauvinistic Ego."

In New York, GLF's involvement with the New Left and support for causes other than gay rights caused a rift among members that lead to a split. In December 1969, donations made to the Black Panthers and Fidel Castro's homophobic regime in Cuba, proved too much for some GLF members, who split to form the Gay Activist's Alliance. However, New York GLF remained active for some time afterwards. One way to combat homophobia in "Movement" groups was suggested by an anonymous author in *Rag*:

> "A Program for Homosexuals
>
> "1) We may not be wanted in some of these groups, but we must struggle against opportunism and demonstrate that bad attitudes toward homosexuals are major props under the male chauvinist system. ... Therefore we must fight to support the struggles of workers and all oppressed people. ... As we prove we are correct the traditional organizations of the left will have to stop writing us off as a special brand of crazies. The facts will force them out of their opportunistic rejection of homosexuals.
>
> "2) But to gain any of this we must defeat in ourselves all of the old defenses. We must stop telling ourselves that we are more artistic, more sensitive and intellectually superior. We will have to stop reciting lists of all the great people who were homosexuals. We must realize that we are not the answer to the population problem, and we must stop claiming to be. We must refrain from imposing our sexuality on others, as we ask others not to impose their sexuality on us."

Raymond Warner wrote of the dysfunctional relationship between GLF and the New Left in the gay *Detroit Liberator*:

> "Recent dialogue within the political science community has led to the statement 'The ineptness of the New Left can be evidenced by its support of Gay Liberation.' The Marxist revival of the '60s called the New Left may very well be the death gasp of dogmatic socialist ideology, the clichés that haunted Europe in 1848 warrant little serious discussion, except in a historic frame of reference.
>
> "This brings us to a negative axiomatic approach–'The ineptness of the Gay Liberation Movement can be evidenced by its association with the New Left.' It can be acknowledged that the Gay Liberation Movement and its activists in Gay Lib are former and present participants in the 'Movement.' ... The New Left failure in the peace movement, their failure to have significant impact upon the American bi-party system, their failure to mobilize the mass of the American people in a modern reform movement, are all a part of their inability to implement real-politik which has resulted in a reactionary trend in this country that threatens to polarize the political system and overwhelm what little freedom exists, much reminiscent of Germany in the 1930s."

In Chicago, *Second City* reported on two new University GLF groups, one in Evanston, at Northwestern (NUGLF), the other at Roosevelt

(RUGLF). On March 8, NUGLF held a "Teach-Out" in the University's Business Building, in conjunction with Women's Liberation and Men's Liberation; the latter "straight" group formed to examine male chauvinistic attitudes toward women and gays. In the *Daily Northwestern* NUGLF co-founder, Bill Dry, urged everyone, both gay and straight, to attend the "Teach-Out." Over 300 attended. The *Daily Northwestern* also published a series of articles by Baran Rosen about "the philosophy behind the increasing openness and spirit of protest of homosexuals." Rosen interviewed NUGLF's four founding members: Robert Birch, a graduate student in German; Maher Ahmad, a speech junior; Bill Dry, a graduate student in religion; the fourth student, a CAS freshman, called himself John. Dry, who Rosen observed was wearing a GLF button reading "Out of the closets and into the streets," said: "The homosexual must stop internalizing the guilt that society imposes on them and begin taking pride in themselves." Birch told the paper:

"The primary reason for establishing Gay Lib groups, is that members hope to liberate themselves and other homosexuals from the social, political and economic prejudice directed at them by heterosexual society, and to liberate heterosexual society from the ignorance and fear that cause prejudice."

The first dance held by University of Chicago GLF (UCGLF) was February 21 at Pierce Tower on the University of Chicago campus, where 660 people attended. A second dance on April 4 drew twice that number. In March, the *Seed* wrote of the first dance: "It was a far cry from the cold, crowded, and impersonal North-Side gay bars. If you give gay people a chance to dance, touch each other, and talk freely, they behave like 'respectable' human beings."

Unfortunately, the two gay on-campus dances didn't sit well with the University authorities. An editorial in the *Maroon* began:

"We were disturbed by the recent announcement by Edward Turkington, director of student housing, that Gay Liberation will no longer be allowed to hold dances in University residences as student activities. The reasons given for the decision were that Gay Lib dances attract too many non-University people."

The *Maroon* noted there were no security problems at either dance, no fights, no stolen coats. The university's decision to eliminate the dances is "weak-willed at best, discriminatory at worst," wrote the paper. UCGLF's response was to hold a Guerilla Dance in the Fred Hampton Gym on May 16. Organized by UCGLF member Step May, the dance was a protest against oppression of all people. Half of the 600 who attended were non-University guests.

This wasn't the only objection to GLF dances on-campus. In August

150 members of GLF and GAA, protested a similar decision made by school officials at New York University. Angela Douglas, in the *Los Angeles Free Press*, reported that several successful dances had taken place at NYU's Weinstein Hall. After a contract had been signed for five dances, officials changed their minds, saying they needed to consider whether homosexuality was immoral, or not. *Women's LibeRATion*, formerly *Rat*, reported that the Administration proposed hiring a psychiatrist to debate a psychiatrist hired by the Gay Student Liberation (GSL). The Administration would then meet behind closed doors and decide whether "gay people were crazy." GSL declined the offer. Another Administration objection, according to Ida Swearingen in *Win*, was that collecting donations endangered NYU's status as a tax-exempt organization. In protest, Swearingen wrote, GSL students occupied the sub-cellar of Weinstein Hall. They only left after fifty members of the Tactical Police Force gave them ten seconds to vacate the building. The protests continued, until school officials acquiesced.

The psychiatrist card was also played at the University of Texas (UT), when it declined to recognize GLF as a student organization. Austin's *Rag* wrote that UT feared GLF "would encourage persons to accept homosexuality rather than to seek professional help." Meanwhile, at the University of Michigan, President Robert Wright Fleming refused Ann Arbor GLF use of college facilities to hold a conference. On May 1, Ann Arbor and Detroit GLF picketed a tea party for the alumni, presided over by President Fleming. Two members of Chicago GLF were present, selling copies of Chicago's *Seed*, which contained a Gay Liberation Supplement. After a protracted battle, the first Ann Arbor GLF dance on the University of Michigan Campus took place on June 12, with entertainment from the Jeweltones, who the *Detroit Liberator* described as "awful," and Leaves of Grass, "indeed a very fine rock band." Two years later, the *Ann Arbor Sun* reported that GLF and Radical Lesbians pressured the University of Michigan into hiring two salaried gay program assistants, Cyndi Gair and Jim Toy.

The third UCGLF dance was off-campus, at the Coliseum Ballroom on April 18. The dance was the first citywide Gay-In. The event was a huge success, with 2,000 gay men and lesbians attending. However, organizing the event was fraught with problems. The first was that the Coliseum required insurance. *Second City* wrote:

> "After Gay Lib obtained an agreement to lease, insurance became an issue. Homosexuals having a dance found themselves a bad risk. A broker for Interstate Fire & Casualty Co. backed out of guaranteeing the insurance four days before the dance, when they found out just who was renting the Coliseum. Finally, insurance was obtained from California one day before the dance by the company that covered the Black Muslims' meeting in the Coliseum some time ago."

As GLF's David Thierry wrote in the *Chicago Gay Liberation Newsletter*: "A faggot dance was too big a risk!" The GLF Coliseum dance was a protest, a boycott of Chicago's Mafia-owned bars. Thierry continued:

"We asked those at the dance to boycott the bars for one night. Instead, they went to the bars after the dance, willing and eager to suck their oppressor's cock, begging to be screwed again. They'll continue to go to the bars until they realize that gay = faggot = nigger. They'll get themselves together when they're ready to be recognized as men, not the nigras they are to the bar owners. ... Forget your massa's voice, and listen to your own. It's telling you to come out. The revolution has just begun."

On March 8, cops from New York's 6th precinct raided the Snake Pit in the West Village, a Mafia-owned dive known to patrons as the Hepatitis Ward. An anonymous GLF reporter wrote in *Rat*:

"167 people were kept there for an hour and a half, then hauled into paddy wagons and unloaded into a big hall in the precinct house. They had not been told that they were under arrest or given information about their constitutional rights. Pigs began asking not only for their names and addresses, but their places of employment. At this, one terrified young man, Diego Vinales, ran from the room up a staircase. A minute later the other prisoners heard a crash, then a scream. He fell through the window and was impaled on an iron fence below. He and a hunk of the fence were taken to St. Vincent's Hospital, where he received quarts of blood, and remains in critical condition."

According to the *Great Speckled Bird*, five spikes went through Vinales' thigh and pelvis. The following day a protest emphasized the divergent philosophies of the Gay Liberation Front and the "one-issue" Gay Activists Alliance. The GLF reporter wrote in *Rat*:

"By Sunday night at 9 o'clock, less than 24 hours after the raid, a throng of radical men and women from the Gay Liberation Front and Women's Liberation and some liberal male chauvinists from the Gay Activists Alliance had assembled at Christopher Street and Sheridan Square. We were about 700 strong, and we were beautiful with a huge GLF banner at the head, we marched through the Village chanting 'Say it Loud-Gay is Proud.' We marched to the Precinct House to confront the pigs who tried to murder our brother. Other people, straights, joined us. After circling the hospital, the plans were to demonstrate at the Women's House of Detention in sympathy with the sisters who had been clubbed there at the International Women's Day demonstration on Saturday, not to mention the sisters who were inside. The Gay Activists Alliance martinets objected. ... They didn't give a shit about demonstrating for women."

After a cursory wave to the women's prison, the protestors arrived back at Sheridan Square:

"Martha of GLF stood on a water fountain to announce that Alternate U. had stayed open for us and that we should pick up food on the way over to the meeting there. Marty O'Brien of GAA then took the podium to say that those radicals who wanted could shout their brains out at Alternate U, but he was going home. He addressed us as 'Brothers … ' 'And sisters,' we shouted back. He ended his stuffy remarks with 'We shall overcome,' and we sang back, 'We shall overthrow.'"

After the Stonewall Riots, the exploitation of homosexuals by gay bars became a top priority for GLF. In "GLF Hits Exploitation," Ralph S. Schaffer wrote in the *Los Angeles Free Press*:

"With few exceptions, those who run gay bars, many of them straights, feed off the pocketbooks of gay people without taking any interest in the welfare of the gay community. Many of these bars actually resist improvement and liberation. … Some bars refuse to admit women, straight or gay, and will actually discourage their presence by spilling beer on them or what have you. Some bars admit only those wearing leather and other bars will reject the leather queens. Some bars, such as the Sewers of Paris, discriminate against different groups at different times. At the Sewers transvestites will be admitted if business is poor that night. But if business is good they will be excluded."

In Seattle's *Sabot*, W.C. wrote about the issue:

"Deep in the canton walls of downtown Seattle are the ghetto caves of Gay People. These dungeons (bars, baths, theatres) where no light shines by day or night and where people turn into cattle and are sold like meat in a butcher shop, become the habitual residency of needy gay people. Gay people who are looking for love or a life, come and find a complex system of exploitation. In return for your money they offer a chance to be placed on the meat rack and if you're really lucky you can have sex … unsatisfying and impersonal. It is a dubious chance at that, but the gay person has no escape, or rather HAD none until recently. It is now the time for us to STOP! … One way to stop this is to refuse to go, another is to become involved in GLF activities. Until you do this the sex they sell you will be little more than masturbation and the shit they cover with tinsel will be just that: shit."

In Venice, CA, the *Venice Beachhead* wrote:

"The police hate us. We're often reminded of this fact when the LAPD sends in some of its graduates of the VICE SQUAD finishing school, those oh-so-uptight sexual beings, to entrap the people in tea rooms, in secluded corners of the beach, and when we openly express our love for each other and go 'topless' at 'kiss-ins' and 'gay-ins."

The article goes on to say that Phil Ewing, an ex-cop who runs the Westwinds Bar, a "membership only" dance club, takes money from the gay community, while refusing to allow the club to be used for Sunday afternoon "Gay Days" on the beach. GLF/Venice promises to "liberate" the bar, saying, "We are organizing for the day when we will make the revolution. Come together!"

Ken Kelley in the *Ann Arbor Argus* attended the second public meeting of the University of Michigan GLF:

"The Flame Bar on West Washington St. is the main gathering place for homosexuals in Ann Arbor, and it's filthy. GLF members plan to present the owner with a list of demands to improve the bar, including the offer of free manual labor to do it, and if that fails, they will organize a boycott."

In another issue of the *Ann Arbor Argus*, GLF members Mike Jones, Genie Linzer, Larry Glover and Fred Uhl are interviewed. One had attended the UCGLF Coliseum dance in Chicago:

"They had a hassle about insurance for the building, which is bullshit, and they called a boycott of the bars in Chicago after the dance. ... I guess the bars really rake in the money, their drink prices are outrageous. Seems most bars in the country are expensive. The Flame isn't, but they have terrible drinks."

Most, but not all, gay bars were anti-GLF. Ads in the gay *Detroit Liberator* for the Lullaby Inn read: "GREATEST, NEWEST SPOT IN TOWN. We welcome Friends and Members of the Gay Liberation Front." In Chicago, the primary focus of GLF was the issue of dancing in bars. Although same-sex dancing wasn't illegal in Illinois, the cops interpreted it as "public indecency." The *Seed* reported that GLF had targeted the Normandy Inn, 744 Rush St., the largest gay bar in the city; the upstairs room held 500-600 people. In the *Roosevelt Torch*, John D. Maybauer, of the Roosevelt University GLF group, described the Normandy as "syndicate operated" and "hostile to its gay patrons." He called for a "freeing of the gay ghetto." In the *Mattachine Midwest Newsletter*, Steve Robertson wrote that on April 24th and 25th, the Normandy got its first taste of Gay Power as GLF picketed and emptied the bar. On April 29 the Bar Committee of GLF met with Wally and Jerry, the owners, who promised to "do everything in their power" to obtain a dancing license. A GLF leaflet entitled, "What the hell does Gay Lib think it's doing?" read: "The oppressive atmosphere of the Normandy must be removed. The right to dance, any tempo, any style, is thus a crucial step towards our personal and collective liberation." On May 14 the bar owners acquired a license and permitted same-sex dancing for the first time in Chicago.

In the spring of 1970, West Coast GLF groups boycotted the bars by organizing social events. The *Berkeley Tribe* reported on a Spring Fair Fling, organized by Berkeley GLF with entertainment by a band called the Buzzards–"three of their members were formerly with Creedence Clearwater Revival." Later, a GLF Olde English Faire was held with free gingerbread and apple cider: "Bring food: feel free to wear costumes. Bring things to the Free Store Trunk and get things from it. Trade things at the Barter Booth. Step right up to the Gay Lib kissing booth, dunk for apples … spin the bottle, anyone?" The event was a flop with only 20-30 people turning up. In the *Los Angeles Free Press*, Douglas Key reported on a GLF sponsored Gay-In, attended by nearly 2,000 people. Among the sideshows, a kissing booth, body-painting, gay guerilla theater, five outlaw marriages of gay people–three female couples and two male couples. The "weddings" were officiated by Helen Niihaus of the Society of Anubis and GLF's Morris Kight.

In March, Chicago's *Seed* published an eight page Gay Liberation Supplement. One article was "Duck and the Dragon Killer" by Michelle Brody, a founding member of UCGLF. The article focused on the lack of women in Gay Lib. Ads like the one in *Maroon* that read, "GAY WOMEN: Gay Liberation is no bastion of male chauvinism. Come join us," did little to swell the numbers of women. Brody wrote:

"There aren't enough gay women in Gay Lib, for a lot of reasons. Probably mostly because Gay Lib, like everything else in Amerika, except Cold Power, Virginia Slims and living girdles, is considered to be for men. While many of the problems of gay women are closely allied with Women's Lib, I think it's important for gay women to become active in Gay Lib. First, because Gay Lib is the best place to work on erasing male chauvinism and creating an atmosphere of sexual equality, and consideration purely as a person. We've achieved it pretty damn well already, and we're really working on it. We (gay women and gay men) don't need to threaten each other. Secondly, as gay women, we've already hassled through a lot of things that Women's Lib is just now dealing with. I see the aims of Gay Lib and Women's Lib as very similar; we're working together somewhat now, and greater unity will come. But we have to get our individual shits together first.

"Another reason that there are so few women in Gay Lib is the fact, for better or worse, there isn't the sense of community (ghetto) among gay women that there is among gay men. Many gay women have no one at all with whom they can relate in a homosexual context. In a sense we have it better than gay guys because society merely dismisses us with a casual wave of its wrist. We're not angry enough to fight back, and since we're just women anyway, we know we're supposed to just be passive, be docile, sit still, shut up, and take it. But it's time to be angry."

Brody's article ends with, "Don't you think it's about time you stopped hiding?"

In June, Atlanta's *Great Speckled Bird* published a press release from GLF at Florida State University in Tallahassee. The group, founded in April, was beset with problems. The University denied them use of campus facilities. A letter in *Flambeau*, the student newspaper, signed by fourteen faculty members, expressed "shock and dismay" that the paper carried GLF ads. A state senator pressured the university to "eliminate" GLF from campus. In addition, the Tallahassee GLF was refused a bank account. Another GLF with banking problems was at the University of Colorado. In January 1971, Philadelphia's *Thursday's Drummer* reported that GLF was refused a bank account at Boulder's National State Bank. After opening the account, National State Bank Vice President A. M. Clearman informed GLF the bank could not act "as your financial medium." The letter included a cashier's check for the GLF's deposit and a request to return its supply of temporary checks. *Drummer* wrote:

> "Clearman said that the GLF is controversial and that because of its nature, 'We don't want their name associated with ours on printed checks.' He also said that the bank had not, to his knowledge, denied checking facilities to any other 'controversial groups.' Clearman said he did not consider Women's Lib has that kind of connotation,' neither did 'peace groups.'"

On April 9, 1970, a GLF was founded at the University of Illinois Chicago-Circle Campus (UIC-CC). The group declared May 7 Gay Liberation Day on campus. *The Daily Illini* wrote: "On this day male and female homosexuals will circulate leaflets, hold a panel discussion in CCC, and speak in classrooms." Three days after the UIC-CCGLF formed, another at Northern Illinois University-DeKalb received recognition as an official student organization by the NIU Students Association.

On April 16, UCGLF celebrated its own Gay Liberation Day, part of a weeklong worldwide protest against the Vietnam War. In Copenhagen and Rome violence broke out as thousands of protestors clashed with police. In the US riot squads and tear gas were used to quell skirmishes in Boston, Detroit, Washington DC, Madison, and Berkeley. In Chicago the protest was peaceful. Nobody was arrested. Not even those marching with Viet Cong flags. At 3:00 p.m. at Civic Center Plaza, gay anti-war protestors marched together to the Federal Building under a banner reading: "POWER TO ALL OPPRESSED PEOPLES–GAY LIBERATION." This was the first time homosexuals marched openly on the streets of Chicago. After the rally some lesbians joined Women's Lib picketing Hugh Hefner's Playboy Mansion, where a $100 a ticket celebrity anti-Vietnam War fundraiser was taking place. While Women's Lib shouted, "Don't go into Hefner's Playboy mansion. His girlie magazine makes women into sex objects," anti-war celebrities crossed the picket line, including Dennis Hopper currently riding high on the hog from *Easy Rider*, Candice Bergen, and science fiction writer and director Rod Serling, who commented on the Women's Lib protestors: "It's a matter of priorities. Women aren't getting killed. The men in Vietnam are."

After the rally, the protestors walked along sidewalks through the Loop to Michigan Avenue where they "liberated" the Tribune Building from the paper's biased coverage of gays. In fact, the *Chicago Tribune* was the only mainstream paper to cover the rally:

"One hundred members of the Gay Liberation Front, protesting alleged harassment of homosexuals by police and society, staged a noon rally yesterday in Grant Park … .The rally's theme, 'out of the closets and into the streets,' was demonstrated by the group as they held hands while sitting on the grass in the park. … Another 150 persons, mostly office workers on their lunch hours, stood nearby, attracted by colorful flags and signs proclaiming Gay Power and Gay is Beautiful."

In Detroit, GLF caused a rift between the Rev. Robert Morrison of St. Joseph's Episcopal Church and Richard Emrich, diocesan Bishop of Michigan. Morrison believed the church should be a sanctuary for young men opposed to the Vietnam War, and as a meeting place for GLF and other revolutionary groups. Morrison's stance so angered the rightist Emrich that he cut off funds to the church. Morrison told *Fifth Estate*: "The bishop is coercing us to kick this group [GLF] out of the church. And we simply won't give in to this type of fascist tactic." On the subject of Emrich, Morrison said: "This man is impossible and should no longer be bishop. Because of his inhuman views, I am convinced that the bishop is unchristian; he is inhuman; he has lost track of the decency of mankind and I call upon him to repent of his evil and of the overt and covert acts he has perpetrated on humanity." The mainstream press spiked the story. An editorial in the *Detroit Liberator* suggested church influence caused the news blackout:

"The Detroit news media have blatantly disregarded their duty to the public by allowing itself to be suppressed by the oldest and one of the most decadent institutions in existence today. … If the Detroit news media can be suppressed in this instance, what else is going on that they aren't telling the public about?"

One controversial protest against Bishop Emrich took place on November 7, 1970 during the Convention of the Michigan Diocese of the Episcopal Church at the University of Michigan. Steve, in the *Detroit Liberator*, wrote that he and other GLF members joined the congregation at the Episcopal Church on Woodward near Wayne State:

> "When it came time for communion we walked hand in hand, in pairs, to the altar, Ken & Bob, Margaret & Terry, Jim & John, Claude & Me, and numbers of others whose spirits were as high as their anxiety. We all received the wafer one by one, then Ken & Bob received the wine. Proudly they stood up, turned around … and spit it over the floor. … They refused to give wine to anymore of us, so Claude and I proudly stood, turned to each other, and kissed in front of the congregation."

The Rev. Robert Morrison, who preferred to be called "Bob," retired and gave his last Sunday service on May 31, 1970. Sunny King in the *Detroit Liberator* described Morrison as a man who gave sanctuary to gay people. King also asked the gay community to attend his final service and give him a "rousing send-off."

In Seattle, there was an "Establishment" gay group called the Dorian Society, founded in 1967 by Nick Heer, a professor at the University of Washington. The group provided referrals for gay counseling, organized social events, and sent speakers into schools. However, in the early months of 1970, there was no radical Gay Liberation Front in Seattle. In April, "Douglas" wrote in Seattle's *Helix*:

> "Gay liberation is off to an uncertain but determined start in Seattle. Much milling about of concerned gay heads, official, and protean unofficial homophile organizations—everyone has ideas, some have plans for action, but very few seem to have any notion of how to get this thing organized on a widespread general basis. … We are aware of our relation to society; we know that we don't fit, don't belong, and, because we groove our trip, we don't want to belong. This makes us social drop-outs ('Heads,' 'Hippies.' 'Commie-fag-pinko-freaks,' by any name). We are in fact gay heads, an oppressed minority among the general culture, a respected faction and well enough received fraternity of the True Faith among the revolutionary counter-culture."

In September, Angela Douglas wrote in the *Los Angeles Free Press*:

> "There is no Gay Liberationist group in Miami, although many younger gays have expressed desires for such a group. A small GLF is functioning in Florida's state capital, Tallahassee. … Many gays in the Miami area do not feel that a GLF is needed or that such a group would be allowed to exist by the repressive forces in this area. Although GLF is not particularly leftist (each GLF is organically developed according to the general climate of the area in which it exists), the U.S. government has placed an official leftist label on GLF as a whole. Considering that Miami has a population of around 100,000 Cuban refugees who are strongly anti-Communist, a GLF in Miami might run into considerable difficulty."

In New York, the Radical Lesbians split from GLF and confronted homophobia in Women's Lib. According to *Rat*, the second annual "Congress to Unite Women" at New York's Intermediate School 70 was a "Congress to Unite White Middle-Class Women," to the exclusion of blacks, the poor, and lesbians. On May 1, the first day of the three-day conference, three hundred women waited for the Congress to come to order:

> "The lights went out, people heard running, laughter, a rebel yell here and there, and when the lights were turned back on, those same 300 women found themselves in the hands of the LAVENDER MENACE. 'Lavender menace' a taunt of the white male press rose incarnate in the persons of the Radical Lesbians of New York who, because of discrimination and sexism within the Women's Liberation, took matters into their own hands to bring their affirmative and compelling awareness to the women of the Congress. For the first time since women's liberation began, the subject of lesbianism was brought into the open. ... As the menaces surrounded the audience and liberated the microphone, rose-colored signs sprang up on the walls and podium: 'SUPERDYKE LOVES YOU; TAKE A LESBIAN TO LUNCH; WOMEN'S LIBERATION IS A LESBIAN PLOT.'"

Lesbians in the "Movement" were "coming out." On January 15, 1970, the first issue of the Berkeley-based *It Ain't Me Babe* was published, the first Women's Lib-era feminist newspaper. The paper was uncompromising, one cover depicting Richard Nixon with a missile penis, raping Cambodian women and children. In the May 21 issue, Judy of Gay Women's Liberation San Francisco wrote "Lesbians As Women." In a sidebar called "Lesbians As Bogeywomen," she wrote:

> "Any form of behavior that doesn't fit into the image that television and *Reader's Digest* believe the American people should be like, is usually categorized as either subnatural or supernatural. The myths about homosexuality fall into both categories, depending on how close it is to being you. Lesbians are subnatural when they live next door and supernatural when they live in Paris and write books."

In May 1970 everything changed. "Blood on Kent State" was the headline in the *Great Speckled Bird*. North Star in the *Berkeley Barb* wrote: "'Rise Up Angry!!! No More Lying Down' ... Tuesday, May 4th, 1970 four students die in front of a National Guard firing squad." The killing of unarmed students at State University in Kent, OH, shocked the nation. *Tin soldiers and Nixon coming, We're finally on our own. This summer I hear the drumming, Four dead in Ohio* wrote Neil Young in his song *Ohio*. National Guardsmen fired sixty-seven rounds into a crowd of students protesting

President Richard Nixon's Invasion of Cambodia. A photograph of a fallen student on the cover of the *Daily Planet* had the word AVENGE scrawled across it. The shootings led to hundreds of universities, colleges, and high schools, closing in protest. Again, on May 15, at Jackson State University in Jackson, MS, another protest against Nixon's Cambodian Incursion, turned deadly when Phillip Lafayette Gibbs, 21, and James Earl Green, 17, were killed by Mississippi Highway Patrol shotguns. Five other men and four women were wounded. Dave Doggett, a *Kudzu* reporter, and Robert Clarke, Mississippi State Representative, wrote in the *Great Speckled Bird*:

> "When the officers finished shooting, they picked up their empty shells and put them in their pockets. Students asked them to help with the wounded and they would not. One officer was finally heard to radio in, 'Send over some ambulances, we've got some niggers in the dorm.' Meanwhile the National Guard came in and helped evacuate the wounded and the dead on stretchers."

In a *Kudzu* editorial published in the *Great Speckled Bird*, an African student at Jackson State University speaking at a Masonic Temple memorial rally, renounced non-violence as a "counterproductive strategy.' He called for new leaders to "replace the tired, unimaginative old guard." Abner Spence in Madison's *Kaleidoscope* wrote: "The revolution is comin' within the next ten years. We gotta understand that pig Amerika is falling apart real fast now. We don't have lots of time anymore. So … first thing is that EVERY KID GOTTA GET A GUN. No shittin'." On page 13 is an article giving tips on how to buy a used gun, what to buy, and a list of "nice guns to have around." Over the next few weeks *Kaleidoscope* published more articles about firearms. In the June 17 issue, Michael Carliner interviewed Abbie Hoffman. Asked about the violent repressions, Hoffman replied: "I think we have to arm ourselves-we have to arm and we have to prepare to defend ourselves militarily. We are in a life or death struggle. … I think young people should begin the task of training themselves to be armed fighters." This fiery rhetoric wasn't limited to the male-dominated radical press. On June 26, the first issue of *Ain't I a Woman?*, a Midwest Women's Lib paper out of Iowa City, IA, taught women how to hold and fire a gun. Firearms also appeared in later issues, including a drawing of a woman waving a rifle aloft on the September 11 issue.

As Women's Liberation publications appeared, more openly lesbian writers found a venue for their work. There was also an increase in lesbian voices in the male-dominated underground press. The *Los Angeles Free Press* published Karla Jay's "Here Comes the Lavender Menace," and Cherie Matisse's "We Are Raised As Sex Objects, Future Wives and Mothers." In the same issue, Virginia Hoeffding "came out" of the closet in a letter entitled "Dear Mom." It begins:

"This is going to be a difficult letter to write; but I've known for some time that it would have to be written sooner or later. For the past several months, I've been trying to come to terms with the fact that I'm homosexual. Before you start having pink and purple fits, at least finish reading this; I want you to understand as fully as possible what's in my mind, and this is the easiest way I know to get it across."

In the *Las Vegas Free Press*, Radicalesbians wrote: "What is a lesbian? A lesbian is the rage of all women condensed to the point of explosion." Milwaukee's *Kaleidoscope*, published Martha Shelley's "Women of Lesbos." Shelley, an anti-Vietnam War activist and member of New York GLF, wrote:

"Lesbianism is one road to freedom-freedom from oppression by men. … I do not mean to condemn all males. I have found some beautiful, loving men among the revolutionaries, among the hippies, and the male homosexuals. But the average man-including the average student male radical-wants a passive sex-object cum domestic cum baby nurse to clean up after him while he does all the fun things and bosses her around-while he plays either bigshot executive or Che Guevara-he is my oppressor and my enemy."

In the *Berkeley Tribe*, Judy Grahn wrote "Lesbians As Women":

"At times the alienation of homosexuals seems more complete than that of any other group. We are kept as far away from the two great spheres of human influence-children and government-as possible. Our sexual preference is so far underground that we cannot ordinarily 'confess' it to our friends, our bosses, our teachers, our parents, or our preachers, and still hope to earn a living or be welcome in their lives. In short, we are a threat to EVERYBODY.

"To deflect the antagonism we arouse by being a disruption in the general order, we have done what every minority group does-taken on the role of jackass. All the traditional American clowns: the witty dyke or drag queen; the grinning black; the giggling Chinese; the giddy and compulsively smiling secretary-are saying in effect; 'Hey boss-you don't have to beat me-I'm not a serious human being.

"Now we are beginning to take ourselves seriously, and slowly getting our heads together to find out how to radically change our position in this country-how to get other people to take our problems seriously."

19

CHRISTOPHER STREET GAY LIBERATION DAY
AND AFTERWARDS

New York, Chicago, Los Angeles, and San Francisco celebrated the first anniversary of the Stonewall Riots with parades, marches and Gay-Ins. In Los Angeles, the giant jar of Vaseline GLF float caused controversy, and at the San Francisco Gay-In cops on "Honda Hogs" made arrests. At the time, police in Los Angeles stepped up their campaign against homosexuals, as they did in New York, Atlanta, San Francisco and New Orleans. In response, militant groups like the Gay Revos threatened to retaliate with bombs and guns. Meanwhile, GLF lashed out at other gay organizations like the North American Conference of Homophile Organizations and Metropolitan Community Church, Radical Lesbians criticized GLF, and GLF and Women's Lib attacked the underground press for publishing pornographic ads. In addition, transvestites and transsexuals spoke out against "communistic" gays. At the end of 1970, some GLF groups were in tatters, while others, like New Orleans, were just starting up.

"Who Am I?

"I lived many thousands of years ago and I still live today. I will die when mankind fails. I am a woman. I am a man. Sometimes I change from one to the other. I am an Atheist. I believe in God. I come from every race, every nation, every little town across the face of the earth. I am always with you. I may be your sister, your brother, your son, your daughter, your mother, your father, or your bedfellow. I may be you. I am an artist, a farmer, a senator, a bricklayer, a cop. Sometimes you recognize me, usually you don't. I used to be silent, but I'm not anymore. Look around! Can you see me? I am a

homosexual."–Seattle's *Sabot* newspaper.

In early June 1970, underground newspapers began publishing articles about the upcoming one-year anniversary of the Stonewall Riots. The *Ann Arbor Argus* published the Chicago Pride Week schedule and listed the Midwest GLF's: Kansas City, MO; Minneapolis, MN; Detroit, East Lansing, Ann Arbor and Kalamazoo, MI; Madison and Milwaukee, WI; and DeKalb, Normal, Champaign, Carbondale, Evanston and Chicago, IL. Chicago Pride Week included a rally and a march, a Gay Liberation dance, and the Midwest Regional Gay Liberation Conference. Philadelphia's *Distant Drummer* wrote:

> "What may be the largest gathering of homosexuals in the history of the world is scheduled for New York City this month. The occasion is Christopher Street Gay Liberation Days-June 26-27-28 being called by New York's Gay Liberation Front along with other homosexual organizations."

Rat published a schedule of New York Gay Pride Week events, including workshops and an erotic art show at the Thompson Gallery, 20 Cornelia St. All events held at the Lesbian Center were restricted to women-only. In *Nola Express,* out of New Orleans, and Austin's *Rag,* Don Jackson wrote about the Christopher Street West celebration in Los Angeles, "co-sponsored by almost all Gay organizations, several churches and underground newspapers." In the article, Jackson embellished the events at Stonewall:

> "The pigs retreated inside the club, barricading the door. The Gays battered at the door with an uprooted parking meter. Suddenly a brick shattered the plate-glass window, showering the pigs with glass. Another brick hit a pig's eye. Seconds later a fire bomb exploded inside the room, setting the place on fire. Seven days of disturbances now called the 'Stonewall Revolt' followed."

The *Las Vegas Free Press* predicted 3,000 gays would join the parade in Los Angeles: "Buses are being chartered to bring groups from San Francisco, San Diego and throughout the state. City officials have indicated that the parade permit will be issued." Permits had been a problem. The *Berkeley Tribe* wrote: "Los Angeles Pig Chief [Edward Davis] claimed 'a parade permit for homosexuals is like giving a parade permit to robbers and burglars.'" Attempting to halt the parade, LAPD demanded $1 million bond to cover injuries from the expected rioting and looting. Police further demanded one male monitor for every twenty demonstrators or, as the *Berkeley Tribe* put it: "Be your own pigs." Also, organizers had to agree the parade would be cancelled if the crowd were less than 2000, or more than

4000. GLF sued the "pigs" and won a permit.

The dispute came during what Don Jackson, in the *Los Angeles Free Press*, called an LAPD "reign of terror" on the gay community. Jackson wrote: "Arrests on trumped-up charges have been greatly accelerated. Two Gay private clubs were raided in a single week. Indiscriminate random arrests are being made. 'Round-ups' on Hollywood Blvd, and Selma Ave. have become nightly affairs." In retaliation, a militant group called Gay Action Element used red and black spray paint to graffiti "Gay Power" slogans, like "Fuck Chief Davis," around the city. Another group suspected of the Gay Power graffiti were the Gaysanos, an ultra-right gay group who fled Cuba and Castro's anti-gay policies. Jackson also noted that militant groups around the nation were taking action, like the Gay Revos in New York, the Freaking Fag Revolutionaries in Chicago, the Weathersuckers in Berkeley, and the Purple Panthers in San Francisco. "The super-militants view Gay Liberation as 'Uncle Toms,'" wrote Jackson. One militant informant told him, "Gay Libbers want to sit around a table and bargain with society for their rights. We will go out and take them."

In Milwaukee's *Kaleidoscope*, an article headlined, "Violent Gay Revolution Now!!" began:

> "The Gay Revos have threatened to bomb underground papers that do not publish their news. ... A letter to the editor of the *Los Angeles Free Press* said 'the staff and editors of FREEP greet members of Gay Lib with giggles and sniggers,' that most radicals view the male homosexual as a 'soft and cowardly fairy,' and that if homosexuals must fight for their rights, 'violence and destruction will be firstly aimed at radical movement organizations. A firebomb for you ... surprises are coming.'"

One Gay Revos member said: "It has begun. Guns are being loaded. Knives are being sharpened. Bombs are being made. We declare war on our oppressors."

Chicago's celebration of Stonewall was a political march and rally, not a parade. There were no drag queens. No floats. It started with a noon rally at Bughouse Square. One speaker, Sunny King of Detroit GLF, told the crowd she had given up her job to work full-time on gay liberation because freedom was more important than job security. Also speaking at the rally were ACLU lawyer Jonathan Smith, psychologist Kitch Childs, and Chicago GLF's Michael Barta, and Henry Weimhoff. The marchers then held hands, linked arms, and chanted, as they marched through downtown Chicago to Civic Center Plaza for more speeches and a circle dance around a Picasso sculpture. "By this time," the *Seed* wrote, "the pig quota was up to five squadrols and two meat wagons." The following day there was a picnic in Lincoln Park. The *Detroit Liberator* wrote: "The police were having a field day with their cameras. It seems the Chicago Police department keeps a complete file, including pictures, of such dangerous radicals." The Chicago Stonewall celebrations ended with a dance at the Aragon Ballroom. The *Detroit Liberator* continued:

"The Aragon management offered the ballroom to Chicago GLF and from there, the dance was entirely managed by Mr. Jerry Cohen, Mr. Gary Chichester, and Mr. Nick Kelly. The gentlemen signed three fine rock groups for the evening's entertainment: Ponch Pilot, Pytheus Tribe, and Corky Siegels' Happy Year Band."

In July, Angela Douglas wrote in the *Los Angeles Free Press* that "1,200 gays freed themselves of almost all inhibitions and fears" to celebrate Christopher Street West, the brainchild of Morris Kight, founder of Los Angeles GLF. Douglas described the parade:

"Several of the floats drew tremendous ovation. One by one, members of the Gay Liberation Front carried a cross with a gay Jesus tied to it, who was being prodded by an 'officer of the law.' ... A fleet of motorcyclists stunned many. A transsexual, Connie Vaughn, rode proudly in an open convertible. She is over six foot tall. A float by the Militant Gay Movement consisted of a funky truck with an eight-foot tall jar of Vaseline, accompanied by the words, 'Ain't nothing no good without the grease.' Greg Byrd, a black gay student who was the first GLFLA chairman, rode on the fender of the 'funky truck.'"

Not everyone appreciated the humor of the Vaseline float, but Lee Heflin defended it from a pagan standpoint in the *Los Angeles Free Press*:

"What was, in reality, a Dionysian Rite was led by a Christian preacher (this is no attack on TP [Rev. Troy Perry]) who frowned heavily at the float which really struck to the heart of the matter, the huge jar of Vaseline. This was the one statement which openly spoke of what homosexuality is all about ... that men can and do find Supreme Ecstasy in each other's bodies."

On August 14, the *Los Angeles Free Press* published a "Gay Supplement" which included three first-hand accounts of Christopher Street West, written by Morris Kight, Lee Heflin, and Geno Vezina. Kight wrote:

"Christopher Street West has become an institution. Just about everybody in the United States who reads a newspaper, listens to the radio, or sees television knows about it; indeed, the European television audience was treated to a special on it. Why an institution? Simply because it was an historic landmark, a high point of pride, and because it worked so well. ... Within two hours of its end, the first pleas came that it be an annual event. This then is the perfect time to announce that it will be–in the *Los Angeles Free Press* All-Gay Special!"

Instead of a parade, San Francisco held a Gay-In in Golden Gate Park. The *Berkeley Tribe* wrote:

"Far out-Fellini/Visconti-psychedelic pig state in Technicolor. … Today pigs riding Hondas, horses, paddy wagons, came to join 800 Gay freaks sitting in the sun, celebrating Christopher Street Liberation Day. … Pigs posted themselves everywhere. … They search jackets, ask all the women for their I.D.'s, bust some more people, maybe seven."

Phil Pukas in the *Berkeley Barb* wrote that at one point a mounted patrolman was circled by gays singing *God Bless America.* The police retaliated with cries of, "Why don't you queers get out of here," "faggot," "punk," and "fairy." After the arrests, GLF's Leo Laurence told the *Berkeley Barb*: "If they continue to persecute minorities like ours, we have no choice but armed revolution."

In the weeks leading up to Christopher Street Liberation Day, the San Francisco "Honda Hogs" arrested gay men in the parks, on the street, and in restrooms. The *Berkeley Tribe* wrote:

"The parks belong to the pigs. They boast of three hundred busts they have made in the last two weeks. Honda donated a bike fleet to the pig's fruit and dope patrol, as they call it–for easy access into the park's private parts to capture society's pariahs engaging in villainous acts against nature. … In one hour, pigs busted 13 people in Macy's T-room."

The *Berkeley Tribe* pointed out that oral copulation was punishable by a $1000 fine and a year in jail. The cover of this issue of the paper had a drawing of a toilet stall with gay graffiti. "UP THE ASS OF THE RULING CLASS," "OFF THE HONDA HOGS," "SUCK COCK BEAT THE DRAFT," "YOU ALWAYS DO BETTER AT MACY'S."

In New York, the turnout was larger. Milwaukee's *Kaleidoscope* wrote: "A force of 10,000 homosexuals, men and women, proud and strong, marched out of Greenwich Village, world capital of gay people, walked briskly up Sixth Avenue and into Central Park for a Gay-In." In the article, Ron Auerbacher, a GLF member, shared his feelings of liberation:

"I spent four and a half years in therapy, feeling guilty and ashamed. The energy spent in keeping my homosexuality a secret dominated every day of my life. This whole weekend was such fantastic reinforcement–we really are sane and we really can be happy. … We saw that gay people could be in couple's, lie down with someone you like, walk through the park with your arm around another man's shoulder. It was really liberating, a real taste of a post-revolutionary situation. It gives gay people something to fight for. I really see that we're not going to be free until we have a gay army ready to defend ourselves and a gay media to educate."

On the presence of women at New York's St. Christopher Day Parade, Ellen DeBoz, another GLF member, told *Kaleidoscope*:

"I thought that far fewer women came out to march than participated in the overall weekend, which indicates to me that there is still a great deal of fear on the part of women. At the Lesbian Center there was a tremendous spirit of camaraderie, a feeling of closeness, at the dinner, and at the workshops. The women who did participate in the march, did so with a tremendous sense of elation and high spirits."

In Washington DC's *Quicksilver Times* "a radical lesbian" reported on "four girls and two dogs" arriving in New York for the celebration. She described activities at the Lesbian Center:

"First a pot-luck supper—what a feast! We swapped recipes and sampled cheeses, breads and salads. ... An all-women's dance downstairs brought over a hundred of us together. (After some previous dances with gay men the women realized that the male-dominated affairs oppressed them and they preferred sisters only events). ... The next day, apprehensive and excited, we joined forces. Over ten thousand of us merged, a coalition of gay groups, militant and moderate, from all over the east coast. ... What a mixture in the movement: pretty girls, strong women, college students, black, oriental, white. We were tired, relieved, happy. We had shared with our sisters a newfound pride."

Several lesbians traveled to New York from Iowa City, IA. One account in *Ain't I a Woman* read:

"We ... met four sisters from Washington D.C. and discussed two divisions between people: Male/Female and Gay/Straight. We mostly agreed that the biggest gap was female/male and that gay women should only ally with gay men in so far as the relation remains unoppressive [sic], however, one GLF woman, who strongly hopes the Gay Liberation Front doesn't split along sex lines, thought that gay people who feel a common oppression must stick together to fight it. ... Politically, we found ourselves more or less together with the sisters from Lesbian Liberation. However, the All-Women Dances on Fri. and Sat. nights pointed out to us how differently we relate to each other in the Midwest. We never dance with each other because there are no places in Iowa City where women can be together. It was so beautiful seeing women dancing with each other."

In Pennsylvania's *Lancaster Independent Press*, "Demos" described the New York celebrations:

"The march was the major event of Gay Pride Week. Other events included a demonstration in support of homosexual law reform at the offices of governor Rockefeller, political workshops, dances, and forums. The final event was a dance Sunday evening at Alternate U, one of the free universities in New York. The crowd at the dance, which was mostly male due to a competing event for women, consisted primarily of movement types and really was, for a change, both gay and liberated. Men danced with women, women danced with women, men with men, and everybody danced together in circle dances which sprang up spontaneously."

In the summer of 1970, while new GLF groups were active in some cities, in others there was no presence at all. In *Nola Express*, Mike Higson interviewed adult bookstore owner Fred Lund:

Q: "How do you explain the absence of an organization like Gay Liberation Front in New Orleans?"

Lund: "In the Quarter anyone from Suburbia is a deviate. The people living here make up a conglomerate of minorities—you have gays, antiquarians, blacks, heads, and so on—therefore the norm here wouldn't be the norm in Gretna. And here we haven't seen the harassment that gays have experienced in New York & San Francisco. The biggest thing in this town is that they arrest a person by entrapment & then expect a payment. But generally they're so bad at it, all the person needs is a competent lawyer."

Lund goes on to say he was involved with the Mattachine Society in "SF, LA, NY, Washington DC and Philly":

Q: "Are any of these organizations here? [New Orleans]."

Lund: "None of them."

A month later, Don Jackson in the *Nola Express* suggested Fred Lund had not been truthful about the status of gays in New Orleans:

"Lund represents the views of the Gay Establishment. Contrary to Lund's statement: 'There's never been a need' for Gay Lib in New Orleans, it is needed very badly. … Gays are constantly harassed, brutalized and blackmailed in New Orleans. Entrapment and enticement arrests are regularly made in the men's room at the Fisherman's Market, in City Park, at the Greyhound bus terminal, and so on. … The oppression of homosexuals in New Orleans is worse than many other places for a number of reasons. The New Orleans gay community is unique. For over a hundred years, New Orleans has been a refugee camp for homosexuals. They came here from all over the South, but not because it was so good, but because other places were so bad. There was no place for gays in the feudalistic and puritanical old south. New Orleans was a lusty, capitalistic island in a feudal sea. Capitalists had darkies from the slave areas to clean the house, shuffle in with drinks and say 'Yassuh,' while queers dyed and curled the hair of ageing matrons, decorated houses and made dresses and gowns for milady to wear. … Gay Liberation says this must all end. We're throwing our curling irons & sewing kits into the trash can of history."

In Atlanta, homosexuals were integrated into the hippie bohemian culture. In the *Great Speckled Bird*, Gene Guerrero, Jr. looked back at its history:

"It grew around the Atlanta Art School, located on Peachtree near 15th. In those days (late fifties) before the corporations decided that art was a necessary part of good business, the Art School was a pretty open, groovy place. One of the first coffeehouses, the Golden Horn, opened near the Art School during the folk music craze begun by the Kingston Trio. … In 1966 a student at the Art School, David Braden, opened an Art Gallery on the north side of 14th. That was Mandorla No.1 and when he moved it to the corner of Peachtree and 14th it became Mandorla No. 2. In the basement Braden opened a coffeehouse–The Catacombs. Braden was gay and was out front about it. People respected him for that and for the openness of his gallery to new art. In the summer of 1967 when kids, mostly from metro Atlanta, began to come into the area, Mandoria was the natural place to go. A few hip people began to sit on the porch or on the wall across the street. Summer of 1967 was the Haight-Ashbury summer, and news media across the country began looking around their towns for hippies. Atlanta was no exception. They found Braden and made him into the 'leader of the hippie colony.' The cops got uptight, and Braden was busted for possession in November 1967. He was sentenced to seven years … "

In Madison's *Kaleidoscope* two anonymously penned articles appeared in August: "Message From a Gay Sister," and "… and From a Straight Sister." Both pieces focused on the redundancy of men. The Gay Sister wrote:

"The lesbian, through her ability to obtain love and sexual satisfaction from other women, is freed of dependence on men for love, sex and money. She does not have to do menial chores for them, nor cater to their egos, nor submit to hasty and inept sexual encounters. She is freed from fear of unwanted pregnancy and the pains of childbirth, and from the drudgery of child-raising."

The Straight Sister added:

"I hate men. They oppress me and make my life miserable. … But, the men in the movement are different–bullshit! … When you find all the naked women with their legs spread apart in the 'movement underground press,' and you complain to the man (the editors of those are ALWAYS men) he says something like, 'Are you ashamed of your body?' … All I know is that you won't find me walking around in a fucking mini skirt. I am not here to give pleasure to men, to feed them or to fuck them. I AM NOT A WHORE. Those that think I am had better watch out. Someday, you will meet a real castrating female."

In the first six months of 1970, pro-feminist Men's Lib groups began to form. According to the *Berkeley Barb*, one Men's Lib group in Berkeley "reversed the roles, got their hands white, and staged a bake sale" to raise money for the Women's Center. In New York's *Liberation*, a monthly started in 1956 by political activists A.J. Muste, David Dellinger, and Sidney Lens, Jack Sawyer wrote:

"Male liberation calls for men to free themselves of the sex role stereotypes that limit their ability to be human. Sex role stereotypes say that men should be dominant; achieving and enacting a dominant role in relations with others is often taken as an indicator of 'Success.'"

In Chicago, Men Against Cool (MAC) described themselves as, "cool radicals," adding: "We had been typical white men, into being superior ballplayers, students, fighters, etc. Then we became radicalized and we rejected all that bourgeois society told us." A MAC press release published in the *Seed* read:

"As Amerikan males we are denied the freedom to express the anguish of insecurity. Instead we are driven to find a false security in our status as superior beings—as those in control. In the same way that we are taught to prove our balls by screwing women, we try to become men by degrading blacks, and exploiting the less powerful countries in the world. Our exaggerated self-importance blinds us and dehumanizes us. Our chauvinism allows us to callously exploit our environment and the people in it. Can you dig this? We are fighting these chauvinistic tendencies in ourselves and urge other men to join us in this struggle for our own personalities."

A month later, *Seed* published "Men Against the Boy," an update of MAC's activities. On June 27, during Chicago's Stonewall celebrations, MAC and GLF protested outside the Playboy club. Approximately eighty men handed out 1,500 leaflets and "got into a lot of raps, both with turned on people and with hecklers." They carried signs that read: "MEN SHOULD BE WARM NOT COOL"; "MEN CAN BE TENDER"; "GAY BROTHERS SUPPORT OUR SISTERS"; "SMASH RACISM, IMPERIALISM AND PLAYBOY."

On August 26–30, 1970 at the North American Conference of Homophile Organizations (NACHO) in San Francisco, the widening gulf between the old guard Mattachine-style "Establishment Gays" and the new post-Stonewall radicals surfaced again. NACHO was an uneasy alliance of homophile groups formed in 1966. The conference was contentious with

GLF taking over and passing resolutions supporting the Black Panthers, the Women's Liberation Front, and anti-Vietnam war groups. In Elizabeth A. Armstrong's *Forging Gay Identities: Organizing Sexuality in San Francisco, 1950-1994*, the author quotes Rev. Jim Rankin in *Gay Sunshine*, who described the Conference as: "The battle that ended the homophile movement." NACHO was slated to meet again on Fire Island in 1971, but the alliance fell apart and dissolved soon after the San Francisco debacle. The report "NACHO Generates Controversy" appeared in the *Mattachine Midwest Newsletter*:

> "Time was given to our friends from the local Gay Liberation Front to hear their views and ideas. Unfortunately we were not able to follow the proposed conference agenda, due to the fact that the local radical GLF people wanted to be seated and have voting rights at the conference, forgetting the NACHO by-laws."

The radical element's take on the NACHO meeting was scathing. Leo E. Laurence wrote in the *Berkeley Barb*:

> "Bitchy, frightened 'Aunties' of the Gay Establishment this week refused to support the Black Panther Party when the Gay Liberation Front included the BPP in a Women's-Lib support resolution passed by NACHO meeting in San Francisco. NACHO is an alleged national homosexual 'movement.' But voting and speaking privileges were restricted only to those paying a $45 fee at the door."

One GLF member accused NACHO of being "a conference only for the rich, racist, male chauvinists of the Gay Establishment," and a Women's GLF member described the meeting as "a do-nothing convention of 'polite reformists.'" On Day 2 NACHO went into closed sessions, excluding the troublemakers. Laurence wrote: "NACHO then became a small tit-tat of 'homophile' (word 'homosexual' is too blatant for their sensitive souls) leaders from around the country ego-tripping to each other, and ignoring the real enemy, the fascist state."

A week later, in the *Berkeley Barb*, Leo Laurence described NACHO as a "Gay Pig Nation, White, racist, rich and male chauvinist." The conference was held at the Society for Individual Rights (SIR) center, "the hub of the Bay Area Gay Establishment." After GLF broke through security waving "flags of revolution," SIR's Larry Littlejohn ordered them out of the building or police would be called. Laurence wrote:

> "The Rev. Troy Perry backed up these orders. He is the handsome pastor of the (gay) Metropolitan Community Church is Los Angeles. He's super-popular in the Gay Establishment and was recently featured in *Time* magazine. Some

consider him a cultural radical, but political reformist. Eyes flashing with Pentecostal fire, 'Brother' Perry shouted: 'Yes, I want the police called!' Then he turned to attack me. 'In one year, Leo Laurence,' he shouted, 'you will be nothing! You will be nothing in one year!' he reiterated, 'You will be shit!'"

Del Martin, co-founder of the Daughters of Bilitis, wrote "Goodbye to All That" in *Sabot*:

"Goodbye to the bulwark of the Mattachine grandfathers, self-styled monarchs of a youth cult which is no longer theirs. As they cling to their old ideas and their old values in a time that calls for radical change. I must bid them farewell. … Goodbye, not just to SIR but all those homophile organizations across the country with an open door policy for women. It's only window dressing for the public, and in the small towns and suburbia, for mutual protection. … Goodbye to all the 'representative' homophile publications that look more like magazines for male nudist colonies. … Goodbye to NACHO. It never really happened. It was a non-organization consisting only of reams of purple dittoed rules and regulations that no one had the time or stamina to read, and big-mouthed, self-appointed and anointed homophile leaders–the steeple without the people. … Goodbye to Gay Liberation … There is a reason for the splits within their own movement, why there is a women's caucus in GLF in New York and why there is a Gay Women's Liberation in the San Francisco Bay Area. … There is no hate in this goodbye–only the bitter sting of disappointment. … I will not be your 'nigger' any longer. Nor was I ever your mother. Those were stultifying roles you laid on me, and I shall no longer concern myself with your toilet training."

On August 21, seven members of Seattle GLF, "a bedraggled and unsightly crew of hippies," met with Mayor Wesley C. Uhlman and Chief of Police Edward Toothman to discuss police entrapment. Eric, a GLF member, reported in *Sabot* that, although against harassing gays, the Mayor insisted the public be protected from men using restrooms for sexual liaisons. Although Seattle GLF were willing to engage elected officials, an October press release, published in *Sabot*, placed them firmly in step with other radical multi-issue GLF groups:

"Gay Liberation Front is part of a fast-growing national movement. It is the militant wing of the 20-year-old Homophile Movement, and the Gay wing of a broader Movement for peace, for human rights and minority integrity, and for preservation of the environment."

On August 29, another confrontation between gays and cops took place in Greenwich Village, as four hundred marched to protest repressive police "clean-ups." It ended in a riot and eighteen arrests. In Milwaukee's *Kaleidoscope* the headline read: "Street-Fighting Gays!" In *Rat*, a "radical lesbian" described events leading up to the protest:

"For a couple of weeks, police brutality against homosexuals rose to a new high with beatings and interrogations on the streets of the Village, and a clean-up campaign in the Times Square area which meant over 300 arrests during one week. A young man who was looking at a window display in Times Square was asked by one of New York's Fascists, 'Were you ever arrested?' 'No,' replied the youth. 'There's always a first time,' said the pig, and without being told any charges, the young man was carted away. For the first time, women have been hassled by the pigs–possibly due to the militancy of the Women's Liberation Movement."

Howard Blum in the *Village Voice* wrote:

"Groups such as the Gay Liberation Front, an organization believing that freedom for homosexuals can only occur through a revolution of all oppressed people, the Gay Activist Alliance, a militant, non-violent group of homosexual men and women, and the Radical Lesbians gathered on the corner of 42nd Street and Eighth Avenue. The purposes of the march were varied: to protest alleged police harassment of homosexuals in the city (the groups claim more than 300 homosexuals have been illegally arrested in the past three weeks); to demonstrate to the 42nd Street community that gay people can organize politically; and to instill a sense of gay pride, that being homosexual is not a sickness or an evil and certainly no cause for shame."

There were a few scuffles and bottles thrown along the route, but the real trouble started outside the Women's House of Detention, where inmates shouted support and dropped burning papers from their cell windows. More police arrived, and after a bottle was thrown into their ranks, the cops charged, swinging their clubs, and making arrests. One undercover cop, dressed as a hippie, hauled in a "street queen," claiming he stabbed a patrolman. Another protestor karate-kicked a cop in the chin, and another, a longhaired man, was dragged into a doorway and beaten by three cops. The protesters dispersed, some regrouping outside the location of the previous Stonewall Inn, others at the Haven, a bar raided the night before. Angela Douglas, in the *Los Angeles Free Press*, wrote that after the raid on the Haven, "a band of over 25 young heterosexual males swept through Christopher Street in Greenwich Village, threatening and attacking gays." Two transvestites were hospitalized, but the thugs disappeared when fifty gay men armed themselves with clubs.

However, not all gay marches were pitched battles. In Provincetown, MA, a popular homosexual resort, a Labor Day Gay Liberation march organized by the Homophile Coordinating Committee of Boston's gay organizations was a great success. According to John Kyper in *Win*, two hundred people participated and the one thousand tourists along the route were friendly, some even joining the march.

Apart from Douglas Key at the *Los Angeles Free Press*, a transvestite, later transsexual, there were no openly "trans" voices in the underground press, until September 1970 in the *Great Speckled Bird*, when drag queen Diamond Lil wrote a campy account of her recent arrest in Savannah:

"As I recall, I had been invited to 'go down,' by special request, of course, to ole SAV-A-NNAH and perform one of my special acts at a masquerade party held in some sort of 'dungeon,' which was operated by an early belle, who went under the guise of 'Cousin Cora,' notoriously known for her assemblage of dirt, ruff trade, derelicts, grease, southern aristocracy, paranoia, closet queens, dowagers, heads, homos, and dynamic, phantasmagorical top-drawer entertainers (sometimes banned from stage): namely DIAMOND LIL.

"Well, it was one helluva romping, stomping evening for right in the middle of my most beguiling number, *The Heat Is On* (Rita Hayworth shopped this one from me in Miss Sadie Thompson, shown frequently on Channel 36), I was informed that the heat and/or fuzz were plenty outside. Now mind you, in an effort for me 'to do' these wild, uninhibited numbers, I get worked up on speed (high blood pressure, I mean)? and I really peaked when word came out about la gestapo. Although I was in mixed company–I was stirring everybody up–I no longer had center attention. Some sissy faggots flew out the back door; a couple hid under a rug; and a hot pair in the boudoir never knew what was going on.

"While some general mayhem continued in front of this tomb, I sort of sleezed on by, hoping desperately to be unnoticed, when a pig snorted in my direction to halt. He asked my name ... I held my breath ... I was so nervous that he scared me to death. Finally, I replied meekly, 'I'm Diamond Lil, Queen of All Glamour, and screaming various assorted sundry stage effects.' He asked my age and I truthfully told him 23. He asked my sex and I replied 'neuter' on the grounds that anything I said further might incriminate me. There was a drag along side me commonly called L. P. (She had nothing to do with records, although she had collected a few here and there). It actually stood for Lady Pat, but she never believed in using her title in ordinary public. She was adorned reverently in a hot fuchsia frock, purple lips, and violet eye shadow, softened by albino white hair, delicately swirled over a Carmen Miranda turban. I thought she was a 'searous gurl' until she openly admitted to Lilly Law that to her own utter regret and dire dismay she was, in reality, a boy! ... Along about this time, a lovely black paddy wagon pulled up and all sheep were loaded cheerfully inside by assorted pigs, who had amassed in numbers to make sure they could handle this violent rip-roaring group, which consisted of three drags, several school teachers from an unnamed small town in south Georgia, some rough trade looking for a 'good' time, a couple of Lesbians, and a vampire called Ollie Owl–a grand total of 18."

Trans issues came out of the closet in the underground press in 1970. In

February, Sue Marshall wrote in the *Berkeley Barb* that Lloyd W. Madison, a missionary at Temple Baptist Church in Los Angeles, was suing the State of Florida for $2 million. Madison was a hermaphrodite. "He has both male and female sex organs," wrote Marshall. After Madison was arrested in Orlando for vagrancy (the charges were later dropped), the police, on discovering he was trans asked him to strip naked for a photograph, "for the purposes of training and educating Law Enforcement Personnel." Madison was told if he did not comply, he would be jailed for thirty days and put on a chain gang where there would be no privacy. Madison acquiesced, telling the *Berkeley Barb*: "There are no laws for anyone who is different. There are laws for the he's and she's, but what if a person is both?"

In the *San Diego Free Door*, Don Jackson wrote: "Ads have been appearing in underground papers placed by a group of transvestites [in Los Angeles] trying to find recruits into an organization of drag queens." Though GLF embraced transvestites, "Establishment" gay groups seeking "respectability and acceptance," often shunned them. Some gay bars refused to serve them. The GLF manifesto read: "There is a tendency among homophile groups to deplore Gays who play visible roles–the queens and the nellies. As liberated Gays, we take a clear stand. Gays who stand out and withstood straight disapproval before the rest of us. They are our first martyrs." On June 2, GLF organized a "Transvestites & Transsexuals Teach-in" at Los Angeles City College campus. Four male transvestites and two transsexuals, members of the Transsexual Action Organization (TAO) and Transsexual Social Organization (TSO), spoke to students. In the *Los Angeles Free Press*, Angela Douglas, presumably this was Douglas Key, wrote that the speakers, "Tammy, Denise, Tracy, Marie, Diane (and myself)," answered student questions, like "what happens when a straight guy picks up a tv and discovers the truth?" Douglas explained the purpose of the two groups:

"TAO is designed for practicing, experienced tvs and transsexuals to eliminate much unnecessary discussion with people not so experienced. TSO is designed to help bring closet tvs out into the sunlight and to provide information about transvestism and transsexualism. Both groups are open to male and female transvestites and transsexuals–straight, gay, bi, or asexual."

A few months later, Douglas wrote "Homosexualize America," a "History of Gay Power," for the *Los Angeles Free Press*. In it she discusses "INCREASED OPPRESSION TOWARD TRANSSEXUALS," notably from gays on the Left:

"Transsexualism and transvestism came under strong attack by gay power. More communistic gays claimed transsexual surgery was only available to a rich, privileged class and was an unneeded accessory to human development. Other gays claimed that transsexuals were only guilt-ridden homosexuals and were detrimental to gay power goals of NORMAL homosexual relationships i.e. male to male, female to female. ... SHOCK TROOPS. Many gay power advocates desired transvestites and transsexuals who were exaggerated caricatures of femininity to be used at demonstrations for shock value and after several such demonstrations, the misuse of people became apparent and most transvestites and transsexuals who were involved withdrew. ... By the summer of 1970 it became apparent to most transvestites and transsexuals that a separate movement or movements was needed."

The *Great Speckled Bird* wrote about a street riot, during which one of Diamond Lil's shows at Atlanta's Club Centaur was tear-gassed: "Saturday night there was a riot in the semiliberatedwarzone called The Strip. People who live near The Strip fought pigs for several hours, sometimes with guns, sometimes with rocks." The trouble started after a "sister" was arrested for dealing drugs. "Laundromat Freak" told the *Great Speckled Bird*:

"I was standing on the corner at Tenth and Peachtree. A cop told me to move down Tenth toward Juniper. I asked to go back to the Laundromat, but he said to get moving. There was a line of cops across Tenth with their guns drawn, advancing down the street. When they had forced the people to Juniper, the cops started throwing rocks at the crowd and I got hit in the leg. Then they began firing their guns. People scattered. Maybe they were using blanks at first, because I didn't see anyone get hit. Other people seemed to think this too and they sort of regrouped. The cops picked up on this, because when they reloaded, they were using real bullets. We knew they were real because the cops started shooting out the streetlights."

While the riot was at its height, Diamond Lil was onstage singing a eulogy to the recently deceased Jimi Hendrix. Standing next to a coffin, he sang, or lipsynced, Aretha Franklin's gospel song *Spirit in the Dark*. Diamond Lil wrote in the *Great Speckled Bird*:

"Outside the Club Centaur, on the famous Strip, spirit of the pigs is competitive to the turbulence of your dynamic star. Why must someone always try to steal my show? Audience is bedazzled by star's captivating performance. Hushed rumors whispered about mayhem outside, but hundreds of fans, including tourists who had driven miles to see the celestial star, remained in reverence enraptured by her radiance and unequalled beauty. Toward the conclusion of the show, audience participation was overwhelming. Handkerchiefs and napkins were used by all, yet a calm silence remained throughout the house. A slight puzzlement was in the air. The star has been known to use unusual props to create illusion, but had this 'special effect' been overdone? A strange gas filtered through the air quickly, but quietly. Everybody became red-eyed, breathless and in awe. ... Had a new gimmick been pulled in show business that made everyone weep so profusely? No, not this time, good brothers and sisters, I am afraid everything was on the up and up. Tear gas was supplied courtesy of the pigs outside involved in an all-out melee, which resulted when the pigs were busting a young girl for dealing. Unbeknownst to the patrons inside, they were more than protected from the hassle outside, for on the rooftop were several well-armed oink-oinks, just ready to 'shoot 'em up' like any ol' Western ya might see on a Saturday night late show."

Soon after the tear-gas incident, Miller Francis wrote in the *Great Speckled Bird*:

"The Centaur Club is no more–closed because of 'underworld connections.' So what else is new? Is there anybody who doesn't know by now how gay bars and clubs all over the country are tight within the clutches of Mafia and syndicate organizations–how else could any gay bar obtain and keep the necessary licenses without dealing directly, on a cash-in-hand basis, with police departments of each city, all of which have fairly smooth working relationships with 'organized crime.' Atlanta is certainly no exception to this rule."

In December, an ad appeared in the *Great Speckled Bird* that read: "Diamond Lil has found a place in the sun at last!! The warmth and doziness of THE CELLAR 355 Peachtree St. (just below the Domino Lounge) is yours to scream as much grease as possible."

Diamond Lil lasted one night at Cellar 355.

Within the ranks of Women's Liberation and Gay Liberation, some questioned the sexist and exploitative ads in underground newspapers. On August 2, 1969, in the *Great Speckled Bird*, Maude wrote about the Radical Media Conference in Ann Arbor the previous month, where women from a dozen newspapers met to discuss sex-ads in radical publications. A resolution, proposed by Sheila Ryan of Liberation News Service, passed on a voice vote. The resolution stated: "Papers should stop accepting commercial advertising that uses women's bodies to sell records and other products, and advertisements for sex, since the use of sex as a commodity especially oppresses women in this country." No matter that some underground newspapers only existed because of the revenue from sex ads. The *Great Speckled Bird* continued publishing sex ads, even though thirteen female staff were named on the masthead. In November 1969, a reader wrote in Florida's *Daily Planet*:

"Could you explain to me how you justify porny ads when you advocate women's lib and in fact the liberation of all peoples? It's one more capitalistic exploitative game, and political papers who are building a movement for a revolution must begin to fight attitudes as well as institutions."

In September 1970, a letter from "A Brother" appeared on the letters page of the *Los Angeles Free Press*:

"The Free Press supplement on Gay Liberation is clearly a positive step for a movement which is thus far deeply misunderstood, mainly for lack of a public forum. However, it is sad that the entire issue's impact and seriousness were diminished by the paid advertisements for gay bars, male movies, gay pornography, photos of male models, etc. Such ads are an indication of the enormous amounts of money being made from the relaxation of sexual restrictions upon homosexual conduct. Already, even before the movement has found its ground, it is being exploited by a growing business community."

In the *Great Speckled Bird*, Barbara Joye, Nan Guerrero, and Sue Jacobs of Atlanta's Women's Lib wrote:

"Many people, including many in the underground press, believe that the sexual revolution is already well on its way. They support this view by pointing to the role of the pill in freeing thousands of girls for premarital sex. They point to the growth of living communes of young people, and add to their tally of 'swingers' clubs where husbands and wives can temporarily escape monogamy. Finally, praising the role of the underground press in aiding sexual liberation, they point to the freer language and to the nudity now seen in print as well as on stage and in women's fashions.

"Many readers of the underground papers welcome the display of female nudity (male nudity is rare) as a stride towards the de-mystification of sex. No longer will young people grow up believing that their bodies are ugly, or that sex is a shameful secret. Atlanta Women's Liberation recognizes some truth to that claim; nor could we object to the fact that women now engage in a wider range of sexual relations.

"What we do find disappointing in the 'New Morality' is that it has so far been directed towards promoting male-dominated and product-dominated sexual relationships, not really transforming the context of sex."

Soon, self-censorship began in the *Great Speckled Bird*:

"We don't accept 'sex ads.' We believe that far from characterizing a position of sexual liberation, they are frequently exploitative of sexuality, especially that of women and homosexuals. (Not all of them are exploitative, of course, but we don't know any simple guideline for determining which are and which aren't, and we don't have the time or energy to debate every ad)."

In November, the *Great Speckled Bird* patted itself on the back, under the headline "R*P":

"Underground papers are one of the new institutions people have been forming. The *Bird*, like other undergrounds, has grown and changed. We want to share these changes, because the *Bird*-product ought not to be separated from the *Bird*-institution. First came the struggle of *Bird* women to free themselves from male oppression. ... Concrete changes are more women on staff, writing, in positions of leadership, and rotating childcare. But just as importantly came a change in women's relations with each other. Love, trust, sisterhood, collectivity-these are only catchwords for the deep emotions women are feeling. ... Four months ago the struggle deepened around gay liberation. Homosexuals have had to exert tremendous effort before being allowed to relate to the *Bird* as such. We try to silence them as much as straight society does, thus activating all their resistance, and denying ourselves their sensitivities. Out of one flagrant incident came a gay editorship and the men's caucus."

In Chicago, a split between GLF radicals, determined to fight for the rights of all oppressed minorities, and those concerned only with gay rights, occurred on September 27, 1970 at a contentious meeting. As with New York GLF nine months earlier, not everyone supported the Black Panthers and other far-left groups. According to the *Chicago Gay Liberation Newsletter*, things came to a head when the Black Caucus, renamed the Third World Gay Revolutionaries, presented a list of demands:

"(1) That political consciousness sessions be a regular function of GLF/Chicago; (2) That consciousness raising sessions on racism be a regular function of GLF/Chicago; (3) That self-defense lessons be made available for GLF members; and (4) That consciousness raising sessions in sexism be a regular function of GLF/Chicago."

The group added: "Third World Gay Revolutionaries will clarify, discuss and help in any capacity to see that the above mentioned demands be met." These "demands" grated on some GLF members, and after the meeting, several split off to form the Chicago Gay Alliance (CGA), an organization focused solely on gay issues. Article 1 of the CGA Constitution read:

"We seek to accomplish the following basic goals: 1) Personal Liberation–to integrate one's sexuality with the total being through a program of social interaction; 2) Gay Community–to instill an awareness of gay brotherhood through mutual respect; to recognize the diversity of lifestyles among ourselves and to unify them into a common culture; and to develop informational programs pertaining to homosexual problems; 3) Reformation–to change oppressive institutions, laws and policies through educational and political activities, thereby initiating a parallel change in human attitudes."

In the *Berkeley Tribe*, a statement from West Coast Third World Gay Revolutionaries began:

"Sisters and brothers of the Third World, you who call yourself 'revolutionaries' have failed to deal with sexist attitudes. Instead, you cling to male-supremacy and therefore to the conditioned role of oppressors. Brothers still fight for the privileged position of man-on-the-top. Sisters quickly fall in line behind their men. By your counterrevolutionary struggle to maintain and to force heterosexuality and the nuclear family, you perpetuate outmoded remnants of Capitalism. By your anti-homosexual stance, you have used the weapons of the oppressor, thereby becoming the agent of the oppressor."

In November, Madison GLF published their "Manifesto" in *Kaleidoscope*:

"We hold that man receives his sex but learns his sexuality; that ideas of 'homosexuality' and 'heterosexuality' are contrivances to discredit the capacity of all persons to sensual pleasure and love in each other; that these contrivances exist to legitimize male supremacy, competition, and the regarding of persons as property. ... WE DECLARE our allegiance to liberation movements of all persons victimized by sexism, racism, and all other direct or indirect forms of exploitation and domination of one person by another. WE CONDEMN as counterrevolutionary any movement for change which ignores the oppression of gay men and women or fosters sexist consciousness among its members."

Among the eleven DEMANDS were:

"2) That all people share equally the labor and products of society, regardless of their sex or sexual orientation; 4) That all political prisoners immediately be released from prisons and institutions; and 10) The abolition of the nuclear family because it perpetuates the false categories of homosexuality and heterosexuality, and its replacement by a system of non-sexist communal care."

In December, Angela Douglas wrote, "A History of Gay Power" in the *Los Angeles Free Press*. In it, she claimed that by October 1970 there were "about 200 gay power groups." One new group was GLF New Orleans. G.W. Weissmann wrote in *Nola Express*: "New Orleans' Gay Liberation Front met ... at the Sphinx Coffee House on Decatur St. to organize support for a gay newspaper and the forthcoming Mardi Gras events." More than forty people attended and coordinator Lynn Miller spoke against Louisiana Statute 14-89 "pertaining to homosexuality." Weissmann wrote: "Miller pointed out that in Louisiana necrophilia ... is not against the law. She said society itself is sick when it's against the law to have sexual relationships with a living body, but legal to screw a corpse or dead animal." The new gay newspaper was to be called *Sun Flower* and its creation would be "assisted by the *Nola Express* until gay journalists and staff get the basics in newspaper production."

After joining three hundred gays in San Francisco for a Metropolitan Community Church (MCC) Christmas service, Nick Benton wrote "Gayule!" in the *Berkeley Barb* on the "allegedly pro-gay" MCC and Santa Claus:

"The essence of what was being said was that 'Christmas is the hope that someday the straight pig society might accept us.' ... Nothing in the service denied that Christmas is the accepted time for wallowing in materialism, for glorifying a past bound up in heterosexual patriarchal family traditions around hearth and tree, for worshipping helplessness in the form of a babe, and for personifying benevolence in a racist, sexist pig figure called Santa Claus. ... How ironic, Christmas is such a straight-pig holiday. But as such it has so little to do with the birth of that cat Jesus–that revolutionary who healed and gave power to the outcast, who stripped power from the forces of oppression, and who was sentenced to execution as a political enemy only to render death itself ineffectual."

The Rev. Howard Wells of the Metropolitan Community Church responded on the *Berkeley Barb*'s Letters Page, saying that after reading Benton's article he felt no anger, just pity:

"Pity because you are in a very special closet of your own, a closet with imaginary police–excuse me, 'pig'–uniforms; enemies with short hair and regular jobs; enemies who are enemies only because they are over 40 years old and happen to be white; enemies who you have relegated to the status of sub-human and hopeless because you refuse to admit that they can love you without agreeing with you."

Benton countered with:

"The more I 'come out,' the more the oppression of the pig becomes clear. It's not a matter for agreeing or disagreeing. It's real. It disrupts dances, harasses gay brothers, shoots them down in streets, ignores our outcries, defines the range of our 'acceptable activities,' does as it damn well pleases in our midst, and defines for us our very existence. ... And I become angry when, in the midst of this struggle, I am met by supposed brothers or sisters who tell me to cease the struggle–to try to lay some guilt trip rooted in fear on me. I disagree. But more than that, you, too, have become my enemy. He who is not for me is against me. You have sided with the pig against my liberation."

At the end of December, the *Daily Planet* published, "A Conversation With Brad Wilson: The Pastor of Miami's Gay Church." When asked about the relationship between GLF and the MCC, Wilson replied:

"Gay Lib, or many of our brothers and sisters who are involved with Gay Lib, hold to a revolutionary Maoist ideology. Some of these brothers believe in blood-letting. Many of them look at us as the Uncle Toms of the gay scene. The radical caucus of GLF maintains that the revolution is already underway in this country, and that unless we adopt a more militant posture, we're likely to be branded counter-revolutionary when revolutionary people take control of the government. I'd only reply that in countries where revolutionary movements have seized control, liberation for homosexuals does not appear to go hand in hand with political liberation. Castro's Cuba is an example. Homosexuals in Cuba are placed in concentration camps. Fidel doesn't have much use for homosexuals, although it appears his brother does."

The rumor of Raúl Castro's homosexuality was repeated in Allen Young's *Gays Under the Cuban Revolution,* where he quoted from an interview he conducted with Allen Ginsberg:

YOUNG: "There are some vague stories going around about your visit to Cuba in 1965 and departure. I'd like to know more about what you did in Cuba and what you said that eventually got you deported."

GINSBERG: "Well the worst thing I said was that I'd heard, by rumor, that Raúl Castro was gay. And the second worst thing I said was that Che Guevara was cute ... "

1970 ended with more police violence against gays. The *East Village Other* reported that Chicago police shot James Clay in the back, while he was "trying to survive in one of the few ways that transvestites can in America–through prostitution." A headline in New York's *Gay Flames, A Bulletin of the Homofire Movement* read: "Street Transvestite Murdered":

"The night before 'Thanksgiving,' the Chicago pigs showed us what we Gays have to be thankful for. James Clay, a transvestite, was murdered in cold blood by James Finnelly and Thomas Bowling, two of Daley's 'finest' fascists. Clay, 'in women's clothes,' was standing by the street early in the morning. The policemen say he was trying to flag down motorists. Finnelly knew Clay. He had arrested him before. The fact that our half-sister was back on the streets was a tremendous insult to his cock privilege. So he tried to arrest Clay. Supposedly, Clay ran. According to the pigs, they tracked him down into an apartment house where he slashed out with a knife and got away. They 'shot to prevent his escape.' Eight shots in the back killed James Clay. He can not tell his story. We can't either but we can say one thing. Clay was in 'men's' clothes when he was killed. When did he change?? During the chase???"

In December, there was another police shooting when Charles Christman was gunned down outside a San Francisco gay bar. According to Nick Benton in the *Berkeley Barb,* after closing time, customers gathered outside the Stud, when police arrived and started swinging clubs to disperse the crowd. *Quicksilver Times* wrote:

"Four pigs leapt from their pigmobiles and charged the crowd. ... They gave no order to disperse nor advance warning, but simply charged into the crowd, shoving and hitting people. Christman climbed into his Toyota and tried to leave, but was stopped by police. In his confusion, Christman moved forward into the intersection and nicked an officer, who opened fire on the car. A police car rammed the Toyota and Christman climbed out and fled the bullets. The crowd heard the police sergeant call: Kill the cocksucking queer!' The crowd in the alley ducked for cover, crawling under cars and into doorways. Then, a smirking pig strutted out of the alley yelling, 'I got him, I got him.' The other police patted him on the back. Christman was shot in the ankle, elbow and back."

20

FREAKIN' FAG REVOLUTION

The trial of the Chicago 7 provided an opportunity for US Attorney Thomas Foran to air his homophobia in public by stating that Dave Dellinger, Rennie Davis, Tom Hayden, Abbie Hoffman, Jerry Rubin, John Froines, and Lee Weiner were a part of the "freaking fag revolution." Foran was later zapped at a speaking engagement, when GLF protestors were pulled out of the building by their hair. Later, YIPPIE leader Jerry Rubin was accused of homophobia by GLF over passages in his book, *Do It! Scenarios of the Revolution.*

"Sacred cows make the tastiest hamburger."–Abbie Hoffman

After the confrontations at the 1968 Democratic National Convention in Chicago, Judge William J. Campbell ordered a twenty-three-member grand jury to investigate the violence. On March 20, 1969, the Grand Jury indicted seventeen persons; eight Chicago police, eight allied with the "Movement," and a member of the press. Chris Singer, in *Fifth Estate*, lists the Chicago 8 as: "Dave Dellinger, *Liberation* magazine editor; Rennie Davis and Tom Hayden, ex-SDS organizers and well-known activists: Abbie Hoffman and Jerry Rubin, of the Yippies; John Froines, an assistant chemistry professor at the University of Oregon; and Lee Weiner, a grad student at Northwestern." The Grand Jury also indicted Bobby Seale, Chairman of the Black Panther Party. All were charged with conspiracy, inciting to riot, and other crimes.

Rubin graciously accepted the "award" in *Fifth Estate*:

"This is the greatest honor of my life. It is with sincere humility that I accept this federal indictment. It is the fulfillment of childhood dreams, climaxing years of hard work and fun. ... I realize the competition was fierce, and I congratulate the thousands who came to Chicago. I hope that I am worthy of this great indictment, the Academy Award of Protest."

The trial began September 24, 1969, presided over by Judge Julius Hoffman, a former law partner to Mayor Richard J. Daley. The problems started straight away, as Bobby Seale requested his trial be postponed until his own attorney could represent him. Judge Hoffman denied the request, also Seale's subsequent request to represent himself. During the back and forth, Seale called the judge a "fascist dog" and a "pig," and was subsequently gagged and shackled to his chair. *Distant Drummer* described Seale: "His boots are loosened and his legs bound with heavy leather straps to the legs of a folding chair. His wrists, wound several times with leather, are buckled to the arms of the chair. Several layers of gauze, adhesive tape and cloth are wound around his mouth and tied to the back of his head." While in his jail cell, Seale wrote and smuggled out, into the hands of Jerry Rubin, a letter, later published in the *Great Speckled Bird*. It began:

"Section 198, title 42 of the United States Government Code says that a black man cannot be discriminated against in any court in any legal defense matter. Why am I handcuffed, shackled to a chair, and gagged in Judge Hoffman's United States District of Illinois courtroom? To say that I made outbursts is erroneous, incorrect, and a lie misleading the American people. I have sat for hours and listened to testimony, most of which is lies, directed against the other seven defendants. The only times I've stood up and demanded my right to legal defense are when a witness says my name. Then I stand up and say, 'I object on the grounds that my lawyer Charles R. Garry is not here. I've been denied his services and I have also been denied the right to defend myself, so I object to this witness testifying against me.' And then the Judge starts telling me that I have a lawyer, one that he the Judge has chosen and not me."

On November 19, 1969, *Dallas Notes* reported that Bobby Seale was sentenced to four years in jail on sixteen counts of contempt of court. Judge Hoffman also ordered a mistrial in his case, removing him from the other defendants, making the Chicago 8 the Chicago 7. On December 11 Allen Ginsberg was in court speaking on behalf of Abbie Hoffman, Jerry Rubin and the Yippie Festival of Life. *Distant Drummer* published "Ginsberg Meets Julius Hoffman," an abridged transcript of Ginsberg's testimony. During questioning Ginsberg played harmonium, chanted, and read poetry, while US Attorney Thomas attempted to focus on the beat poet's homosexuality.

After Ginsberg was dismissed, Foran was overheard muttering, "That goddamn fag." On February 18, 1970, all seven defendants were found guilty of conspiracy. Froines and Weiner were acquitted, while the others were convicted of crossing state lines with the intent to incite a riot. Two days later they were sentenced to five years in prison and fined $5,000 each. On November 21, 1972, the convictions were overturned by the United States Court of Appeals for the Seventh Circuit.

After the trial, Thomas Foran continued his bigotry with a ninety-minute speech at the Loyola Academy Booster Club in Wilmette, IL, where he questioned the masculinity of the Chicago 7 defendants. In "Fags Versus Fuzz" in the *Los Angeles Free Press*, Art Kunkin quotes him as saying:

> "We've lost our kids to the freaking fag revolution and we've got to reach out to them. ... Our kids don't understand that we don't mean anything by it when we call people niggers. They just look at us then like we're dinosaurs when we talk like that. Bobby Seale had more guts and charisma than any of them (the Chicago Conspiracy defendants) and he was the only one I don't think was a fag."

Kunkin goes on to say that the *Chicago Sun-Times* reported that while Foran was speaking he "walked about mincingly or gave limp handed waves."

In December, a headline in the *Chicago Seed* read: "Gays Zap Foran." This wasn't an organized zap, but a zap of opportunity. In his book *Dancing the Gay Lib Blues,* Arthur Bell describes a "zap" as "When the 'good guys' publicly embarrass the 'bad guys.'" On November 23, the University of Chicago GLF (UCGLF) held an open forum on "Coming Out as Gay in the Straight Movement" in the South Lounge of the Reynolds Club. Allen Young, Liberation News Service editor, was speaking on "Gays and the Old Left," when news arrived that Thomas Foran, who had aspirations of becoming the Democratic candidate for governor, was across the street holding a fundraiser. About thirty GLF members crossed the street and began chanting. Other protestors arrived. Prior to the cops' arrival, six GLF members entered the club and found Foran onstage. "Hey Tom, what about the faggots," shouted one protestor. "Gay power" and "freaking faggots are here to stay," yelled others, before being dragged out by the hair. Outside, thirty or so protestors surrounded a police car, but the cops managed to disperse the crowd. According to Allen Young in the *Berkley Barb*, police beat the protestors with their fists and elbows. Handcuffed and arrested were Kevin Burke, Lucas Kemp, Murray Edelman, and Brad Edwards. The incident lead to a protest on December 18, starting with a rally in Bughouse Square, followed by a march to the 18th District Police Station where the GLF demanded that police stop harassing gays. They were joined by YIPPIE group, Students for Violent Non-Action. The police appeased the crowd by promising to meet with GLF at a later date. A promise they broke.

In 1975, Bob Fish and Ray Nelson interviewed Allen Ginsberg and William Burroughs in the *Chicago Gay Crusader*. Ginsberg recalled the Chicago 7 court case:

"I was giving testimony about our peaceable intentions in the assembly in the parks, and then, in order to discredit me as the so-called religious advisor or the religious ritual advisor for the Yippies and their organization, Foran and the Government prosecutors got out a couple of my books, especially early poems— *Empty Mirror* and, I think, *Reality Sandwiches*, which is the only thing they had around—and they found some dirty words in the poems, and they asked me to read them aloud to the jury, including a number of gay poems, thinking that this would discredit me as the supposed religious advisor to the political scene— I don't know if 'religious' was the right word, whatever it was, you know— meditation advisor. So I eagerly grabbed the texts and began reading them in the most charming manner possible, so that the jury saw the humor of it and saw the ridiculousness of what Foran was trying to do, and he went out of the court when it was adjourned, muttering 'freaking fag revolution' or 'fucking fag revolution—it's nothing but a fucking fag revolution.' ... The poems read were *In Society* and *Nightapple*. *In Society*, which is like a cocktail party which mentions eating a sandwich with a dirty asshole, and then *Nightapple*, which is sort of an impressionistic description of a wet dream ... "

While the Chicago 7 trial was at its height, Jerry Rubin's book *Do It! Scenarios of the Revolution* was published and criticized for being anti-gay. In Madison's *Kaleidoscope*, Step May of UCGLF wrote, "An Open Letter to Jerry Rubin Which May Fix His Big Mouth." May wrote: "Your book *Do It!* is one of the most anti-gay pieces of literature I've seen in current writing— movement or otherwise. Throughout the book you denigrate the villains of Amerika by suggesting they are homosexuals." May provides examples:

"[Page 163] Dick Daley fell asleep every night scratching his crabs (which he got from his closed-door meetings with J. Edgar Hoover)," and "[Page 227] The entire university administration was drunk, sucking each other off in the back rooms of the university," and "[Page 215] Fuck bureaucrats, especially the 'nice' Deans of Men who put one hand around your shoulders, while the other hand gropes for your pants."

21

ALPINE COUNTY UTOPIA

In 1970 GLF planned to take over the sparsely populated Alpine County, CA, build a gay Utopia, and raise the consciousness of the "natives." The project was set to proceed, but while gay groups argued over the plan, the authorities in Alpine County found a way to stop the invasion.

"The newspapers of Utopia ... would be terribly dull."–Arthur C. Clarke, in "2001: A Space Odyssey."

In the October 21, 1970, *Las Vegas Free Press*, Don Jackson wrote:

"I have a recurring dream. I imagine a place where gay people can be free. A place where there is no job discrimination, police harassment or prejudice. A place where love rules instead of hate. A beautiful valley in the mountains, remote enough from cities so we will not be hassled, yet close enough so transportation is rapid. A place where a gay government can build the base for a flourishing gay counter-culture and city. Anyone who is interested in participating in the establishment of a gay colony, contact GLF."

In the *Los Angeles Free Press*, Paul Eberle wrote: "Nearly 500 homosexuals are planning a takeover of one of California's most sparsely populated counties. Since Alpine County has only 430 residents, about 300 of them registered voters, the gays could easily succeed." The plan, according to GLF spokesman, Don Kilhefner, was to move en masse, establish residence, then ninety days later, initiate a recall of every county official, hold a special election and elect out-gays to all county offices, including County Supervisors, Superior Court Judges, and County Sheriff. However, Herbert Bruns, chairman of the Alpine County Board of Supervisors, vowed to stop the invasion, backed by Sheriff Merrill who said that gays couldn't tolerate hardships like snow and snakes. Reports in the mainstream press echoed the concerns in *The Invasion of the Body Snatchers*, the movie about space aliens taking over a small California town. Only instead of becoming infected with pods of Communism, the straight residents of Alpine County would turn gay overnight. Another issue was that nearly fifty percent of Alpine County residents were Washoe Native Americans. Kilhefner said: "One of the most important things is the neighbors: we do not want to disturb the lifestyle of the people already living there in any way. Efforts will be made to raise the consciousness of the residents there, so that they might accept their gay neighbors in peace."

Don Jackson, in the *Berkeley Tribe,* warned prospective pioneers of hardships: "Hostile natives. Chopping wood, drawing water from a stream, severe Alpine winters living in tents and quonset huts." However, as Jackson pointed out, the reward would be "the joy of accomplishment in creating a city especially suitable for the Gay lifestyle." He ended with GOD SAVE THE STONEWALL NATION. In the same issue of the *Berkeley Tribe*, Nick Benton added that "gay liberation separatists" were planning to meet with representatives of the Indian community about "making a treaty" with the Washoe Indians. According to the *Berkeley Barb* in November 1970, 1179 gays signed up to move to Alpine County. A month later, the *Los Angeles Free Press* reported that Sheriff Merrill was "holed up in his fortress" in Markleeville, the county seat of Alpine County. Merrill, who was organizing a vigilante group, warned: "A few of these critters will be found in the river sewn up in a flour sack." Another group, the Northern California Alpine Liberation Front, joined the mission to make Alpine County a place "where people can do anything they want so long as they don't harm anyone." Their spokesperson was Sexual Freedom League founder, the Rev. Jefferson Fuck Poland, of the San Francisco-based sex and pot-focused Psychedelic Venus Church.

Not everyone was on board with the plans. Milwaukee's *Bugle-American* reported that Berkeley GLF considered the move to be "separatist." Nick Benton in the *Berkeley Barb* wrote that New York GLF also opposed the idea, and that Smedley of Berkeley GLF wrote a paper, distributed by the Gay Switchboard, that read: "The whole Alpine County trip seems to be a put-down of Gay Liberation. … Gay men struggling to be free, can only be horrified at the macho manipulative approach of the organizers." He goes on to accuse Don Jackson and Morris Kight of Los Angeles GLF of "reveling in the oppression of male homosexuals." James Coleman in the *Detroit Liberator*, wrote that it was "a thoroughly reactionary idea and deserves condemnation." On the use of the phrase "hostile natives," he wrote: "Doesn't something sound a little wrong? For there is possibly no word so chauvinist, so dripping with imperialist condescension, so infuriating as 'native.' Nor is it just an unfortunate phrase. Precisely this contempt for the 'natives' as less than human underlies the whole scheme."

In March 1971, Don Jackson reported in the *Berkeley Barb*:

> "Many problems are now plaguing the Gay Liberation Front's plan to liberate Alpine County by moving in enough homosexuals to outvote the 387 registered voters. Dissension, fear and alternative proposals have taken their toll of supporters. Ron Gibson, one of the main promoters of Alpine, has deserted the cause, charging that 'elitists' in the GLF power structure were ruining the project by using it as a 'publicity stunt.'
>
> "Another controversy has developed along political lines. Homophile (establishment Gays) Alpiners charged that Gay Libbers ruined the project with all the publicity. Worse, say the homophiles, the Gay Libbers are planning to attract thousands of drop outs and penniless 'push outs' who will turn Alpine into a new Haight-Ashbury with stoned freaks running naked through the snow to pot orgies while waiting for their relief checks."

The Los Angeles GLF accused the "Establishment" homophile groups of planning to turn Alpine County into an expensive gay resort, by hiring the company that developed DisneyLand, Mineral King, and Busch Gardens to build an $8 million resort. Homophiles countered by saying the resort would create jobs for the influx of gay residents. GLF suggested the proposed resort was nothing more than a brothel for wealthy homosexuals. While the two sides bickered, the authorities in Alpine County enacted a new building code, banning trailers, campers, and tents, with a "grandfather clause," exempting the temporary structures of older residents. The GLF vision of an Alpine County Utopia was dead in the water.

22

GAYS AND THE BLACK PANTHERS

In 1970, Huey Newton, the Minister of Defense for the Black Panthers, published an open letter supporting gay and women's rights. GLF was also invited to participate in the drafting of a new US Constitution at the Black Panther's Revolutionary People's Constitutional Convention in Philadelphia, where a delegation of lesbians had their meeting hijacked by Mother Makeba. The follow-up meeting in Washington DC was a chaotic affair, effectively cancelled, but not before gay activists smashed up a local straight bar who refused to serve them.

"Everybody's journey is individual. If you fall in love with a boy, you fall in love with a boy. The fact that many Americans consider it a disease says more about them than it does about homosexuality."–James A. Baldwin.

In August 1970, support for the Gay Liberation Front came from an unexpected source. *Black Panther*, *Great Speckled Bird*, and numerous other papers, published a pro-gay missive from Huey P. Newton, the Minister of Defense for the Black Panther Party. In its entirety, it read:

"During the past few years, strong movements have developed among women and homosexuals seeking their liberation. There has been some uncertainty about how to relate to these movements.

"Whatever your personal opinion and your insecurities about homosexuality and the various liberation movements among homosexuals and women (and I speak of the homosexuals and women as oppressed groups) we should try to unite with them in a revolutionary fashion.

"I say 'whatever your insecurities are' because, as we very well know, sometimes our first instinct is to want to hit a homosexual in the mouth and to want a woman to be quiet. We want to hit the homosexual in the mouth as soon as we see him because we're afraid we might be homosexual and want to hit the woman or shut her up because she might castrate us or take the nuts that we may not have to start with.

"We must gain security in ourselves and therefore have respect and feelings for all oppressed people. We must not use the racist-type attitudes like the white racists use against people because they are black and poor. Many times the poorest white person is the most racist because he's afraid that he might lose something or discover something that he doesn't have. You're some kind of threat him. This kind of psychology is in operation when we view oppressed people and we're angry with them because of their particular kind of behavior or their particular kind of deviation from the established norm.

"Remember we haven't established a revolutionary value system; we're only in the process of establishing it. I don't remember us ever constituting any value that said that a revolutionary must say offensive things towards homosexuals or that a revolutionary should make sure that women do not speak out about their own particular kind of oppression.

"Matter of fact, it's just the opposite; we say that we recognize the woman's right to be free. We haven't said much about the homosexual at all and we must relate to the homosexual movement because it is a real movement. And I know through reading and through my life experience, my observation, that homosexuals are not given freedom and liberty by anyone in this society. Maybe they might be the most oppressed people in the society.

"What made them homosexuals? Perhaps it's a whole phenomena that I don't understand entirely. Some people say that it's the decadence of capitalism-I don't know whether this is the case, I rather doubt it. But whatever the case is, we know that homosexuality is a fact that exists and we must understand it in its purest form; that is, a person should have freedom to use-his-body whatever way he wants to.

"That's not endorsing things in homosexuality that we wouldn't view as revolutionary. But there is nothing to say that a homosexual can not also be a revolutionary. And maybe I'm now injecting some of my prejudice by saying, "even a homosexual can be a revolutionary." Quite the contrary, maybe a homosexual could be the most revolutionary.

"When we have revolutionary conference, rallies and demonstrations, there should be full participation of the Gay Liberation Movement and the Women's Liberation Movement. We understand there are factions within the Women's Liberation Movement. Some groups might be more revolutionary than others. We shouldn't use the actions of a few to say that they're all reactionary or counterrevolutionary because they're not.

"We should deal with factions just as we deal with any other group or party that claims to be revolutionary. We should try to judge somehow whether they're operating sincerely in a revolutionary fashion from a really oppressed situation (and we'll grant that if they're women they're probably oppressed.) If they do things that are unrevolutionary or counterrevolutionary, then criticize that action. If we feel that the group in spirit means to be revolutionary in practice but they make mistakes in interpretation of the revolutionary philosophy or they don't understand the dialectics of the social forces in operation, we should criticize that and not criticize them because they are women trying to be free. And the same is true for homosexuals.

"We should never say a whole movement is dishonest when in fact they are trying to be honest; they're just making honest mistakes. Friends are allowed to make mistakes. The enemy is not allowed to make mistakes because his whole existence is a mistake and we suffer from it. But the Women's Liberation Front and Gay Liberation Front are our friends, they are our potential allies and we need as many allies as possible.

"We should be willing to discuss the insecurities that many people have about homosexuality. When I say 'insecurities' I mean the fear that there is some kind of threat to our manhood. I can understand this fear. Because of the long conditioning process that builds insecurity in the American male, homosexuality might produce certain hang-ups about female homosexuality and that's a phenomena in itself. I think it's probably because that's a threat to me maybe, and the females are no threat. It's just another erotic sexual thing.

"We should be careful about using terms which might turn our friends off. The terms 'faggot' and 'punk' should be deleted from our vocabulary and especially we should not attach names normally designed for homosexuals to men who are enemies of the people such as Nixon or Mitchell. Homosexuals are not enemies of the people.

"We should try to form a working coalition with the Gay Liberation and Women's Liberation Groups. We must always handle social forces in an appropriate manner and this is really a significant part of the population–both women and the growing number of homosexuals that we have to deal with."

The *East Village Other* reported that Los Angeles GLF responded by writing a letter of support to Newton recognizing the Black Panther Party as "the vanguard of the people's revolution in America." The letter ends with a pledge that GLF "is fighting for the total liberation of all its people and for true equality of all people." In the *Great Speckled Bird*, Jerry Dreva of Milwaukee GLF wrote:

"In the August 21, 1970 issue of the Black Panther Party paper, there appeared a letter from Huey P. Newton concerning the Women's and Gay Liberation Movements. The publication of this letter is an important event in the development of the revolutionary movement in the United States. The Gay Liberation Front welcomes Huey's letter as an honest attempt to understand and assess the revolutionary nature of the women's and gay movements. We appreciate Huey's sincere efforts to deal with his own anti-gay feelings and his recognition that sexism, particularly the sexism of anti-homosexuality, is based on an individual's own insecurities and fears."

The Black Panthers and Gay Liberation Front first publicly held hands in 1970 over Labor Day weekend in Philadelphia, at the Black Panther's Revolutionary People's Constitutional Convention (RPCC). The purpose of the Convention was to write a new Constitution. According to *Rat*: "The original Amerikan Constitution is not only totally outdated, but is oppressive to all people other than those who wrote it (white heterosexual ruling class men)." Prior to the Philadelphia Convention, there was an August 8th and 9th planning meeting held at Howard University Law School, in Washington DC. The *Great Speckled Bird* reported:

"There was a representative of the Mothers of Black Liberators from Winston-Salem, N.C., who said she had been educated by her children. Migrant workers from the neo-slave camps of Long Island, N.Y., Puerto Ricans from all over the East Coast, Black students from Kent State, Women's liberationists, Gay people from coast to coast, Black and white lawyers, Greasers from Daley's Chicago, and white people from the Allegheny hills of Pennsylvania with accents thicker than black strap molasses."

Radicalesbians and GLF attended the preparatory meeting in Washington DC at the behest of Afeni Shakur, mother of rapper Tupac Shakur. In *Ain't I a Woman*, out-lesbian Lois Hart described Shakur as "a beautiful black woman, virile, revolutionary." However, after the DC meetings, Hart was skeptical:

"As groups we represented the THIRD WORLD GAY REVOLUTION, RADICALESBIANS and GLF men and women. ... I was a white woman coming into the Panther presence–active in the movement a little more than a year– freshly awakened and growing consciousness of Women's and Gay oppression–sick and angry at almost everyone except radical Gay sisters, questioning the validity of working with gay men and their infuriating unconscious sexism–ruling out straight men categorically as SUPER PIG–and here were the Panthers, a straight man's trip in cinemascope and Technicolor. Super butch, the brown, muscled bare-armed, deep-voiced African American– their words cracked with rage and self-righteousness. They moved the meeting along tracks of their pre-arranged program oblivious of everyone unless she or he was in agreement or of use. They insulted us with words of democratic procedure while bulldozing through their agenda. I felt intimidated, angry and defensive."

There were high hopes for the Black Panther's Revolutionary People's Constitutional Convention in Philadelphia. Out of New Brunswick, NJ's *All You Can Eat*, a piece proclaimed: "The 'Movement,' that amorphous conglomeration of parties, organizations, collectives, affinity groups, cadres, cliques, communes, clubs, chapters, crowds, individuals, is entering a particularly crucial stage in its development. So is the United States." The paper predicted the Convention would unite Afro-Americans, Puerto Ricans, and Chicanos, and their three revolutionary parties, the Black Panthers, the Young Lords and the Brown Berets, as well as women and gays.

At the time of the Convention, Philadelphia was a tinderbox of racial tension. Vin McLellan, in the *Boston Phoenix*, reported that Frank Von Colin Jr., an officer in Philadelphia's Fairmount Park police, had been fatally shot and it was rumored to be the work of the Black Panther Party (BPP). Within days, the police ruled them out, saying the officer was killed by a Panther splinter group called the Black Unity Council. However, that didn't stop the police raiding three Panther offices and arresting the entire leadership of the Philadelphia BPP. *Rat* reported:

"The Gestapo forces of Philadelphia Police Commissioner Frank Rizzo viciously attacked Black Panther Party offices. ... The pigs, numbering 150, armed themselves to the teeth with shotguns and rifles, and tear gas and rammed their way into the branches at Germantown, West Philadelphia, and North Philadelphia. People living at the North and West Philly branches fought back when the pigs came on. They defended themselves up to a point, but it was useless because they were outnumbered. ... The Panthers were stripped naked in the streets outside their offices and carted off."

Observer Media Watch in *Distant Drummer* accused the media of pandering to Police Commissioner Rizzo: "In this city, in this era, freedom of the press has come to mean that Frank Rizzo is not only the commissioner of police, but also editor-in-chief of the mass media. Once again the commissioner has effectively manipulated this city's press into submissively and selectively reporting only what fits his editorial vision." A headline in one mainstream paper read: "3 More Policeman Shot, 15 Arrested in Dawn Raids on Black Militants." Under the headline was a photograph of Black Panthers lined up against a wall, suggesting they were responsible for the murder of Frank Von Colin Jr., while buried deep in the story it was revealed the Panthers were not involved.

Highlighting the corruption of Philadelphia politics, the *Boston Phoenix* wrote:

"Fourteen Panthers were brought in for arraignment before Judge Anne Clark; then, during the arraignment, Judge Clark was called off the bench to confer with Commissioner Rizzo. As Judge Clark left the courtroom, a red police car pulled up at the courthouse with Judge Leo Weinrott, a close associate of the commissioner, inside. Judge Weinrott took over the arraignments and each of the Panthers was held on $100,000 bail."

The raids were part of Rizzo's campaign to close down the BPP altogether. In *Distant Drummer*, Donald Cox quoted the warning of Zayd Shakur, the Panther's Deputy Minister of Information: "We will schedule the convention in the streets if necessary." On the subject of the high bail, Shakur said: "This is the type of fascistic justice used in the courts against the Blacks. The courts work hand in hand with the police." At a press conference, when asked about the Black Panthers, Rizzo replied: "These creeps lurk in the dark. They should be strung up. ... I mean, within the law." According to Milwaukee's *Kaleidoscope*, ten thousand people attended the Panther Convention. At the registration desk, attendees were greeted by a flagpole bearing the red, green and black, revolutionary flag, emblazoned with Che Guevara's profile. The first plenary session, attended by 5,000 people, was at Temple University gym, where Michael Tabor, a New York Panther, spoke on American history, "All people are created equal. But women and black people were not considered people." Later Huey Newton spoke to over 10,000 people in the gym. "It is a fact that we will get change; we will transform the society," asserted Newton, adding:

> "It is up to the oppressor to decide if this will be a peaceful thing or ... we will use whatever means that is effective regardless of the consequences because it is our conclusion and our principle that a slave who dies a natural death will not balance two dead flies on the scale of eternity. We will have our manhood–even if we have to level the face of the earth in an attempt to get it!"

Not everyone praised Newton's speech. *Kaleidoscope* reported that women's groups were disappointed at Newton's use of the word "manhood." Also, a woman was scheduled to speak on the same platform as Newton, but was canceled without reason. That led to a group of radical lesbians walking out the next day, arguing that, "Huey's prior statement of support for women's liberation and gay liberation was a mere attempt to co-opt the rage of women and gays." The *Berkeley Tribe* published "Gay Sisters Speak." On Michael Tabor's speech, the anonymous author wrote:

> "Most of us dug it and were pleased with the frequent references to women and homosexuals, however, we were also disturbed at the superficiality of the presentation, which did not spring from a real awareness of our oppression. The words 'women' and 'homosexual' were attached to the talk much like a caboose, easily detachable, is tacked on to the end of the train."

On Sunday, workshops were scheduled at the Convention. In the evening the attendees gathered in the gym to share the results of their various meetings. The *Berkeley Tribe* explained that some of the lesbians walked out because the women's workshop was presided over by Panther women with male Panther guards protecting them. Some women found this intimidating. Also, the statement and list of demands drawn up by lesbians and due to be presented to the Convention, was hijacked by Mother Makeba, who was described in the *Berkeley Tribe* as "another trip entirely." Makeba insulted the lesbians in the workshop by calling them "men." Then when Joan Bird, spokeswoman for the women's workshop, tried to walk on stage, she was elbowed out the way by Makeba, who claimed she was representing the women's workshop. Needless to say, the lesbians' statement and demands were not read. A delegation of sixty male gays fared better, holding a workshop on sexual self-determination and then reading their statement and eighteen demands to the Convention:

1) The right to be gay anytime, anyplace.
2) The right to free physiological change and modification of sex.
3) The right to free dress and adornment.
4) That all modes of human sexual self-expression deserve protection of the law and social sanction.
5) Every child's right to develop in a non-sexist, non-possessive atmosphere which is the responsibility of all people to create.
6) That a free educational system present the entire range of human sexuality, without advocating any one form or style; that sex roles and sex-determined skills be not fostered in schools.
7) That language be modified so that no gender takes priority.
8) That the judicial system be run by the people thru people's courts; that all people be tried by members of their peer group.
9) That gays be represented in all governmental and community institutions.
10) That organized religions be condemned for aiding in the genocide of gay people and be enjoined from teaching hatred and superstition.
11) That psychiatry and psychology be enjoined from advocating a preference for any form of sexuality and from enforcing that preference by means of shock treatment, brainwashing, imprisonment etc.
12) The abolition of the nuclear family because it perpetuates the false categories of homosexuality and heterosexuality.
13) The immediate release of and reparations for gay and other political prisoners from prisons and mental institutions; the support of gay political prisoners by all other political prisoners.
14) That gays determine the destiny of their own communities.
15) That all people share equally the work and products of society regardless of sex or sexual orientation.
16) That technology be used to liberate all people's of the world from drudgery.
17) The full participation of gays in the people's revolutionary army.
18) Finally, the end of discrimination of one person over another.

No Revolution Without Us! An Army of Lovers Cannot Lose! All Power to the People!

In Plato's *Symposium*, an "army of lovers" is how Phaedrus described the Sacred Band of Thebes, a 4th century BC Greek army comprising 150 pairs of male lovers. One of the sixty gay male delegates at the People's Constitutional Convention was Ortez E. Alderson, an anti-war campaigner. Born in Buffalo, NY in 1952, Alderson spent his formative years growing up on the South Side of Chicago. At eighteen he presented a striking figure in his red bellbottom pants, yellow sweater, maxi-trench coat, floppy black hat, necklace with a black fist on it, and GLF button. Alderson was chairman of Chicago's Third World Gay Revolutionaries. On July 29, 1970, he and three companions–Phyliss Burke, Kevin Clark, and Pat Pottinger– were arrested and charged with seizing and destroying Selective Services records in the draft board office at Pontiac, IL. The police caught up with them in the nearby town of Minonk, where they were charged with breaking into the draft board office and removing records of draftees. Richard Chin of Chicago GLF wrote in *Win*:

"The Pontiac 4 Defense Committee has been set up to raise money for the trial which will be held in Peoria and to spread the word about the case. Several groups in the Chicago area have endorsed the Committee including Clergy & Laymen Concerned, Chicago Moratorium, Non-Violent Training & Action Center, Alliance to End Repression, Chicago Gay Liberation."

Alderson, who was represented by ACLU lawyer, Ronald Barnard, was the last to be released on bail of $5,000. He was sentenced to one year in prison, spending the first three months in Peoria County Jail. In a 1972 interview with *Motive*, entitled "On Being Black, Gay, and in Prison," Alderson described his incarceration in Peoria:

"When I was there, I was the only black on the tier for a long time. The rest of the people seemed to be poor whites from around that area and they also seemed to be–or were–racist; something I put up with at the time. There were quite a few hangups going around at that time about whether or not I was actually gay. I of course am … and very proud of it. And then being a black man, too, everyone was rather afraid to try and hassle me or try to do anything with me. I guess this had something to do with that All-American black male myth."

Alderson served the rest of his term in Ashland, KY, the same federal correction center where Bayard Rustin was incarcerated during World War II for refusing to register for the draft. While in Ashland, Alderson and three other gay prisoners, Craig (Puerto Rican), Green (Black) and Davis (Full-blooded Sioux Indian), tried to organize a Gay Pride Day on June 28, 1971. Not surprisingly, prison officials denied their request and the three were thrown into the hole.

Another founding member of Chicago's Third World Gay Revolutionaries was Ron Vernon. In an interview in the *Great Speckled Bird*, Vernon was asked if, during his time in jail, people were talking about the Black Panther Party and Malcolm X:

"Yes, there was quite a movement in jail. Most of the people in jail are black, first of all. I was in jail when I first heard of the Black Panther Party, and related to it very positively, but in a blackness sense and not out of a gayness sense, because the Panthers were offing gay people, verbally offing gay people. You know, saying things like this white man who is fucking you over is a faggot, and that was getting to me, because I was a faggot and I wasn't no white man! Finally their consciousness has changed, and they have begun to relate to homosexuals as a part of the people. That's when I became a revolutionary, really began to live my whole life as a revolutionary. … If they offed every revolutionary, they'd have to off me too. I think that more and more third world and also gay white people are coming into the movement because they know that they'll have a fighting chance somewhere to be gay people, whether they're third world or white, you know, they'll have the opportunity, so they're going to get in there and struggle for it."

The ties between GLF and the BPP were tenuous at best. The *Great Speckled Bird* reported on the hundreds of people "Black, brown, white, many gay" who gathered in front of the Women's House of Detention in New York's Greenwich Village on October 13, 1970 to protest the arrest of Angela Davis. Davis, a black philosophy professor and BPP member, was arrested in a New York Howard Johnson Motor Lodge, after evading a nationwide police hunt. She was on the FBI's Ten Most Wanted list after being tied to Jonathan Jackson's attempt to release prisoners from California's Marin County courthouse. Jackson, a seventeen-year-old high school student, took control of the courtroom, armed the black defendants, and then took Judge Harold Haley and three women hostage. The police shot into the getaway vehicle, the judge and three black men were killed, while two of the women, a juror and the prosecutor, were injured. Davis had purchased the firearms used in the attack.

In another protest supporting Angela Davis, gays didn't fare well. Ken, in the *Detroit Liberator*, wrote about a protest at Detroit's Federal building. Michael D. was speaking on behalf of the Black Panther's National Committee to Combat Fascism (NCCF). Nearby were anti-Angela Davis protestors led by Donald Lobsinger and his group Breakthrough, who wanted to arm whites in preparation for guerilla warfare against blacks. While Michael D. was speaking, he suggested Breakthrough were homosexuals, less than men. He said: "Not only will I come over there and kick yo head in, I just might bring my Blue seal grease with me and make you a woman."

In the *Detroit Liberator*, Ken wrote:

"After this comment, being one of the demonstrators on the pro-Angela Davis side of the street with Michael D, Black and a member of GLF, I was enraged by this statement of black-heterosexual-male-supremacy. At the same time I felt like a goddamn fool marching in support of a member of a so-called politically responsible party that maintained such a sexist/politically irresponsible spokesman as Michael D.

"Those of us who are black homosexuals are painfully aware that this is not an uncommon public statement to be made by a member of the NCCP/BPP. Although national Panther policy dictates an alliance with the Gay's and Women's Lib movements, local Panther practices are far from alliance, or even silent support. … In our black communities the Panthers are establishing sexual roles in the mirror image of inhumane white Amerikkka. Roles that only guarantee the continued dehumanization of male and female homosexuals and women."

The irony, of course, is that in 1997 Angela Davis came out as a lesbian in *Out* magazine.

Another anti-gay Black Panther incident occurred in San Francisco. In the *Berkeley Barb*, Leo Laurence wrote that twenty blacks "who obviously hate queers and whiteys" raided the Gay Liberation Front and the Resurrection Medicine Show commune at 330 Grove Street. The building was leased by a "negro slumlord" called Lafayette Jamieson, who had earlier sent two of his henchmen to threaten the commune. Other threats followed. Darwin Dias, of GLF, claimed that Richard Brown, former Captain of the Black Panther Party, burst into his bedroom and threatened to beat him up if he didn't move. When GLF asked the Black Panthers for help, they were told, "We'll investigate." No help came. The twenty members of GLF and the Resurrection Medicine Show commune were forcibly evicted and the building occupied by the blacks. Roger Green, a former chairman of San Francisco GLF, told the *Berkeley Barb*:

"A lot of Gay Lib members are disappointed with the non-help we got from the Panthers. When the Panther offices were threatened last year with a vamping, over a dozen GLF members quickly and without question rushed to the Panthers headquarters in the Fillmore and in Oakland to join a 24-hour vigil. We put our bodies on the line. Had the pigs started shooting, it might have been our lives. But we didn't take a week to 'investigate' first."

The third part of the Black Panther's Revolutionary People's Constitutional Convention was set to take place in Washington DC on November 26-28, 1970. The *Great Speckled Bird* reported that at the last minute Howard University refused to allow its buildings to be used. A press release from Tim Hayes of the Revolutionary People's Constitutional Convention Information Center, published in the *Great Speckled Bird*, read:

> "In Washington the political vultures escalated their harassment to a much higher level by putting pressure on the nigger pig lackey James Cheek, president of Howard University. ... This is a classic example of a pawn in the hands of the pigs and a traitor in the eyes of the people."

In *Fifth Estate*, a conventioneer from Chicago summed it up: "There's plenty of revolutionary people here but 'convention' means getting together. And that's what we're not doing." In the *Great Speckled Bird*, a "sister," who arrived in DC in a van with other women from Atlanta, wrote that they were met with chaotic organization, and took shelter in the DC Women's Liberation Center. They attended a Panther Rally in Malcolm X Park and gay-danced to Lumpen, the Black Panther R&B band, who sang lyrics like "Bullets in the air, snipers everywhere–for freedom." Barbara, who wrote a report in Iowa City's *Ain't I a Woman*, wrote that "a lot of gay women and men danced in a snake dance and shouted 'Ho, Ho, Homosexual, the ruling class is ineffectual." In the *Great Speckled Bird*, Roger, a gay activist from Atlanta, wrote of his disappointment that Howard University students didn't take it over to support the Black Panthers. With no venue, there was no event.

Mike Silverstein who was also in Washington DC, wrote in the *Berkeley Barb*: "Yes we had our own collective, our own organization and communications system, and our own place to stay. That made the convention something of a success for GLF when as a whole it was a disaster." Silverstein stayed in a GLF collective, which he described as "an old Brownstone filled with the usual Gay revolutionary hippie chaos." Silverstein described the arrival of the Louisville, KY delegation, then Tallahassee, FL, Lawrence, KS, Boston and New York. He ended with: "What the Panthers accomplished I have no idea. They didn't have much to say to the rest of us. But we haven't got time to wait around listening. We've got a revolution to build." In the same issue of *Berkeley Barb*, Nick Benton wrote that the fifteen-member Boston GLF delegation left early, with member Craig Smith explaining:

> "We walked out on the Washington convention because we didn't think that we had to spurt semen all over the place in order to be an army of lovers. ... We, in Boston, over the past months had lived and worked together and had begun to define for ourselves a sense of gayness that was closer to an intimate loving brotherhood not affected by the popular bourgeois images of what constitutes sexual appeal."

Washington DC's *Quicksilver Times* wrote: "While the rest of the

Revolutionary People's Constitutional Convention (RPCC) was looking for a place to happen, on Thanksgiving Day three hundred gay people met at the American University 'to define their relations with each other, the rest of the movement, and the 'straight' world." Not an easy process, given the widening divisions within GLF. *Quicksilver Times* continued:

"The gay men who identify themselves as 'femmes' don't want to be put down by the 'butch' anymore. The transvestites and transsexuals effectively raised the consciousness of their brothers and sisters who had ignored or even mocked their situation. Most gay women met separately from the gay men. Third World gay men also held several separate caucuses."

However, *Quicksilver Times* noted that all disagreements were forgotten at the soul food Thanksgiving dinner at St. Stephen's church, which GLF shared with a delegation of YIPPIES. Also reported in the *Quicksilver Times*, twelve GLF members at the "cancelled" RPCC (three from DC, nine from other cities) were arrested after "trashing" an all-white "redneck bar" that refused to serve four gay men: two Puerto Ricans, one black, and one white. After the incident, the gay men recruited fifty others and returned to the bar. When they entered, the bar manager attacked them. Police arrived and arrested four people, releasing them when reporters arrived. Shortly afterwards a van load of gay men was stopped, the men arrested. At the police station the men were verbally abused with names like "fags" and "fairies." *Quicksilver Times* concluded: "There was one major flaw in the police case however; the twelve were arrested in a Volkswagen bus blocks away from the bar. Lawyers defending the twelve anticipate the prosecution will have a hard time pinning particular actions to particular people." The twelve GLF members were the only people arrested at the RPCC in Washington DC. This was the beginning of the end of the flirtation between GLF and BPP. In March 1971, Michael Jacobi in the *Bugle-American* asked, "Is the Black Panther Party Dying?" after Huey Newton purged members of the New York Panthers and, in *Black Panther* newspaper, accused Eldridge Cleaver of being a "male chauvinist." In retaliation, Cleaver, in exile in Algeria, expelled Newton and David Hilliard from the BPP.

In the *Bugle-American*, Jacobi wrote:

"The Black Panther Party is in deep trouble. Split by factionalism and internal disputes, harassed by the police, with many of their leaders murdered, jailed or in exile, the Panthers have sunk to an all-time low. And when the Panthers do surface from this obscurity, they are too often caught up in their own rhetoric and surrounded by a self-styled aura of elitism—which is not at all the way to reach 'the people' or to construct any kind of revolutionary base. ... Official confirmation of the split, which has been brewing for some time, comes at a time when white radicals are re-evaluating their alliance with the Panthers, realizing that any bond of solidarity can no longer come from feelings of white guilt, but rather from recognition of mutual expression."

23

VENCEREMOS (WE SHALL WIN)

The US embargo against Cuba began October 19, 1960. In 1969, members of the Students for a Democratic Society founded the Venceremos Brigade, including gay activist Allen Young. The Brigade sent young volunteers to show solidarity with the Cuban revolution by working in the sugarcane fields. However, gay and lesbian participation in the Brigade was short-lived when it became clear that the much-vaunted revolution was, as one paper put it, a "heterosexual revolution."

"Cuba, Vietnam y nosotros-Venceremos!"–a favorite chant of the Venceremos Brigade.

The United States embargo against Cuba was put in place two years after Fulgencio Batista y Zaldívar was deposed by the Cuban Revolution. In March 1968, Thorne Dreyer in *Rag* reported that six San Francisco Bay Area antiwar activists were "abducted" at Mexico City airport. The six were heading for Cuba as graduate students and journalists. They had applied for permission from the State Department, received tacit approval, but no official reply. The six were Karen Wald and Bobbi Cieciorka, both from the editorial board of the *Movement*, and organizers for Students for a Democratic Society (SDS) and Stop the Draft Week; Jack Bloom, a Teaching Assistant at Berkeley and an organizer of the International Student Strike; Hal Jacobs, also a Berkeley SDS member; Connie King, San Jose SDS; and Stuart McRae, an organizer for the Resistance in Palo Alto.

At Mexico City airport they were approached by ten men, taken outside, and told to get into two cars. When they asked for identification, they were bundled into the vehicles, held for twenty hours, driven to the border and told not to enter Mexico again. They were given no explanation.

In January 1970, the *Great Speckled Bird* reported that in late 1969, 250 members of the Venceremos Brigade visited Cuba in three planes via Mexico City (other sources say Czechoslovakia). The Venceremos Brigade was an organization founded by members of SDS and officials of the Republic of Cuba. Among the US founders were Carl Oglesby, Bernardine Dohrn, Julie Nichamin, Brian Murphy, and gay activist Allen Young. In his book *Gays Under the Cuban Revolution*, Young wrote about his personal conversations with Carlos Rafael Rodriguez, a top Communist minister who served in both the Batista and Castro cabinets. The organization was named after the 1969 book, *Venceremos! The Speeches and Writings of Ernesto Che Guevara*. The purpose of the Venceremos Brigade was to show solidarity with the Cuban Revolution by working alongside Cuban laborers in the cane fields, in violation of the US embargo. The *Great Speckled Bird* wrote: "These young people broke the political sound barrier and produced a sonic boom to add to the distress of the Washington policy-makers, who have fought so long and so hard to isolate the American people from Cuba." The first brigadistas landed at Jose Marti Airport and were taken to the campamento, where they lived for the duration of the zafra (harvest). Javier Ardizones, chief of the international relations section of the Young Communist League of Cuba and the director of the camp, explained: "Their contribution to the cane harvest is important, especially from a symbolic point of view. We will do all we can to guarantee that our American visitors are healthy, that they enjoy their stay with us and that they learn the truth about the Cuban revolution." In June 1970, the *Great Speckled Bird* reported that almost 1,000 members of the Venceremos Brigade had been macheteros in the sugar cane fields.

Two months later Nan Guerrero, in the *Great Speckled Bird*, wrote that thirty local members of the Venceremos Brigade left Atlanta on the first leg of their journey to Cuba's Island of Youth to cut cane. Their first stop was New York to pick up more brigadistas, then Canada to board a Cuban ship. "This third brigade of close to 500," wrote Guerrero, "is the first to include a formal contingent of gay men and women and has a higher percentage of women and third world people than the first two brigades." That's not to say they were welcomed. They weren't. In the same issue of the *Great Speckled Bird*, Atlanta GLF member Guy Nassberg wrote:

"The Cuban revolution, we think, must not be a revolution for men first, women second, and homosexuals who stay in the closet. It is precisely the contradiction between the promise of that liberation and its practice towards homosexuals that has convinced us of the need to organize GLF within this country and to confront both capitalist society and the movement which hopes to change it.

"There is little positive to say about the Cuban revolution's treatment of homosexuals. Cubans regard homosexuality as a natural product of capitalist decadence; they have always associated homosexuality with the decadent bourgeoisie of the United States who ran the country, stole the profit's of the people's labor, and built the chief whore-supplying city of the western hemisphere, Havana, in the image of 42nd Street and the Upper East Side of Manhattan. ... The Cubans, with their inheritance of the Spanish Catholic culture which labeled homosexuality a sin, have traditionally stuck to a rigid cult of machismo which sanctifies male heterosexual dominance as THE way. ... All homosexuals suffer as a consequence of Cuban practice. The model country of liberation sent known homosexuals to workcamps where a truly communist work experience was supposed to cure them of their 'deviation.' It didn't work, of course, and a combination of world-wide protest and the discovery of brutality in the camps led Fidel to disband them."

In March 1971, in New York's *Women's LibeRATion*, gay members of the Venceremos Brigade were interviewed after returning from Cuba. Earl explained how Venceremos and GLF came together at the 1970 Christopher Street Liberation weekend:

"GLF had contracted for use of the Elgin Theatre on the Friday night of that weekend, and it turned out that the Brigade had also contracted to use it the same night. And so we had an explosive encounter there. It was our feeling that people from the Brigade should have been sensitive to the fact that this was a special weekend for Gays. Strangely, it led to a demand that Gay people go on this Brigade. A number of Gay people applied and we were supposed to be a quota of 25–that was our impression. When we got on the ship, there were four of us."

Two more women "came out" and that made six.
Jesse told *LibeRATion*:

"In my work brigade I was the only Gay person, and there was anti-gay feeling among a lot of people. There were a series of words that were used indirectly toward me–this was by North Americans–mariposa, gavillota, maricon, and high voices and whistling. I also ran into physical threats. One time I was threatened to be thrown through a wall. The most revolutionary thing I could do, I was told, was to confront my homosexuality, and that if I was really proud of being a faggot, I should stand up and punch this guy in the mouth. He said 'Punch me in the mouth.' I didn't. Then he went away and the whole dorm started applauding at his little speech."

Heidi Steffens, a brigadista, wrote in San Francisco's *Good Times*:

"The Cuban exclusion of homosexuals from the revolution became an excuse for the North Americans who had intellectually accepted Gay Liberation as part of the U.S. revolutionary movement, but who still held emotional prejudices, to take the easy way out. They no longer had to struggle around their feelings about gay people–if homosexuality was pathological in Cuba it couldn't be revolutionary in the U.S."

On their return from Cuba, several gay brigadistas spoke at a forum held at Alternative U in New York City. The event was tape-recorded and a transcript published in *Out of the Closets: Voices of Gay Liberation*, edited by Karla Jay and Allen Young. Chicago GLF member, and brigadista, Step May, addressed the argument that homosexuality was not illegal in Cuba:

"The Communist Party rules Cuba, and I really disagree ... that there are no laws against homosexuals. There might not be laws in the sense that we know them, in the sense that they're legislated by a house of representatives or a senate, but there are policies that exist and are enforced. Like the way open homosexuals can't be teachers and can't be in the Communist Party. This is enforced right down the line, and if you want to call that a policy or a rule of law, the truth remains that it's made to work and it has an effect. As a part of the Communist Party's position, there's even a word for it; they call it peligrosidad, which means a dangerous thing, or a danger to society. And because of the way the Communist Party or government operates in Cuba, there is a policy that once the government takes a position on something, or determines that something is a peligrosidad, such as marijuana or homosexuality or whatever, then it's considered to be a closed matter, in the sense that people cannot propagandize or agitate for a position that's in opposition to the position that the Communist Party has taken."

This open criticism of the Cuban Revolution led to the National Committee of the Venceremos Brigade issuing the dictate, "Venceremos Brigade on Gay Recruitment," reprinted in Allen Young's *Gays Under the Cuban Revolution*:

"Through many discussions in the past few months by the National Committee and the Regionals, we have formulated a policy concerning recruitment to the BV (Brigada Venceremos) of gay North Americans. The BV is not pretending to analyze the potential or the validity of the gay liberation movement in the United States. (The potential or validity of any sector in the U.S. will be determined by their practice within the context of the struggle carried out inside the U.S.) Our policy is based on practical considerations of the Brigade in Cuba: Cuba's position toward homosexuality, the Political Objectives of the BV, our purpose in Cuba, thus our position toward Cuban policies, and the past practice of gay Americans on the Brigade.

"The Cuban people, as a whole, do not accept homosexuality. There is no material base for the oppression of homosexuals in Cuba. They are not repressed in work camps or anything of the sort. But it should be clear that Cuba does not encourage homosexuality.

"The First Congress of Education and Culture [attended by Fidel Castro, according to New Brunswick's, N.J. *All You Can Eat*], a congress of three years of work and hundreds of thousands of participants, published a report of major importance in the creation of a Cuban culture, a culture which in the past had been robbed, denied, and infiltrated by U.S. imperialist domination.

"Concerning homosexuality, this congress took the position that homosexuality is a social pathology which reflects left-over bourgeois decadence and has no place in the formation of the New Man which Cuba is building.

"This position was formulated by the Cuban people for the Cuban people. It was not formulated for the U.S., or any other country. Cuba is for Cubans, and while progressive and revolutionary people are always welcome in Cuba, the Cuban culture is not created for them in particular.

"'As to the BV, the past activities of gay North Americans have generally been destructive. A list of specific activities would include 're-educating the Cubans' (assuming that the situation in Cuba must be the same as in the U.S.), outright attacks and denunciations of the Cuban Revolution, imposing North American gay culture on the Cubans (for example, parading in drag in a Cuban town, acting in an overtly sexual manner at parties). Also, some gay North Americans have shown a greater interest in finding out about Cuban homosexuals than in finding out about the Cuban people and their Revolution. This kind of activity has been a flagrant insult to Cuban culture. And it has demonstrated a lack of understanding of the position of the Brigadistas in Cuba as guests of the Cuban Revolution. One of the objectives of the BV is to show solidarity with the Cuban Revolution–to affirm the Cuban peoples right to self-determination. While this does not mean that we deny the importance of dialogue, we are not in Cuba to carry out confrontations over our disagreements. The BV involves activity within the Cuban setting. As guests of the Cuban Revolution, we must realize that internal questions concerning Cuba's development can only be answered by the Cuban people; answers cannot be imposed from the outside. Only the Cuban people have all of the essential elements to analyze and solve their problems correctly.

"The attitudes and actions described above are particularly dangerous at this time because they join a cultural imperialist offensive against the Cuban Revolution, carried out by U.S. imperialism in an attempt to discredit the Revolution and alienate North Americans from it.

"There are gay Americans who share the objectives of the BV. Our policy is not meant to exclude them. However, given the gay North American position, the Cuban position on homosexuality, and the problems that have arisen from this situation, we will require of gay North Americans a clear understanding of revolutionary anti-imperialist priorities and total identification with the Political Objectives of the BV. It must be understood that going to Cuba means respecting Cuban culture."

In response, the Gay Committee of Returned Brigadistas issued a statement:

"We, as gay North Americans who have identified with and supported the Cuban revolution and our gay sisters and gay brothers in Cuba through our participation in the Venceremos Brigade, denounce the anti-homosexual policy formulated at the recent Conference on Education and Culture and endorsed by the Cuban government. ... Gay people owe allegiance to no nation. The anti-homosexual policy of the Cuban government does not simply fail to include gay people in the revolutionary process–it specifically excludes them from participation in that process and the right to self-determination. We have been told that it is reactionary for us to criticize and condemn our oppressors when they call themselves 'revolutionary' or 'socialist.' A policy of ruthless and incessant persecution of gay people is contradictory to the needs of all people, and such a policy is reactionary and fascist. ... Also, we denounce the national committee of the Vinceremos Brigade as the agents of a sexist hierarchy. They, in their liberalism, have not engaged in critical relationship with either the Cuban people or with revolutionaries here. We call upon all progressive people to join in our protests against this reactionary policy and to make their feelings known by writing to the Cuban Prime Minister and First Secretary of the Communist Party in Havana. Turn it out!"

In January 1972, Step May and Robbie Skeist wrote in Minneapolis' *Hundred Flowers* that on November 13, 1971, at a Brigade Dance, Chicago GLF members and brigadistas circulated a petition protesting the anti-gay policy of the Venceremos Brigade. They collected 110 signatures. May and Skeist wrote: "Those who refused to sign included blatantly prejudiced people who seemed disgusted just to read the word 'gay' and think about homosexuals, plus members of 'revolutionary' organizations who express virtually total support for Cuba and show very little concern for the rights of gay people in the United States or in Cuba."

In spite of GLF efforts, no more openly gay people traveled with the Venceremos Brigade to the sugarcane fields of Cuba. In the *Columbus Free Press*, Jon wrote:

"Through communications with gay people of past Venceremos Brigades, amerikan gays have come to see the truth about the 'heterosexual revolution' in Cuba. ... Gays are arrested for their clothing, hairstyles, and group meetings. For a while homosexuals were confined to (may I use the words concentration camps?) military units to increase production. ... ('And they ain't no Fire Island, either Mary')."

In *Gays Under the Cuban Revolution*, Allen Young described the plight of gays in Cuba:

"On New Year's Day in 1959, the overwhelming majority of the people of Cuba was celebrating the flight of Fulgencio Batista, a rightwing dictator who had just been tumbled from power by the guerrilla army of the 26th of July Movement led by Fidel Castro, his brother Raul Castro, and the handsome Argentine physician-adventurer-revolutionary Ernesto "Che" Guevara. Among the many places where rum and beer were flowing in jubilation were the gay bars of Havana. Some of the gay men and lesbians who joined in celebrating the victory of the insurrection were veterans of an heroic resistance movement, rural and urban that extended even to the United States where an anti-Batista Cuban exile community lived in the hope of a better day for their native land. Little could these gay men and lesbians, so full of joy and optimism, imagine that within a few short years the freewheeling 26th of July Movement would be taken over by the dogmatic bureaucrats of the Cuban Popular Socialist Party, as the Cuban communists then called themselves."

After the apologists at the Venceremos Brigade expelled gays, many in the Movement became despondent with the New Left, on which they had unwisely hung their revolutionary hat. Young wrote:

"Confronting the homophobia of Cuban communism led inevitably to a questioning of Marxist doctrine itself, especially the idea that central planning by a state apparatus could erase inequalities. ... For a while, perhaps, I was equally doctrinaire in my embracing of feminism, but it has become to clear to me that my rebellion is not against Marxist dogma, but against the idea that a particular set of ideas can hold all the answers to all questions. ... I feel an affinity for the Cuban lesbian who wrote to an American friend, 'Marxism is beautiful theoretically, but in practice it is a GREAT LIE. I am a lesbian and a homosexual of integrity and I would never lean on Marxism in order to achieve it.'"

Published in 2005, *The World Was Going Our Way: The KGB and the Battle for the Third World* by Christopher Andrew and Vasili Mitrokhin, sheds light on the issue of gays and the Venceremos Brigade. The book is based on thousands of documents that Vasili Mitrokhin, a senior KGB archivist, smuggled out of the Soviet Union in 1992. The book claims that while Fidel Castro publicly supported the Venceremos Brigade, he "looked askance at the presence of gay and women's liberation movements among his American New Left supporters." The Dirección General de Inteligencia (DGI), Cuba's KGB, told Castro that, "the New Left brigadistas were homosexuals and drug addicts," and that the DGI were looking into using homosexuality "to bring about the physical degeneration of American imperialism."

It didn't work.

24

GAYS VS. PSYCHIATRISTS

Aversion therapy with electric shocks and brain surgery were two suggested methods of curing homosexuality in the late 1960s/early 1970s. Psychiatrists were targeted for zaps by GLF, including those attending the American Medical Association convention in Chicago, the American Psychiatric Association convention in San Francisco, and the conference on Behavior Modification in Los Angeles.

―――――――

"My mother took me to a psychiatrist when I was fifteen because she thought I was a latent homosexual. There was nothing latent about it."―Amanda Bearse.

―――――――

In July 1970, the *Las Vegas Free Press* reported on a new cure for homosexuality, coming from the University of Goettingen, Germany:

> "Although homosexuality is considered a psychological, rather than a physical, ailment by most researchers, they have been puzzled by the fact that many homosexuals do not respond to psychological therapy. Now, neurosurgeons report 'good success' in curing homosexuality with brain surgery. Dr. Othner … says that all of the homosexuals he operated on have been cured, 'None,' he said, 'have lapsed into their former perversion.'"

The *Las Vegas Free Press* was quick to note: "The above report is presented only for the enlightenment of the reader. It reflects the statements and opinions of certain head shrinks and most certainly does not reflect the views of the editors or the writer, nor probably 95% of the homosexuals in the world."

In Boston's *Broadside and the Free Press*, Don Jackson explained Dr. Othner's procedure:

> "The operation consists of destroying the portion of the brain which regulates the sexual urge. The surgery is done with an electronic probe sunk into the brain. A portion of the brain is destroyed with electric shocks. The patient remains conscious during the entire procedure. ... Dr. Orthner calls the destruction of the sexual and aggressive drives a social recovery, since the treated patient is better able to function in society. So far, the operation has only been used to cure homosexuality, but it holds great promise as a cure for rebellious students, racial agitators, revolutionaries, and other trouble makers."

The medical profession had long been the enemy of homosexuals, as psychiatrists, quacks, and snake-oil salesmen, lined up to air their opinion on all-things gay. One of the first targets of the GLF was the psychiatric profession. In January 1970, the University of Chicago's *Maroon-Grey City Journal* published an article by Henry Weimhoff, co-founder of The University of Chicago GLF, entitled, "The 'Problem' of Homosexuality":

> "Homosexuality is neither an affliction to be cured, nor a weakness to be resisted. ... Why then does society persist in treating homosexuality as something less than acceptable? Currently the argument is that homosexuality is a 'sickness,' a symptom of a deeper personality disorder. However, previous to widespread public acceptance of psychoanalytic theory, homosexuals were seen as criminals, threats to the state and the established order of society, and before that as heretical sinners, blasphemers of the 'natural' order established by God and subject to appalling and barbarous persecution. What the designations of homosexuality as 'sinful,' 'criminal' or 'pathological' have in common is neither fact nor logic, but rather a subjective negative attitude–in short, prejudice."

Weimhoff took aim at the virulently anti-gay Irving Bieber, MD, "a renowned psychoanalytic 'authority' in the field." He quoted from Bieber's book *Homosexuality: A Psychoanalytic Study of Male Homosexuals*, that "all psychoanalytic theories assume that homosexuality is psychopathologic." As late as 1973, when the American Psychiatric Association voted to remove homosexuality from its list of illnesses, Bieber wrote: "A homosexual is a person whose heterosexual function is crippled, like the legs of a polio victim." Bieber wasn't alone in his theories. One contributor to his book was Cornelia B. Wilbur, the psychiatrist who treated Shirley Ardell Mason aka Sybill, whose story of multiple personality disorder was made into a bestselling book. Wilbur's diagnosis of Mason's "illness" was later called into question and her credibility shot to pieces. In his article, Weimhoff argued that psychiatrists judged homosexuals from those they saw as patients, but what of the millions of others they didn't see who enjoyed a happier, more stable existence? Weimhoff added that the problems of homosexuals weren't medical but sociological, due to "entrenched prejudice and discrimination." Weimhoff explained:

> "The problems of the gay person are the direct result of a relentless barrage of assaults upon his self-esteem and his dignity, the results of which are manifested in damaged self-image, lack of self-confidence, and unwillingness to come forward as a homosexual in society."

On June 23, 1970, the American Medical Association (AMA) convention in Chicago was zapped during Gay Pride Week. Eighteen members of GLF infiltrated to protest Dr. Charles Socarides, a physician noted for his anti-gay writings. The AMA zap took place during "Family Medicine," a workshop where Socarides was due to speak. In May 1970, in the *Journal of the American Medical Association* (JAMA), Socarides wrote:

> "The pattern arises from faulty sexual identity, a product of the earliest years of life. Typically, we find a pathological family constellation in which there is a domineering crushing mother who will not allow the developing child to achieve autonomy from her, and an absent, weak, or rejecting father."

The protestors were dispersed throughout the hall. When Socarides said the word "homosexual," a GLF member shouted, "Homosexuals are beautiful." Socarides continued but was interrupted again with calls of "you're making things up" and "do you cure your straight patients of heterosexuality?" A report by Step May in an undated *Gay Flames* housed at the McCormick Library of Special Collections at Northwestern University, Evanston, IL, reads:

> "After Socarides finished, one furious doctor demanded to know by what authority we were attending the session. Another doctor suggested that the issue that the Gay Liberation people were raising should be given legitimacy, and that one homosexual should join Socarides and the other authorities on the panel. A gay guerilla raised the objection that there were women homosexuals and men homosexuals and that both groups would have to be represented. A gay woman and a gay man then took their places on the panel and explained that homosexuals are not inherently sick, but that society and psychiatrists force them to think of themselves as sick. Socarides reiterated his position about gender identity being confused by childhood trauma, which by now must have sounded pretty lame to just about everyone present. That evening a man called the number on the leaflet and said that he approved of the action we'd done. 'I'm a doctor,' he explained. 'I'm gay.'"

A GLF leaflet handed out at the AMA zap read:

"The establishment school of psychiatry is based on the premise that people who are hurting should solve their problems by 'adjusting' to the situation. For the homosexual, this means becoming adept at straight-fronting, learning how to survive in a hostile world, how to settle for housing in the gay ghetto, how to be satisfied with a profession in which homosexuals are tolerated, and how to live with low self-esteem.

"The adjustment school places the burden on each individual homosexual to learn to bear his torment. But the 'problem' of homosexuality is never solved under this scheme; the anti-homosexualist attitude of society, which is the cause of the homosexual's trouble, goes unchallenged. And there's always another paying patient on the psychiatrist's couch.

"Dr. Socarides claims, 'a human being is sick when he fails to function in his appropriate gender identity, which is appropriate to his anatomy.' Who determined 'appropriateness?' The psychiatrist as moralist? Certainly there is no scientific basis for defining 'appropriate' sexual behavior. In a study of homosexuality in other species and other cultures, Ford and Beach in 'Sexual Patterns of Sexual Behavior' conclude 'human homosexuality is not a product of hormonal imbalance or 'perverted heredity.' It is the product of a fundamental mammalian heritage of general sexual responsiveness as modified under the impact of experience."

"Other than invoking moral standards, Dr. Socarides claims that homosexuality is an emotional illness because of the guilt and anxieties in homosexual life. Would he also consider Judaism an emotional illness because of the paranoia which Jews experienced in Nazi Germany?

"We homosexuals of Gay Liberation believe that the adjustment school of therapy is not a valid approach to society.

"We refuse to adjust to our oppression, and believe that the key to the mental health of all oppressed peoples in a racist, sexist, capitalist society, is a radical change in the structure and accompanying attitudes of the entire social system.

"Mental health for women does not mean therapy for women–it means the elimination of male supremacy. Not therapy for blacks, but an end to racism. The poor don't need psychiatrists (what a joke at 25 bucks a throw!)–they need democratic distribution of wealth. OFF The COUCHES, INTO THE STREETS!

"We see political organizing and collective action as the strategy for affecting this social change. We declare that we are healthy homosexuals in a sexist society, and that homosexuality is at least on a par with heterosexuality as a way for people to relate to each other (know any men that don't dominate women?)

"Since the prevalent notion in society is that homosexuality is wrong, all those who recognize that this attitude is damaging to people. And that it must be corrected, have to raise their voices in opposition to anti-homosexualism. Not to do so is to permit the myth of homosexual pathology to continue and to comply in the homosexual's continued suffering from senseless stigmatization.

"A psychiatrist who allows a homosexual patient–who has been subject to a barrage of anti-homosexual sentiments his whole life–to continue in the belief that heterosexuality is superior to homosexuality, is the greatest obstacle to his patient's health and well-being.

"We furthermore urge psychiatrists to refer their homosexual patients to Gay

Liberation (and other patients who are victims of oppression to relevant liberation movements). Once relieved of patients whose guilt is not deserved but imposed, psychiatrists will be able to devote all their effort to the rich–who do earn their guilt but not their wealth, and can best afford to pay psychiatrists' fees.

"We are convinced that a picket and a dance will do more for the vast majority of homosexuals than two years on the couch. We call on the medical profession to repudiate the adjustment approach as a solution by working in a variety of political ways (re-educating the public, supporting pickets, attending rallies, promoting social events, etc.) to change the situation of homosexuals in this society.

"Join us in the struggle for a world in which all human beings are free to love without fear or shame."

In June 1970, in the *Chicago Defender*, an African-American publication, Faith Christmas reported on a meeting of the Chicago Mental Health Association. Brian O'Connell, the executive director, spoke of the high incidence of mental illness in "ghetto" areas and how poor blacks had inadequate health care. He also urged the medical profession to stop diagnosing "homosexuals, student activists, anti-war protestors and Black Panthers" as being mentally ill. The debate within the medical profession spilled over into the mainstream press. In August, Steven Roberts wrote "Homosexuals in Revolt," published in the *New York Times*. The article pitted the new gay militants against the older "in the closet" homosexuals afraid to rock the boat. On the subject of gay militants, homophobic Dr. Lionel Ovesy told the *New York Times*:

"Homosexuality is a psychiatric or emotional illness. I think it's a good thing if someone can be cured of it because it's so difficult for a homosexual to find happiness in our society. ... It's possible that this movement (Gay Lib) could consolidate the illness in some people, especially among young people who are still teetering on the brink."

In July 1970, GLF zapped the National Convention of the American Psychiatric Association (APA) in San Francisco. Gary Alinder described the Convention in the *Los Angeles Free Press*:

"White, straight, male middle-aged, upper middle class. ... Men who are 'insulated' ... separated in their immaculate garb, cars, country clubs, planes, expensive hotels–protected from emotional involvement by a gibberish vocabulary which translates humanity into 'scientifically' quantifiable and 'objective' terms."

The zap is aimed at "one of the worst mind pigs," Dr. Irving Bieber, Professor of Psychiatry at New York Medical College." On the day of the

Convention, the Veteran's Memorial Auditorium was filled with three hundred psychiatrists. Secreted about the room were twenty members of Women's Lib, and fifteen from GLF. As soon as the Convention started, the speakers were shouted down and the meeting adjourned. Alinder wrote:

"We are in a room of enraged psychiatrists. 'They should be killed,' shouts one. 'Give back our air fare,' shouts another.' Maria DeSantos reads from a Women's Liberation statement: 'Women come to you suffering from depression. Women ought to feel depressed with the roles society puts on them … Those roles aren't biological; those roles are learned … It started when my mother gave me a doll and my brother a ball.' Michael Itkin reads the Gay Liberation demands. Anarchy. Knots of people talking loudly all over the room. Shrinks coming up and asking what we want. Finally, some discussion."

One of GLF's demands was the abolition of psychiatry as a tool of oppression. When GLF finally located Bieber, he was on a panel entitled "Transsexualism vs. Homosexuality." Alinder confronted him:

"You are the pigs who make it possible for the cops to beat homosexuals; they call us queer; you–so politely–call us sick. But it's the same thing. You make possible the beatings and rapes in prisons; you are implicated in the tortuous cures perpetrated on desperate homosexuals. I've read your book, Dr. Bieber, and if that book talked about black people the way it talks about homosexuals, you'd be drawn and quartered and you'd deserve it.

"Bieber answers 'I have never said homosexuals are sick; what I said was that they have displaced sexual adjustment.' Much laughter from us. 'That's the same thing motherfucker.' He tries again. 'I don't want to oppress homosexuals; I want to liberate them, to liberate them from that which is paining them–their homosexuality.'"

In October 1970, Tony De Rosa wrote "Gays in a Shocking Situation" in the *Los Angeles Free Press*. In it, he quoted from "The Application of Anticipatory Avoidance Learning to the Treatment of the Homosexual," by psychologist Dr. M. P. Feldman:

"The patient (homosexual male) is presented with a large series of slides of men, both clothed and unclothed. He is asked to assess them for their degree of attractiveness. A hierarchy of female slides is set up in the same way. A level of electric shock is then established, which the patient describes as 'very unpleasant.' The room is darkened; the slides are projected; the patient is told that he will see a male picture and that some seconds later he will receive an electric shock. He is told that he can turn off the slide by pressing a switch whenever he wishes to and that the moment the slide leaves the screen the pain will stop. He receives no shock when a slide of a woman is shown, and he can ask for a female slide at any time. He thus learns that the absence of the female slide means that a male slide, soon associated with electric shock and pain (and hence anxiety-provoking) may reappear."

After hearing that Dr. Feldman was attending the second annual conference on Behavior Modification at the Biltmore Hotel in Los Angeles, GLF and Women's Lib turned up to an early-morning meeting in large numbers. De Rosa wrote: "Dr. Feldman was obviously nervous, pausing often before saying the word 'homosexual,' noticing the arrival of long-haired yawning freaks and their more wide awake and ready sisters." A film of Feldman's methods was shown. De Rosa described it as having "the quality of a Tijuana stag film, almost sepia in tone." The film shows a male homosexual strapped to a chair being electrocuted "like a lizard prodded by children." Steve Morrison, a GLF member, interrupted the film, shouting out, "How long are we going to let this thing go on! What's wrong with these people?" The film stopped and the lights went up to reveal that GLF had taken over the stage. Don Kilhefner said: "We are taking over this session! We don't accept the premise that homosexuality is something that must be cured. We reject the entire idea of electric shock treatment for homosexuals!"

25

GLF UNSTUCK

The political differences that caused the split in New York GLF surfaced in Chicago and on the West Coast, while Georgia GLF was just starting up. Trans issues come out of the closet in popular culture, thanks to Andy Warhol and the Kinks, the latter leading to a GLF zap of a Philadelphia radio station. Meanwhile, a GLF convention in Austin, TX, is a great success, as was the Midwest Regional Gay Liberation Conference in Illinois. However, as GLF meetings in Washington DC became farcical, gay liberation groups nationwide shrunk further when lesbians jumped ship to Women's Lib because of gay male chauvinism.

"The movement began to devour itself. There was an absence of all the things that made the movement so powerful; absence of trust; absence of love; absence of a sense of humor; absence of commitment; absence of-this is communal, we're all in this together. All this stuff seemed to have been blown apart."–Kathleen Cleaver in *The Weather Underground*, a documentary by Sam Green and Bill Siegel.

In the August 21, 1970 issue of *Berkeley Barb*, Leo Laurence reported that when the co-founder of Berkeley GLF, Konstantin Berlandt, tried to sell the first issue of *Gay Sunshine* in the White Horse, a straight-owned gay bar, he was ejected by "a baldish fat man in his fifties." The first issue of *Gay Sunshine* was a labor-of-love compiled by Gary Alinder and Konstantin Berlandt, though the editorial collective for the first five issues was anyone who turned up. In the *Berkeley Barb*, January 8, 1971, an article began: "The January issue of *Gay Sunshine* features a confrontation between a member of the Cockettes performing drag troupe and a San Francisco pig on the cover, [and] is 20 pages of right-on revolutionary Gay Liberation articles." Soon afterwards the collective disbanded, and publication stopped. *Gay Sunshine* was saved in the spring of 1971 by British born Winston Leyland who moved it to San Francisco, kept the GLF flavor but added literary content, like interviews with William Burroughs, Jean Genet, Allen Ginsberg, Christopher Isherwood, Gore Vidal and Tennessee Williams. Later in the month, the *Berkeley Barb* reported that the GLF founded Gay Switchboard was "on the breadline." "Expenses of the switchboard include not only rent of an office and cost of the phones, but materials for the enormous amounts of mimeograph printing of articles relevant to gay liberation. ... The Gay Switchboard has served as the 'glue' for gay liberation in the Bay Area." The glue came unstuck in April when the *Berkeley Barb* reported that the Gay Switchboard was defunct. Elijah, of the Committee of Concern for Homosexuals, who founded the Switchboard, claimed the project had become counter-revolutionary. "It was not a revolutionary switchboard," he told the *Berkeley Barb*, "Most of the calls we handled were for where the nearest gay bar was, or something like that. A revolutionary switchboard serves a different purpose." It didn't help that they were $200 in debt "with no-one interested in helping us pay our bills."

Six months after Stonewall, some members of New York GLF split to form the Gay Activists Alliance, to focus on one issue, gay rights, and not take on the plight of all oppressed people. In Chicago, the same thing happened in the fall of 1970, when the Chicago Gay Alliance rejected the dogma and rhetoric of the New Left and split from GLF. Soon the split spread to the West Coast. In January, Nick Benton wrote "Gay-Lib Activist Split Foreseen Here" in the *Berkeley Barb*. In the article, Benton quoted Konstantin Berlandt who, after attending the Black Panther's People's Constitutional Convention in Washington DC, spent a month in New York, where he found GLF meetings sparsely attended: "It's the Gay Activists Alliance which has the large meetings and the impressive structure. ... It's made up of young, hip types who still basically believe in the Constitution and change through law reform, but aren't quite as uptight establishment as San Francisco's Society for Individual Rights." Berlandt predicted a similar split would occur in Berkeley GLF. Benton noted that Berkeley GLF was already reduced to weekly consciousness-raising meetings, the *Gay Sunshine* collective, and the Gay Switchboard. All were struggling with "a few committed souls." Benton acknowledged the trend away from revolutionary to one-issue politics, citing the Gay Students Union (GSU), as a group focused on "issues of homosexuality, as they relate to the University":

"Members of GSU generally advocate working within the established order, and are heavily into encounter group structures. ... So are many attending Gay Lib meetings, and the constant strife between those who are struggling to find a revolutionary gay consciousness and those who identify with the system and continue to perpetuate sexist and racist patterns, are bogging down the meetings."

Konstantin Berlandt's prophecy came true in May, when the *Berkeley Barb* reported "Gay Lib Splits":

"What happened a year ago in New York has happened at last in the Bay Area. There has been a split in Gay Liberation and there is now a Gay Activists Alliance West. ... The foundation marks a splitting off by the less-than-revolutionary from the San Francisco Gay Liberation Front. Just as happened in New York, GAA split off from GLF to adopt policies of non-violence and one-issue activist politics, reports founding father Rev. Ray Broshears."

In February, Milwaukee's *Kaleidoscope* reported a similar GLF split in that city. Also, many women were leaving GLF to form the Radical Lesbians, while others joined a new trans group, the Radical Femmes. There was also an exodus to other organizations like the Radical Queens, the Gay People's Union, and the Homosexual Freedom League. In Chicago, some GLF members formed the Fiery Flames Collective, and ads appeared in the *Seed* for a lesbian YIPPIE group called the Flippies. Their ad read:

"The Flippies (Feminist Lesbian Intergalactic Party) are a female nationalist, gay nationalist political party that works for the overthrow of everything in society that oppresses women and gay people (namely everything). We're publishing a paper called *Killer Dyke*. Contact us through our men's auxiliary by writing Flippies Men Auxiliary 2314 E. 70th Pl. Chicago 60649. We love you."

While some GLF groups split, some diluted their Marxist dogma and others still continued to fight the revolution. *Fifth Estate* reported that on January 30, Detroit GLF protested "in solidarity with all people and resistance to the police/court system of American injustice." A GLF spokesman told the paper: "Contrary to what many believe, Motor City gays suffer heavy repression from police and court agencies. The bar scene is cooler here than on the West Coast, but Detroit is not a fun place for gays." Twenty-five members of GLF picketed Murphy Hall of Justice, Wayne County Jail, the main branch of the Detroit Police Department, and Recorders Court. However, the five degree weather with twenty-five mile per hour winds cut the protest short, to half an hour. In the Deep South GLF groups were fighting an uphill battle against religious bigotry. The

Daily Planet, out of Coconut Grove, FL, published a feature on GLF Tallahassee, at the time mired in a prolonged battle with the authorities at Florida State University. The article ended with:

"'The Killing of Sister George' never played in Tallahassee. It's next to impossible to get a copy of the *Los Angeles Free Press*. There are no gay bars (some of us have never even seen one). Yet, a lot of very together kids have managed to pull off something which has drawn the attention of the whole state. From this uptight little southern town, 20 miles from the Georgia border, has come the impetus which we hope will soon see the spread of the Gay Lib Movement into the larger southern cities."

"Why Do You Stomp Us?" asked Steve Abbott in Atlanta's *Great Speckled Bird*:

"What is the Gay Liberation Front? Is such an organization needed in Atlanta? If so, what should it be like? Gay men in Atlanta discuss these questions with increased seriousness and frequency. Some think an Atlanta GLF should be a center for information and social activity and that our main work should be to help closet brothers come out. Some think GLF should mainly agitate for legal reform. Some fear an Atlanta GLF will be a small band of fanatics who will jeopardize the Gay community by over-hastily pushing dogmatisms, marches and confrontations. Recently a group of us interested in starting an Atlanta GLF have been getting together and rapping. Most of us are in our twenties though some are younger and some older. ... Most of us have been involved in Leftist politics before (some of us would describe ourselves as revolutionaries) but our raps have been refreshingly free of political rhetoric and its accompanying uptight atmosphere."

On February 4, the first publicized Georgia GLF meeting took place at the Morningstar Inn in Atlanta and drew a crowd of over one hundred. Larry Fisher spoke, stating the twofold goals of GLF: "First, to serve the Gay Community; secondly, to challenge straight society about where it is going." Concerns from attendees echoed other GLF meetings around the nation: one woman warned against using nude photographs in their literature; another reminded everyone that in New York City women split from GLF because of chauvinism; and a gay man suggested women co-chair meetings and share responsibility for the planning and operating of GLF. One of the first actions of Georgia GLF was to garner the support of the American Civil Liberties Union (ACLU) in challenging the state's sodomy law. Under "Sodomy Appeals" the *Great Speckled Bird* wrote that over two hundred gay men were incarcerated in Georgia's prisons under the state's sodomy laws.

In February 1968, author James Baldwin, interviewed in the *Los Angeles Free Press*, described himself as "bisexual," as did Kate Millet, author of

Sexual Politics, a critique of patriarchy in Western society and its literature. While many writers in the underground press "came out" after Stonewall, nobody ruffled as many feathers as Jill Johnston, columnist for the *Village Voice*. San Diego's *Goodbye To All That*, a radical women's paper, described her speaking engagement at the University of California, San Diego, as "disappointing to many us because of her condescension, egocentricity and repetitiveness." Johnston believed that "coming out" in large numbers and being visible would change the way society viewed homosexuals. *Goodbye to All That* wrote:

"She believes a social convulsion will follow the discovery that homosexuality is extremely widespread. A sexual revolution and the freedom it would bring women and men to express their love and sensuality towards members of their own sex would certainly cause widespread social change, but Jill's belief that this revolution will come when the public is simply made aware that homosexuality is more prevalent than generally believed in individualistic and naive to say the least. In our analysis sexual and every other freedom can be brought about only through political revolution and when the repressed structures of the state have been brought down."

In 1973, Johnston spoke in Chicago at a women-only Pride event. In Chicago's *Reader*, Sally Banes described Johnston's book *Marmalade Me*, a collection of *Village Voice* columns published between 1960-1970, as charting the author's "transition in that decade from a lively and sensitive critic of dance, various plastic arts and happenings to an incisive critics' critic to a dreamy visionary surrealistic streamofconsciousness exploding chronicler of the endless performance of her own life from day to day." Banes, who eschewed most uppercase lettering–mrs., english, amerika, etc.– quoted from Johnston's speech:

"Until all women are lesbians there will be no true political revolution until in other words we are woman I am a woman who loves herself naturally who is other women is a lesbian a woman who loves women loves herself naturally this is the case that a woman is herself is all women is a natural born lesbian so we don't mind using the names it naturally I am a woman and whatever I am we are we affirm being what we are saying therefore Until all women are lesbians there will be no true political revolution meaning the terminus of the heterosexual institution through the recollection by woman of her womanhood her own grace and eminence by the intense identities of our ancestors ... "

Presumably this was Johnston's "dreamy visionary surrealistic streamofconsciousness" at work. Perhaps you had to be there. Jobwise, "coming out" was easy for a columnist at the *Village Voice*, but in other professions it meant the end of a career, especially if the "coming out" is attached to radical ideas about restructuring the hierarchical education system. In February, the *Berkeley Barb* reported on Hayward State Sociology Prof. Mike Silverstein, a Berkeley GLF member, who "came out" to his students in October 1970. Silverstein told the *Berkeley Barb*:

"I knew at the time it was all over for me as a professor here. At the same time I sought to expose the unwritten policies of the department–such things as the demand to flunk a certain percentage of students in order to keep the supposed quality of education at the highest level."

Silverstein admitted the committee that fired him didn't mention his homosexuality. "They claimed that I didn't grade hard enough and that I identified too much with the students." Silverstein explained:

"Gay liberation is not a movement for homosexual civil rights. It is the right of people to love each other through the elimination of the power relationship that forces people to encounter each other in a competitive situation. ... Because I am gay I want to destroy those things that keep me from encountering other people as people, by forcing myself and others into roles. That means that I want to destroy my role of professor as professional. Therefore, when I am fired because I identify too much with students or because of alleged 'unprofessionalism' then I am fired because I'm gay."

Some Berkeley GLF members were clearly Maoists. In the *Berkeley Barb*, Nick Benton described State Assemblyman Willie Brown's attempt to strike down California's Sodomy Law as "A Pig Bill":

"Our black brother and representative to the California State Legislature (currently running for mayor of San Francisco) has called himself 'the faggot's friend' in his attempt over the past few years to pass his bill which would legalize all sexual acts in private by consenting adults. ... What is bothersome, however, is the fact that homosexuals feel that this law represents some sort of liberation for them or even that it represents a step in the right direction. The fact is, it represents the opposite. The limitations imposed by the bill speak louder than the so-called freedoms it would provide. First of all: What freedoms? The concept that a state, by law, would ALLOW consenting adults to have sex with each other in private is repulsive. It is not a privilege to be allowed to do such things legally. It is a RIGHT. Brown's bill is not GIVING us anything. As homosexuals–no, as humans–we have got to stop thinking of ourselves as perverse creeps begging for privileges and some sort of social consolation."

Benton noted that the bill increases penalties against "heterosexual acts involving minors." He adds:

"Sexual repression is thinking that sex should be legal only if it is set within definite limitations–i.e. in private between adults only– that is the clue to our oppression as a people. Brown's bill reinforces that way of thinking. People who accept the sick morality of the distinction between public vs. private and adult vs. minor imposed by our society are going to exhibit repressed sexual behavior whether or not it is in public or private or with adults or minors."

In 1970/1971 images of trans persons began to appear in pop culture. Andy Warhol and Paul Morrissey's *Trash*, a movie about New York junkies starring Joe Dellesandro and "drag queen" Holly Woodlawn, played in underground movie theatres nationwide. In his review in the *Great Speckled Bird*, Smokey Kaufman described the audience in Atlanta: "Lots of gay people in glad rags, lots of hair-heads. Some people seemed to know the gay scene–titters when a girl wants to give Joe a rim job, etc." Kaufman continued:

"Most of the people in the movie–the shoe fetishist social worker, the bored New York housewife, Holly's pregnant sister–are junkies, too. They're not on the needle but they're exploiting their own deviancies in a hurtful way. Nobody really has much of a good time in *Trash* and a lot of people hurt themselves and others."

Kaufman ends his review: "Go see *Trash*, even if you walk out."
Mike Neville in Madison's *Bugle-American* wrote:

"It is difficult to say if *Trash* is a parody of itself or a whole genre of film. Dellesandro is certainly the anti-hero to beat all anti-heroes. Though he looks like King Stud, he plays an impotent junkie living with a transsexual lover-protector. Despite his inability to get his monstrous engine to turn over, he is chased throughout the film by a variety of representative erotomaniacs."

Another trans turned up in the song *Lola* by the Kinks. In the *Detroit Liberator* in December 1970, M. Moone and S. Martin claimed *Lola* belonged "at the vanguard of 'revolutionary' music." *I can't understand why she walks like a woman and talks like a man*, sings Ray Davies of his new paramour. Of course, at the end of the song, when he realizes the gender of the "woman," he sings, *Well, I'm not the world's most masculine man. But I know what I am and I'm glad I'm a man. And so is Lola, L-L-Lola, L-L-Lola*. Moone and Martin conclude: "The unabashedly frank lines ... demonstrate that genital polarity is not necessarily a requirement for sexual/emotional fulfillment. Rather, it's where one's head is at that determines compatibility." However, *Lola* proved too much of a temptation for Long John Wade on his WIBG radio show in Philadelphia. *Thursdays Drummer* reported that on March 15, Wade played the Kinks' *Lola*, after which he "hurt and insulted gay people with a lisping-fag stereotype ... splitting his esses and falsetto-ing the comment that the song was for his friends at the city's homosexual bookstore." Within hours GLF were at the Radio 99 studio chanting "Gay Power to the People! Gay Power to the People!" *Thursdays Drummer* wrote:

> "Freaking out [Wade] spun around to face angry fairies in his closet-sized studio. … Eljay [Wade] started into a tacky number with words with one Gay Liberation Fellow, as another flew behind him and pushed the on-the-air button and resumed the GAY POWER TO THE PEOPLE chant in the middle of a record. Kids doing their homework were now tripping out on the first shot of energy into LJW's otherwise tired program … Eljay was feeling his tight-assed program being loosened up by freaking fag revolutionaries."

Meanwhile, Austin GLF announced they were sponsoring a four-day nationwide conference from March 25-28, 1971, in response to the failures of the Black Panther Revolutionary People's Conventions in Philadelphia and Washington DC. *Rag* wrote:

> "Gay people can not adequately deal with the vital questions affecting their lives in brief caucuses associated with other conventions–especially when these conventions are planned by and for straight people. … This conference, planned by and for gays, can be an opportunity to talk openly about how we are oppressed by our traditional lifestyle. We are making the arrangements, especially with respect to housing, in a way that we hope will reduce the tendency for us to see each other as sex objects."

This was in response to complaints from GLF members–notably Boston GLF–that some men were being treated as sex objects at the Panther Conventions. Later, it was reported in *Quicksilver Times* that the Austin Gay Lib Convention was a success, with a picnic and workshops, including one with former Venceremos brigadista talking about the cleansing of gays in Cuba. In a letter addressed "Dear J.," published in the *Great Speckled Bird*, Steve Abbott penned his personal impressions, saying the most "head-changing" part of the conference was not the meetings, workshops, or picnic:

> "It was meeting Frank from Berkeley. Frank had longish hair and a beautiful reddish brown beard. Unlike others he did not talk at meetings, yet I felt that his presence was one of the most influential. He simply walked in wearing long orange stockings, navy blue dress with white polka dots and an army jacket. And sitting down he would proceed to knit. Frank was part of the Radical Fems Against Sexism Caucus. Unlike drag queens, these brothers did not hide their gender. They emphatically did reject the Patriarchal masculine role, however, the manly 'need' to dominate, control, make verbal ideological points and so on. One brother told me that he felt that while the goal of GLF was to go beyond sex roles, even Gay Men could not do so without first rejecting the

status of pants. Maybe Nixon can't pull out of Vietnam for the same reason he can't put on a dress–he's afraid to lose face."

In the *Great Speckled Bird*, Steve Abbott reported on the 1st Midwest Regional Gay Liberation Conference at Northern Illinois University (NIU), held on April 16, 1971. Fourteen colleges from six states were represented. The gathering included thirty-eight members of NIUGLF, and University groups from Louisville, KY; Wisconsin State, Platteville; Chicago; Oberlin College, OH; U of Illinois, Urbana and Chicago Circle; U of Southern Illinois, Carbondale; U of Iowa, Iowa City; and U of Kansas, Lawrence, who arrived in a "sea-green Volkswagen love-bug." According to a report by Al, an NIUGLF member, archived at the McCormick Library of Special Collections at Northwestern University, the opening night "was a groove with Gay Libbers dancing to the sounds of Diana Ross and the Jackson Five, wearing everything from Farmer John overalls to hot pants." At the General Session, the GLF groups introduced themselves and updated their status. The University of Kansas GLF said they were founded in August 1970 and were still trying to get recognition from the university. Oberlin College had only been in existence for one month and already had thirty men and five women members. The University of Louisville had legal problems after two women applied for a marriage license. The University of Iowa also had legal problems after one member was sued for corrupting a minor after speaking before a high school class. The subject of the first workshop was "Gay Civil Rights," lead by Chicago lesbian lawyer Renee Hanover, who suggested GLF move away from universities and take root in the surrounding communities. She asked: "What are you young people going to do with your degrees? Are you going to use them to help fight sexism and promote Gay Liberation?"

In late-May Thomas Shales wrote "Gay Liberation in DC" in the *DC Gazette*, casting a jaundiced eye over a GLF Meeting:

"Meetings of the Gay Liberation Front in DC don't exactly come to order. They aren't supposed to. There is no president, no chairman, no recording secretary. There is really no organization. ... An awful lot of people wanted to speak their pieces–and did. Sometimes the more interesting personal experiences related would be subsequently put down by the alleged radicals in the group who said that time had been wasted on trivia. There was constant stress between radical, liberal, moderate and semi-conservative elements of the group. Worse, there was the continuing game of what's-my-guilt? being played. One person would accuse another of racism and then he would be accused of classism. 'Where are all our black sisters?' somebody asked one night. 'In women's lib,' somebody answered. Then a former SDS leader declared, 'Women were feeling a whole lot of (male) chauvinism within the organization, so they split.' He then accused most people in the group of sexism. ... One member, older than many, was continually castigated because he wore a hairpiece. It came to symbolize his bourgeois capitulation to the straight world, apparently; he had a respectable job, that sort of thing. The issue of his toupee kept coming up until one week it came off–he tore the thing from his head and threw it on the floor."

Not surprisingly, attendance at Washington DC GLF meetings was in decline. In other parts of the country, GLF was just starting up. *Outlaw*, in St. Louis, MO, published "Gay Militancy" about St. Louis GLF, which read like a revolutionary press release from the Berkeley GLF a year before. On the cover of Spokane's *Provincial Press*, a headline read: "This issue deals mainly with WOMEN'S LIBERATION and GAY LIBERATION (if these two issues offend you, you should read them twice). ALL POWER TO ALL PEOPLE."

While some lesbians left GLF to join Women's Lib, they weren't welcomed with open arms there either. Kate Millet, author of *Sexual Politics*, caused a storm of controversy when she "came out" as bisexual. It started with an article in the August 31, 1970 issue of *Time* magazine that described Millet as the "Mao Tse-Tung of Women's Liberation." A follow up article on December 8 "outed" her. Earlier, while sitting on a panel at a conference on sexual liberation at Columbia University, an audience member asked Millett: "Why don't you say you're a lesbian, here, openly. You've said you were a lesbian in the past." In response, Millett said she was bisexual. Unbeknownst to her, the exchange was taped by a *Time* magazine reporter who concluded that Millett's bisexuality would "reinforce the views of those skeptics who routinely dismiss all liberationists as lesbians." The reporter noted that Irving Howe, in *Harper*'s magazine, had described *Sexual Politics* as "a farrago of blunders, distortions, vulgarities and plain nonsense." Even though Howe was unaware of Millett's bisexuality at the time, he sensed a sexual ambiguity in its author. He wrote that Millett "shows very little warmth toward women and very little awareness of their experience. There are times, one feels, the book was written by a female impersonator." Helen Lawrenson in *Esquire* was more direct, describing Millett's book as "the splenetic frenzy of hatred for men" and Women's Lib as "these sick, silly creatures."

The reaction to Kate Millett's bisexuality in the Women's Liberation movement was mixed. In the *Great Speckled Bird*, Vicki reported that several prominent members of the women's movement held a press conference in New York in response to the *Time* article, where they expressed "their solidarity with the struggle of homosexuals to attain their liberation in a sexist society." Vicki wrote:

"Gloria Steinem, a journalist; Ruth Simpson, president of the New York chapter of Daughters of Bilitis; Florynce Kennedy, a black woman lawyer; Sally

Kempton and Susan Brownmiller, journalists and members of New York Radical Feminists; and Ivy Bottini, Dolores Alexander and Ti-Grace Atkinson of NOW. Supporting statements from Bella Abzug, Democratic Representative from the 19th Congressional District; Caroline Bird, author of *Born Female*; and Aileen Hernandez, national president of NOW were read. The statement said in part: 'Women's liberation and homosexual liberation are both struggling towards a common goal: a society free from defining and categorizing people by virtue of gender and/or sexual preference. 'Lesbian' is a label used as a psychic weapon to keep women locked into their male-defined 'feminine role.' The essence of that role is that a woman is defined in terms of her relationship to men. A woman is called a Lesbian when she functions autonomously. Women's autonomy is what women's liberation is all about.'"

In March, Millett spoke at Emory College in Atlanta, where she reiterated her support for gay liberation. Maude in the *Great Speckled Bird* wrote that Millett criticized the "patriotic heterosexuality" of America, and said: "No woman can be free as long as 'faggot' is a pejorative term." In *Village Voice*, Vivian Gornick found the *Time* article "appalling":

"Hundreds of women in the feminist movement are lesbians. Many of them have worked in the women's movement from its earliest days of organized activity. … Sitting next to a heterosexual feminist who might rise in distress at a meeting to say: 'Oh, let's not do that. They'll think we're a bunch of lesbians,' the lesbian in the next seat could not rise and say: 'But I am a lesbian,' because her admission would have forced to the surface a wealth of fears only half understood which would then quickly have been converted into panic and denunciation."

The debate played out in the letters pages of the underground press. In the *Great Speckled Bird*, Tor Bay wrote:

"It is amusing indeed to hear straight sisters say that it is a gross insult to the really great feminists of herstory, Susan B. Anthony and Lucy Stone, to get so tarnished an image by association since these two, along with Gertrude Stein, Emily Dickinson and many more, have already made their place in the herstory of Lesbians as intellectual giants."

26

GLF BURN OUT

The Gay Activists Alliance in New York, San Francisco, and Washington DC recognize the power of the "Gay Vote" as a weapon in the battle for gay rights. The 2nd annual Christopher Street celebration of the Stonewall Riots was a great success, with little participation from GLF. Articles begin to appear in the underground press about the New Left, the Venceremos Brigade, and others in the "Movement," abandoning gay rights. The last nail in the coffin is when the Socialist Workers Party attempt to co-opt GLF, leading to more defections. In Atlanta, when only two people turn up for a Georgia GLF meeting, they vote to disband the group.

"In truth my homosexuality made me a nigger, a blameless person neither good nor evil suffering at the hands of his fellow men, never knowing why; suffering for no reason save my existence. The words 'queer' and 'nigger' are dirty words. Faggot and darkie. Symbols of degradation just as the Cross was a symbol for all the ugliness that the Roman Empire could heap upon the heads of its oppressed peoples. The Cross became in the hands of Europe the symbol for one of man's most sublime hopes, some of its great art, one of his most beautiful loves. The words nigger and queer will function in a like manner in the future of the world."–"Homosexuality Made Me a Nigger" in *Rag*.

In the spring of 1971, veteran homosexual rights activist Franklin E. Kameny became the first openly gay person to run for Congress, as the Personal Freedom Candidate for DC's non-voting seat in the House of

Representatives. The *D.C. Gazette* published this biography from his campaign literature:

"Franklin E. Kameny, 45, is an astronomer, physicist, author, lecturer, and D.C. resident for 15 years. He holds a Ph.D. in astronomy from Harvard University and has taught at Georgetown University. Kameny is a WWII combat veteran, former Executive Board member of the Congress of Racial Equality, and founder and President of the Mattachine Society of Washington. A champion of human rights, Kameny led the Washington homosexual contingent during Martin Luther King's 1963 March on Washington. A prolific writer, Kameny has had articles published in many prominent periodicals, including the *New Republic*, the *Humanist*, and *Sexology*."

Kameny came in fourth among six candidates. In June, Tony Jackubosky wrote in the *D.C. Gazette*, that Kameny's campaign workers discovered a segment of the gay population who wanted to be politically active but didn't fit into Washington DC's gay organizations: "Gays who couldn't hack GLF's 'burn the bars' rhetoric, or who were turned off by Mattachine's discreet conservatism were, politically speaking, still in the closet." When New York's Gay Activists Alliance (GAA) volunteered on the Kameny campaign, the campaign workers were impressed by their commitment to "direct action to achieve the one goal which gays of every political persuasion can agree on: equal rights for homosexuals." Kameny's campaign workers set about founding a GAA chapter in Washington DC.

In the *D.C. Gazette* Jackubosky wrote:

"Consciousness-raising, rather than political action, has been and will probably continue to be GLF's most effective contribution. GLF is hampered from political action, both by its radical disdain for electoral politics, which soured many GLFer's on the Kameny effort, and by a concern to deal with a whole lot of isms other than sexism. In trying to purge your self of racism, male and beauty-chauvinism, classism, and capitalism, GLF members developed a multi-issue concern, which spread their struggle thin over every conceivable political front. ... Looking back, GLF's success in bringing gays out of the closet, and helping us overcome internalized oppression, leads directly to a group like GAA to work at eradicating that oppression from society. While GLF lacks organization in order to encourage consciousness-raising and self-expression, GAA has to be organized–with elected officers and the whole show–in order to be an effective source of zaps."

Over the next few months, GAA-style single-issue groups sprang up nationwide. In New Brunswick's *All You Can Eat*, a letter from John talks about the "rapid growth from two dozen to five dozen men and women" in the Gay Activist Alliance of New Jersey; in the *Venice Beachhead*, out of

Venice, CA, Lavender People formed to focus on gay-issues only. The *Columbus Free Press* noted that the city's GLF formed in early 1971, but in the fall became the Columbus Gay Activist Alliance. By November 1971 the Tulsa Gay Alliance had "Come Out of Mothballs" as *Osmosis* put it. *Fifth Estate* wrote that on November 20th 1971, Detroit Gay Activists picketed the J.L. Hudson Co. department store protesting the entrapment of gay men in their restrooms. And in early 1972, Mary in Oregon's *Eugene Augur*, reported that Eugene's Gay People's Alliance was meeting the Human Rights Commission in the City Council Chambers, trying to extend the human rights ordinance to include protection of homosexuals.

One event that foretold the future of gay activism, but was anathema to GLF and their disdain for electoral politics, occurred in October 1971 when San Francisco Gay Activists Alliance organized a "Candidates for Mayor Night." The *Berkeley Barb* explained:

"In 1969, all of San Francisco was shocked when Dianne Feinstein received more votes than any other candidate running for the Board of Supervisors. At first, no one could explain it, but it has become clear to San Francisco politicians and public media since then that a new political force that had to be taken seriously had emerged in the city. The force is the so-called homosexual community, numbering perhaps as many as 130,000 of SF's total 725,000 population. The city's most established homosexual rights organization, the Society for Individual Rights [SIR], claimed credit for mustering support for the surprise election of Dianne Feinstein to the supervisor presidency."

All the candidates agreed to be there: Harold Dobbs, Scott Newhall, Fred Selinger, Nathan Weinstein, and Dianne Feinstein. Nick Benton later reported in the *Berkeley Barb* that Dianne Feinstein failed to show-up: "Her conspicuous absence ... raised conjecture among some that she might have been advised to avoid alienating establishment gays by appearing at a GAA-sponsored meeting–since GAA has sharp differences with the much larger and more established SIR." It was becoming clear that the "Gay Vote" was a more potent weapon in the gay armory than angry GLF threats of an armed revolution. Articles began appearing in the underground press soliciting support from candidates seeking elected office. Don Jackson, in the *Los Angeles Free Press*, wrote: "Scores of politicians are making promises in bids for the Gay vote. Shrewd politicians sense that the Gay vote is a slumbering giant about to wake. And a giant it is indeed: the 21 million voting-age homosexuals outnumber all racial minority voters combined." In the *Lincoln Gazette*, the Lincoln Gay Action Group listed the candidates in Nebraska's primary ballot and their positions on gay rights. The *North Carolina Anvil* reported that the Raleigh Triangle Gay Alliance asked candidates "from the courthouse to the Capitol" where they stood on gay issues. Congressional candidates were asked:

"Would you work for an end to income tax discrimination against single persons?

"Will you support federal laws forbidding discrimination against homosexuals in employment, housing, and public accommodations?

"Will you support an end to federal aid to institutions discriminating against homosexuals?

"Will you support recognition of the constitutional rights and respects due people without regard to their sexual orientation?"

"Christopher Street Liberation Week June 19-27" read the headline in Milwaukee's *Kaleidoscope*, an article urging gay readers to join the celebrations in Chicago organized by the Chicago Gay Alliance. On May 4, 1971 the city of Chicago granted Permit #71-114 to CGA for the Gay Pride parade on Sunday, June 27. The Gay Pride Week Committee published *Chicago Gay Pride*, a twenty-four page newspaper containing news, a schedule of events, articles about the various gay groups involved in Pride, photographs of Pride 1970, and a list of resources and advertisements. Pride Week 1971 kicked off with the Gay Pride Week Committee discussing Pride Week on Chuck Collins' *Underground News*, a TV show offering a radical take on political and cultural events, with guests like the Grateful Dead, John Lennon, and the Chicago Seven. After a week of events, the Pride Parade, attended by 1,000 people, snaked through Lakeview, the gay neighborhood, and ended with a Gay-In in Lincoln Park. The only Chicago GLF event was a Kiss-In at the Civic Center protesting the April 30 arrest of John Cantrell and Richard Chinn, two gay men charged for what Chinn, in *Chicago Gay Pride,* called "a peck of a kiss that would have been overlooked had we been two men from the 'old country.'" Chinn wrote:

"To the plainclothes pigs who arrested us, the sight of two men kissing is indecent. They are not moved to anger by the death and mayhem this country is causing in Southeast Asia. They are not moved to anger by hundreds of years of racism and inequality for American minorities. They are not touched by hungry children whose lives are damned from the beginning by their poverty. ... But the sight of two men kissing they find 'indecent.'"

The GLF Kiss-In on June 25 followed a protest outside the courthouse at 321 N. LaSalle St. where John Cantrell and Richard Chinn were on trial. The indecent peck occurred after they alighted from a bus and parted ways, only to be pounced on and charged with disorderly conduct, public indecency, and lewd fondling. They were released on $1,000 bond each. Virginia wrote in Chicago's *Seed* that after the Kiss-In the protestors danced around the Civic Center, holding hands, waving signs and chanting: "Say it loud, gay is proud! 3, 5, 7, 9, lesbians are mighty fine! 2, 4, 6, 8, gay is just (twice) as good as straight. Ho-ho-homosexual, the ruling class is ineffectual!" She continued:

"There were about ten pigs standing around looking uptight, but they weren't into hassling us. The vibes from the crowd surrounding us didn't feel particularly hostile. I think many of the people were interested in what we had to say—some seemed very sympathetic."

The trial lasted until July 13, when the charges were dropped.

"In the court of Judge Dunn, Branch 46, the state and the city both dropped their trumped up charges to the surprise of the two pigs who arrested the Gay brothers. Before the judge dismissed them he said that they would not use his courtroom to advance their cause and that now they 'wouldn't get the publicity.'"

Cantrell and Chinn were members of the Fiery Flames Collective and their rhetoric was fiery indeed. One of their leaflets read:

"SMASH IMPERIALISM! ... We, Gay Women, Gay Men, Transvestites, and Transexuals in Amerikkka, who have been systematically and deliberately oppressed and exploited in this country through sexism, male supremacy, racism, and capitalism, feel that the war waged against the South-East Asian people by the government of the United States is an extension of our oppression. War, Amerikkkan style, is a male chauvinist's game, where to prove his masculinity, he must maim, or kill Women and Children, the very old and the very young, and his own brothers. ... We, as Gays, are part of the struggle of the Vietnamese, Laotian, Thai, and Cambodian people and feel solidarity with them. In this spirit we sign this treaty of peace, love and struggle."

According to the *Berkeley Barb*, San Francisco celebrated the 2nd anniversary of Stonewall earlier than other California cities like Los Angeles and San Jose. San Francisco's festivities began with a rally at Union Square with speakers in support of the passage of AB437, the Willie Brown sponsored bill in the State Assembly that would legalize all sexual acts between consenting adults in private. The rally was followed by the Long March, led by the Rev. Troy Perry, pastor of the Metropolitan Community Church in Los Angeles, from Oakland's Lake Merritt to Sacramento, to support and publicize Willie Brown's Bill. In the *Berkeley Barb*, Leo Laurence wrote that there were thirteen marchers, a few more joined along the way, while others fell by the wayside. The marchers camped out overnight, arriving in Sacramento eighty-two miles and five days later. At the State Capital, there was another rally. As Perry described it: "We opened and closed with prayer, sang THIS IS MY COUNTRY, heard Assemblyman Willie Brown shout Power-to-the-People, and saw dozens of clenched fist salutes." Laurence wrote:

> "Then a strange trip in the sky. Directly overhead during the rally, a circular dark cloud formed, the sun was behind it, and there was a rainbow around its perimeter. I've never seen anything like it before. San Francisco's Assemblyman John Burton was speaking at that moment. He looked up and said, 'I've heard of Gay Power, but this is ridiculous.'"

In October a *Berkeley Barb* headline read: "Ass-Holes Preserve Sodomy Statute." The article blamed bible-thumpers for rejecting 41 to 25 Willie Brown's third attempt at passing the "homosexual bill of rights."

Cyclops, in the *Great Speckled Bird*, described Atlanta's first Gay Pride celebration in flowery prose:

> "Brightmorning on the corner Anxiousfaces relaxed clothes huddledtogether. 'Only ten,' i thought, "no more?" Then arms, legs, faces, warpaint, robes, signs, bongos, buttons. And the sound grows from chirping to chatter; and there's a group of women from NOW, and YSA socialists selling their paper, and Moe from the *Bird* giving freely his smile, and Fisher (i think) giving freely his chanting: 'Ho, Ho, Homosexual, Sodomy laws are ineffectual!' And joyfully we begin to overflow our little corner. 'Has anybody got a cigarette?' Cars driving by 7th and Peachtree Sunday saw this picture behind a lavender sheen banner proclaiming GAY POWER. People in the cars (Sundaybest) took leaflets and stared. This had never been seen in Atlanta before, Gaysexuals getting it together on public street number one, saying it LOUD, saying it PROUD. ... The size of the March: Bill counts over eighty, Phil counts over 100, Mike says 200, UPI later writes 50, but the spirited chants sound like 500. It is a respectable many. And we tambourine our way to the park."

In *Quicksilver Times*, an anonymous author penned "Christopher Street West," writing that 2,000 gays, fifty-four groups, and fifteen floats, were in the Los Angeles parade after a week of activities, including the Western Regional Gay Men's Conference. One popular float, a giant caterpillar with sixteen dancing legs, symbolized how a caterpillar changes into a butterfly. However, Sergeant Sherman of the Los Angeles Police department thought it was "a giant penis," and threatened to arrest those inside:

> "GLF spokesman Ralph Schaffer said: 'Apparently the policeman's cock looks like a worm so he thinks all cocks look like worms. I've seen thousands of penises, but I've never seen one with eyelashes.' ... The flaccid worm was captured by police as it lay dying on Hollywood Blvd, after the people inside the worm had split."

In the same issue of *Quicksilver Times*, another anonymous author wrote "Christopher Street East," saying 5,000–10,000 people celebrated the

Stonewall Riots in New York City by marching from Christopher Street in Greenwich Village to Central Park. In the article, Anon suggested the New Left had rejected gay rights:

"This year, though, it is clear from the mood of the crowd, we are more sober. … We are more sober now because we realize that unity and victory will come only after long and bitter struggle–nearly all of which lies ahead. … At this moment in history the eradication of sexism toward gay people as an integral part of a whole revolutionary process in which capitalism, imperialism, male supremacy, sexism toward women, and racism would be destroyed is anything but certain as a goal or even an issue for struggle with perhaps most revolutionaries. When gay people were so much involved in Mayday [anti-Vietnam War protest in Washington, DC] at all levels, it disgusted me to read in the liberated *Guardian* and elsewhere reports of that week with not one mention of the way many gay people were fucked over or of their presence in the actions. Our very existence and our struggle are still negligible to far too many people who claim to be revolutionaries and liberators. … The weekend commemorating the Christopher Street riots coincided with my first chance to talk with a gay brother who had been on the fourth Venceremos Brigade. … [He] told me about watching on live Cuban TV the declaration of the First National Congress on Education and Culture, which denounced Cultural Imperialism and included a statement on homosexuality. The whole Brigade and the Cuban leadership were sitting at the tables in a large hall. When the extremely anti-gay repressive passages on homosexuality was read, the Cubans and the most anti-gay of the North Americans began pounding the tables and cheering in the presence of the gay Brigadistas. … To repeat the description of the scene is not vindictiveness toward the Cubans but an attempt to point out the limits in practice and theory of dogmatic Marxism-Leninism as an approach to eliminating sexism. … The most vicious and hypocritical of the North Americans were some of those who were most 'adept' in Marxist theory."

The betrayal to gay people of the Cuban Revolution and the Venceremos Brigade continued to be a sore point. In August, in the *Berkeley Barb*, Ralph Hall wrote:

"In short, the Cuban declaration means that after 10 years of revolution in Cuba, homosexuality still exists. Therefore, a systematic process would be invoked against gay people excluding them, in every conceivable way, from the Revolution, and that all forms of mental and physical persecution, including a cure treatment for notorious and open-about-it gays and/or shipment to concentration camps or farms, isolation and extermination would ensure and be the solution to the problem, the eradication of gay people in Cuba and their dreadful disease plaguing their people and the Revolution. I'm going to be sick!"

In St. Louis' *Outlaw* two local brigadistos attempted to put the issue in context:

"It is important … to understand the context in which the resolutions were passed. Before the Revolution, almost all visible homosexuality was part of the decadent Havana life that wealthy Northamericans brought to Cuba. Homosexuality was rightly seen at that time not as a liberating human relationship, but as an exploitation and enslavement. The Cubans are legitimately trying to destroy this kind of homosexuality, along with other forms of decadence such as prostitution, gambling and drugs. But in the same way that growing sugar was bad for Cuba when the profits went to Northamerican companies but is good for Cuba now that the profits make Cuba's economic development possible, so homosexuality which was enslaving and decadent under capitalism is not necessarily so under socialism."

In the *Great Speckled Bird*, Steve Abbott wrote about how hurt he was when he read Jerry Rubin's book *Do It* and found homophobic statements, and also by the actions of the First National Congress and Education and Culture in Cuba. Abbott asked:

"How am I as a Gay socialist who has always supported Cuba, to feel? Should I say, 'Well, it's just a tiny part of a long document.' Should I say, 'Well, they have tremendous pressure from US Imperialism and they've made tremendous gains for the poor, the sick, the illiterate, so it's okay if they decide to scapegoat and stomp us queers? And where is the public defense from my straight-identified sisters and brothers on the Left? Would you be as passive if Blacks or women were attacked as 'social pathological deviants?' Or do you too think my 2,000-year-old struggle for liberation is secondary or irrelevant to the 'main issues' on the Left?"

It was clear that GLF was in decline, as members dropped out, or joined one-issue groups like GAA. GLF played less of a role in organizing the second Christopher Street Liberation than they did the first. In the *Village Voice*, Arthur Bell, author of *Dancing the Gay Lib Blues*, wrote:

"Happy birthday, gay liberation, happy birthday to you! The baby is two years old and the song is sung by Martha Shelley and Allen Young and Judy from New York's defunct Gay Liberation Front, under a Christopher Street banner, a stone's throw from the old Stonewall Inn, so long ago and far away. … Early gay liberation faces–Jerry Hooze and Craig Rodwell and Marty Nixon–have come out for the celebration. Young serious politicos, wearing granny glasses and toting knapsacks, buss the likes of Eben Clark and Jean De Vante. … Sylvia of STAR is there–and Marsha and Bebe and Natasha. … Jill Johnston was there. … Pete Fisher and Marc Rubin pass by, arm in arm, caressing. Kate Millett arrives. … Three days prior to the march, I spotted Bob Kohler in front of the *Voice* office. Kohler is one of the founders of the Gay Liberation Front. He's quieted down lately, seldom seen at marches, no longer a fixture outside the late Women's House of Detention with his dog and his pamphlets. He's kvetching less and looking better. 'I lived, ate, slept, shit gay liberation for two years,' he said. "I was leading a closed, incestuous existence. A few months ago, I just dropped out. Now I'm getting myself back into the mainstream and putting my body where my mouth was. You can talk gay lib forever and picket until you're blue in the face, but the time has come for me to relate to the department store clerks, the sanitation people, the workers of the world who don't know 'movement' to try to raise their consciousness. I no longer feel the need of an organization for a crutch. Gay Liberation Front in New York, as it had been set up, is no longer in existence. It was used as a springboard from which other organizations and collectives were formed. We have a Gay Activists Alliance now, but for anyone to hang onto an organization is wrong. I'd like to see the movement use its sixth sense like an animal and kick its young out when they're ready and push them into something better. Encourage people to leave the great father and go into the world and relate."

While some GLF groups struggled to survive, others were just starting up. The *Great Speckled Bird* published a letter from Roger Benson, an inmate at Washington State Prison, Walla Walla:

"We here at the prison are trying something that I think is new to prisons in the United States. We have started a Gay Liberation Front. We are still in the process of organizing but already we have made some steps forward that we had doubts of ever making. First, the administration is admitting that we are here and that we are human. Second, they are letting us organize our group and even giving us some badly needed help. Third, we are no longer segregated when it comes to our celling units or job assignments."

Other GLF groups remained active, though the degree to which they fit the criteria of being "revolutionaries" is questionable. San Jose's *Red Eye* reported that the GLF Community Drop-In Center would be opening its doors with a potluck dinner. In the Texas *Rag*, Austin's GLF promised consciousness-raising groups in the "Y" auditorium every Monday night. Madison's *Kaleidoscope* reported that GLF were opening a new rap center at 10 Langdon Street. And the *Great Speckled Bird* noted that Atlanta GLF elected new officers: Alex Joyce, Co-chairwoman; Phil Lambert, Co-chairman; Bill Smith, Treasurer; and Shelby Cullom, Secretary.

The idea of elected officials or any form of hierarchy was anathema to most GLF groups, including the University of Chicago GLF. The *Chicago Gay Alliance Newsletter* reported that UCGLF had opened an office on campus at the Ida Noyes Hall. A "Gay Message" flyer, composed by "some gays who have just abdicated their leadership positions, nasty and subversive as it is to be leaders," and housed at the McCormick Library of Special Collections at Northwestern University, Evanston, IL, reads:

"The office is just a place to meet and talk with other gay people–for whatever purpose you want. The important thing is that it's your office–not the 'leaders' or the 'doers.' If you want to come and answer the phone, answer some questions or ask them, or just talk to other people, this is your office to do it in. The office has no organization or leaders; it is operating only when people are there. Come for as long or as short a time as you want, but please come, otherwise there is no office."

In the summer of 1971 more members of GLF doubted the role of homosexuals in the Movement. Donald in the Rag wrote:

"To write an article on gays and the revolution for a straight radical newspaper is a strange thing for me to do. I find it next to impossible for various reasons to relate to any kind of straight revolutionary movement. Male radicals are (in my own experience anyway) as infested with sexism as other straight men in our society. It takes many forms: casual imputations of homosexuality to certain vile establishment figures, degrading attitudes toward women as sex objects (despite endless 'right-ons' for women's liberation), and the subtle male egotism of being a 'revolutionary leader.' Although it is risky to debunk culture heroes, a particularly striking exemplar of all these forms of sexism is Eldridge Cleaver. From reading Soul on Ice, it is clear that he is obsessed with the symbols of masculinity (guns and violence) and is contemptuous of gay people and women. What of the countries that are supposedly revolutionary socialist, that are held up as models for the fledgling second American revolution (of undeniable evil) with the bloody purges and convulsive violence of the People's Republic of China? What is Chairman Mao but another 'great man,' another monstrous male ego? Cuba is a favorite example for American radicals. Yet the dictatorship that now rules Cuba has an official policy of persecuting gay people. ... We should (we are told) try to convince Cuba that we are part of the revolution. Having discovered the growing strength and militancy of the Gay movement, straight radicals are trying to co-opt it. ____ Power to ____ People. Fill in the blanks with the appropriate minority; it is a formula to fit any movement into the ranks of their revolution. The history of the 20th century is the history of revolutions betrayed. Each time, one set of 'big men' is replaced by another, this time called revolutionary leaders. I want no part of another male-dominated sexist revolution. It has nothing to offer gay people."

The disintegration of the relationship between GLF and the New Left lead to skirmishes with the underground press. In the Gay Pride issue, the *Seed* published a humorous article called "We Are Who We Eat," which prompted a letter from John:

"I still cannot believe that the *Seed* would publish such a thing. ... A heavy handed un-funny parody of aspects of the movement, with a special swat in the face for Gay Lib (Cannibal Pride Day, CA, ELF, 'out of the kitchens and into the streets). ... Consider the message and make the translation as follows:

'Another movement. Don't we have enough important causes already? What are those queer cannibals into now?' 'Will a fellow employee be safe having lunch with a cannibal? Do cannibals eat every part of the anatomy?' 'Of course there are always some who wear bones in their noses at parades?' And over all, the clear implication: If we tolerate those queers I suppose cannibals will be next. And who will we have to put up with after that?"

On the same page is a letter from the Third World Gay Revolution (TWGR) and Gay Liberation Front, accusing the *Seed* of racism and sexism. The complaint related to an article submitted by TWGR that was laid-up badly. The *Seed* replied:

"We are sorry about the layout of this article. Lack of proofreading is evident throughout the last issue and happens many times to articles staff write. However, we found problems in getting the writers of this letter to work with us. We asked them to come in and help layout the article. We asked them to meetings. ... Many organizations when submitting articles for consideration come in and talk to us about them, are open to revisions, assist us in the layout of the article, insuring that it will come across as meant. This was not the case with the Gay Liberation Front in the last issue."

Similarly, an article in Dallas' *Iconoclast*, under the headline "Gays Call Meeting" read:

"Thirteen gay brothers and two friendly reporters came into the News office July 5, singing and fluttering. For four hours the Sugar Plum Fairies Gay Liberation men cited their complaints over the 'Gay Pride' issue of the *Dallas News*; there wasn't much gay news; the cover of a man walking down a road by himself was unsatisfactory; the 'gay' advertisements were sexist; the 'Gay brothers and sisters unite' graphic of a naked man and woman should have been two men or two women or both, according to the gay men. ... As the gay brothers left the office they sang, 'I don't want no straight men fuckin' over me.'"

In the *Berkeley Barb*, Ralph Hall accused the Liberation News Service (LNS) of censoring a letter written by gays in Cuba:

"I ... condemn one of the American Revolution's foremost news services, the Liberation News Service ... for their bungling and hesitant release of the publicity surrounding Cuba's inane and anti-gay policy; as well as for the censorship of portions of the letter by Gay Cuban brothers who smuggled their letter out of Cuba to North American gays. LNS took it upon themselves to revise, transform and delete (censor) words, sentences and paragraphs of the letter in question, which were most pertinent to both its continuity and its meaning, and the gay constituency it was written to, gays the world over."

The letter was published in *Rag*. One paragraph read: "The homosexual here is hurt and attacked, obliged to conceal what the authorities consider an aberration or repudiable defect. This concealment varies from forcing us to marry and appear to live a 'normal' life to confining us to farms where the treatment is brutal."

In early December 1971, Diamond Lil wrote in the *Great Speckled Bird* about her trip to California, which brought this response on the Letter's Page from Campy Simplex:

"I am writing to you as a Gay person, a revolutionary anarchist, and an ardent admirer of the *Great Speckled Bird*. In all three capacities I was dismayed and perplexed to find in your December 6th issue an article by Atlanta's foremost 'drag queen,' Diamond Lil, on a trip she took to California. I have nothing against drag queens writing about trips to California, but I'm at a loss to understand why the *Bird* staff considered this material appropriate to any of its editorial purposes. There are plenty of Gay magazines (like *David*, published in Florida) that are panting for exactly this sort of campy, sexist, crypto-elitist, Sunday-Brunch-Drag-Show-at-the-Snottiest-Gay-Bar patter. Why did the *Bird* feel obliged to publish it? I have noticed that fewer and fewer substantive articles on the Gay movement have been appearing in the *Bird* in the past few months, and this makes the publication of Diamond Lil's piece all the more disconcerting, by shifting the emphasis from progressive aspects of Gay liberation to stereotypical representations of the old unliberated "faggot" (no other word for it). Does the absence of articles reflect the death of the Gay Liberation movement, at least in Atlanta? Diamond Lil's piece throws considerable light on the reasons for the failure of the GLF to change consciousness, the way the women's liberation movement has done. Traditionally, Gay people have been considered, and have considered themselves, 'advanced' and 'free' because they are not tied down by society's sexual standards and because their self-expression does not conform to the definitions of 'masculine' and 'feminine' behavior generally agreed upon and followed in western civilization. Yet the alternative modes of conduct that most Gay people have chosen have not represented genuine liberation from meaningless restrictions, but pathetic and exaggerated copying of the worst features of 'straight' society. ... One would hope that if GLF means anything, it means the liberating of Gay people to find and be themselves, not to try and be Joan Crawford or Bette Davis."

In Boston, GLF had been a short-lived affair for a few months in 1970, but out of it came Gay Women's Liberation, the Gay Male Liberation collective (GML), and the Monday Night Study Group. In the August *Win*, Charles Shively, not a member of GML, reported on the collapse and modus operandi within the gay commune, living in a dilapidated house beyond repair:

"The economy and management of its finances were never worked out. A basic problem was that those with jobs and resources were hesitant to entrust everything to the community. And those without jobs often criticized those working for 'selling out.' ... With inadequately coordinated finances, the commune suffered. At the very beginning, a gay brother ripped off hundreds of dollars from the community funds. At one coffeehouse, most of the money was taken from the contribution jar. ... What is indisputable is that groups within the house (and within gay liberation) related to one another in a very macho way. Brother would call brother 'pig' or 'queen' in order to make a point; brothers speaking would often be interrupted. The contest was sometimes who could stamp their foot the hardest, who could yell loudest, or even who could hit hardest. The less macho brothers felt understandably intimidated, fearing abuse from their brothers if what they said was not acceptable and as a result fewer and fewer brothers tended to speak at meetings."

Also in *Win*, John Kyper, a member of GML, explained that the individual who stole money called himself Wade and later stole funds from other GLF's in Washington DC and Milwaukee. Kypers' article gives an insight into how radical gays "lost it" with the New Left and how the Socialist Workers Party co-opted the Gay Liberation Front:

"At first we had to build our own movement for ourselves. We received little help from the rest of the Movement, just the jeers that homosexuality was 'a bourgeois disease that does not exist under Socialism.' Sadly, here the Left has been as bigoted as the Right. Read Eldridge Cleaver: 'Homosexuality is a sickness, just as are baby-rape or wanting to become head of General Motors.' Or the snide attempts of Tom Hayden and Jerry Rubin to lampoon their enemies by insinuating that they were fags. Presumably the dedication of the early homophile organizations was not revolutionary enough to inspire their enthusiasm. Presumably, also, fag-baiting, prevalent throughout the Left, expressed anxieties about a subject that was too hot for many of its members to handle. ... Like the Socialist Workers Party [SWP]. Until six months ago they, too, had found us too hot to handle and would have nothing to do with us. Homosexuals who were discovered were immediately expelled from the Party. And when they [SWP] advocated Socialism, they proudly pointed to the example of Cuba, a nation that has harshly repressed its maricons. Now, without a word of apology, they assure us that they are on our side. I do not trust them."

Kyper goes on to say that three SWP members attended meetings of the planning committee for Boston's Gay Pride Week:

"I and several other members of the planning committee were openly suspicious of their motives. Our misgivings were quickly confirmed. Apparently, as its contribution to our Gay Pride observance, SWP sponsored its own 'Forum on Gay Liberation,' without the committee's prior consent or knowledge. The first that any of us learned of it was from handbills, which implied that it was a part of the Week's activities."

In November 1971, the *Berkeley Barb* reported that two gay contingents would participate in a November 6 peace march in San Francisco–a Gay Pride and a Gay Women's group. There was also to be a pre-march dance at San Francisco State College sponsored by the SF State GLF. According to the march's organizers, the rationale for joining the peace march was that some gay men forced to stay in the closet were fighting and dying in Vietnam. However, the Gay Activists Alliance opposed gay participation in the peace march. GAA president Ray Broshears told the *Barb*: "Even though the organizers are gay, themselves, we feel their politics are influenced by Socialist Workers Party thinking, and do not represent gay people's interests." The Daughters of Bilitis also refused to endorse the march, denouncing the SWP's "co-option tactics" of the march's organizers.

In January 1972, in the *Berkeley Barb*, William Beardemphl, the first president of SIR, spoke on the subject:

"Nothing has been so laughable in American political life as the inept boorishness of American Communists. Oh I guess, the KKK, the American Nazi Party, the John Birch Society and the Black Panthers have tried very hard to outdo the American Communists for stupid incompetence, but none have quite come up to the Communists ability to do everything incorrectly. Now we have some of these jerks attempting to pervert the homosexuals. Damn Women's Lib or Men's Lib, or religious faggotry exploitation of Nazism, or Communism, or anything else that takes away from the homosexualism of the homosexual movement. In 1972, let's try to get back to plain virile homosexuality."

Beardemphl also said the Women's Liberation Front, "has put lesbians back into the thumbsucking fetal position, and effectively taken lesbians out of the homosexual movement." In July 1972, the SWP infiltration of GLF was again in the news. The *Berkeley Barb* reported that forty-four gays walked out of the Southwest Conference of the National Coalition of Gay Organizations in Bakersfield, CA. Ray Broshears, of the San Francisco GAA, and Mike Itkin of the Hollywood Lavender People, lead the walk-out saying the conference had been hijacked by the Socialist Workers Party and International Socialists. Broshears told the *Berkeley Barb*: "We are facing a time when the gay movement is the 'in' thing. We must resist the temptation and pressure to be used by partisan political interests. Allowing ourselves to be used by them is to have no freedom at all." The SWP infiltration of GLF was the last nail in the coffin of the early 1970s revolutionary gay rights movement. In the winter of 1971 the UPS News Service published two spoof items under the headline "Gay Marx Day.

December 25."

"A Gay Christmas

"800 gay Cubans, men and women, jammed Havana's central square on Christmas Day to protest the Cuban government's repressive position against gay people.

"The plan was to stage a massive 'blow-in' to affirm the right of people in a socialist country to free sexual activity, without interference or condemnation from the state. The action was also planned to celebrate Gay Marx Day–a day which has been set aside in recognition of the fact that Karl Marx himself was actually gay, but could not come out as a gay person because of the strict 'morality' of Victorian England.

"But the demonstration was upstaged by the appearance of Fidel Castro, who arrived unexpectedly as the protest reached its height. Fidel strode to the center of the crowd and announced that he had signed a decree 'ending forever the revisionist anti-gay policy,' and that Cuba 'will never again stand among the ranks of nations which deny their citizens complete identity.'

"Then he left, hugging demonstrators along the way."

And:

"Letter to God

"The recent discovery by a wrecking crew of an unpublished letter by Karl Marx, hidden under the closet floor of a London flat he once occupied, has moved Gay Marxists the world over to proclaim Dec. 25 'Gay Marx Day.' The letter reads as follows:

"Dear God,

"Just thought I would write you an obscene letter to let you know I think you are the hunkiest, most gorgeous, sexiest man in the whole world.

"Listen, I know you have some sort of hang-up about sex. But if you try it just once, you might dig the hell out of it. I mean we homo sapiens really groove on it, and since we were made in your image you may really be latent and not know it. You may not be able to recognize me as one, but I am a qualified, certified Grade 'AA' choice queer. Now, before you get offended, just remember, your only begotten son ran around with 12 dudes all his life. Maybe he was a gay blade, too. Maybe that cross should have said 'Queen of the Jews,' not 'King.'

"Too bad they pulled that shit. He was nice.

"Anyway, if you think we might be compatible, just put on your heels or wings or whatever and boogie on down to Earth, Great Britain, London, king-size bed next to the w.c., and HOLD ON, BABY."

"Love Karl."

In June 1973, Franz Martin looked back on the rise and fall of Detroit GLF in *Fifth Estate*:

"Gay Liberation had a modest beginning in Detroit. One gay person put a small classified ad in *Fifth Estate* asking for responses from people interested in forming a group. Responses were good. … Early meetings of the group were chaotic, with as many as 100 people attending, having wild disparities in interests, goals and political views. Despite disagreements the influence of GLF in its first year was enormous. Gays speaking out in public, demonstrating, leafleting and publishing their own newspaper were all unheard of events in the local gay community."

Martin goes on to say that soon after several controversial demonstrations against the Episcopal Church, GLF disbanded in April 1971. He explained:

"This was because of a splintering process–it went from a broad-based and largely apolitical beginning, to a smaller loose-knit coalition of caucuses (women's, student, third world) all sharing a vaguely New Left perspective but with no direction. Racial, sexual and political divisions split the group, making agreement on any significant issue nearly impossible while keeping membership down."

A month later Bill Smith wrote "Gay is Gone" in the *Great Speckled Bird*:

"The Georgia Gay Liberation Front [GGLF] was established in Atlanta in February of 1971. Billie McClaine and I were elected temporary chairpeople. It was the third organizational meeting for Gay people in Atlanta and more than one hundred people were packed into the New Morningstar Inn. Two people attended the last meeting held by the GGLF. They voted to officially end operations on July 14. After two and a half years of struggle the Georgia Gay liberation Front has closed. Why? … To me the Southeastern Gay Conference, held in Athens, Georgia during November of 1972, marks the point at which the conflicts within the Georgia Gay Liberation Front that eventually ended its effectiveness were brought to the surface. The conflict between gay men and gay women, drags, cosmic drags, anti-drags, the socialists, liberals, marxists, non-marxists, liberal democrats, system and nonsystem people, the organizationalists, the communalists or non-organizationalists, the political and the non-political, was voiced loudly. Returning to Atlanta each group had found strength and support from like-minded people from other cities. The facade of unity fell away, the work of the organization slowed as each group, with renewed vigor, pressed its particular idea or program as the 'right' one. Visitors to our meetings were treated to three and four hours of in-fighting, rhetoric, political diatribes, and large doses of bullshit. I harangued as much as anyone, fighting for my particular viewpoint, leaving the meetings exhausted, uptight and angry. People began to drift away. … Like the politicians in GLF New York, the politicians of GLF Atlanta fought for control, for power over the Gay community, and as a result lost the support of the Gay community and ended up fighting each other and destroying the organization they each cared for, each in their own way, so deeply. The women who left GGLF joined by many others who were never members have formed a strong organization, the Atlanta Lesbian Feminist Alliance. The Metropolitan Community Church, a religious service organization, is firmly established and growing. Other former members have joined political groups such as the Young Socialist Alliance, International Socialist, Socialist Workers Party, etc., forming gay caucuses within these organizations. Hopefully the cycle will be followed completely and Atlanta will have, in the near future, a viable political service organization along the lines of the Gay Activist Alliance."

In October 1971, Nick Benton, one of the most radical gay voices in the underground press, revealed in the *Berkeley Barb* that the revolutionary bravado of GLF was nothing more than a paper tiger:

"Last November, at the Revolutionary People's Constitutional Convention in Washington D.C., the Gay Liberation Front movement was fatally wounded when a chapel-full of young, white middle-class faggots discovered much to their dismay that they weren't revolutionaries at all. Faced for the first time with a collective 'moment of truth' when told that they may be called to participate with the Black Panthers in an armed takeover of Howard University, everyone, myself included, fell apart. The Panthers decided against such action, but not before Gay Liberation exposed itself to itself, a frightened confused bunch of kids who really came to Washington for other reasons than revolution. ... We need to destroy the reactionary remnants of a necessary but false start called Gay Liberation. ... It must be destroyed."

The Underground Press too was on its last legs. In July 1973, in *Northwest Passage*, out of Bellingham, WA, Roxanne Park wrote:

"The underground press sustaining milieu disappeared in recent years; one could read sex ads in other types of papers, nudes were everywhere, four-letter words no longer shocked people, and the anti-Establishment rhetoric grew stale. Underground papers either had to expand their definition–or die. In the wake of this turnabout, the term 'underground' became an anachronism. A new term emerged–the 'alternative press'–and with it came scores of new papers across the country. It is estimated that there are 200 such papers in existence now."

In *Uncovering the Sixties: The Life and Times of the Underground Press*, Abe Peck wrote that by June 1973 many of the radical papers had gone under:

"The *Oracle*'s paisley pages lay buried amid the rubble of the Haight-Ashbury, its ex-readers tripping more quietly, living in the country. ... The *Fifth Estate* hung on in Detroit, but *EVO*, [*East Village Other*] ledgers had turned murky, then terminal. The *Barb* was drowning in sex ads. ... The *Rat* became *Women's*

Liberation, then incandesced in Weatherwoman frenzy. The *Tribe* choked on the Kim Il Sung style book. ... The *Ladder* and the *Furies*, two generations of lesbian papers, were giving way to other journals. *Kaleidoscope, Good Times, Helix*–gone."

It was the end of an era.

BIBLIOGRAPHY

PREFACE

Ink 3 Dec. 1971:1

INTRODUCTION

"Berkeley Explodes Again: This Time it's War." *International Times*, 12 Dec. 1966, 8

Bobo. "New York." *International Times*, 14 Oct. 1966, 6

"Busted!" *International Times*, 5 Dec. 1969, 1

"Consenting Adults." *International Times*, 27 Oct. 1967, 1

de la Croix, St. Sukie. *Chicago Whispers: A History of LGBT Chicago Before Stonewall*. Madison: University of Wisconsin Press, 2012

"Dick Gregory." *International Times*, 28 Nov. 1966, 7

"Dwarf Fuzzed: Organs Menaced!" *International Times*, 23 May 1969, 28

Glauberman, Stuart. "Panthers." *International Times*, 12 July 1968, 3

"Guilty!" *International Times*, 19 Nov. 1970, 2

"Homosexuality and the Law." *OZ* Aug.-Sep. 1969: n.p.

Honselman v. People. 48 N.E. 304 (1 Nov. 1897)

"It and Oz Trial." *International Times*, 11 Oct. 1970, 1

"IT in Court. What is Decency? Jury to Decide." *International Times*, 12 Feb. 1970, 10

"*it* Vanishes' shock! Underground Buried?" *International Times*, 13 June 1969, 1

Jeremy. "Gay Liberation: An Introduction." *Kaleidoscope* (Milwaukee), 13 Feb. 1970, 6

"Letter From America." *International Times*, 1 Aug. 1969, 11

"Letters." *International Times*, 31 Aug. 1967, 2

Mairowitz, David. "Presidents and Pigs." *International Times*, 6 Sep. 1968, 21

"Males." *International Times*, 20 Sep. 1968, 40

Pope, Alexander. *The Poetical Works on Alexander Pope*. New York: MacMillan and Co. Ltd., 1904

Rees-Mogg, William. "Who Breaks a Butterfly on a Wheel?" *London Times*, 1 July 1967, n.p.

"Sabotage!" *International Times*, 23 May 1969, 1

"Small-Ads." *International Times*, 20 Sep. 1968, 14

"Suck for Peace." *OZ* Dec. 1968: 10

"Unclassified Advertisements." *International Times*, 5 Oct. 1967, n.p.

"We Are the People Our Parents Warned Us Against." *International Times*, 25 Apr. 1969, 1

"Who's Got the Fear?" *International Times*, 9 May 1969, 1

The Wolfenden Report: Report on the Committee on Homosexual Offenses and Prostitution. New York: Stein and Day, 1963

CHAPTER 1
HOMOSEXUALITY IN THE EARLY RADICAL PRESS

Anderson, Margaret. "Mrs. Ellis' Failure." *Little Review*, Mar. 1915, n.p.

"Dagger in Heart, Last Will." *Chicago Tribune*, 31 Jan. 1910, 1

Fox, Margalit. "Walter Bowart, Alternative Journalist, Dies at 68." *New York Times*, 14 Jan. 2008, A23

Goldman, Emma. "Anarchy and the Sex Question." *Alarm*, 27 Sep. 1896, 3

Fähnders, Walter. "Anarchism and Homosexuality in Wilhelmine Germany: Senna Hoy,Erich Mühsam, John Henry Mackay." *Journal of Homosexuality 1995* Vol. 29 Issue 2/3, 117-154

"Harman's Body Escapes Dirk." *Chicago Tribune*, 1 Feb. 1910, 5

Hirschfeld, Magnus. *Homosexualität des Mannes und des Weibes*. Berlin: Unknown, 1914

"Homosexual Probe Group Encounter." *East Village Other*, 14 May 1969, 23

Kissack, Terence. *Free Comrades: Anarchism and Homosexuality in the United States,1895-1917*, Oakland: AK Press, 2008.

Leamer, Laurence. *The Paper Revolutionaries*. New York: Simon and Schuster, 1972

McElroy, Wendy. *The Gender-Feminist Attack on Women*. Jefferson, N.C.: McFarland & Company, 2001

Ostertag, Bob. *People's Movements, People's Press: The Journalism of Social Justice Movements*. Boston: Beacon Press, 2006.

"Penitentiary For An Editor." *Chicago Tribune,* 27 Feb. 1906, 9

Smith, Joan. "Farewell to Norman Mailer, a sexist, homophobic reactionary: He hated authority, homosexuality, women and almost certainly himself." *Guardian,* 12 Nov. 2007, n.p.

Szittya. Emil. *Das Kuriositäten-Kabinett*. Berlin: Konstanz, 1923

"The Underground and the Establishment." *Provo*, 16 July 1967, 7

W. "Comstock the Censor." *Lucifer the Light-Bearer*, 13 Mar. 1885, 1

CHAPTER 2
SEXUAL FREEDOM

"ACLU Policy Statement About Sexual Behavior." *Berkeley Barb*, 31 Dec. 1965, 3

"An Angry Young Magazine." *Realist*, June-July 1958, 1

"Bi-Sexual Bi-Circle Dissolves." *Berkeley Barb*, 3 Jan. 1969, 3.

Brackman, Jacob. "The Underground Press," *Playboy*, Aug. 1967, 151

"Censure U. of I. For Manner of Firing Dr. Koch." *Chicago Tribune*, 6 Apr. 1963, 12

Chason, Gary. "Sexual Freedom League: The Naked Truth." *Rag*, 17 Aug. 1966, 1

"Classified Ad." *Berkeley Barb*, 29 Apr. 1966, 11

Coult, Allen. "On 'n' Off on Sensible Sex." *Berkeley Barb*, 18 Mar. 1966, 4

"Expect Final U. of I. Action Soon on Koch." *Chicago Tribune*, 18 Apr. 1960, 6

"Fair Gay Laws." *Open City*, 15 Dec. 1967, 17

Goodman, Paul. Etd. by Taylor Stoehr. *Crazy Hope and Finite Experience: Final Essays of Paul Goodman*. Hoboken, N.J.: John Wiley & Sons, 1994

Goodman, Paul. "Memoirs of An Ancient Activist." *Win*, 15 Nov. 1969

Havemann, Ernest. "Homosexuality in America: Why?" *Life*, 26 June 1964, 76

Hope, David. "Sexual Liberty Movement to Follow Civil Rights." *Los Angeles Free Press*, 9 Apr. 1965, 2.

Hughes, Frank. " University Head's Action OK'd By Board." *Chicago Tribune*, 15 June 1960, 1

"In Defense of Homosexuality." *Los Angeles Free Press*, 22 Oct. 1965, 6

"Koch Appears Before U. of. I Board Today." *Chicago Tribune*, 14 June 1960, B16

"Koch Ouster Hit by 229 On U. of I. Staff." *Chicago Tribune*, 17 July 1960, 14

"Koch Suggests Care in Using Biblical Rules." *Chicago Tribune*, 31 May 1960, B10

Krassner, Paul. *Confessions of a Raving Unconfined Nut*. New York; Simon and Schuster, 1993.

Laurence, Leo. "Charges SFL Neglects Bisexuality." *Berkeley Barb*, 22 Dec. 1967, 4.

Leamer, Laurence. *The Paper Revolutionaries*. New York: Simon and Schuster, 1972

Levi, Allen. "Sexual Freedom in Miami." *Daily Planet*, 10 Oct. 1971, 19

Lipton, Lawrence. *Holy Barbarians*. New York City: Grove Press, 1959

Lipton, Lawrence. *The Erotic Revolution*. Los Angeles: Sherbourne, 1965

"Live and Let Live. Part One." *Realist*, Aug. 1962, 1

"Live and Let Live. Part Two." *Realist*, Sep. 1962, 9

"Live and Let Live. Part Three." *Realist*, Oct. 1962, 8

Lovell, Vic. "Free U Course Asks 'All Sexual Question.'" *Midpeninsula Observer*, 3 June 1968, 1

"Milwaukee Sexual Freedom League." *Kaleidoscope* (Milwaukee), 9 Aug. 1968, 27

"Parts That Were Left Out of the Kennedy Book." *Realist,* May 1967, 1

Poland, Jefferson. "Letter: Beatniks' So Sexually Conservative." *Berkeley Barb*, 20 May 1966, 6

Poland, Jefferson. "Sex Courses Cinch For 'Shadow College.'" *Berkeley Barb*, 11 Feb. 1966, 3

"Police Raid Nude Fest … Like 'Gangbusters.'" *Berkeley Barb*, 20 May 1966, 1

Seranini, Maxine. "On Sick Sex." *Berkeley Barb*, 25 Mar. 1966, 7

"Sex Freedom League to Cover Nation." *Modern Utopian*, Circa. Late-fall, 1967

"Sexual Freedom Blooms at Nude Beach Parties." *Berkeley Barb*, 8 Apr. 1966, 1

"Sexual Freedom League Aims Clarified." *Berkeley Barb*, 15 Apr. 1966, 1

"Sexually Free?" *Open City*, 19 July 1968, 5

"Students: The Free-Sex Movement." *Time*, 11 Mar. 1966, 66

"U. of I. Faces Court Fight in Koch's Ouster." *Chicago Tribune*, 15 July 1960, B10

Welch, Paul. "Homosexuality in America." *Life,* 26 June 1964, 66

CHAPTER 3
NUDITY

Aldrich, Robert. The Seduction of the Mediterranean: Writing, Art, and Homosexual Fantasy. London: Routledge, 1993

"Allman Brothers Band." *Great Speckled Bird*, 8 Dec. 1969, 2

Barnes, Clive. "It's Fresh and Frank." *New York Times,* 29 Apr. 1968, n.p.

Black, Jonathan. "'Che!' Eight Judged Guilty of Obscenity." *Village Voice*, 5 Mar. 1970, 44

"Chicago [John and Yoko]." *News From Nowhere*, Feb. 1969, n.p.

Gover, Robert. "''Che Busted in New York." *Los Angeles Free Press,* 28 Mar. 1969, 23

"J "Fuck" Poland." *Berkeley Tribe,* 20 Feb. 1970, 16

"Jim Morrison Jacks Off." *Dallas Notes*, 19 Mar. 1969, 3

"Jim Morrison on Trial." *Los Angeles Free Press,* 4 Sep. 1970, 1

"John and Yoko Slapped Hard." *Rolling Stone*, 15 Mar. 1969, 12

Latimer, Da. "Decomposition Che!" *East Village Other*, 14 Mar. 1969, 5

"Longhair Arrested." *Great Speckled Bird*, 12 Apr. 1968, 11

Miller, Scott. *Rebels With Applause: Broadway's Groundbreaking Musicals.* Portsmouth, N.H.: Heinemann Drama, 2001

"More Nude-Ins For SF State." *Berkeley Barb*, 6 Oct. 1967, 4

"Morrison Commemorative." *Daily Planet*, 21 Sep. 1970, 1

CHAPTER 4
THE TWILIGHT WORLD OF THE HOMOSEXUAL

Adams, Joe. "Love and the Bisexual." *Vanguard*, Sep. 1967, n.p.

Anderson, Nels. *On Hobos and the Homeless*, Chicago: University of Chicago Press, 1998.

"Backtalk." *Open City,* 12 Jan. 1968, 4

Brother Don. "Letters Page: Custer Was a Fag." *East Village Other*, 15 Sep. 1967, 8

"Critique." *Vanguard*, Sep. 1967, n.p.

Eisenbach, David. *Gay Power: An American Revolution*, New York: Carroll & Graf, 2006

Glessing, Robert J. *The Underground Press in America*. Bloomington, Ind.: Indiana University Press, 1970

Grenshaw, Corbet. "What Homosexuals Want." *Open City*, 2 Feb. 1968, 8

"Homosexual." *Washington Free Press*, 23 Nov. 1967, 2

"The Homosexual in America." *Time*, 21 Jan. 1966, 40

Leamer, Laurence. *The Paper Revolutionaries*. New York: Simon and Schuster, 1972

Moldenhauer, Jearld. "Homophile on Record." *Scimitar*, 1 Nov. 1968, 15

"On Sexuality." *Prosperos Newsletter*, 9 Nov. 1969, n.p.

Schumach, Murray. "Columbia Charters Homosexual Group." *New York Times*, May 3, 1967, 1

Speltz, Frank. "The World of Washington Homophiles." *Washington Free Press*, 4 Aug. 1967, 3

Tate, Laurence. "Exiles of Sin, Incorporated." *Paper,* 20 Oct. 1966, 1

Thorp, Charles. *What It's Like to Be a Homosexual*. San Francisco: Prosperos, 1969

"Why Drugs in the Tenderloin?" *V*, Nov. 1966, n.p.

CHAPTER 5
SADOMASOCHISM

Allen, Chris. "A Visit to the Leather Bars." *Open City*, 11 Oct. 1967, 5

"Aardvark." *Seed*, 22 Sep. 1967, 9

Barrios, Greg. "Anger's 'Scorpio Rising' Finest Underground Film." *Rag*, 8 May 1967, 10

Burton, Shelly. "Conversation With Kenneth Anger." *Fifth Estate*, 1 Dec. 1967, 5

Rolling Stones, *Metamorphosis*. CD. ABKCO. Writ. Jagger/Richards. Prod. Andrew Loog Oldham, 1975

The Velvet Underground and Nico. Vinyl. Verve. Writ. Lou Reed. Prod. Andy Warhol and Tom Wilson, 1967

Welch, Paul. "Homosexuality in America." *Life,* 26 June 1964, 66

CHAPTER 6
TROUBLE WITH THE LAW

"Agencies Aid Hippie Invasion, Lamport Says," *Los Angeles Times*, 21 June 1967, A-1

Ancona, Barry. "Cops Cripple Yippies." *Pterodactyl*, 5 Apr. 1968, 8

Bloice, Carl. "Notes From a Black Reporter in Orangeburg." *Seed*, 15 Mar. 1968, 3

"CAUTION." *Buffalo Chip,* Summer 1968, 4

Ellin, Joe. "U.S. Police State." *Western Activist*, 25 Jan. 1968, 3

Frischberg-Jezer-Bloom, "Police Riot at N.Y. Yip-In." Fifth Estate, 16 Apr. 1968, 2

Garcia, Bob. "Cops Hassle Hustlers." *Open City*, 27 Sep. 1967, n.p.

"Gay Advice." *Open City*, 4 Oct. 1967, 7

"Hippie Restricting Ordinance Passed," *Los Angeles Times*, September 5, 1968, C-1

Kight, Morris. "The Truth About Gay Scene." *Open City*, 4 Nov. 1967, 7

Joachim, Jerry. "Cops Visit Homosexuals." *Open City*, 18 Oct. 1967, 16

K.G. "Where It's At: In the Streets." *Berkeley Barb*, 5 July 1968, 5

Kid, Hickory, "Campus Cops Peek Under Toilet Doors for Homosexuals at … Fondlin' Library." *Dallas Notes*, 2 Apr. 1968, 6

"Laguna Councilmen War on Gay Bars." *Los Angeles Free Press,* 16 Feb. 1968, 16

"L. A. Homophile Leaders To Meet With Hollywood Vice Chief." *Advocate,* Sep. 1967, 1

Lenny the Red and Black, "Berkeley Burns." *Los Angeles Free Press*, 5 July 1968, 1

"Letter to the Editor." *Fifth Estate,* 5 Sep. 1968, 12

"Manifeste des 343 salopes." *Tout! Ce Que Nous Voulons.* 23 Apr. 1971, n.p.

Marcuse, Herbert. "Impression of the French Revolution." *Midpeninsula Observer,* 1 July, 10

Michaels, Dick. "Anatomy of a Raid." *Open City,* 19 July, 1968, n.p.

Novak, Peter. "We're Going to Get Every Nigger and Long-Haired Son of a Bitch." *Rat*, 19 Apr. 1968, 11

"Police Abuse Prisoner." *Kaleidoscope* (Milwaukee), 2 Feb. 1968, 2

"Police Resume Haight Raids." *Rolling Stone,* 24 Feb. 1968, 8

"Press release regarding the raid on the Black Cat bar New Year's Eve, 1966." Tavern Guild of Southern California. 5 Jan. 1967

"Police Meet With Homosexuals." *Los Angeles Free Press,* 27 Oct. 1967, 2

"Racist Cops Beat Black Mother." *Inner City Voice,* June 1968, 1

"The Social Plague: Group 5 of the F.H.A.R." *Actuel,* Nov. 1972

"Vice Busts Gays." *Ungarbled Word,* 17 Oct. 1968, 2

Welch, Paul. "Homosexuality in America." *Life,* 26 June 1964, 66

W, Jim. "Victim Tells How Hollywood Vice Fracture the Law." *Open City,* 22 May 1968, 4

Young, Allen. "Rebellion at Berkeley." *Georgia Straight: Vancouver Free Press.* 12 July 1968, 6

CHAPTER 7
CLAMPDOWN ON ALTERNATIVE LIFESTYLES

"Andy Warhol's 'Chelsea Girls.'" *Berkeley Barb*, 1 Sep. 1967, 11

"Andy Warhol's Chelsea Girls Busted." *Seed*, 11 Aug. 1967, 7

Averitt, Conrade. [No headline] *Washington Free Press*, 19 Apr. 1967, n.p.

Bailey, Steve. "Special Showing of 'Obscene' Film Arranged for Today." *El*

Gaucho, 28 Sep. 1967, 1

Benner, Richard. "Vice Guerillas Bust Film, Keep Isla Vista Minds Pure." *Los Angeles Free Press* 6 Oct. 1967, 5

Bloom, Marshall. "Underground Press Un-American? HUAC Investigates the 'Syndicate.'" *News Project*, 8 Dec. 1967

Bowart, Walter. "Good Bye Groovy Tuesday, Memorial Day Debacle." *East Village Other*, 3 June 1967, 3

Bowers, Jim. "Chicago Windchimes." *Kaleidoscope* (Milwaukee), 6 Oct. 1967, 7

Burns, Jeffrey M. "Lenore Kandel: Historical Essay." *Argonaut*, Spring 1994, n.p.

"Chelsea Girls." *Chicago Tribune,* 5 Aug. 1967, 4

"Classified Ads." *Berkeley Barb*, 21 Apr. 1967, 14

"Classified Ads." *Los Angeles Free Press*, 18 Aug. 1967, 22

Clifford, Terry. "Warhol Focuses on Greenwich Village Hotel." *Chicago Tribune*, 26 June 1967, B17

Cross, Robert. "The Immortals: LSD and the Hippie Life in Chicago." *Chicago Tribune*, 20 Aug. 1967, J20

"Death of Hip–Birth of the Free." *Seed*, 14 Oct. 1967, 2

"Detroit Love In." *Seed*. May/June 1967, n.p.

Dreyer, Thorne. "High Camp." *Rag*, 17 Aug. 1966, 12

"'Erotica of Underground' DA in film Crackdown." *Gazette Citizen*, 11 Jan. 1968, 1

"Free Wells St. Liberate Old Town; Police Trained by Former SS Officers?" *Seed*, Apr. 1967, n.p.

Grant, H. Roger. *Spirit Fruit: A Gentle Utopia*. DeKalb, Ill: Northern Illinois University Press, 1988

"Hippies on the East Village and the Revolution." *New Left Notes*, 6 Nov. 1967, 4

Jassen, Jeff. "Slug-Happy Cops Wreak Havoc in the Haight." *Berkeley Barb*, 7 Apr. 1967, 1

Jay, Karla and Young, Allen. *Out of the Closets: Voices of Gay Liberation*. New York; Douglas/Links, 1972.

Katzman, Allan. "Community Action." *East Village Other*, 3 June 1967, 7

Lanier, Thomas. "Magic Lantern 'Smut' Bust." *Isla Vista Argo*, 4 Oct. 1967, 1

Latimer, D.A. "The Persecution and Assassination of Reality as Performed by the Inmates of 100 Center Street Under the Direction of his Honour and the Riot Squad." *East Village Other*, 3 June 1967, 5

Morang, Joe. " $100,000 in Dope Found in Old Town." *Chicago Tribune*, 29 Jan. 1971, B9

Mothers of Invention, We're Only In It For the Money. CD. Writ. And prod. Frank Zappa. Rykodisc, 1968

Mungo, Raymond. Duberman, Martin. *Liberace (Lives of Notable Gay Men and Lesbians)*. New York: Chelsea House, 1994

Mungo, Raymond. *Famous Long Ago: My Life and Hard Times With Liberation News Service*. Boston: Beacon Press, 1970

Nordhoff, Charles. *The Communistic Societies of the United States*. New York: Dover Publications, 1966

Pearson, Drew. "Is Ronnie [Reagan] gay?" *Open City*, 11 Nov. 1967, 1

Perry, Charles. *Haight Ashbury*. New York: Wenner Books, 2005

"Psychedelic shop." *Rag*, 28 Nov. 1966, 7

Salasnek, Sheil. "Love-In." *Fifth Estate*, 15 May 1967, 1

"Spirit Fruit Founder Dead." *Chicago Tribune*, 25 Nov. 1908, 3

"Stop 'Spirit Fruit' Meeting." *Chicago Tribune*, 13 June 1904, 9

"Sunday Serenade in Square Causes Morris to Yield." *Village Voice*, 13 Apr. 1961, 1

"Tells How Haight Cops Exploit Hips." *Berkeley Barb*, Apr. 7, 1967, 7

"Tribes Assemble on North Avenue Beach." *Seed*, May/June 1967, n.p.

"U of I Be-In." *Seed*, May/June 1967, n.p.

Van Ronk, Dave. Wald, Elijah. *The Mayor of MacDougal Street: A Memoir*. Cambridge, Mass.: Da Capo Press, 2009

"Vigs and Pigs Vamp on Fags" *Liberation News Service*, 3 July 1969, 3

Walker, Valerie. "Hair Piece." *Seed*, Aug. 11, 1967, 18

"Why Don't You Make It Safe For Me?" *Seed*, Apr. 1968, 5

Wiedrich, Robert. "State Official Charges Slander, Sues: Karnes Asks for $600,000 for False Arrest." *Chicago Tribune*, 21 Apr. 1966, C28

CHAPTER 8
UNDERGROUND PRESS SYNDICATE

Allen, Chris. "A Homosexual Views the Draft." *Open City*, 27 Oct. 1967, 13

"End Anti-Sex Law." *Fifth Estate*, 15 Sep. 1967, 9

"Gay Marine to Get Aid." *Berkeley Barb*, 22 Dec. 1967, 2

"Gay Vote Scramble." *Berkeley Barb*, 13 Oct. 1967, 2

"I Read the News Today, Oh Boy." *Fifth Estate*, 1 Jan. 1968, 11

Peck, Abe. *Uncovering the Sixties: The Life & Times of the Underground Press*. New York: Pantheon Books, 1985

Ritalin, Thane Gower. "The Hippies and the Hypocrites." *Seed*, 11 Aug. 1967, 6

"The Underground and the Establishment." *Provo*, 16 July 1967, 7

"Underground Organs For Deviates, Sez Pool." *Middle Earth*, 6 Nov. 1967, 12

"Underground Press Has Tribal Meeting." *Fifth Estate*, 15 May 1967, 5

CHAPTER 9
HOMOSEXUALS AND THE DRAFT

Allen, Chris. "A Homosexual Views the Draft." *Open City*, 27 Oct. 1967, n.p.

Anderson, Jervis. *Bayard Rustin: Troubles I've Seen*. Berkeley: University of California, Reprint 1998

Colton, James. "Backtalk." *Open City*, 12 Jan. 1968, 4

"The Draft Counselor–Rejecting Homosexuals." *Chicago Sun-Times*, 16 Apr. 1970:98

G. "Guernica." *Seed,* May 1968, 11

"Gay Army Life." *Fifth Estate*, 1 Apr. 1968, 9

"Gays Are Drafted. *San Diego Free Door*, 13 Mar. 1968, 2

Gerberg, Mort. "The Fag Battalion." *Realist*, Sep. 1966, 16-17

Guthrie, Arlo. *Alice's Restaurant.* Vinyl. Reprise, 1967

"Homosexuals and the Armed Forces." *Natural,* 3 May, 1968, 6

"The Homosexual and the Draft–A Moral Dilemma." *Mattachine Midwest Newsletter* May 1966:3

"Homosexuals Rally For Equal Draft." *Berkeley Barb*, 20 May 1966, 1

"Homos In." *Berkeley Barb,* 8 Mar. 1968, 2

"How to Stay Out of the Army." *Seed,* May 1968, 16

Kupferberg, Tuli. Bashlow, Robert. *1001 Ways to Beat the Draft.* New York City: Grove Press, 1967

Lester, Julius. "To Hell With Protest." *New South Student: Newsletter of the Southern Student Organizing Committee*, Feb. 1968, Vol. 5

Lynn, Conrad. *How to Stay Out of the Army: A Guide to Your Rights Under the Draft Law,* New York: Monthly Review Press, 1967

Ochs, Phil. *I Aint Marching Anymore.* Vinyl. Columbia Records. Writ: Phil Ochs. Prod. Jac Holzman and Paul Rothchild, 1965

"Panthers Voice Defy." *Berkeley Barb*, 12 May 1967, 3

Pearson, Drew. "Is Ronnie Gay?" *Open City,* 10 Nov. 1967, 1

Randolph, Bob. "Peace Action: GI's Cheer; Trainmen Jeer." *Berkeley Barb*, 13 Aug. 1965, 1.

R.R. "August 12 ... Black Day For Berkeley." *Berkeley Barb*, 13 Aug. 1965, 1

Russo, Vito. *The Celluloid Closet,* New York; Harper Collins, 1987

Rustin, Bayard. *Down the Line*, Chicago: Quadrangle Books, 1971

Sanford, David. "Boxed In." *New Republic* 21 May 1966, 8

Slater, Don. "Protest on Wheels." *Tangents*, May 1966

Timmins, John L. "Letter from a Homosexual." *Realist*, May 1967, 2

CHAPTER 10
LEADING UP TO CHICAGO'S PERFECT STORM

"150 Police Raid Women for Peace," *Seed,* Apr. 1967, 2

Ancona, Barry. "Cops Cripple Yippies." *Pterodactyl*, 5 Apr. 1968, n.p.

Bailey, Jim. "Police Harass Gay Bars." *Second City,* 12 Dec. 1968, 16

"Control the Cops." *Berkeley Barb*, 2 Dec. 1966, 1

de la Croix, St. Sukie. *Chicago Whispers: A History of LGBT Chicago Before Stonewall.* Madison: University of Wisconsin Press, 2012

"Eye on the News." *Chicago Gay Crusader,* Aug. 1973, 4

"Fairmont Demonstrators Are Brutally Attacked." *Midpeninsula Observer,* 22 Jan. 1986, 16

"Festival Marks Riot Anniversary." *News and Courier*, 14 Aug. 1966, 3A

Garson, Marvin. "What Happened in Chicago-An Analysis. The Whites: A Clown Show." *Berkeley Barb*, 15 Sept. 1967, 9

Heyman, Barton. "Ginsberg Raps at GU." *Washington Free Press,* 19 Mar. 1968, 7

Illinois Criminal Code of 1961. Enacted 28 July 1961, effective 1 Jan. 1962. *Laws of Illinois 1961*. p. 1983

"Killer Cop Loose." *Kaleidoscope* (Chicago), 22 Nov. 1968, 2

Lack, H. Lawrence. "Exclusive: Rap Brown Raps With Free Press." Los Angeles Free Press, 18 Aug. 1967, 1

"Malpractice by Police Trigger to Watts Riots." *Los Angeles Free Press*, 20 Aug. 1965, 5

Martin, Del. "New Illinois Penal Code–What does It Mean?" *The Ladder* 6, no 6, (Mar. 1962): 14-15

"New Criminal Code In Effect Jan. 1." *Chicago Sun-Times*, 21 Dec. 1961: 43

"New Penal Code in Illinois." *Mattachine Review* 8, no 1 (Oct. 1962)

"Operation Dragnet." *Mattachine Midwest Newsletter,* Sep. 1965, 1

"Panthers Voice Defy." *Berkeley Barb*, 12 May 1967, 3

Reynolds, Larry. "Dear Seed." Seed, Circa End of Oct. 1967, 18

"Rich Nuccio As Mad Dog." *Seed,* Aug. 1968, 4

"Rich Nuccio Is Guilty." *Kaleidoscope* (Chicago), 28 Mar. 1969, 3

Rosenfeld, Al. "Arms and the Man." *Seed,* Aug. 1968, 4

Rustin, Bayard. "The Watts." *Commentary,* March 1966, n.p

"Secret Police in Chicago-A Comic Opera." *Kaleidoscope* (Chicago), Mar. 14, 1969, 14

Schmiechen, Bruce. "Leary in Chicago: Finding Fault With he Family Doctor." *Rag,* 21 Nov. 1966, 14

Smith, Tom W. "Oakland Police Brutality Plants Seeds of White Revolution." *Rag,* 23 Oct. 1967, 2

"Some Music, Some Flesh, Some Delights." *Le Chronic,* 3 Apr. 1968, 6

Steve. ["Title unintelligible"] *Seed,* Circa. Apr. 1968, 9

"Summary of NCNP Resolutions." *Seed,* 22 Sep. 1967, 2

"Third Party Convention." *Seed,* Mid-Aug. 1967, 3

"Town Hall On Fire." *Mattachine Midwest Newsletter*, Jul-Aug. 1968, 5

"Unsigned Letter to the Editor." *Seed,* 22 Sep. 1967, 18

Wexler, Morris J. "Sex Offenses under the New Criminal Code." *Illinois Bar Journal,* Oct. 1962, 152-54

CHAPTER 11
THE YIPPIES ARE COMING

"Chicago Community Catches Cop." *Movement*, Sep. 1968, 4

"Chicago Police Riot." *Great Speckled Bird*, 30 Aug. 1968, 3

"Cop Caught Convicted." *Movement,* Oct. 1968, 15

Donaldson, Stephen. "Bill of Rights For Homos." *Black* Panther, 12 Oct. 1968, 17

Draper, Robert. *Rolling Stone Magazine: The Uncensored History*. New York: Doubleday, 1990

Edelman, Cynthia. "New Politics-Too Late." Seed, 22 Sep. 1967, 3

Eisenbach, David. *Gay Power: An American Revolution.* New York: Carool & Graf, 2006

"Freedom of the Press Department." *Seed*, Circa. Feb. 1968, 2

"Electric Theatre Busted." *Seed*, Circa June 1968, 3

Farber, David. *Chicago '68*. Chicago: University of Chicago Press, 1994

Frischberg-Jezer-Bloom, "Police Riot at N.Y. Yip-In." Fifth Estate, 16 Apr. 1968, 2

"Garson in Jail." *Helix*, Dec. 1968, n.p.

G. "Protest at the Civic Center." *Seed*, Late Apr. 1968, 4

Garson, Marvin. "The Whites: A Clown Show (conclusion)." *Berkeley Barb*, 22 Sept. 1967, 8

Golden, Stephen A.O. "200 Hippies Stage an 8th St. 'Be-Out.'" *New York Times*, 7 Aug. 1967, 26

"Hippie Killed by Policemen in Old Town." *Chicago Tribune*, 23 Aug. 1968:C14

Hoffman, Abbie. *Soon to be a Major Motion Picture*. New York: Perigree Books, 1980

"Homosexual Bill of Rights." *Haight Ashbury Maverick*, n.d., 10

"Homosexual Bill of Rights." *Kaleidoscope* (Chicago), 22 Nov. 1968, 4

"The Homosexual Fights Back." *Sepia*, Sept. 1968, n.p.

"Homosexuals Ask Candidates' Ideas: Seek Views on Penalties." *New York Times*, 19 Aug. 1968, n.p.

"It's Illegal to be a Kid in Chicago." *Rat*, 15 June 1968, 3

Jezar, Martin. "Notes on New Politics: Black Humor at the Palmer House." *WIN*, 30 Sep. 1967, 4

Lipton, Lawrence. "Allen Ginsberg in Chicago." *Georgia Straight: Vancouver Free Press*, 11 Oct. 1968, 8

Lipton, Lawrence. "Letter from a Police State: Billy Clubs Blitz Noncovention." *Los Angeles Free Press*, 30 Aug. 1968, 1

Peck, Abraham. "Chicago: An Open Letter To Mayor Daley." Helix, Circa May 1968, 7

Peck, Abe. *Uncovering the Sixties: the Life and Times of the Underground Press*. New York; Pantheon Books, 1985.

Remy, Harold. "Police Pull Electric Theater Plug; Nab 29." *Chicago Tribune*, 21 May 1968, C7

Retherford, James. "What's Left After Chicago?" *Spectator*, 25 Sep. 1967, 4

Ridgeway, James. "The Cops & the Kids." *New Republic*, 7 Sep. 1968, 11

Rights in Conflict: "The Chicago Police Riot." New York: New American Library, 1968

Rubin, Jerry. "The Year of the YIPPEES." *American Dream*, Circa. Jan. 1968, 9

Rubin, Jerry. "Jerry Rubin's Future Plans." *Berkeley Barb*, 14 Jan. 1966, 1

Seymour, Sunshine. "The Seed's First Bust (All true!)" *Seed*, Circa. Feb. 1968, 2

"Turn Electric Theater Back On Tonight." *Chicago Tribune*, 22 May 1968, 12

Varbrough, Arthur. "New Politics." *Rag*, 17 July 1967, 9

Wasserman, Harvey. "Chicago: Festival of Life & Death." *Le Chronic*, 3

Apr. 1968, 6

"Wayne University Destroys Files Protested by Students." *New York Times*, 5 May 1967, 19

Webb, Lee. "Chicago in 68." *Washington Free Press*, 19 Mar. 1968, 5

Wenner, Jann. "Musicians Reject New Political Exploiters." *Rolling Stone*, 11 May, 1968, 1

"The YIPPEES in Chicago." *Seed*, Feb/Mar. 1968, 8

"Yip Yip Yip." *Seed*, Jan. 1968, 2

CHAPTER 12
AFTER THE "PIG" RIOT

"2, 3 Many Chicagos." *Fifth Estate*, 5 Sep. 1968, 1

"A Free Press Interview With James Baldwin." *Los Angeles Free Press*, 23 Feb. 1968, 3

Burroughs, William. "The coming of the Purple Better One." *Esquire*, Nov. 1968, 89

"Chicago Police Riot." *Great Speckled Bird*, 30 Aug. 1968, 3

Cleaver, Eldridge. "Notes on a Native Son." *Ramparts*, June 1966, 51

"Cover [naked woman with rifle]." *Georgia Strait: Vancouver Free Press*, 15 Nov. 1968, 1

"Cops Ride Again." *Mattachine Midwest Newsletter*, Sep. 1968, 1

"Czechago U.S.A." *Berkeley Barb*, 30 Aug. 1968, 1

Dreyer, Thorne. "Law Harasses Underground Papers." *Guardian*, 7 Dec. 1968, 7

"Eldridge: Reagan is a Punk, Sissy, Coward." *Los Angeles Free Press*, 11 Oct. 1968, 25

"Evidence of Pigs Run Amok." *Black Panther*, 28 Sep. 1968, 5

"Expose: Short-Haired Anti-Intellectual Queers." *Kudzu*, 12 Nov. 1968, 3

"Freakin' Fag Revolution." *Berkeley Tribe*, 3 Mar. 1970, 1

"Gay Vote Scramble." *Berkeley Barb*, 13 Oct. 1967, 2

Genet, Jean. "The Members of the Assembly." *Esquire*, Nov. 1968, 86

"Homosexuals Ask Candidates' Ideas." *New York Times*. 19 Aug. 1968, 29

Jones, LeRoi. (Amiri Baraka) *Home Studies*. New York; William Morrow & Co., 1966

Kingston, Barbara. "Esquire castrates Chicago." *Peninsula Observer*, 18 Oct. 1968, 12

Kurtis, Ron. "On Gay Bars." *Open City*, 30 Aug. 1968, 5

Kurtis, Ron. "On Gay Bars." *Teaspoon Door*, 27 Sep. 1968, 14

Kurtis, Ron. "Why Homosexuals Trick." *Open City*, 6 Sep. 1968, 1968, 8

Lipton, Lawrence. "Letter from a Police State: Billy Clubs Blitz Noncovention." *Los Angeles Free Press*, 30 Aug. 1968, 1

Marshall, Sue. "On Tour for Panthers and Conspiracy." *Los Angeles Free Press*, 27 Mar. 1970, 1

"Miss Craig's Face-Saving Exercises." *Ain't I a Woman*, 25 Sept. 1970, 5

"Never Having Been Sure of Anything." *Ain't I a Woman*, 11 Sep. 1970, 1

"NOW!" *Fifth Estate*, 20 Feb. 1969, 1

"Oh Mary." *Seed*, Undated 1970, 15

Patterson, Gary. "Homophile Campaign on Against Der Max." *Berkeley Barb*, 13 Sep. 1968, 9

Patterson, Gary. "SIR Ball Relaxed and Gay." *Berkeley Barb,* 12 Apr. 1968, 7

Patterson, Gary. "Straight Scribe Gets Bent." *Berkeley Barb,* 9 Sept. 1968, 9

Sack, John. "In a Pig's Eye," *Esquire,* Nov. 1968, 91

Sides, Josh. *Erotic City: Sexual Revolutions and the Making of Modern San Francisco.* Oxford, United Kingdom; Oxford University Press, 2009

Sorcic, James. "From the Second Floor." *Kaleidoscope* (Milwaukee), 11 Apr. 1969, 3.

Southern, Terry. "Grooving in Chi." *Esquire*, Nov. 1968, 83

"Take Up the Gun." *Kaleidoscope* (Madison), 19 May 1970, 1

"Vice Busts Gays: Bumrap Band for 'Vag.'" *Ungarbled Word,* 17 Oct. 1968, n.p.

"Watts, Jerry Gafio. *Amiri Baraka: The Politics and Art of a Black Intellectual.* New York; New York Press, 2001

Winston, Sam. "Be Gay AND Hip." *Open City,* 22 Nov. 1968, 6

CHAPTER 13
THIRD SEX IN THEATER AND MOVIES

Eberle, Paul. "Los Angeles Times Kills Sister George." *Los Angeles Free Press,* 7 Feb. 1969, 32

The Field Marshall. "Foxy Smut." *Kudzu,* 12 Nov. 1968, 3

"Films: The Detective." *Rat,* 6 Sept. 1968, 16

Forsyth, Robert, "Why Can't 'We' Live Happily Ever After, Too." *New York Times,* 23 Feb. 1969, D1

Francis, Miller Jr. "Portrait of Jason." *Great Speckled Bird*, 24 Mar. 1969, 15

Francis, Miller Jr. "A Review and More." *Great Speckled Bird,* 15 Sep. 1969, 6

Francis, Miller Jr. "The Queen." *Great Speckled Bird*, 14 Oct. 1968, 7

"The Gay Scene." *Kaleidoscope* (Milwaukee), 7 June 1968, 7

Gussow, Leon. "The Queen." *Rat,* 1 July 1968, 15

Hayes, Bob. "The Boys in the Band." *Berkeley Barb,* 21 Nov. 1968, 15

"Homosexuality in Men and Women." *Los Angeles Free Press*, 22 Dec. 1967, n.p.

Itkin, Michael Francis Rt. Rev. "Reinforcing Stereotypes." *Berkeley Barb,* 21 Nov. 1968, 15

Lahr, John. "Homosexual Theater." *New York Free Press,* 18 Apr. 1968, 7

"LA's First Homosexual Film Festival Breaks Every Attendance Record!" *Los Angeles Free Press*, 5 July 1968, 13

Leamer, Laurence. *The Paper Revolutionaries.* New York: Simon and Schuster, 1972

Moss, Nancy. "Sex Fills the Screen as Fox Takes a Fall." *Midpeninsula Observer*, 6 May 1968, 12

"No More Glory of the Fuck or Smut Hunt." *Great Speckled Bird*, 25 Aug. 1969, 5

Ogar, Richard A. "Gentlemen … The Queen." *Berkeley Barb,* May 10, 1968, 12

Pellman, Diane. "The Killing of Sister George." *Great Speckled Bird*, 31 Mar. 1969, 12

Raymond, Dennis. "The Queen: A Lovely Human Being." *Fifth Estate,* 6 Feb.

1969, 7

Schrader, Paul. "Rod Steiger is the Sergeant." *Los Angeles Free Press*, 31 Jan. 1969, 33

Senn, David. "Boys in the Band." *Seed,* Undated Vol. 3 No. 13. 1970, n.p.

"Smut in Dallas." *Great Speckled Bird*, 18 Nov. 1968, 2

Stevens, Richard L. "Letter to the Editor." *Great Speckled Bird,* 7 Apr. 1968, 5

"Underground Theater." *Seed,* Circa. Apr. 1967, n.p.

"Underground Film Seized by Raleigh Police." *North Carolina Anvil*, 3 Aug. 1968, 1

Waters, John. "Silver Screen." *Baltimore Free Press*, 1 Oct. 1968, 13

"Where the Boys Are." *Time,* 28 June 1968, 80

CHAPTER 14
THE "PIG RIOT" TO THE STONEWALL RIOT

"Bad Vibes." *Great Speckled Bird*, 12 May 1969, 3

Bird, David. "Trees in a Queens Park Cut Down as Vigilantes Harass Homosexuals." *New York Times*, 1 July 1969, 1

"Classified Ads." *Great Speckled Bird,* 26 May 1969, 19

Flammonde, Paris. *The Kennedy Conspiracy: An Uncommissioned Report on the Jim Garrison Investigation.* New York; Meredith Press, 1969

"Gay Rebel Gets Shafted by Uptight Boss." *Berkeley Barb*, 4 Apr. 1969, 11

"Gays Join Strike." *Berkeley Barb,* 16 May 1969, 9

"Gay S'Board Unplugs." *Berkeley Barb*, 23 Apr. 1971, 4

"Gay Strike Hits Southern Front." *Berkeley Barb,* 2 May 1969, 11

"Gay Strike Turns Grim." *Berkeley Barb,* 25 Apr. 1969, 7

"Gays Win: Record Dealer Bow to Gays, Rehires Clerk." *Berkeley Barb,* 6 June 1969, 11

Himmler II, Jose. "Letters." *Great Speckled Bird*, 9 June 1969, 4

"Homo Death Group Will Act." *Berkeley Barb*, 2 May 1969, 11

"Homo Group Gets Some New Brooms." *Berkeley Barb,* 7 Feb. 1969, 6

"Homo Mag Editor Vows to Hold Out to the End." *Berkeley Barb,* 4 Apr. 1969, 9

"Homo Murder Complaint Set." *Berkeley Barb,* 16 May 1969, 12

"Homo Revolt Blasting Off on Two Fronts." *Berkeley Barb,* 11 Apr. 1969, 11

"Homo Revolt: 'Don't Hide It.'" *Berkeley Barb,* 28 Mar. 1969, 5

"Homos Strike Back." *Berkeley Barb,* 7 Feb. 1969, 10

"Homos to Vote." *Berkeley Barb,* 31 Jan. 1969, 7

Jackson, Don. "Gay Liberation Front." *Berkeley Barb*, 10 Oct. 1969, n.p.

Jackson, Don. "Howard Efland: Gay Memorial Services Planned." *San Diego Door,* 26 Feb. 1970, n.p.

Laurence, Leo. "Homos Not Homogeneous." *Berkeley Barb,* 27 June 1969, 11

Laurence, Leo. "Widespread Backing for Brown Sex Bill." *Berkeley Barb,* 14 Mar. 1969, 3

Laurence, Leo. "S.I.R. Secretary Quits in Disgust." *Berkeley Barb,* 6 June 1969, 11

"The Lavender Panthers." *Time,* 8 Oct. 1973, 73

MacLeod, Amos. "Sexual Deviation: A Documented demonstration." *Distant Drummer,* 3 Apr. 1969, 10

"Nudes Protest Playboy at Antioch" *Liberation News Service,* 5 June 1969, 19

"Pink Panther Gay Revolution Toughening Up." *Berkeley Barb,* 18 Apr. 1969, 11

Pinney, Morgan. "Telling It Like It Is: State College From A Homosexual Perspective." *Vector,* Jan. 1969, n.p.

"Rev. Raymond Broshears Interviewed by Garrison." *Los Angeles Free Press,* 13 Sep. 1968, 30

Romaine, Howard. "Parks Belong to Alderman." *Great Speckled Bird,* 16 June 1969, 7

Romaine, Howard. "The Park Belongs to the People." *Great Speckled Bird,* 26 May 1969, 2

Singer, Chris. "Strike at S.F. State." *Fifth Estate,* 23 Jan. 1969, 3

"Thousands Ring Campus at SF State." *Guardian,* 11 Jan. 1969, 3

"Watts, Jerry Gafio. *Amiri Baraka: The Politics and Art of a Black Intellectual.* New York; New York Press, 2001

"Wedding Rights." *Berkeley Barb,* 18 Apr. 1969, 11

Young, Allen. "Sitting On." *Spectator,* 1 July 1969, 4

CHAPTER 15
THE STONEWALL UPRISING

"2 Clubs Catering to Homosexuals Closed by Police." *New York Times,* 25 Nov. 1967, n.p.

"3 Deviates Invite Exclusion by Bars." *New York Times,* 22 Apr. 1966. 43

"4 Policemen Hurt in 'Village' Raid." *New York Times,* 29 June 1969, 33

Anderson, Lincoln. 'I'm sorry,' says police inspector who led Stonewall raid."

Downtown Express, June 25, 2004, n.p.

Come Out! 14 Nov. 1969, n.p.

"Court Limits Taverns on Homosexuals." *New York Times,* 30 Dec. 1967, 6

Detwiler, Bruce. "Squirrel Starts Riot. 'Liberate the Trees.'" *Peninsula Observer,* 9 Sep. 1968, 7

Di Brienza, Ronnie. "Stonewall Incident." *East Village Other,* 9 July 1969, 2

Dreifus, Claudia. "Smut Control." *East Village Other,* 9 Apr. 1969, 3

Dreyer, Thorne. "Lower East Side United Against Pigs." *Washington Free Press,* 1 Aug. 1968, 3

Gabree, John. "Homosexuals Harassed in New York." *Guardian,* 12 July 1969, 14

"Gay Power." *Logos,* Aug. 1969, 5

Goulianos, Joan. "Book Review: Police Abuses in New York." *Rat Subterranean News,* 9 July 1969, 23

Grutner, Charles. "Mafia Buys Clubs for Homosexuals." *New York Times,* 30 Nov. 1967, 1

Jon. "Revolt of the Street People." *Rat Subterranean News*, 2 May 1969, 3

Komisar, Lucy. "Three Homosexuals in Search of a Drink." Village Voice, 5 May 1966, 15

Ladder, Oct.-Nov. 1969, n.p.

Leitsch, Dick. "Vendetta: Letter to the Editor." *Village Voice*, 10 July 1969, 49

Laurence, Leo. "Gays hit NY Cops." *Berkeley Barb*, 4 July 1969, 5

Laurence, Leo. "Gays hit NY Cops." *San Diego Free Door,* 31 July 1969, 14

"Liquor License is revoked At Tony Pastor's Night Spot." *New York Times*, 18 Mar. 1967, 15

Liscoe, Kevin. "Scared No More: Letter to the Editor." *Village Voice*, 10 July 1969, 4

Lisker, Jerry. "Homo Nest Raided, Queen Bees Stinging Mad." *New York Daily News*, 6 July 1969, 1

"Offensive: Letter to the Editor." *Village Voice*, 10 July 1969, 4

"Police Again Rout 'Village' Youth." *New York Times*, 30 June 1969, 22

"Police Begin Times Sq. Cleanup After Night Workers Complain." *New York Times*, 6 Feb. 1969, n.p.

Smith, Howard. "Full Moon Over Stonewall." *Village Voice*, 3 July 1969, 1

Truscott IV, Lucien. "Gay Power Comes to Sheridan Square." *Village Voice*, 3 July 1969, 1

"Queen Power–Fags Against Pigs in Stonewall Bust." *Rat Subterranean News*, 9 July 1969, 5

Spencer, Walter Troy. "Too Much My Dear." *Village Voice*, 10 July 1969, 36

CHAPTER 16
THE AFTERMATH: JULY TO DECEMBER 1969

"A Walrus Interview-The Committee for Homosexual freedom." Walrus, 25 Nov. 1969, 12

Baim, Tracy. *Gay Press, Gay Power*. Chicago; Prairie Avenue Productions, 2012

Berlandt, Konstantin. "Been Down So Long, it Looks Like Up to Me." *Berkeley Tribe*, 12 Sep. 1969, 5

Berlandt, Konstantin. "On Gay Liberation." Great Speckled Bird, 13 Oc. 1969, 8

Brown, Julie. "Women's Liberation." *Great Speckled Bird*, 11 Nov. 1968. 5

"Classified ads." *Kaleidoscope* (Chicago) 3 Jan. 1968, 14

Cooke, Michael. "Homosexuality and Capitalism: Why Don't They Like Us?" *Liberation News Service*, 28 Aug. 1969, 12

Crocker, Larry. "Sexual Role Exploitation." *Old Mole*, 13 Sep. 1968, 4

"Court May Okay Cocksucking." *Dallas Notes*, 3 Dec. 1969, 7

Dreifus, Claudia. "Gay Power Comes to the Village Voice.' East Village Other, 4 Sep. 1969, 11

Duberman, Martin. *Stonewall*. New York; Dutton; 1993

"Excerpts from an Interview ... " *Great Speckled Bird*, 15 Sep. 1969, 7

"Farber, Jerry. "The Student As Nigger." *Great Speckled Bird*, 23 Sep. 1968, 3

Farber, Jerry. "The Student As Nigger." *Rag*, 8 May 1967, 6

"Fuck Him In His Motherfucking Ass." *Berkeley Barb*, 12 Dec. 1969, 5

"Gay Confab Comes Up With Three-Way Split." *Berkeley Barb*, 2 Jan. 1970

"Gay Lib Stirs Up Fem Lib." *Berkeley Barb*, 2 Jan. 1970, 3

"Gay Liberation Front." *Walrus*, 25 Sep. 1969, 11

"Gay Lib Weekend." *Berkeley Tribe*, 27 Nov. 1969, 18

"Gay Power." *Spokane Natural*, 26 Sep. 1969, 4

"Gay Revolution Comes Out." *Rat Subterranean News*, 12 Aug. 1969, 7

"Goons Gang Gay Guerillas." *Berkeley Barb*, 7 Nov. 1969, 6

Goodman, Paul. "Memoirs of An Ancient Activist." *Win*, 15 Nov. 1969

Israeli, Phineas. "The Gay Blues." *Berkeley Tribe*, 7 Nov. 1969, 7

Itkin, Michael Francis Rt. Rev. "The Homosexual Liberation Movement: What Direction." *Berkeley Barb*, 5 Dec. 1969, 16

Jackson, Don. "Gay Liberation Movement Invades Los Angeles." *Berkeley Barb*, 24 Oct. 1969, 5

Jackson, Don. "Gays Not Thankful." *Berkeley Barb*, 5 Dec. 1969, 5

Jackson, Don. "Homosexual Gov't Planned." *Los Angeles Free Press*, 9 Jan. 1970, 1

Jay, Karla and Young, Allen. *Out of the Closets: Voices of Gay Liberation*. New York; Douglas/Links, 1972

"Joel Fabricant Perverts Gay Power." *Come Out!*, 14 Nov. 1969, 3

"Kill a Queer for Christ." *San Diego Free Door*, 20 Nov. 1969, 2

"Koreen Phelps: Interview." Twin Cities Gay and Lesbian Community Oral History Project at the Minnesota Historical Society.

Laurence, Leo. "Gay Fifteen Get Shaft." *Berkeley Tribe*, 7 Nov. 1969, 7

Laurence, Leo. "Gay Pickets Bounce Ball." *Berkeley Tribe*, 24 October 1969, 4

Laurence, Leo. "Gays Bend KFOG." *Berkeley Tribe*, 27 Nov. 1969, 27

Laurence, Leo. "Gays Get Panther OK." *Berkeley Tribe*, 25 July 1969, 7

Laurence, Leo. "Gays Rising." *Berkeley Tribe*, 5 Sep. 1969, 7

Laurence, Leo. "Mafia in the Middle." *Berkeley Tribe*, 18 July 1969, 13

Laurence, Leo. "Wear Your Gown all Year Round." *Berkeley Barb*, 31 Oct. 1969, 8

LeMieux, Dotty. "Gay Liberation-A Straight View." *Old Mole*, 6 Feb. 1970, 18

Marcus. "Gay Roundup." *Berkeley Tribe*, 10 Oct. 1969, 21

Martello, Dr. Leo Louis. "Gay Power in Pay Power." *Gay Power*, Issue no 8, n.d.

Martello, Dr. Leo Louis. "Sexual Fascism Sucks." *Corpus "The Main Body,"* 29 Nov. 1969, 15

Martin, Bob. "The New Homosexual and His Movement." Win, 15 Nov. 1969, 15

Martin, Del. "New Illinois Penal Code–What Does It Mean?" *The Ladder*, No. 6 (March 1962): 14-15

McReynolds, David. "Notes for a More Coherent Article." *Win*, 15 Nov. 1969, 8

"Minneapolis Movement." *Berkeley Tribe*, 18 July 1969, 13

Mrazek, Marcia. "In Defense of the 'Gay World'" *Aquarian*, 30 Oct. 1969, 3

"New Criminal Code in Effect Jan. 1." *Chicago Sun-Times*, 21 Dec. 1961, 43

"New Penal Code in Illinois." *Mattachine Review*, no. 1 (Oct. 1962)

"Playboy Meets Sex." *Rat*, 14 Feb. 1968, 7

Plexus, Solar. "Gay Is Good: Letter to the Editor." *San Diego Free Door*, 17 July 1969, 2

"Radical Homosexual Group Starts Newsletter." *Ann Arbor Argus*, 17 Sep. 1969, 17

"Radical Homosexual Group Starts Newsletter." *Liberation News Service*, 23 Aug. 1969, 27

Streitmatterm Rodger. *Voices of Revolution: The Dissident Press in America*. New York; Columbia Press, 2001

"VD and the Homosexual." *Rag*, 3 Nov. 1969, 6

Weisstein, Naomi. "Woman As Nigger." *Second City*, Feb. 1970, 12

Wittman, Carl. "Gay Power: A Manifesto." *Kaleidoscope* (Madison), 11 Feb. 1970, 5

Wittman, Carl. "Refugees From Amerika: a Gay Perspective." *Berkeley Tribe*, 26 Dec. 1969, 12

Wingell, Bill. "A Time for Holding Hands." *Distant Drummer*, 10 July 1969, 8

CHAPTER 17
WOMEN'S LIBERATION IN THE UNDERGROUND PRESS

Balser, Henry. "The Ballsy Chicago Report." *First Issue*, 29 Jan. 1968, 18

Cassell. "Miss (Plastic) America." *Kudzu*, 18 Sep. 1968, 3

"Chicago Women Form Liberation Group." *New Left Notes*, 13 Nov. 1967, 2

Clamage, Dena. "Women's Liberation: the Only Path is Revolution." *Fifth Estate*, 5 Mar. 1969, 7

"December Conference impressions." *New Left Notes*, 28 Jan. 1966, n.p.

Goldfield, Evi. "Radical Women's Movement in Chicago." *Radicals in the Professions*, Feb. 1968, 11

Homer, Nancy. "Women Protest Mindless Boob Symbol." *Fifth Estate*, 19 Sep. 1968, 5

"The Homosexual in America." *Time*, 21 Jan. 1966, 40

Ignatin, Noel. "Revolutionary Struggle for Women's Liberation." *New Left Notes*, 23 Dec. 1968

Isobel, Dodie and Jenny. "Fair Head Bristles As Women Unveil Shuck." *Berkeley Barb*, 21 Feb. 1969, n.p.

Kilian, Melody. "Sexual Guerillas." *Peninsula Observer*, 2 Dec. 1968, 12

Koedt, Anne. "Myth: Vaginal Orgasm." *Kaleidoscope* (Milwaukee), 7 Nov. 1969, 6

"Liberation of Women." *New Left Notes*, 10 July 1967, 4

Martin, Del and Lyon, Phyllis. "The Realities of Lesbianism." *Los Angeles Free Press*, 9 Jan. 1970, 1

Martin, Del and Lyon, Phyllis. "The Realities of Lesbianism." *Kaleidoscope* (Milwaukee), 7 Nov. 1969, 6

Morgan, Robin. "Miss America Goes Down." *Rat*, 20 Sep. 1968, 14

Orvino, Jennie. "To Begin With." *Kaleidoscope* (Milwaukee), 7 Nov. 1969, 6

Schneider, Beth. "Ann Arbor Beauty Pageant." *Ann Arbor Argus*, 28 Mar.1969,

1

Smith. Jack A. "SDS Sets Out On Radical Path." *Guardian*, 15 July 1967, n.p.

"Students Get Naked With Playboy." *Rolling Stone*, 15 Mar. 1969, 12

Tornquist, Elizabeth. "Women's Liberation Marches Again." *North Carolina Anvil*, 5 Apr. 1969, 5

Truth, Sojourner. "Ain't I a Woman." *Ain't I a Woman*, 26 June 1970, 1

Rubin, Gayle. "Woman As Nigger." *Ann Arbor Argus*, 28 Mar. 1968, 7

Rubin, Gayle. "Woman As Nigger (Part II)." *Ann Arbor Argus*, 14 Apr. 1968, 7

"Women's Liberation: A Part of People's Liberation." *Pterodactyl*, 3 Feb. 1968, n.p.

"Women's Liberation Group Forming in Baltimore." *Peace and Freedom News*, Aug. 1968, n.p.

CHAPTER 18
1970: A NEW DECADE

"100 Protest Harassing of Homosexuals." *Chicago Tribune*, 17 Apr. 1970:11

"Ain't I a Woman Face-Saving Exercises." *Ain't I a Woman*, 25 Sept. 1970,5

"Avenge!" *Daily Planet*, 25 May 1970, 1

"Bank Rejects Gay Account." *Thursday's Drummer*, 7 Jan. 1971, 6

Bieber, M.D., Irving. *"Homosexuality: A Psychoanalytic Study of Male Homosexuals."* New York: Basic Books, 1962

"Blackout." *Detroit Liberator*, 22 May 1970, 2

Boats, Mother. "Lesbian Hit WACS Hard and Live." *Berkeley Barb*, 20 Feb. 1970, 11

Boroff, Dan. "Come Out!" *Seed*, circa Jan. 1970, 8

Bradford, Jim and Kelly, William B. "Cops Hit More Bars." *Mattachine Midwest Newsletter*, Oct. 1969:1

Bradford, Jim. "The New Militancy Emerges." *Mattachine Midwest Newsletter*, Oct. 1969:2

"Break Out of the Closet." *Berkeley Tribe*, 19 June 1970, 13

Burton, Don. "Gay Head Hits Liberal Shits." *Berkeley Barb*, 20 Mar. 1970, 2

Burton, Don. "Gay Lib's Free Fair." *Berkeley Barb*, 1 May 1970, 10

Canady, Alexa. "Strange Priorities." *Detroit Liberator*, 22 May 1970, 7

Carliner, Michael. "Abbie Says get a Gun." *Kaleidoscope* (Madison), 17 June 1970, 19

Caselman, Mike. "Gay Lib Pickets Bar." *Roosevelt Torch*, 4 May 1970, 11

Chisman, Nancy. "Gay Lib Talks to Detective." *Maroon*, 6 Feb. 1970: n.p.

"Classified Ads." *Maroon*, 6 Mar. 1970:11

De Rosa, Tony. "'Some of Your Best Friends Are Gay.'" *Los Angeles Free Press*, 19 June 1970, 9

Doggett, Dave and Clarke, Robert, "Jackson State." *Great Speckled Bird*, 25 May 1970, 2

Dorfman, Ron. "Mattachine Editor Arrested; Gays Picket Sergeant Manley." *Chicago Journalism Review*, Apr. 1970: n.p.

Douglas, Angela. "Gay Liberation News Front." *Los Angeles Free Press*, 18 Sep. 1970, 24

Douglas. "Hard On!" *Helix*, 16 Apr. 1970, 9

Dry, William. *Daily Northwestern* 3 Mar. 1970: n.p.

Freddie, Captain. "We Are Here: Gay Liberation." *Liberator*, Jan. 1970, 4

"Gay Editor Arrested." *Second City*, (Vol. 2 No 5), n.d.

"Gay Fest." *Berkeley Tribe*, 27 Mar. 1970, 10

"Gay Is Beautiful." *Ann Arbor Sun*," 4 Feb. 1972, 3

"Gay Lib." *Ann Arbor Argus*, (Vol. 11 No 5) n.d., 10

"Gay Lib." *Great Speckled Bird*, 30 Mar. 1970, 21

"Gay Lib Charges Prejudice." *Maroon*, 17 Apr. 1970: n.p.

"Gay Lib Dances." *Maroon*, 14 Apr. 1970:4

"Gay Liberation." *Venice Beachhead*, 18 Nov. 1970, 2

"Gay Liberation." *Great Speckled Bird*, 29 June 1970, 18

"Gay Liberation." *Quicksilver Times*, 19 Jan. 1970, 22

"Gay Liberation: Free the Normandy." *Seed*, circa Feb. 1970, 6

"Gay Liberation Sponsors First City-wide Dance." *Second City*, (Vol. 2 No. 7) n.d., 7

"Gay Liberation Supplement." *Seed*, Mar. 1970:13

"Gay Liberation Week Begins This Monday." *Daily Illini*, 4 May 1970:5

"Gay Lib Faire." *Berkeley Tribe*, 24 Apr. 1970, 20

"Gay Meeting Causes Church Dispute." *Fifth Estate*, 15 Apr. 1970, 6

"Gay Minority Militancy on the Rise." *Berkeley Barb*, 20 Feb. 1970, 11

"Gay OK at UofM." *Detroit Liberator*, July 1970, 1

"Gay Pickets." *Berkeley Barb*, 23 Jan. 1970, 7

"Gays' Camp Banned." *Berkeley Barb*, 3 July 1970, 7

Grahn, Judy. "Lesbians As Women." *Berkeley Tribe*, 19 June 1970, 16

Hoeffding, Virginia. "Dear Mom." *Los Angeles Free Press*, 14 Aug. 1970, 52

"Homosexual & Movement." *Rag*, 30 Mar. 1970, 14

Jackson, Don. "Gay Liberation News." *San Diego Free Door*, 1 Jan. 1970,16

Jackson, Don. "Gay Liberation in N.O." *Nola Express*, 21 Aug. 1970, n.p.

Jackson, Don. "Suck Cock, Beat Draft." *Berkeley Barb*, 1 May 1970, 10

James, John. "Gays Blow Minds." *Good Times*, 22 Jan. 1970, 6

James, John. "Gays Blow Minds." *International Times*, 27 Mar. 1970, 2

Jay, Karla. "Here Comes the Lavender Menace." *Los Angeles Free Press*, 14 Aug. 1970, 55

Judy. "Gay Power." *Amazing Grace*, Vol. 1 No. 8, 1970. 13

Judy. "Lesbians As Women." *It Ain't Me Babe*, 21 May 1970, 7

Jackson, Don. "Gay Memorial Services Planned," *San Diego Free Door*, 12 Mar. 1970, 6

Jackson, Don. "Gay Power Strikes." *Los Angeles Free Press*, 26 June 1970, 18

Jackson, Don. "Gays Blast Barney's." *Berkeley Barb*, 13 Feb. 1970, 11

Jackson, Don. "Gays Demand Ninety Billion." *Los Angeles Free Press*, 20 Feb. 1970, 18

Kelley, Ken. "Come Out!" *Ann Arbor Argus*, Apr. 1970, 3

Kelly, William B. "I.D. Check Escalates to Melee." *Mattachine Midwest Newsletter* Sep. 1969:7

Key, Douglas. "Gay Liberation News Roundup." *Los Angeles Free Press*, 13 Feb. 1970, 3

Key, Douglas. "Homophile Hassled in San Dimes." *Los Angeles Free Press*, 2 Jan. 1970, 8.

Key, Douglas. "Homosexual Gov't Planned." *Los Angeles Free Press*, 9 Jan. 1970, 1

Key, Douglas. "More on Gay Conference." *Los Angeles Free Press*, 20 Feb. 1970, 18

King, Sunny. "The Rev. Robert E. Morrison." *Detroit Liberator*, 22 May 1970, 8

Laurence, Leo. "Hard On! Gay Lib." *Berkeley Tribe*, 20 Feb. 1970, 13

Laurence, Leo. "Leo's Hearing: KGO Blows." *Berkeley Tribe*, 24 Jan. 1970, 11

Laurence, Leo. "Leo Wins!!" *Berkeley Tribe*, 13 Feb. 1970, 14

Laurence, Leo. "Roland Raps Leo Listens." *Berkeley Tribe*, 26 Dec. 1970, 8

Malone, Bob. "Blood on Kent State," *Great Speckled Bird*, 11 May 1970, 3

Matisse, Cherie. "We Are Raised as Sex Objects, Future Wives and Mothers." *Los Angeles Free Press*, 14 Aug. 1970, 55

"Mattachine Editor Discharged." *Second City*, (Vol. 2. No 8), n.d., 9

Mary. "Gay Rights Hearing." *Eugene Auger*, 12 Jan. 1972, 5

"New Gay Lib Groups." *Second City*, 1970 (Vol. 2, ?), 7

North Star. "Rise Up Angry!!! No More Lying Down." *Berkeley Barb*, 8 May, 1970, 1.

"Other Side," *Seed*, (Vol. 5 No 6), n.d., 19

"Out of the Closets." *Rat*, 28 Mar. 1970, n.p.

"Out of the Closets and into the Subcellar." *Women's LibeRATion*, 6 Oct.1970, n.p.

Radicalesbians. "What is a Lesbian?" *Las Vegas Free Press*, 17 June 1970, 8

Robertson, Steve. "Dancing Comes to the Normandy." *Mattachine Midwest Newsletter*, June 1970, 6

Rosen, Baran. "Gay Lib Hopes for Liberation From Prejudice." *Daily Northwestern*, 5 Mar. 1970:4

Rosen, Baran. "Gay Lib Rally in Loop Protests Harassment of Oppressed Groups." *Daily Northwestern*, 17 Apr. 1970: n.p.

Schaffer, Ralph S. "GLF Hits Exploitation." *Los Angeles Free Press*, 14 Aug. 1970, 54

Spence, Abner. "Take Up the Gun!" *Kaleidoscope* (Madison), 19 May 1970, 1

Shelley. Martha. "Women of Lesbos." *Kaleidoscope* (Milwaukee), June 1970, 2

Steve. "See How They Snide." *Detroit Liberator*, Dec. 1970, 3

Stienecker, David. "A Gay Deceiver-Or Is He?" *Mattachine Midwest Newsletter*, Sep. 1969, 3

Swearingen, Ida. "Gays Confront N.Y.U." *Win*, 1 Nov. 1970, n.p.

Thierry, David. "On the Dance." *Chicago Gay Liberation Newsletter*, 28 Apr. 1970, n.p.

Tiresias. "Ultimate Liberation." *Good Times*, 22 Jan. 1970, 6

Truth, Sojourner. "Ain't I a Woman." *Ain't I a Woman*, 26 June, 1970.

"Vice Squad's Manley Infiltrates Gay Lib." *Maroon* 3 Mar. 1970, n.p.

Warner, Raymond. "Our Movement and the A.P.A." *Detroit Liberator*, July 1970, 5

W.C. "Gay Ghetto." *Sabot*, 1 Oct. 1970, 6

Weimhoff, Henry. "The 'Problem' of Homosexuality." *Maroon-Grey City Journal*,

30 Jan. 1970:1

"What the Hell Does Gay Lib Think it's Doing?" Gay Lib leaflet, Northwestern University Library's Special collections.

"What Pride Liberation." *Rag*, 2 Nov. 1970, n.p.

Whittington, Gale. "Queer Stamp: Gay Postman Canceled." *Berkeley Tribe*, 6 Feb. 1970, 21

Whittington, Gale. "Queer Killers." *Berkeley Tribe*, 30 Jan. 1970, 11

CHAPTER 19
CHRISTOPHER STREET GAY LIBERATION DAY AND AFTERWARDS

"3,000 Gays to March." *Las Vegas Free Press*, 24 June 1970, 5

A Brother. "Gay Lib Supplement." *Los Angeles Free Press*. 11 Sep. 1970, 5

"A Conversation With Brad Wilson: the Pastor of Miami's Gay Church Raps on Sexual Liberation." *Daily Planet*, 29 Dec. 1970

" … and From a Straight Sister." *Kaleidoscope* (Madison), 19 Aug. 1970, 11

A Radical Lesbian. "Gay Liberation." *Quicksilver Times*, 14 July 1970, 8

A Radical Lesbian. "We're Not Gay, We're Angry." *Rat*, 11 Sep. 1970, n.p.

Armstrong, Elizabeth A. *Forging Gay Identities: Organizing Sexuality in San Francisco*, 1950-1994. Chicago; University of Chicago Press, 2002

Benton, Nick. "Gay Shooting War Council." *Berkeley Barb*, Dec. 18 1970, 3

Benton, Nick. "Gayule." *Berkeley Barb*, 25 Dec. 1970, n.p.

Blum, Howard. "Gays Take On the Cops: From Rage to Madness." *Village Voice*, 3 Sep. 1970, 1

"Chicago Mid-West Gay Conference." *Detroit Liberator*, Aug. 1970, 1

"Cockettes Benefit Jan. 23." *Berkley Barb*, 15 Jan. 1971, 12

Demos. "Gay Power: A New Cry for Liberation." *Lancaster Independent Press*, 9 July 1979, 3

"Diamond Lil." *Great Speckled Bird*, Dec. 14, 1970, 19

Douglas, Angela. "A History of Gay Power: Homosexualize America." *Los Angeles Free Press*, 11 Dec. 1970, 20

Douglas, Angela. "Gays March on Hollywood Blvd." *Los Angeles Free Press*, 3 July 1970, 5

Douglas, Angela. "Transvestites & Transsexuals' Teach-In." *Los Angeles Free Press*, 5 June 1970, 12

"Drag Queen Murdered in Chi." *East Village Other*, 3 Jan. 1971, 4

Flaming Faggot. "We Are Not Gay, We're Angry." *Rat*, 11 Sep. 1970, 3

Francis, Miller. "Centauricide." *Great Speckled Bird*, 30 Nov. 1970, 13

"Gaybreak." *Berkeley Tribe*, 3 July 1970, 10

"Gay Liberation Day." *Distant Drummer*, 11 June 1970, 14

"Gay Liberation Week!!" *Kaleidoscope* (Milwaukee), 24 July 1970, 4.

"Gay Pride Week." *Ann Arbor Argus*, 10 June 1970, n.p.

"Gay Pride Week." *Rat*, 26 June, 1970, n.p.

Guerrero, Gene. "Community." *Great Speckled Bird*, 6 July 1970, 2

Heflin, Lee. "The Great Parade Christopher Street West." *Los Angeles Free Press*, 14 Aug. 1970, 51

Higson, Mike. "Fred Lund's Adult Books." *Nola Express*, 10 July 1970, n.p.

Jackson, Don. "Drags Organize." *San Diego Free Door*, 12 Feb. 1970, 4

Jackson, Don. "Gay Lib." *Nola Express*, 12 June 1970, 25

Jackson, Don. "Gay Lib." *Rag*, 15 June 1970, 11

Jackson, Don. "Homosexual Violence Predicted." *Los Angeles Times*, 16 Jan. 1970, 20

Joye, Barbara. Guerrero, Nan. Jacobs, Sue. "Sex Right." *Great Speckled Bird*, 22 Dec. 1969, 14

Kight, Morris. "The Great Parade Christopher Street West." *Los Angeles Free Press*, 14 Aug. 1970, 51

Kyper, John. "Gay March in Provincetown." *Win*, 15 Oct. 1970, 3

Larsen, Richard. "Ho-Ho-Homosexual." *Seed* (Vol. 5 No 7), n.d., 7

Laurence, Leo. "Gay Pig Nation Liberated." *Berkeley Barb*, 4 Sep. 1970, n.p.

Laurence, Leo E. "Strait Gays Badrap Blacks." *Berkeley Barb*, 28 Aug. 1970: 9

Lil, Diamond. "Diamond Lil, Most Glamorous Queen in the World, In Captivity." *Great Speckled Bird*, 28 Sep. 1970, 10

Lil, Diamond. "Gassed Grease." *Great Speckled Bird*, 19 Oct. 1970, 5

Livingston, Brian. "Barb Drops Sexist Ads." *Eugene Augur*, 24 Aug. 1972, 17

"Manifesto." *Kaleidoscope* (Madison), 18 Nov. 1970, 4

Marshall, Sue. "Hermaphrodite Sues Curious Cops." *Berkeley Barb*, 20 Feb. 1970, 15

Martin, Del. "Goodbye … " *Sabot*, 25 Nov. 1970, 17

Maude. "Sex Ad Sell-Out?" *Great Speckled Bird*, 4 Aug. 1969, 10

"Men Against Cool." *Seed*, (Vol. 5 No 10) n.p.

"Men Against the Boy." *Seed*, (Vol. 5 No 6), n.d., 19

"Men' Lib Bake Sale." *Berkeley Barb*, 26 June 1970, 7

"Message From a Gay Sister." *Kaleidoscope* (Madison), 19 Aug. 1970, 11

"NACHO Generates Controversy." *Mattachine Midwest Newsletter*, Sep. 1970, 1

"Out of the Closets & Into the Streets." *Ain't I a Woman*, 10 July 1970, 11

"Panther Busts." *Rat*, 11 Sep. 1970, 17

"Porny ads." *Daily Planet*, 24 Nov. 1969, 2.

Pukas, Phil. "Lonely Porkers Crash Gay-In." *Berkeley Barb*, 3 July 1970, 1

"R*P." *Great Speckled Bird*, 9 Nov. 1970, 14

Sawyer, Jack. "On Male Liberation." *Liberation*, Autumn 1970, 32

"Schism in Chicago Gay Lib." *Chicago Gay Liberation Newsletter*, Oct. 1970, 1

Seed Circa. Summer 1970, n.p.

"Street Fighting Gays." *Rat*, 11 Sep. 1970, 5

"Street Transvestite Murdered." *Gay Flames*, Dec. 1970, n.p.

"Third World Gay Revolution." *Berkeley Tribe*, 13 Nov. 1970, 8

"Violent Gay Revolution Now!!" *Kaleidoscope* (Milwaukee), 7 Aug. 1970, 15

Weissmann, G.W. "New O's Gay Libs Come Out." *Nola Express*, 25 Dec. 1970, 17

Well, Rev. Howard. "JC & The Gay Community." *Berkeley Barb*, 1 Jan. 1971, 13

"What Is Gay Liberation?" *Sabot*, 1 Oct. 1970, 6
"Who Am I?" *Sabot*, 23 Sep. 1970, 16

CHAPTER 20
FREAKIN' FAG REVOLUTION

"Allen Ginsberg Meets Julius Hoffman." *Distant Drummer*, 25 Dec. 1969,3
Bell, Arthur. *Dancing the Gay Lib Blues*. New York: Simon and Schuster, 1971
"Bobby Seale: 4-Year Sentence." *Dallas Notes*, 19 Nov. 1969, 7
Fish, Bob. Nelson, Ray. "An Interview With Allen Ginsberg and William
    Burroughs." *Chicago Gay Crusader*, June 1975, 6
"Gays Zap Foran." *Seed*, circa Dec. 1970, n.p.
Kunkin, Art. "Fags Versus Fuzz." *Los Angeles Free Press*, 6 Mar. 1970,1
May, Step. "An Open Letter to Jerry Rubin: Which May Fix His Mouth."
    Kaleidoscope (Madison), 12 Aug. 1970, n.p.
"Panther Leader Shackled, Silenced at Chicago Trial." *Distant Drummer*, 7 Nov.
    1969, 3
Rubin, Jerry. *Do It! Scenarios of the Revolution*. New York; Simon and Schuster,
    1970.
Rubin, Jerry. "The Academy Award of Protest." *Fifth Estate*, 3 Apr. 1969, 3
"Seale An Ordeal a Voice." Great Speckled Bird, 10 Nov. 1968, 6
Singer, Chris. "The Chicago Conspiracy." *Fifth Estate*, 3 Apr 1969, 3
Young, Allen. "Chicago Gay Zap Zapped." *Berkeley Barb*, 10 Dec. 1971, n.p.

CHAPTER 21
ALPINE COUNTY UTOPIA

"1179 Gay Libbers Sign Up to Go Up." *Berkeley Barb*, 20 Nov. 1970, 8
Benton, Nick. "'Alpine Liberation.' – Green Gay Ghetto?" *Berkeley Barb*, 18
    Dec. 1970, 11
Benton, Nick. "Treaty With Indians." *Berkeley Tribe*, 30 Oct. 1970, 20
Coleman, James. "Brother Don's Nightmare." *Detroit Liberator*, Dec. 1970, 16
Eberle, Paul. "Gays Plan to Liberate a County." *Los Angeles Free Press*. 23 Oct.
    1970, 10
"Gays Ready for Alpine Assault." *Bugle-American*, 10 Dec. 1970, n.p.
Jackson, Don. "Gaycity." *Berkley Tribe*, 30 Oct. 1970, 20
Jackson, Don. "Gay Highland Plan Goin' Down." *Berkeley Barb*, 26 Mar. 1971, 4
Jackson, Don. "Gays Seek to Take Over Small Calif. County." *Las Vegas Free
    Press*, 21 Oct. 1970, 7
"Vigilantes to Fight GLF." *Los Angeles Free Press*, 11 Dec. 1970, 2

CHAPTER 22
GAYS AND THE BLACK PANTHERS

"Angela," *Great Speckled Bird*, 26 Oct. 1970, 4
Barbara, Sally and Karen. "Three Women Talk on the Revolutionary People's

Constitutional Convention." *Ain't I A Woman*, 29 Jan. 1971, 9

Benton, Nick. "We Bombed." *Berkeley Barb*, 11 Dec. 1970, 2

Chinn, Richard. "Pontiac, Illinois Hits Draft Raiders." *Win*, 15 Oct. 1970, 30

"Constitutional Convent." *Kaleidoscope* (Milwaukee), 12 Sep. 1970, 10

Cox, Donald. "Convention Will Meet: In Streets if Necessary." *Distant Drummer*, 3 Sep. 1970, 6

Dreva, Jerry. "In the August 21, 1970 issue … " *Great Speckled Bird*, 4 Oct. 1970, 4

"Gay Brothers Unite in Rage." *Quicksilver Times*, 8 Dec. 1970, 8

"Gay Power: Gays Support BPP." *East Village Other*, 20 Oct. 1970, 5

"GLF Presents Program Despite RPCC Chaos." *Quicksilver Times*, 8 Dec. 1970, 15

Hart, Lois. "A Woman Speaks." *Ain't I a Woman*, 9 Oct. 1970, 9

"Huey Newton's Letter." *Great Speckled Bird*, 31 Aug. 1970, 9

Jacobi, Michael. "Is the Black Panther Party Dying?" *Bugle-American*, 11 Mar. 1971, 5

Ken. "Same Chain." *Detroit Liberator*, Dec. 1970, 6

Laurence, Leo. "SF Gay Lib Commune Raided After threats." *Berkeley Barb*, 2 Oct. 1970, 7

McLellan, Vin. "Prelude to a New Constitution." *Phoenix*, 12 Sep. 1970, 8

Observer. "The Media Watch." *Distant Drummer*, 3 Sep. 1970, 2

"On Being Black, Gay, and in Prison: 'There is No Humanity.'" *Motive*, 1972:26

"People's Constitution." *Great Speckled Bird*, 24 Aug. 1970, 2

"People's Convention." *Fifth Estate*, Dec. 10, 1970, 2

"Philly Convention." *Rat*, 11 Sep. 1970, 17

Silverstein, Mike. "We Bombed." *Berkeley Barb*, 11 Dec. 1970, 2

"Third World and Gay: 'They'd Have to Off Me Too.'" *Berkeley Barb*, 15 Mar. 1971, 10

"We the People." *Great Speckled Bird*, 7 Dec. 1970, 10

CHAPTER 23
VENCEREMOS (WE SHALL WIN)

Andrew, Christopher and Mitrokhin, Vasili. *The World Was Going Our Way: The KGB and the Battle for the Third World*. New York: Basic Books, 2005

"Cuban Congress Declares Homosexuality to be Pathological." *All You Can Eat*, 24 Jan. 1971, 9

Dreyer, Thorne. "Abducted on Route." *Rag*, 18 Mar. 1968, 1

"Gay Feelings on the Brigade." *Women's LibeRATion*, 30 Mar. 1971, 19

Guerrero, Nan. "Si Cuba!" *Great Speckled Bird*, 31 Aug. 1970, 2

Jay, Karla and Young, Allen. *Out of the Closets: Voices of Gay Liberation*. New York: New York University Press, 1972

Nassberg, Guy. "Flaming Faggots." *Great Speckled Bird*, 31 Aug. 1970, 8

Steffens, Heidi. "Maricón Go Home." *Good Times*, 25 Nov. 1971, 12

"Venceremos." *Great Speckled Bird*, 1 June 1970, 12

"Venceremos!" *Great Speckled Bird*, 26 Jan. 1970, 10

Young, Allen. *Gays Under the Cuban Revolution*. San Francisco; Grey Fox Press,

1981

CHAPTER 24
GAYS VS PSYCHIATRISTS

The primary sources include McCormick Library of Special Collections at Northwestern University, Evanston, Illinois.

Alinder, Gary. "Off Dr. Bieber." *Los Angeles Free Press*, 14 Aug. 1970, n.p.

Bieber, M.D., Irving. *Homosexuality: A Psychoanalytic Study of Male Homosexuals.* New York: Basic Books, 1962

"Brain Surgery New Cure for Homosexual." *Las Vegas Free Press*, 1 July 1970, 1

Christmas, Faith C. "Mental Illness Is High." *Chicago Defender* 13 June 1970:1

De Rosa, Tony. "Gays in a Shocking Situation." *Los Angeles Free Press*, 28 Oct. 1970, 11

Jackson, Don. "The Homofile." *Broadside and the Free Press*, 15 July 1970, n.p.

Roberts, Steven V. "Homosexuals in Revolt." New York Times, 24 Aug. 1970, n.p.

Socarides, Charles, "Homosexuality and Medicine." *Journal of the American Medical Association*, 18 May, 1970, n.p.

Weimhoff, Henry. "The 'Problem' of Homosexuality." *Maroon-Grey City Journal*, 30 Jan. 1970:1

CHAPTER 25
GLF UNSTUCK

The primary sources include McCormick Library of Special Collections at Northwestern University, Evanston, Illinois.

Abbott, Steve. "Atlanta Gay Liberation Uncaged." *Great Speckled Bird*, 15 Feb. 1971, 6

Abbott, Steve. "G.L.F. Conference." *Great Speckled Bird*, 3 May 1971, 13

Abbott, Steve. "GLF Conference: Changes." *Great Speckled Bird*, 19 Apr. 1971, 4

Abbott, Steve. "Why Do You Stomp Us." *Great Speckled Bird*, 25 Jan. 1971, 6

"A Free Press Interview With James Baldwin." *Los Angeles Free Press*, 23 Feb. 1968, 3

Banes, Sally. "Jill Johnson in Chicago. Grande Dame of Dykes." *Reader*, 6 July 1973:3

Bay, Tor. "Dear Bird." *Great Speckled Bird*, 22 Mar. 1971, 5

Benton, Nick. "Gay-Lib-Activist Split Foreseen Here." *Berkeley Barb*, 15 Jan. 1971, 8

"Brothers and Sisters." *Rag*, 15 Mar. 1971, 13

"Detroit Gays Come Out." *Fifth Estate*, 4 Feb. 1971, 16

"Gayga-zette." *Berkeley Barb*, 8 Jan. 1971, 9

"Gay-In." *Provincial Times*, May 1971, n.p.

"Gay Lib Splits." *Berkeley Barb*, 14 May 1971, 12

"Gay Militancy." *Outlaw*, 28 May 1971, n.p.
"Gays to Hit Cops/Courts." *Fifth Estate*, 14 Jan. 1971, n.p.
"Gay Switchboard on the Breadline." *Berkeley Barb*, 22 Jan. 1971, 4
Gornick, Vivian. "Lesbians & Women's Lib." *Village Voice*, 18 Mar. 1971, 5
"Hayward Fires Gay Lib Prof." *Berkeley Barb*, 26 Feb. 1971, 2
"Jill Johnston Comes Out." *Goodbye to All That*, 10 Feb. 1971, n.p.
Kaufman, Smokey. "Trash." *Great Speckled Bird*, 4 Jan. 1971, 6
Maude. "Kate Millett." *Great Speckled Bird*, 15 Mar. 1971, 6
Moone, M. Martin. S. "Lola." *Detroit Liberator*, Dec. 1970, 5
"National Gay Lib Conference." *Quicksilver Times*, 31 Mar. 1971, 10
Neville, Mike. "Warhol Surfaces With 'Trash.'" *Bugle-American*, 8 May 1971, 11
"Sodomy Appeals." *Great Speckled Bird*, 15 Mar. 1971, 11
"What is Gay Liberation?" *Daily Planet*, 18 Jan. 1971, 17
"Who's Come a Long Way, Baby?" *Time*, 31 Aug. 1970, 16
Vicki. "Gay Sisters & Brothers." *Great Speckled Bird*, 1 Mar. 1971, 22

CHAPTER 26
GLF BURN OUT

The primary sources include McCormick Library of Special Collections at Northwestern University, Evanston, Illinois.

"A Gay Office Opens at the University of Chicago." *Chicago Gay Alliance Newsletter*, May 1971, 5
"Anything Gays." *Red Eye*, 2 Dec. 1971, 15
"Ass-Holes Preserve Sodomy Statute." *Berkeley Barb*, 8 Oct. 1971, 9
Bell, Arthur. "Toward a Gay Community." *Village Voice*, 1 July 1971, 7
Benson, Roger. "Brothers and Sisters." *Great Speckled Bird*, 4 Oct. 1971, 27
Benton, Nick. "Anti-GLF." *Berkeley Barb*, 8 Oct. 1971, 9
Benton, Nick. "Dianne No-Shos Gay Boosters." *Berkeley Barb*, 15 Oct. 1971, 14
Campy Simplex. "Dear Birdflock." *Great Speckled Bird*, 27 Dec. 1971, 9
Candidates on Gay Rights." *Lincoln Gazette*, 8 May 1972, n.p.
Chinn, Richard. "Gay Not Guilty." *Seed*, 30 July 1971, n.p.
"Christopher Street Liberation Week June 19-27." *Kaleidoscope* (Milwaukee), 17 June 1971, 10
Cyclops. "Celebration ... Very gay." *Great Speckled Bird*, 5 July 1971, 2
"Dialogue." *Seed*, circa July 1971, 5
Diamond Lil, "California 'Diamond' Rush." *Great Speckled Bird*. 6 Dec. 1971, 25
Donald. "Role of Gays in Revolution." *Rag*, 12 July 1971, 12
"Gay Action Depends on You." *Rag*, 30 Aug. 1971, 14
"Gay Activists." *Columbus Free Press*, 26 Jan. 1972, 15
"Gay Flower Blooms." *Kaleidoscope* (Madison), 4 Aug. 1971, 16
"Gay Fray Rocks SF." *Berkeley Barb*, 7 Jan. 1972, 10
"Gay Liberation Front." *Great Speckled Bird*, 2 Aug. 1971, 8
"Gay Lib Poll Hits Antiquated Laws." *North Carolina Anvil*, 15 Apr. 1972, 3
"Gay Marx Day." *UPS News Service*, 24 Dec. 1971, 2
"Gay Pride Issue." *Dallas News*, 2 July 1971, 1

"Gays From the West to the East." *Quicksilver Times*, 17 July 1971, 10

"Gays Picket Hudson's." *Fifth Estate*, 25 Nov. 1971, 9

"Gay Walk Out." *Berkeley Barb*, 7 July 1972, 6

"Hall, Ralph. "Gay Radical Rips Into Cuba." *Berkeley Barb*, 20 Aug. 1971, 2

Jackson, Don. "Gay Political Power Growing." *Los Angeles Free Press*, 24 Mar. 1972, 20

Jackubosky, Tony. "Gay Activist Group Formed." *DC Gazette*, 21 June 1971, 14

John. "Gay Movement Grows in New Jersey." *All You Can Eat*, 24 Nov. 1971, 22

"Kameny for Congress." *DC Gazette*, 15 Mar. 1971, 7

Kyper, John. "Will success Spoil Gay Lib." *Win*, 1 Oct. 1971, 20

Laurence, Leo. "Long March for Gay Pride," *Berkeley Barb*, 2 July 1971, 7

"Lavender People." *Venice Beachhead*, Dec. 1971-Jan. 1972, 2

Martin, Franz. "Christopher Street Story." *Fifth Estate*, 23 June 1973, 6

"My Homosexuality Made Me a Nigger." *Rag*, 20 Sep. 1971, 9

Park, Roxanne. "Undergrounds Become Alternatives." *Northwest Passage*, 9 July 1973, 20

Pritchett, Rod. "Tulsa Gay Come Out of Mothballs." *Osmosis*, circa Nov. 1972, 14

"Repression of Gays in Cuba." *Rag*, 13 Sep. 1971, 7

"Schedule of Events." *Chicago Gay Pride*, June 1971, 1

"Cuban Controversy: Understanding the Context … " *Outlaw*, 9 Sep. 1971, 10

"SF's Gays–A New Political Force." *Berkeley Barb*, 1 Oct. 1971, 16

"Smith, Bill. "Gay is Gone." *Great Speckled Bird*, 23 July 1973, 7

"Some Gays Going, Others Hang Tuff." *Berkeley Barb*, 5 Nov. 1971, 2

Virginia. "Gay Pride Kiss-In." *Seed*, circa July 1971, 5

INDEX

275–276, 278, 280, 283–284
Gay News (Britain), 9
Gay Revos, 201, 203
Gaysanos, 203
Gay Student Liberation (New York), 190
Gay Sunshine, 210, 257–258
Gazette Citizen, 72
Genet, Jean, 91, 112–113, 115, 258
Georgia Straight, Vancouver Free Press, 62, 108, 116
Gerberg, Mort (cartoonist), 86
Gessner, Pete, 98
Gibbs, Philip Lafayette, 199
Ginsberg, Allen, 7–8, 22, 27, 63, 66, 68–69, 76, 82, 98, 108–109, 113–114, 123, 221, 224–226, 258
Gittings, Barbara, 106, 158
Gleason, Ralph, 103
Glessing, Robert J., 40
Glide Foundation, 43
Glide Memorial Church, 43
Glover, Larry, 193
Golden Gate Park, 34, 69, 168–169, 205
Golden, Stephen, 101
Goldfield, Evi, 175
Goldman, Emma, 15–16, 19
Goodbye to All That, 261
Goodlet, Carleton (doctor), 135
Goodman, Murray (judge), 36
Goodman, Paul, 25, 167
Good Times, 182, 184, 245, 285
Gornick, Vivian, 267
Goulianos, Joan, 148
Gover, Robert, 35
Grahn, Judy, 200
Grant Park, 100, 113, 141, 196
Great Speckled Bird, 2, 36–37, 110, 112, 121, 124–125, 129, 131–132, 142, 160, 162, 164–165, 176, 191, 195, 198–199, 208, 213, 215–217, 224, 230, 232–233, 238–240, 260, 263–267, 275–276, 279, 283

Green, James Earl, 199
Green, Lawrence, 110
Green, Roger, 239
Greenwich Village, 6, 19–20, 22, 27, 67, 72, 101, 113, 144–145, 147, 152, 154–155, 205, 211–212, 238
Greer, Michael, 83
Gregory, Dick, 9, 118
Grenshaw, Corbet, 40
Griffith Park, 56, 119
Grutzner, Charles, 146
Guardian (New York), 121, 135, 143, 155–156, 174, 274
Guérin, Daniel, 61
Guerrero, Gene, 208
Guerrero, Nan, 217, 244
Guevara, Ernesto "Che," 2, 5, 200, 221, 235, 244, 249
Gundy, Walt, 98
Guns of the Trees, 123
Gurdjieff, George, 41
Gussow, Leon, 130
Guthrie, Arlo, 98–99

Hagen, Sandy, 187
Haight Ashbury, 6–7, 66–68, 75, 93, *Haight Ashbury Maverick*, 106–107
Hair: The American Tribal Love-Rock Musical, 34–35
Hall, Dave, 10, 12
Hall, Ralph, 274, 278
Hanover, Rene, 185, 265
Harman, Moses, 17–18
Harper's, 266
Harris, Benjamin, 14
Harrison, Rex, 129
Hart, Lois, 163, 233
Havemann, Ernest, 25
Have You Seen Your Mother, Baby, Standing in the Shadows?, 6
Hayakawa, Samuel Ichiye, 135
Hayden, Tom, 89, 223, 280
Hayer, Talmadge, 1
Hayes, Tim, 240
Haymarket Riot, 15, 92
Hazlewood, Grady (state senator),

Miller, Francis, 125, 131–132, 216
Miller, Lynn, 219
Miller, Virginia, 31
Millet, Kate, 260, 266–267, 275
Minneapolis Daily, 159
Mitrokhin, Vasili, 249
Modern Utopian, 31
Moldenhauer, Jearld, 43
Moore, Jack, 9
Morgan, Robin, 176
Morrison, Jim, 36–37, 118
Morrison, Robert (reverend), 196–197
Morrison, Steve, 256
Morrissey, Paul, 263
Mother Makeba, 230, 236
Motive, 237
Movement, 106, 243
Mrazek, Maria, 164
Mühsam, Erich, 16
Mungo, Raymond, 98
Murphy, Brian, 244
Murphy, Claudia, 69
Muste, A.J., 209

Naked Lunch, 22, 116
Nassberg, Guy, 244
National Association for the Advancement of Colored People, 83, 92
National Conference on New Politics, 96
National Lawyers Guild, 92
National League for Social Understanding, 55
National Urban League, 83
Nation of Islam, 1
Natural, 82
Neebe, Oscar, 15
Needham, Sherry, 20
Nelson, Ray, 226
Nelson, Ronald, 105
Neville, Mike, 263
New England Courant, 15
New Left, 1–2, 21–22, 35, 74–75, 95, 167, 178, 186–188, 249, 258, 268, 274, 277, 280, 283

New Left Notes, 75, 174–175, 177
New Masses, 20
New Republic, 84, 106, 269
News and Courier, 91
News from Nowhere, 37
Newman, Tom, 98
Newton, Huey, 9, 116, 230, 235, 241
New York Daily News, 82, 149, 154
New York Free Press, 128
New York Radical Feminists, 179, 267
New York Times, 20, 34, 42, 82, 98, 101, 106, 110, 126, 142, 145–147, 154, 254
Nichamin, Julie, 244
Niihaus, Helen, 194
Nixon, Marty, 275
Nixon, Richard, 104, 121, 198–199
Nola Express, 202, 207, 219
Normandy (gay bar), 193
North American Conference of Homophile Organizations, 105, 201, 209
North Carolina Anvil, 124, 176, 270
Northern Illinois University, 195, 265
Northwest Passage, 284
Northwestern University, 252, 265, 276
Notes from the Underground, 41, 76
Notting Hill Gate, 7, 10
Nouvelles questions féministes, 61
Noyes, John Humphrey, 67
Nuccio, Richard L. (police officer), 105

Ochs, Phil, 74, 79, 81, 98–99, 103
Ockene, Bob, 98
Ogar, Richard, 130
Oglesby, Carl, 244
Oglesby, Richard J. (governor), 15
Old Mole, 141, 170
Omega Delta Nu, 55
One, 40
Oneida Community, 67
One Inc., 25, 28, 40–41, 55
One Thousand and One Nights (The

www.ingramcontent.com/pod-product-compliance
Lightning Source LLC
Chambersburg PA
CBHW031234090426
42742CB00007B/188